OBERLANDOR

Planning Theory
in the 1980's

Planning

List of Contributors

Robert A. Beauregard
Brian J. F. Berry
Robert W. Burchell
Chang-I Hua
Janice Cogger
Paul Davidoff
Otto A. Davis
John W. Dyckman
Amitai Etzioni
John Friedmann
William G. Grigsby
Britton Harris
Chester W. Hartman
David Harvey

Carl F. Horowitz
Irving Louis Horowitz
Morton Hoppenfeld
James W. Hughes
Jerome L. Kaufman
Donald A. Krueckeberg
Norman Krumholz
John Linner
Lawrence D. Mann
Ian McHarg
Lisa R. Peattie
George M. Raymond
George Sternlieb
Melvin M. Webber

Julian Wolpert

Theory in the 1980's

a search for future directions

Edited by
Robert W. Burchell
and George Sternlieb

THE CENTER FOR URBAN POLICY RESEARCH
RUTGERS UNIVERSITY
BUILDING 4051 / KILMER CAMPUS
NEW BRUNSWICK, NEW JERSEY 08903

Cover design by Francis G. Mullen

Copyright 1978, Rutgers—The State University of New Jersey

Published in the United States of America
by the Center for Urban Policy Research
New Brunswick, New Jersey 08903

Library of Congress Cataloging in Publication Data
Main entry under title:
Planning Theory in the 1980s.

  Bibliography: p.
  1. City planning—United States—Addresses,
essays, lectures. 2. Regional planning—United
States—Addresses, essays, lectures. 3. United
States—Social policy—Addresses, essays,
lectures. 4. United States—Economic policy—
1961-   —Addresses, essays, lectures.
  I. Burchell, Robert W. II. Sternlieb, George.

HT167.P56   309.2′12′0973   78-12929
ISBN 0-88285-048-2

Contents

SECTION V: WHAT ARE PLANNERS? WHAT DO PLANNERS DO? AND HOW ARE THEY PREPARED FOR THEIR TASKS?

BIBLIOGRAPHY

About the Contributors

Robert A. Beauregard is Assistant Professor of Urban and Regional Planning, Department of Urban Planning and Policy Development, Rutgers University.

Brian J. F. Berry is Williams Professor of City and Regional Planning and Director of the Laboratory of Computer Graphics and Spatial Analysis, Graduate School of Design, Harvard University.

Robert W. Burchell is Research Professor, Center for Urban Policy Research, Rutgers University.

Chang-I Hua is Professor, Center for Population Studies, Harvard University.

Janice Cogger is a former City Planner, Planning Commission, City of Cleveland, Ohio.

Paul Davidoff is Executive Director, Suburban Action Institute, New York.

Otto A. Davis is Dean—School of Urban and Public Affairs, Carnegie-Mellon University.

John W. Dyckman is James Irvine Professor of Planning, School of Urban and Regional Planning, University of Southern California.

Amitai Etzioni is Professor of Sociology and Director, Center for Policy Research, Columbia University.

John Friedmann is Chairman, Planning Department, School of Architecture and Urban Planning, University of California, Los Angeles.

William Grigsby is Professor of City and Regional Planning, University of Pennsylvania.

Britton Harris is Dean, School of Public and Urban Policy and UPS Professor of Transportation Planning and Public Policy, University of Pennsylvania.

Chester W. Hartman is an author of numerous planning articles and a practicing planner in the San Francisco Bay Area.

David Harvey is Professor of Geography, Department of Geography and Environmental Engineering, Johns Hopkins University.

Carl F. Horowitz is Research Associate, Center for Urban Policy Research, Rutgers University.

Irving Louis Horowitz is President, Transaction Inc. and Professor of Sociology and Political Science, Rutgers University.

Morton Hoppenfeld is Chairman, Department of Urban Planning, School of Architecture, University of New Mexico.

James W. Hughes is Professor of Urban and Regional Planning, Department of Urban Planning and Policy Development, Rutgers University.

Jerome L. Kaufman is Professor of Urban and Regional Planning, Department of Urban and Regional Planning, College of Letters and Science, University of Wisconsin.

Donald A. Krueckeberg is Chairperson, Department of Urban Planning and Policy Research, Rutgers University.

Norman Krumholz is Director of the Planning Commission, City of Cleveland, Ohio.

John Linner is Chief Planner, Department of Community Development, City of Cleveland, Ohio.

Lawrence D. Mann is Chairman, Urban Planning Program, Department of Public Administration, University of Arizona.

Ian McHarg is Chairman, Department of Landscape Architecture and Regional Planning, University of Pennsylvania.

Lisa R. Peattie is Professor of Urban Anthropology, Department of Urban Studies and Planning, Massachusetts Institute of Technology.

George M. Raymond is President, Raymond, Parish, Pine and Wiener, Inc. Tarrytown, New York.

George Sternlieb is Director, Center for Urban Policy Research, Rutgers University.

Melvin M. Webber is Director, Urban and Regional Development Program, University of California.

Julian Wolpert is Henry G. Bryant Professor of Geography, Public Affairs and Urban Planning, School of Architecture and Urban Planning, Princeton University.

Preface

Theory and practice in city planning are uneasy bed companions. The stress on the operating planner; dealing with the personalities at work in a variance board meeting, the realities of coping with fund raising, of political realities and the like, seemingly can find little immediate guidance in the theory of the trade. Certainly, this level of discontinuity is not unique to planning; it is shared by all of the professions. What heightens it in the former case, however, are the enormous human problems to which the planner in our own day is increasingly called. The issues of poverty groups, whether rural or urban, the provision of services and the packaging of them in a fashion, and at a level, which must meet increasing standards, are seemingly insuperable. The sheer frustration in the inability to deliver, which so many planners feel, makes for a vast impatience and a questioning of the relevance of theory.

While this state of affairs is understandable, it cannot be accepted. While short range meliorism without sense of perspective may be good for the practitioner's individual psyche, the cost may be borne by the long-run best interests of the groups to be served. The gap between the planner's capacities to deliver and the nominal goal structure can often seem so vast as to encourage short-sightedness. The risks of a lack of perspective and the experiences generated by this phenomenon are too serious in their implications to permit the process to continue. In an area allied to our own, for example, it was just a very few years ago that community education planners, in an effort to bring relevance to schools, called for decentralization of authority and standard setting. They have lived to see that genie now invoked for far less laudible goals. The failure to maintain conceptual grasp in the face of an immediate problem resolution is a form of self indulgence and is unworthy of the professional. Planners without concept, without long-range perspective, without a sense of their craft in the broadest of terms all too easily can end up drifting into either or both of the classic sins: of short-run optimization/survival or romantic subjectivism, bringing band-aids to a select few, without ever being in a position to heal the basic wound.

This is strikingly the case in our own time. Ours is an era in which the vision of a materialist millenium came closer to hand than perhaps ever before. It is only a decade ago that the wealth of the United States was thought to be beyond cavil, its growth the wonder of the age. The economists were busily seeking out new fields, now that the business cycle had been reduced to quibbles about the level of fine tuning required by the economy. The poor had been discovered; the bridge between surplus wealth and the rectification of their pain, seemingly required little but good will for cure.

The planner of the '60s had in his knapsack not a Napoleonic Field Marshal's baton but rather a seeming cornucopia of strategems to lick urban wounds, restore Appalachia, and rectify the sins of the generations. We were about to send a man to the moon. Certainly there would be little problem in ensuring that his return to U.S. Earth would be to a site of much more human beneficiance than had before been the case. Environmental limitations were just being discovered by the popular mind. A barrel of oil cost $2.10. The major issue in designing automobiles was to ensure large enough gas tanks to minimize the inconvenience of occasional refueling.

Certainly it was difficult to gain the attention which planners felt the applications of their craft required. But assuming that this public attention could be secured, the resources would be assembled. A decade of disillusionment (and let me suggest an overdone disillusionment) has followed into our present day. It has left many planners with the aspirations of an earlier time, yet a growing frustration about the failure to be able to *deliver*.

The classic responses to frustration gaps whether in this or any other in the field, are simply ennumerated. The flight into fantasy—"Let us simplify the world, it is too difficult to cope with in its present complexity," and thus in a world of 4 billion people—"Think small." The movement to nihilism, "If the world will not respond the way I would like; Bomb it, Rip it, Tear it, Shred it"—It may not convince anyone but it feels so good! The retreat into day-by-day mechanics, of trivia routinely done and routinely conceived, in order to avoid the necessities of direction. And so very, very many more.

The age of affluence came and has left as its residual an immobilizing fear of its loss. The spirit of social adventure of the early 60s in retrospect may have been overly sanguine but certainly had more to commend it than the overt pessimism of our own time.

With the current loss of public vitality the necessity for theory as a unifying concept becomes even more important. In this new age of anxiety it is an essential input enabling us both to understand our own roles as well as providing guidance in shaping them. For the moment, in all too many areas, the planners' actions and movement can seem terrifyingly small. But this is precisely the time when theory and the firm grasp of principle are most useful.

Gathered here are a variety of individuals all of whom in their separate and distinct fashions are seasoned, both in practice and in theory. It is our hope that their statements, shared puzzlements and insights may prove useful to all of us fellow practitioners in the planning field.

George Sternlieb
Director,
Center for Urban Policy Research

Introduction

Planning Theory in the 1980's— A Search for Future Directions

Robert W. Burchell

James W. Hughes

The invited papers which comprise this work are an attempt to provide insight to future directions for planning theory of the next decade. They represent substantial statements on predicted movement in this area from a group of experienced theorists and practitioners.

As is the case for any assemblage of individuals, opinions differ as to future form and focus. This is a strength not a limitation of this monograph. This difference of perspective and orientation, however, occasions a difficult problem when attempting to disseminate ideas to the field. Since the authors represent, in most instances, the leading edge of thought for their particular niche in planning theory/practice, the richness of their individual as well as collective insight is lost without an appropriate base of reference from which to draw. When these papers were introduced to planning students at various levels of sophistication, even the most advanced found a framework a necessary accompaniment to view both the direction and potential for growth of the various strains of planning theory.

It is the purpose of this introductory essay and the organization of the monograph: (1) to first group authors into several dominant strains or currents of planning theory, (2) once grouped, to develop a theoretical base upon which to view their latest contributions, (3) to present a summary of the author's statements within the context of the theoretical base, and finally, (4) to make brief comments, reflecting the substance of the included papers, as to the projected direction and pace of change in theory and practice.

Two points of caution. First, the grouping presented here represents but one view of the developing components of planning theory. A bibliography is cited throughout this essay to attempt to substantiate this view but also to provide a range of reading materials in plannnig theory from which alternative views may be derived.

Second, papers of authors categorized within a particular grouping could in several instances be placed in another group or multiple groups. For some papers the fit within any group is a difficult one. The format of this reader provides a necessary beginning to view the contributions of the invited authors. It is the obligation of the user of this text to augment, alter or abbreviate the structure that is provided here, according to his/her individual interpretation of the evolution of planning theory.

Background

The river of American planning theory indeed may be broader than it is deep. It is theory which, in developing in less than half a century, has many currents and tributaries. As such, it is a theory which has wrestled with the interpretation of these components for most of its history [504: 233-234].*

The paper which follows views planning theory as significantly influenced by four main currents over its gestation period. Planning theory by choice and by necessity has had to embrace a structure of explanation for: physical development, economic control, social priorities, and policy initiation.

Physical planning is thus defined as a concern for the physical development of an area emphasizing primarily form and function. Its theory, over time, has been concerned with (1) a single, end-state plan reflecting an overriding public interest and (2) the size, scope, legal standing and position of this plan relative to derivative regulations (official map, zoning, subdivision control, etc.) [144:31].

Social planning and a derivative, advocacy planning, emphasize the needs and preferences of the plan's consumer population—people. They are a reaction to the functional and efficiency orientation of physical planning, and are intimately concerned with the systemic distribution of resources to counter social inequity. The advocacy plan pertains to a very specific client and is a much more politicized document than the physical plan [263:80].

---

* Numbers refer to citations of authors and page numbers as indicated in the general bibliography to this monograph.

Economic planning, in its simplest sense, deals with the planned as opposed to market distribution of goods and services. The theory of economic planning is concerned with who controls, the scope of control and the legitimacy of controlled goods distribution [412:371].

Policy planning is concerned with decisionmaking in both the private and public sectors. Its theory involves who decides, how much information is brought to the decisionmaking process, how alternatives are evaluated and the probability of a decision's success or implementation [329:18].

While each of these currents of planning theory have long histories and in some form or another are present today, there are also clear periods or eras when one or another current became the "in" way of explaining or teaching planning theory. For instance, physical planning was in vogue from the 1920s through the 1950s and is in resurgence again as part of the environmental movement of the early and mid-1970s. Social planning, taking its beginnings from the early reform movements of the 1920s-1930s, did not really come into its own until the 1960s. Economic planning, more or less rejected by all "New Deal" fearers in the 1930s, is in vogue as we approach the 1980s, from both traditional and radical political perspectives. Public policy planning while also having numerous roots in earlier periods received its greatest attention in the late 1960s and early 1970s.

In the material which follows no attempt is made to interpret the river of planning theory via some form of *summation* of its principal currents. This is an exercise that has been done in the past e.g., planning theory as a continuous debate over *substance versus process* (physical (urban) planning versus a combination of social, economic and policy planning) or planning theory's currents as *elements of a maturing theory,* e.g. seeking first substance (physical planning), then issues (social planning), then power and feedback (economic/policy planning) [516]. Other examples obviously exist and need not be elaborated here. It is an exercise that will be continued in the future and is best left to the field's prime paradigm builders—Webber, Etzioni, Friedmann, Harvey, Harris, Dyckman, Mann, etc.

The Physical Current

American urban planners trace their physical origins to ideas of planning which emerged from the development of the British model garden suburbs. These suburbs, a reaction to the burgeoning industrial city, were low density, open space communities which emphasized form and function. They were essentially physical solutions within a static set of economic and social parameters [611:xvii].

Planners came away from the Chicago World's Fair in 1893 with an idea that indeed at least the *aesthetics or form* of a city could be predetermined. This was an era known in planning as "City Beautiful." Plans of this period, developed by civic improvement organizations and private consultants (primarily architects), were concerned with public buildings, parks, streets and transportation. During the next fifteen years, a planning field, consisting only of a limited number of professionals, developed a plan for the Boston park system, a revised plan for Washington, D.C. and the Plan of Chicago. Soon came city plans for Rochester and Dallas [626:54-56]. At about this same period of time, the Pittsburgh Survey was completed and represented one of the first data-supported plans addressing the physical needs of the city and its resident populations.

During the 1920s a second generation of planners concentrated on the *function* of the city. This was the era of the "City Efficient" and was characterized by the development of *master plans,* drawn by newly created planning boards, encompassing programs for streets, transportation, central business districts, and parks/recreation. Emphasis was on the physical layout of the community with function as important as form. Financial and engineering considerations became paramount. Zoning and subdivision ordinances were developed as necessary regulations to carry out the plan. Comprehensive municipal zoning was upheld by the Supreme Court in Euclid, Ohio (1926); Radburn, the first American "garden city" was developed in 1927 and the Standard City Planning Enabling Act was drawn in 1928 [626:57-61].

Just prior to 1930, the *Regional Plan of New York and its Environs* was completed. It represented a broadening of scope of the plan to include economic and population problems as well as the more standard physical elements. Planning continued to expand during the 1930s and 1940s with the physical plan being extended to redevelopment and slum clearance activities. Again in terms of largely physical solutions to urban problems, planning was also a part of the Reform movement. Real property inventories and blight surveys became essential "pre-plan" activities.

In 1949, a National Housing Act was created which stated that federally-aided urban developments should conform to a planned program for the entire community. Five years later, in the Housing Act of 1954, the federal government's position that a plan is a mandatory precondition to publicly funded activities was reenforced with statements concerning the necessity of a "Comprehensive Plan" as well as general community acknowledgement of this plan (a "Workable Program"). In so doing, the federal government offered matching funds under the 701 Planning Assistance Program to assist municipalities in preparing a plan. The 701 Program increasingly specified the type of background studies which should be included in the plan: transportation, housing, economic base studies, community facility assessments, etc.—the emphasis continued to be on hard-ware.

The plan was acknowledged as a single document, not municipally adopted (i.e., not legally binding) but rather used for guidance purposes, reflecting the desires and directions of an overriding public interest. The plan had to reflect a single and consistent set of values and hence suppose a fundamental agreement among those with an interest in the outcome of the plan. To safeguard the public interest an *independent* planning commission was to oversee the plan. This then became the local planning model.

Following the 701 Planning Assistance era was a turn by physical planning to the importance of geographic location (within cities and metropolitan areas) and the relationship of location and land use [101:5]. This spawned a land use plan that was sensitive to both the economics and efficiency of location. This trend within planning has continued to the present day and is referred to by Marxists as the "planners fettish with space" [419:12].

In the mid-1960s, the significance of geographic location was internalized within the confines of a single development or project. The large scale new community experiments under Title VII and even the smaller planned unit developments (PUDs) were concerned with concepts of neighborhood as the focus of the community, the size of a "social intensive unit" as the basic building block of neighborhood, and harmoniously arranged, "mixed uses" as the essence of community. The physical plan in this sense was keyed heavily to the success of the "built environment". This period was characterized by a proliferation of theory concerned with the degree to which administrative discretion would replace the rule of law (ordinances, regulations etc.) in the development process and resultingly, the power relationships of an appointed planning board which would pass on a specific planned development, versus elected municipal officials, who would be responsible for the overall appropriateness of the zoning plan [158:5-10].

As developments grew larger (early 1970s) and a feeling developed that the tempo and sequence could be controlled within the confines of a single project, the desire to control timing and location of development at the community scale reemerged from the earlier debates of the 1950s. Could the master plan itself specify where in the community and at what pace development could take place? Initial enthusiasm emanating from the growth control movement said that it could; the results of such schemes in Ramapo, Petaluma and the Twin Cities found that it could not. The continued role for the plan was as a guidance document with zoning, subdivision control, capital facilities ordinances and now, development systems (for tempo and sequence of development) the teeth of the plan, as legally-binding, implementing regulations.

Again the plan was viewed as essentially a document to coordinate the hardware of land development. Robert Freilich's comment to the field on numerous occasions reflected other professions' view of the specific competence of the planner: "at a time when we badly need physical land planning, most of the field has forgotten how to draw a plan."

In the mid-1970s, the McHargian view began to have an impact on the physical plan. Land was partitioned not according to the most favorable land use but rather according to natural science criteria affecting its holding capacity. The land had "value to nature as well as value to society." [143:7].

Over time, there have been continuous disagreements as to the true effectiveness of the plan due to scope and term [611:218]:

> . . . confusion as to coverage generates additional confusion as to function.
>
> . . . its complexity and bulk and the cumbersome procedures involved in its preparation rule out any simple process for modifying it or bringing it up to date.

Yet its focus has not been altered significantly. Although we have passed through periods calling for policy plans, concept plans, plans for limited areas (PUD's), plans for limited purposes (Urban Renewal, CRP's, Model Cities), the master plan has remained an essentially physical (form and function) development vehicle.

Mel Webber's statement to the field in 1963 wherein he claimed that city planners' responsibility relates primarily to the physical and locational aspects of development improvements has remained as a guide for a definite wing of the planning profession [274:35]. It is ironic that Webber today notes that although scores of 701 Master Plans have been produced, in the aggregate, they have failed to alter the course of urbanization.

Physical Planning in Change*

Amid the urban unrest of the 1960s, and the national economic difficulties of the early 1970s, physical planning has regained a momentum that could not have been perceived a decade ago. While new permutations have evolved in the applied realm—no doubt due to the vagaries of federal program shifts and evolving public consciousness—the persistence of older tenets is a basic reality. Indeed, as is demonstrated in several of the contributions to this section, a virtual reaffirmation of long standing,

---

* Quotes secured from the papers in this section are not directly referenced to page numbers, nor are comments taken from the initial conference transcripts.

but debated principles is taking place, and will probably represent a constant in the coming decade. As Norman Krumholz concludes, the changes which appear from time to time to ripple the surface of the profession are often superficial and transient.

Similarly, alternative posturings and diverse paradigms also promise to be tensions persisting into the 1980s. While certainly not schisms, a uniform consensus does not appear on the horizon.

The authors of the papers of this section, more than any other, are rooted in professional practice, hence influencing their theoretical perspective heavily to the descriptive rather than the prescriptive. And as they differ in their professional roles, so too does their basic framework of planning.

PHYSICAL PLANNING AS CONCERNED WITH THE "NUTS AND BOLTS" OF LAND USE

In the first paper, George Raymond explores the role of the physical urban planner, and his conclusions would probably be ratified by the bulk of those involved in professional consulting practice. The neo-architect's role is accepted, and broader political and social dilemmas relegated to secondary status. Indeed, Raymond's conclusions appear as extrapolations of the basic physical planning heritage:

1) A true physical planner is one who understands the socio-economic-political context in which he operates, and who is concerned with the socio-economic-political implications of physical planning objectives.

2) Older objectives of planning's heritage are still paramount, however —the aesthetic focus of the "City Beautiful" movement and the concern with the rational distribution of land uses of the "City Efficient" period.

3) Raymond questions the logic of later periods in the history of planning which sacrificed physical planning objectives on the altar of social utopias. Stemming physical deterioration, preserving neighborhood values, restoring dwindling tax bases, achieving safety, beauty and convenience, and other similar objectives are not yet obsolete notions.

4) While the ascendency of "environment" in the 1970s has sharpened awareness of the broad implications of development patterns on the macro-scale, the micro-scale arena—where most physical planning efforts are concentrated—finds little in the environmental movement's text that hasn't been present in the traditional principals of sound physical development practices. The real problem today is that the diverse strands of the planning profession have been unable to talk to one another.

5) Rationality and the formulation and articulation of the "plan" are still viewed by Raymond as the central focus of planning.

6) Yet the ineffectiveness of physical planning at the local level cannot be refuted.

a) A major reason is that physical plans are not developed by, or under the aegis of, local governing bodies, with the latter not required to enact them as official policies. Governing bodies cherish their freedom to respond to pressures for land use changes.

b) Similarly the courts do not often give full credence to plans that, under our present laws, are required to be adopted by planning boards—appointed advisory bodies.

c) Planning will continue to lose credibility without a legal requirement mandating that plans be adopted by local government bodies.

d) Within the context of the latter provisions, the plan should be a general decisionmaking guide, not the depiction of an ideal "end state." It would establish a unitary planning and regulatory system, assuring that proposed land use changes would be examined through a disciplined process, open to public scrutiny and debate.

7) Physical planning at higher-than-local levels has been very effective in a number of substantive areas—transportation, sewerage and the like. There are really only two issues that are intimately involved with physical planning that we have not been able to resolve on a regional basis—regulation of land use and the equitable and rational distribution of the working population.

8) The planning education design advocated by Raymond is congruent to his conceptualization of the physical laws of planning—the schools must teach the student to see the world as it is rather than as the instructor would like it to be.

Physical Planning as Assuring Ecological Determinism

Ian McHarg sharply delineates the functional roles and tasks of planning within an even more tightly defined sector of the planning spectrum—ecological planning. Resurrected are a number of premises subject to sustained debate in the past two decades.

1) The environment and its preservation through correct use is the prime basis of planning.

2) Within this context, the planner is a catalyst, suppressing his/her personal ego while attempting to bring forth and explain numerous planning options.

a) The planner offers scientific predictability about the consequences of different courses of action.

b) The planner helps the community make its values explicit and identifies alternative solutions with their attendant costs and benefits.

3) Resisted is the philosophy of planning imposing values or exercising the will of the constituency. The planner is viewed as external to the political realm.

4) The analytic orientation is defined in a full systems approach to the process which produces the phenomena constituting the region (itself a system).

Rationality, a systems orientation, and non-biased, apolitical perspectives dominate the McHargian tenets of environmental planning.

PHYSICAL PLANNING AS PROMOTING A WORKABLE BUILT ENVIRONMENT— SUBURBAN-EXURBAN

Via an equally narrow partition—planning as a holistic urban design— Morton Hoppenfeld also reflects the biases of the physical solution to urban problems.

1) While all of the millions of pieces of artifacts that make up the built environment are, in fact, "designed" for some purpose, they are not consciously designed to add up to a "good city."

2) It is the phenomenon of relatedness to each other and the whole which is the critical public interest and it is that urge and knowledge of how to relate that distinguishes planning and its practitioners.

3) Planning is the process of stating goals, articulating issues, value creation, and policy and program identification for resource allocation and activities aimed at achieving goals—all of this enroute to the "good city."

While these concepts are not antithetical to those of the preceding authors, the client relationship differs. Although Hoppenfeld states that the designer is subservient to and participant with client groups, a role beyond that of pure technician is implied.

4) Part of the problem of not valuing "good design" process and environmental awareness is the fact of an undemanding, unsophisticated clientele. Only with inroads into the "educational" processes will young people become first sensitized, then educated, and ultimately demanding of, a better urban environment.

Inherent in these statements is not the articulation of the client group's values in design, but rather convincing them of the superiority of professional insight—the planner's unique competence to interpret and relate the physical environment.

Further, great stress is placed by Hoppenfeld on physical determinism.

5) The physical development process can properly and creatively be used as a lever for social and institutional change/development which is one of the essential activities of a healthy democratic society.

Given these viewpoints, it is understandable that Hoppenfeld eschews the small scale focus in favor of large scale development. Recognizing the likely limits to the latter in our present era, there is nonetheless the belief that improved urban environments can only be achieved through large scale, self-contained projects.

Physical Planning as Assuring a Workable Built Environment—Urban

But standing in sharp contrast to these conventions is another heritage of more recent vintage—the institutionalization of political activism by the traditional physical planning function in the urban arena. Norman Krumholz rejects the roles described above, and takes an aggressive stance toward expanding the conventional modes of action characterizing municipal planning practice.

1) Planning is both in a state of flux and quite static. Despite the current ascent of environment, and the emergence and complementary descent of other substantive issues, planning remains unchanged in many fundamental ways.

2) Planners have traditionally lacked access to the decision-making process, have had little impact on important public policy issues, have tended to avoid political conflict, have been technique-oriented rather than goal oriented, and are facilitators rather than initiators.

3) Recognizing these limitations, as well as being in a context of negative growth, Krumholz while embracing the traditional activities of physical planning—general land use, transportation, and public facilities plans—adopts an alternative paradigm for evaluating plans for the built environment.

4) A normative posture is established, whose goal is the promotion of a wider range of choices for those residents who have few, if any, choices. The analytical process is rational with respect to these ends, with alternatives evaluated in terms of "who pays" and "who gets," *i.e.*, cost-benefit analyses with respect to affected clienteles.

5) Within this context, it is asserted that the planner's obligation is to realistically point out what is possible and what is probably impossible to accomplish in a declining city, and to advocate the interests of the city's less affluent residents with respect to the built environment.

6) This, however, means abandoning one of the planning profession's most cherished myths—that the planner is an apolitical professional, promoting goals that are widely accepted through the use of professional standards that are objectively correct.

7) Planners must become more innovative, more entrepreneurial and more aggressive than they have been in the past. They must become "activists" seizing responsibility where power vacuums exist, and expanding their array of clients.

8) A corollary effect of these thrusts is to embed planning in conflict situations, requiring risk-taking not normally accepted in traditional professional roles.

Physical Planning—A Search for Future Directions

It seems clear that planning's physical roots remain strong. The debate between Thomas Adams and Lewis Mumford that took place at the time of the publication of the *Plan for New York* remains current today. Is a plan for an area a predominantly physical vehicle, which in its development process pays attention to but is not dominated by current economic and social forces, or is it rather a reflection of the economic and social forces with the physical solution contingent upon their correct interpretation/synthesis [611:xix]?

Physical planning into the 1980s has been correctly defined by McHarg, Raymond, Hoppenfeld and Krumholtz. It will be dominated by environmental determinism; traditional planning/regulatory vehicles will be sought to interpret the physical environment and developed planning solutions or planning "principles" will mold the built environment. The planner as an apolitical agent, an articulator of multiple solutions, will preside in the first instance, the planner as a land use technician will be called upon in the second, and the planner as a unique professional to deal with problems of the built environment will be summoned in the third.

This is a world of the natural resource inventory, critical area/issue legislation and environmental impact statements combining to state the ability of the land to receive development; master plan, zoning subdivision controls, growth management systems, planned shrinkage concepts dictating tempo and sequence of development; and planned unit development ordinances, "reworked" new community legislation, energy conservation regulations, holding capacity schemes, and transfer of development rights, helping to prescribe ways to achieve this development.

Geographers, natural scientists and attorneys will continue to encroach upon the traditional planner/architect as interpretors of the physical environment. Techniques and approaches such as remote sensing, fiscal impact analysis, etc., will be sought as pseudo-scientific ways to keep abreast of and predict the impact of land development.

Equity in land use will continue to be sought. Increasing restrictions will be placed on the ability of communities to zone out populations—fair share plans, housing assistance plans, consistency between regional and local plans will continue to be the criteria upon which intergovernmental revenue transfers are based.

The Social Current

Social planning as defined by John Dyckman involves the "application of social values to programs undertaken in pursuit of economic or political goals" [223:68].

Social planning came to the fore in response to:

1) the physical and economic bias of the comprehensive plan [226:5],

2) the political inequities fostered by recasting questions of public policy in terms of technical solutions [263:80],

3) the necessary redistribution of resources brought about by the inequities of the workings of the private market [229:312].

In the first case a segment of the planning field became concerned that the most prolific outgrowth of their expertise, the comprehensive plan, seemed to slight a very vital part of community development—i.e., social rehabilitation. There was a definite impact of physical and economic development upon *people,* yet social problems seemed to be continuously slighted in favor of physical problems which could be answered by technical/economic rather than behavioral solutions. Elizabeth Wood characterizes the current and suggests at least one possible reason for the flagrant social inactivity [383:9-10]:

> It is increasingly clear that planners and administrators are not planning effectively or appropriately with or in behalf of people, and that they must begin to invoke measures shaped by a new kind of knowledge broadly characterized as social because it deals with people. What this means is that planning must somehow be enabled to deal better with the invisible but potent social and economic characteristics, capacities, and desires of people as well as tangible and visible characteristics of physical structures. It is not that planners have not recognized that people are the materials of which the city is made . . . they have not known how to do anything about that knowledge.

"Social" rehabilitation within the field of planning (especially urban planning) became such a pervasive issue that it soon posed serious disfunctional effects to the on-going, and by now, technically smooth, physical and economic planning. The existing situation caused a mild yet clearly concerned statement by Frieden [229:311]:

> Within the planning profession there has been considerable dismay over the impact of planned programs . . . shortcomings in scope tend to work in direct opposition to what little is otherwise being attempted . . . this has given rise to a reexamination of purposes and methods.

This reexamination of purpose took the form of an expanded comprehensive plan and a realization that those who were affected by the plan were to be viewed at least as partial clients of the planner, if only in the sense of unfulfilled consumers.

> The Comprehensive Plan can be turned into a more valuable instrument through the conscious incorporation of social policy decisions . . . The physical form, facilities and features of a community affect the social life and opportunities of its members and therefore should be designed in a manner to meet social objectives [226:4].

> Planning which is responsive to professional discretion and political leadership, might in the process forsake the preferences, needs and desires of the consuming population . . . What we are calling for is a new technology which could develop new standards by feeding new information into the planning process—namely data derived from social-scientific inquiries about the preferences of present and potential service users [266:234].

The ultimate product of the profession's searchings was a general agreement on what would constitute the scope of social planning.

Three variables were considered primary components of any formula essential to the establishment of social policies [226:6]:

1) *Social Needs*—The total amount of assistance required to serve a given population.

2) *Social Capital*—The total amount of effort and latent capacities of all social groups measured as a community resource.

3) *Social Services*—Recreation, education, individual and family guidance, health assistance, welfare and housing.

The second condition favoring development within the field of a current of social planning, was a feeling of general apathy induced by a heavily influential technological society. The "mainstream" planner, characteristic of many of his professional peers in other fields, was recognized as a withdrawn *technician*. The planner formed in the image of the classical model was primarily a technician, an analyst, a model builder, and as such, relatively isolated from the vital forces of change in society [332:316]. His professional jargon and analytical approach cast planning in a context which was too distant from and lacked understanding by other ordinary citizens. Lower groups of the social strata were put to a further disadvantage as their ability to comprehend their "planned" future was lessened by a single unchallengeable, self-declared expert—a middleman dealing exclusively in a "world of maps, diagrams and statistical tables" [332:316].

A field of planners developed that would not only be available to interpret plans to those who could not comprehend their full import, but also to represent the interests of such individuals by providing an alternative plan more favorable to their cause. The planner became an "advocate" of group interests and his alternative plan "a reaction to, rather than an enactment of", the basic plan [263:81].

The third and probably most striking condition which led to the rise of social planning was a feeling that the private market was compounding existing social inequities and thus had to be assisted to enable programs geared to reducing these inequities to gain necessary footholds. This took the form of a redistribution of resources. Further, social planners believed that indeed an excess supply of resources was needed, over and above what would be required by actual demand. Although confined only to supplying decent housing and recreation facilities to the disadvantaged in urban areas, it was still a fundamental change in the "neutral-efficient resource stand" maintained by the "mainstream" planner [229:312].

In terms of decisionmaking, the social planner does not work in behalf of an overriding public interest; instead the planner is the neutral agent of two specific clients. The immediate client is his employer (municipality, agency, etc.); the ultimate client is the populace affected by the plan. The acceptable plan is a compromised version containing the views of both clients.

This neutral stance of the social planner made explicit by Davidoff/ Reiner and others evoked serious criticism from the more active members of social planning's rank and file [320:110]. This group was composed primarily of planners brought under the social umbrella in reaction to the power inequities of technical plan. The theory of widening choice basic to social planning was given the modifier "opportunity" and soon became the rallying point of "advocacy" planning.

Advocacy planners took the view that any plan is solely the embodiment of particular group interests and therefore "it is imperative that any group with interests at stake in the planning process have these interests articulated" [263:81].

This group in similar fashion to the main body of social planners, rejects the idea of a "single best planning solution" however, does not see their role as neutral bargaining agents between an immediate and ultimate client. The advocacy planner actively seeks those at the bottom of the social structure and uses his expertise to plead their case in the planning process [321:335]:

> There are many possible roads for a community to travel and many plans should show them. Explication is required of many alternative futures presented by those sympathetic to the construction of each future.

In this case planning is no longer neutral but rather "pluralistic and partisan—in a word overtly political." Advocacy planning in one sense is thus a new type of politics, a medium through which [263:81, 87]:

1)   local interests are expressed in the larger political system.

2   issues which pertain to specific kinds of communities (urban renewal —urban areas) build coalitions of support.

3)   technical society may be harnessed and bureaucracy controlled.

There was a belief in the social wing of planning that social scientists, social/advocacy planners and policymakers in search of change could redirect national policy, largely through influence on federal programs, toward social rather than economic objectives. System change was possible through the introduction of new streams of voices—voices whose power was weighted inversely to their position in society. The legitimacy of social objectives was to be maintained by continuous challenge by and fear of replacement with an alternative political system.

Advocacy planning moved the field significantly ahead in that the planner was an active decisionmaker—one who sought *implementation* of the plan as well as the plan itself as an achievable end.

Social Planning in Change*

The abrupt differentiation between the socio-economic-political context of the 1970s when compared to the 1960s has also been evidenced by the evolution of social planning. However, while persistence appears to be the appropriate description of the trajectory of physical planning, adaptation and change appear more to characterize the realm of social planning.

The contributions of this section tend to define three distinct loci of the broader subject matter; the relationships of social planning to social science; the evolution and adaptation of advocacy planning (which in itself is marked by three separate dimensions); and the emergence of and identification of new social service client groups. Cutting across these partitions are varying theoretical shifts as well as different professional strategies and postures. It is readily apparent that the changes in society as a whole are mirrored by the conceptualizations of the individual contributors.

Social Planning as a Reluctant Social Science Disciple

Irving Louis Horowitz refutes the powerful tendency to think of social planning and social science in strictly cumulative and interactive terms. In fact, he presents powerful arguments that there is a substantial inertia to the gulf between the two which appears to represent a historical continuity.

1) In the 1960s, amidst the heady wine of movement and rebellion, there seemed no question that social planners, policy makers, and social scientists would come together in a grand assault against the establishment. Yet, it is clear from the perspective of only a decade, that the much heralded unity of social planning and social science has not taken place.

2) Social planning and social science, far from being "handmaidens" in a common concert, are in fact exceedingly different and for the most part profoundly antithetical in their missions.

3) The "commonsense" of planning rests on maximum utilization of resources and perfect equilibrium of economics. The "commonsense" of social science rests on maximum equity and liberty, and entails producing an excess of supply to satisfy demand.

---

* Quotes secured from the papers in this section are not directly referenced to page numbers, nor are comments taken from the initial conference transcripts.

4) As a result, the dynamic of social science discovery, the interpretation of research and criticism, and the consequent emergence of new paradigms, tends to be ignored, even suppressed in the mechanistic renderings of social science innovation by the planning communities.

Advocacy Planning as a Radical Political Movement

Social planning is also marked by the evolution and adaptation of its advocacy component. It is possible to discern within the contributions of this section three threads of the gradual transformation—a more explicit elaboration of its redistributive nature, the increasing presence of the Marxist (or class) perspective, and a broader reformulated conceptual framework.

Paul Davidoff is a proponent of the first thread, which is a close extrapolation of the modes of thought of the recent past. Perhaps the least ideological of the viewpoints with respect to the broader institutional structure of society—or its potential restructuring—the redistributive function of planning is nonetheless stridently normative.

1) The redistributive function in planning is aimed at reducing negative social conditions caused by great disparities in possession, by classes of the population, of important resources resulting from public or private action.

2) The redistributive goal is substantive—a political and ethical issue—as well as relating to process—a system of decisionmaking open to all.

3) And the battlelines are etched sharper and deeper. If a planner is not working directly for the objective of eradicating poverty and social and sexual discrimination, then she or he is counterproductive. If the work is not aimed at redistribution, then a presumption stands that it is amoral—there is an ethical imperative for a single direction in planning.

Chester Hartman broadens the thrust maintained by Davidoff, directing the analytical posture to the functional capitalist structure of the economic institutions of the nation.

1) It is a system that has proved itself incapable of providing all of its people with a decent standard of living.

2) Within the context of the unprecedented fiscal and urban crises of the 1970s, the work of social planning centers on the perspective of class conflict.

    a) Support of defensive struggles to maintain urban services and offensive struggles to improve urban services.

    b) Political organization to unify class groups impacted negatively, of the pervasive urban crises.

    c) Development of strategies to counter the tendencies to divide the working class, and to unite the class in common struggle against its enemies.

3) Consequently, it is the struggle to transform the class system that sets the stage for the coming period of activity for planners and everyone else involved in urban policies and strategies.

In contrast, Lisa Peattie focuses on the processes by which planning, politics and ideas change over time in interrelationship and discerns the need for advocacy planning to adopt a conceptual framework suitable for long term processes of social change.

1) In the 1960s, advocacy planning could form purposes and organize groups around ameliorating an issue or pieces of that issue, but not around transforming it.

2) A different system could only happen through a set of consecutive and cumulative modifications in both the political and technical order, each opening up new constituencies, new possibilities, new ideas and new purposes, each building on previous developments.

3) But two modes of 1960's advocacy planning—the classic model, bringing pluralism into the decisionmaking process; and a variant of classical radical political organizing, whose real output was growth of radical consciousness—tended to focus on isolated issues.

4) With regard to the latter, their results tended to assume a negative format—a vetoing operation. But even the generation of positive alternatives would, if practical in nature, be but a modification of the existing system, or a variation of an existing institution.

5) And with the focus on constituencies defined by concrete, but usually small scale, situations—constituencies whose longevity proved questionable —continual interaction was missing, as was the attempt to place local organization within the structural context of large-scale policy.

6) The task for advocacy planning in the future thus has to move: from transplanting plight into problem, problem into purpose, purpose into programatic action or planning—and building a political framework in which the outcomes of such a process can themselves be further modified by the people affected in a cumulative process of social change.

SOCIAL PLANNING AS A "STOREWATCHER" OF DEFINITE SERVICE POPULATIONS

An emerging focus of social planning has less to do with methodological, normative, or procedural aims than it does with the expansion of the arena of application. Julian Wolpert concentrates on one sector of an expanding matrix of concern—the mentally and physically handicapped—growing special service populations.

1) Substantial evidence reveals relative stability in the concentration of handicapped people in central cities and suggests a highly significant new role for the urban planner.

2) Two models, among others, can find validation in the social service delivery systems for handicapped people in urban areas.

a) One approach assumes the economic, cultural and social service systems have casualties and victims. It is easier to redress through public programs, the gaps in the market basket of the handicapped and the needy than to create a support structure which has no casualties. In this framework, the handicapped strive to approximate normalization.

b) Another model assumes that progress in creating open and acceptable societies requires a stage of labeling and even stereotyping its casualties so that corrective action can be taken. This approach assumes that the segregation of the handicapped permits conspicuous attention to be focused on the imperfections of our society.

3) As a result, the efforts of the social service system are uncoordinated, diffuse, and insufficient. This implies that special populations will continue generally to be concentrated where housing costs are least and where "free" public services are in abundance—urban areas of capital disinvestment.

4) The social planner who understands how to deinstitutionalize center city life for the handicapped population has the requisite skills for intervention. Two major issues become the responsibility of the community based social service planner: (1) the support system of the individual within the community and (2) the community as a viable unit.

Social Planning—The Search for Future Directions

Social rather than economic or physical priorities will continue as the main thrust of this wing of planning. A concern about the problems of people rather than their artifacts—structures and public facilities—will shape emerging theory. Theory will continue to be concerned with whose voices affect policy and the balancing of those voices to better reflect those unable to be heard. Social planners will consistently be involved in the advocacy of major economic system changes if their objectives are not achieved or achieved at less than adequate pace.

A national system of minimum health care and the guaranteed welfare or minimum income for those who are economically handicapped become short-range social objectives. Lobbies for economically handicapped cities and regions, and the staffing of the federalized city (brought about through necessary intergovernmental transfers for fiscal stability) are current roles/ occupations for the social planner.

Social planning will continue to be provided with a constituency-by-default —the physically and mentally handicapped. The needs of these populations are legion and almost totally unaddressed from a planning perspective.

The Economic Current

Recognizing the dangers of oversimplification when attempting to classify economic allocation in the dichotomous grouping of the "market and the mastermind" [319:3], it is necessary to turn to the comparative economist, George Halm [404:14-21] when such a classification becomes unavoidable.

In Halm's *Economic Systems* two basic alternatives are suggested to the unidimensional system of "Robinson Crusoe." These are the "market economy" and the "centrally planned economy." The central issue of course is when private enterprise, markets and prices shall be relied upon as control mechanisms for operating the economy and when these mechanisms shall be replaced by state action [404:16].

March and Simon in *Organizations* specify the alternatives from an organizational approach [372:200]. Consider a single organization with a goal which may simply be to maximize profit. The organization has at its disposal certain resources, and its problem is to achieve a maximum attainment of its goal, subject to the limits of its resources. Clearly if one person or group of persons possesses all the relevant information connecting possible courses of action, with the utilities resulting therefrom, he or they could discover which course of action was best for the organization. **This would be central planning in its simplest form.**

As an alternative procedure we could simulate within the organization the operation of markets and the price mechanism. We could designate various subparts to the organization, establish a separate criterion for each subpart (profit) and create markets for all commodities that would flow between parts. Then each part of the organization would purchase its inputs and sell its outputs whether to other parts of the organization or outside the organization. **A procedure of this kind is called decentralized decisionmaking through prices.**

For the development which follows it is necessary to portray the means of economic allocation as two conceptually-opposite delivery systems. This is unavoidable for the bulk of the literature presents the alternatives of commodity distribution as such. Throughout the debate which has raged since the late 1920s, two dichotomous economic delivery systems are consistently linked with the philosophical question of "to plan or not to plan." Planning of course was identified with a centrally directed economic system whereas non-planning pertained to the free market variety [404:17].

Those who favored a centrally guided economy would agree with Joan Robinson's statement [416:2]:

> Under a system of private enterprise . . . there is no central control, *no plan of action,* and whatever actually occurs in economic life is the result of innumerable, independent, individual decisions. *The course which is best for each individual to pursue in his own interests is rarely*

> *the same as the course best calculated to promote interests of society
> as a whole* (emphasis added) and if its economic system appears
> sometimes fantastic or even insane—as when foodstuffs are destroyed
> while men go hungry—we must remember that it is not surprising
> that the interaction of free individual decisions should lead so often
> to irrational, clumsy, and bewildering results.

On the other hand, those who opposed central control in favor of the
market drew heavily upon the "bounded rationality" argument and viewed
man as a limited being incapable of developing a scale which could equi-
tably rank an entire society's values. Planning via any centralized means
carried with it a distinctive taint of individual bias and therefore of latent
discrimination [405:15]:

> To direct all our activities *according to a single plan* presupposes
> that every one of our needs is given its rank in an order of values
> which must be complete enough to make it possible to decide among
> all the different courses which the planner has to choose. It presup-
> poses, in short, the existence of a complete ethical code in which all
> different human values are allotted their due place . . .
>
> The planning authority cannot confine itself to providing opportuni-
> ties for unknown people to make whatever use of them they like. . It
> cannot tie itself down in advance to general and formal rules . . . There
> can be no doubt that planning involves deliberate discrimination be-
> tween particular needs of different people and allowing one man to do
> what another must be prevented from doing. It means in effect a
> return to the rule of status.

The view which is expressed above draws from the prose of Manheim,
Mumford, and Tugwell and interprets planning as only [613:3]:

> . . . a field for practical social reform, for utopian thinking, for norm
> setting, for widening the scope of rationality and order in society and
> for sharing in the exercise of power.

An alternative view would be to selectively extract the economic guidance
claims of Manheim, link them with the power features of Tugwell and
together with March and Simon's realistic interpretation of the plan or no
plan debate (i.e., as merely an argument over centralized versus decentralized decisionmaking), portray planning as directly concerned with influencing and charting the direction of a national economic delivery system
in an effort not to induce utopia, but rather to provide badly needed economic stability [345:33]:

> The rapid growth and reorganization of the economic structure,
> coupled with the expiration of the dogma of laissez-faire, have endowed
> government with a largely expanded role as regulator or policemen
> over our *economic republic* . . . the acceptance of the philosophy that
> government should *act* to help citizens in economic distress and even
> more that government should *plan* to avoid or at least cope with un-
> avoidable distresses has further added to the role of modern government.

Renewed interest in economic planning as we know it in the mid and late 1970s has been brought about by similar economic uncertainty that spurred its original calling: unemployment, inflation, monetary imbalances and resource/conservation difficulties. It is brought about also by a curious alignment of business leaders/conservatives and liberals/Marxists who seem to agree as to the necessity of a planned economy yet wait patiently to violently disagree as to who will eventually control it [412:372].

Business leaders, reflecting corporate experience and business school training, believe that the time for rational economic planning is here—what is good for the goose (the corporation) is good for the gander (the nation). Long range national economic intent is essentially for stable corporate planning [412:373].

Liberals view any alteration of the existing system which would move from a private to a planned economy as a situation which would bring meliorative revenues, however fragmented, to the problems of the poor. Marxists believe that it will be virtually impossible to remedy urban ills without a fundamental alteration of the political economic system. The crisis of the city is a symptom of deep seated tensions lying within capitalistic social relations. Since the most essential material base of a society is the way production is organized, it is essential to control this process. He who controls the process is the direct beneficiary of its rewards [419:6].

Thus the modern view of economic planning is not heated debate over to plan or not to plan or over economic planning as an anti-American concept, but rather, how it will be done, how much of the supply sector will be controlled and who will control it.

Questions surrounding the implementation of economic planning posed by Meyerson are whether Americans who generally distrust their leaders will give them this kind of power, the tools of economists/planners are sufficiently sophisticated to control a planned economy and finally, there exists an atmosphere in an essentially recessional economy for this type of social experiment. Peter Schuck concentrates on the second and concludes [418:68]:

> We simply do not know how to build urban communities, fashion a national transportation system or eliminate social disintegration, much less accomplish all of these objectives simultaneously through an integrated strategy or plan.

Economic Planning in Change[*]

PLANNING REASONS FOR MOVING AWAY FROM A MARKET-BASED ECONOMY

David Harvey presents a classic essay describing the future role of the planner in a capitalist society. According to Harvey it is an ideological

---

[*] Quotes secured from the papers in this section are not directly referenced to page numbers, nor are comments taken from the initial conference transcripts.

mismatch (capitalism and planning) which dooms the planner to a life of perpetual frustration with the high sounding ideals of planning theory so frequently translated to the grubby experiences of planning practice. "Planners are taught to appreciate how everything relates to everything else in the urban system, to think in terms of costs and benefits, and to have some sympathetic understanding of the problems which face the private producers of the built environment, the landlord interest, the urban poor, the managers of financial institutions, the downtown business interests and so on." The planner then armed with these sensitivities, administers band-aids to extremely serious wounds.

According to Harvey, the late 1970's presents economic conditions (unemployment, stagflation, etc.) which signal a need for major systemic change. With change, planning for reconstruction of society is possible. Without change, and working within an ideology that allows capital to dominate labor, we will be merely "planning the ideology of planning."

The Disbenefits of Planning in a Capitalist State

Robert A. Beauregard, also advocating major change in the economic system as it is currently constructed, seeks to describe the dysfunctional role of the planner (from a Marxist perspective) in capitalist state. He defines public policy planners in terms of what they hold in common:

> . . . the belief of the importance of technical rationality for public policy, the requirement that complex systems must plan, and the political acceptance of State intervention into societal affairs.

With this orientation, planners apply their technical expertise to the manipulation of the State surplus (the distribution and redistribution of excess goods and services). According to Beauregard, they do so with a decided bias for efficiency considerations and thus have an implicit orientation towards preserving the status quo of power and privilege. Planners are thus fully implicated in the imbalances that capitalist society to date has wrought.

Beauregard's solution is a change in the criteria by which planning decisions are made. Equity considerations must be substituted for those of efficiency and the pursuit of greater distributional justice must replace the goal of minimizing the State surplus. The contribution of the planning theorist to the planning practitioner is unearthing planning's implications for inequality and suggesting various paths to radical reform.

The Capacity of Planners in a Controlled Economy

Brian J.L. Berry comments on the capacity of the planner, his skills and the data he employs to move to and participate in a controlled economic system. He views that capacity as limited because:

1) Policy research, the task of the planner in a controlled system, is different from disciplinary research in that it is ill-defined, not susceptible to precise design, and usually must be completed within an abbreviated time period.

2) Available data is oriented to those who exercise power in society. What is available may be very different from what is necessary to measure progress. Planners are data consumers rather than data producers.

3) More information in the decisionmaking process can only result in challenges to the decisionmaker's policies and programs.

The professional planner, according to Berry, has little chance of contributing more than enlightened guesses in such a society.

THE BENEFITS OF A MARKET BASED ECONOMY

Otto Davis and Chang-I Hua are reluctant to leave the market-oriented society that the planner has been a part of in the United States. The market orientation provides for efficient allocation of resources in society, not necessarily at the sacrifice of equity. According to Davis and Hua, urban renewal and various urban housing strategies were planned responses of limited success applied in the absence of a full understanding of the market mechanism.

Further, they point to fundamentalist planners' assertions of current social problems as a product of capitalist society, as essentially unfounded—"equity and efficiency are basically two distinct problems and in a real suboptimum world there is usually room for increasing efficiency at no one's cost." Further, "efficiency is a technical problem which forms the basis for a Pareto utopian's professionalism and equity is a political problem and no profession is entitled to claim expertise in it."

Davis and Hua agree that national redistribution of resources is an important problem but do not proclaim this task as the professional role of the planner. To accomplish such reallocation is a complex task—sufficient training to deal with this is currently not available to the planning profession. Courses in analytical methods, applied economics, quantitative techniques and modelling skills must prepare the planner for such tasks. Finally, the shift from supply-oriented to demand-oriented goods, characteristic of the current trend in federal programs, indicates a societal reaction to the incapacity of planners to plan.

PLANNING AS SOCIAL LEARNING IN A LAISSEZ-FAIRE ECONOMY

Britton Harris presents a planning paradigm of "social learning", similar to Friedmann's and Webber's ideas, which would operate also within a traditional laissez-faire economy. (According to Harris even if we were to subscribe to the principles of social reorganization the problems that face planners would still persist.) Planners would have the more or less traditional role of cultivating and evaluating feedback from other levels of government and other geographic areas as national planning concentrated in a single agency is an unworkable alternative and thus an improbable outcome. Harris sees ample room for both efficiency and equity —both are valuable concepts for social organization and not in conflict.

The social learning paradigm suggested by Harris would be composed of:

1. Methods which provide us with a better understanding of the way in which society functions and evolves.

2. Ways to specify value systems which govern the development and choice of plans.

3. Ways of finding or inventing good plans.

In Harris' view our potential for working towards realization of the first two components of his paradigm is much more advanced than it is for the third.

Economic Planning: A Search for Future Directions

The messages of Harvey and Schuck ring clear. Although there will be continued pressure from multiple political camps to move ahead with national economic planning on a grand scale, the societal enertia required to accomplish such an objective is obviously lacking.

Further, the Nixon-Ford Administration started a trend, continued in the current Administration, towards demand rather than supply oriented public goods. This will be difficult to reverse in the short-run. This trend obviously flies in the fact of attempts for more rather than less control of the public economy.

Crisis is often the prerequisite for major change in a democracy, however. Crisis could indeed be precipitated in the next decade by the externalities of inflation and increasing international economic competition. The causal and responsive elements have been delineated in two opposite directions. Government over-regulation could serve as one focus with less control seen as a precondition for effective response. Diametrically opposite would be the assertion that the private market has failed and the problems can only be solved by more centralized government control. The arguments over the centralized control function will be set in this arena.

The Public Policy (Rational/Technical—Social Action) Current

The public policy current has two main tributaries—a rational/technical component and a social action component. The first involves the introduction of knowledge and structure to the decisionmaking process, the second is concerned with the linkage between knowledge and action such that decisions, properly made, stand a reasonable chance for implementation.

RATIONAL/TECHNICAL COMPONENT

The rational/technical public policy current views planning as a process and thus heavily influenced by the theory of decisionmaking [344:331]. The view of planning as a process is important because through it, planning can be extended to the whole field of social development and not just a singular physical environment. In addition, planning would take on an ongoing or dynamic nature and not be characterized by a static and predetermined end state. This would be possible because planners would collect, analyze, and publicize information required to make decisions. The resulting most appropriate course of action would be determined through a sequence of choices—choices arrived at in a rational manner with significant technical assistance from systems analysis, operations research, the computer, model building, etc. [324:141].

The concept of rationality is no stranger to the social science literature. Its early origins associate it with the utility element in classical economic theory and with the concept of traditional economic man. "Man by acting rationally secured the necessary means to satisfy his increasing wants" [262:164]. In the economic view, necessary is defined as correctly designed to maximize goal achievement and may simply be replaced by the phrase "most efficient."

The type of rationality that has been identified most frequently with planning, however, is not the economic concept "to be rational man must be efficient" but rather a behavioral approach advocated by Meyerson and Banfield "to be rational one must follow a set of procedural steps" [352: 314]:

1) A decisionmaker considers all the alternatives open to him,
2) He identifies and evaluates all of the consequences which would follow from the adoption of each alternative,
3) He selects that alternative, the probable consequences of which would be preferable in terms of his most valued ends.

Dror adds the requirements of the "establishment of operational goals" and "the inventory and weighing of values" to the Meyerson-Banfield concept and terms this the "pure rationality" model [324:141].

Frequently cited alternatives to Dror's "pure" model besides those previously mentioned are the "bounded rationality" model of Simon and the "incrementalist" approach of Dahl-Lindblom.

Simon observes that most decisionmakers do not even try to optimize but settle for "satisficing" solutions, those which provide a relatively satisfactory realization of their values. Only if the realization of a value is frustrated is a search initiated for an alternative solution. There is no attempt to find maximum service of the value or the optimal combination of services which would be required in the "pure" model. Thus a decision-maker can test a number of alternatives either hypothetically or actually and reject them one after the other until he finds the one that "will do." This procedure is far less exacting than the one which is advocated by the pure model [371:80]. The incremental approach of Dahl-Lindholm is deliberately exploratory. Rather than attempting to foresee all of the consequences of the various routes, one route is tried and the unforeseen consequences are left to be discovered and treated by subsequent increments [319:25].

These latter forms of limited rationality sustained recognition as the pure model was unworkable and lacked relevance to practice—too much information was required to be processed, alternatives were legion, and far too many values had to be taken into account in the decision process.

After viewing the panoply of rationality types, Mann reacts negatively to their individual significance and attempts to summarize their influence on planning by saying: "In public urban planning (some kind of rationality) is most likely to lead to the best possible results".

The rational/technical component of the public policy current may be summarized as perfecting the decisionmaking function in a more decentralized type of local planning. Increased scientific and technical knowledge was sought to expedite and make consistent the interim stage between initial policy and ultimate plan implementation. Planning is viewed as a process and the comprehensive or master plan as a flexible guide to public policy.

The planner, using expertise as a mask, retreated from the political sector to protect his rational effort "from the folksy inconsistency of the local politician" [511:299]. The planner's prime concern was objective decisions whether or not the product of these decisions was implemented.

SOCIAL ACTION COMPONENT

The social action component of the public policy current draws from both the economic and social currents in planning and recognizes that the scope of planned action must be sufficiently large to be purposeful (national, societal) and further, must contain some level of assurity of completion by encompassing a correct blend of both power and congruity of objective. The focus of planning is shifted from decisions to actions. The question is no longer how rational a decision is but rather how to improve the quality of a decision-implementation sequence (action). Planning is thus viewed as a means of correctly articulating a "control-concensus" mix. Control, consisting of decisionmaking and power, enables society to move forward in pursuit of its goals. Consensus, with responsiveness to insure authenticity, enables society to implement the above action with a minimum of sustained resistance. This essentially is the language of Etzioni in *The Active Society* [326] which has been adjusted and interpreted for planning by Friedmann in *Retracking America* [329].

Dyckman notes that planning at this level requires the selection of social goals for the nation or state and the setting of targets for their achievement. It requires: "a ranking of these goals and an assessment of the cost of achieving them and judgments of the feasability of such programs" [223: 67]. According to Friedmann, the role of the planner is to evaluate societal performance and identify strategic points which require massive innovation [332:312].

This would be accomplished through the application of scientific and technical intelligence to organized actions. It would require a *transactive* planner—one that was adept at bringing together the processed knowledge of the planner and the experience knowledge of those who were being planned for [329:172-173].

The planner as a professional is part of an expert or elitist class—the client is the one who is planned for and is a member of some less-than-elitist class. While an exchange of information between planner and client is inherent in their relationship, nothing is said by Friedmann or others about role changes.

Public Policy Planning in Change*

It is clear that the bulk of policy planners continue to view planning as a legitimate policymaking activity, intimately involved with decisionmaking in its active or "implementation" mode, yet most (Etzioni in particular) look to less grand tasks for planners to influence and effectuate.

Lawrence D. Mann and Jerome Kaufman begin with general descriptions of planning and policymaking; the former to prescribe planning as a legitimate policymaking activity, the latter to suggest that planning become more politicized within this basic public sector role. John Friedmann specifies alternative activities for planners in the policymaking process as well as the expected outcomes of these activities. Melvin Webber calls for a single role for the planner in the policymaking arena—a facilitator of debate.

PLANNING AS A POLICYMAKING ACTIVITY

Lawrence D. Mann, adding fuel to a dialogue that has been within the planning/public administration literature for a decade, attempts to lay to

---

* Quotes secured from the papers in this section are not directly referenced to page numbers, nor are comments taken from the initial conference transcripts.

rest any notion that planning is not a legitimate professional policymaking activity. He admits that this is a difficult question to discuss as over the last decade there has been no serious and sustained effort to describe what (the process of) planning is—rather planners have attempted to focus on specific substantive problems of the city, blindly aping techniques borrowed from economics, quantitative geography and engineering.

Contrary to the above notion, Mann sees planning as a unique activity of policymaking which attempts to understand how organizations work and through that understanding, make things within and affected by organizations happen.

Mann believes that the core of a professional definition of *urban* planning, for instance, will center much more around a general knowledge of the *behavior* of urban places than a specific understanding of the composition of one subpart: "many specialists claim specific knowledge of how communities work—few claim to plan them in any sense." Indeed, it may be much more accurate to talk of a "professional federation of planning" each with its own functional or topical specialty.

PLANNING AS A STRATEGY OF SELECTIVE INTERVENTION

Jerome Kaufman is not concerned with legitimizing planning as a policymaking activity—he views this as a given. It is the planner's role within the policymaking sphere that he would like to alter.

Kaufman characterizes the previous role of the planner as a neutral advisor to decisionmakers. This is achieved by the planner's introduction of more rationality and objectivity to the decisionmaking process. Kaufman indicates that this is a less than satisfactory role for the planner as "real world" decisions are seldom made rationally and when they are, the role of the planner in this process is further diffused by its sharing with other professionals.

An alternative strategy is available to the planner—he may act as an *interventionist, i.e.,* inject himself in policy issues in which he is interested, by exercising various degrees of political behavior. This involvement might take the form of (1) initiating, (2) modifying, or (3) preventing local policy.

To achieve influence, a team with certain skills is required: a strategist, boundary spanner (coalition builder) and a substantive specialist. Support, information, and power are drawn upon at the time of specific intervention.

Intervention poses potential pitfalls for the policy planner—the outcome of unsuccessful intervention is probable loss of existing power and resources. To Kaufman the risk is worth it—the current alternative is ineffectual influence.

PLANNING AS AN ACTIVITY WHICH KEYS SOCIETAL LEARNING

Friedmann in his latest essay is careful to react to the elitist allegations concerning the respective roles of planner and client in a social guidance system.

He initially reaffirms that the linkage of knowledge and action is the true meaning of planning. According to Friedmann: "planning deals with neither concept exclusively but rather is concerned with mediation between them." Institutions must be designed to guide nations through turbulent times—capable of responding to diverse stimuli. To live with turbulence the social guidance system must be transformed into a social learning system. This social learning system would replace a central guidance system (earlier advocated by societal guidance enthusiasts) of separate headwork and handwork—knower and doer would be one and the same.

In conclusion, Friedmann briefly describes a structural network to carry out social action. The basic element of the learning society would be the cell of *territory*—horizontally integrated units related to each other on the basis of shared destiny and sentiment. This would be opposed to the growing trend toward vertical *functional* alignments of which the corporation is a prime example.

PLANNING AS THE ARTICULATOR OF MULTIPLE
VIEWS ENROUTE TO AN EQUITABLE PLAN

Mel Webber, although in basic agreement with Friedmann, sees the planner less as scientist and technocrat and more as a facilitator of debate. According to Webber, the planner is one who, through previous experience, knows, for instance, that alternative programs have divergent distributional outcomes and these outcomes effect who benefits and who loses from the implemented plan.

Planning viewed by Webber is a cognitive style predisposed to ways decisions get made rather than their substantive content. Planners have a special way of thinking about pluralities of individual and group wants and a special way of satisfying these variously competing wants.

Webber believes that neither the planner nor the plan is value free and what may be called for far down the line of professional development is a variety of advocate planners each representing different points of view and value constructs. The plan, participated in by multiple advocates, does not represent the correct or most efficient solution—rather it is the one which, within the confines of maximizing equity, is procedurally acceptable.

Public Policy Planning—A Search for Future Directions

Public policy theorists will continue to search for appropriate roles for planning within the policymaking field. The role of planning and planners will be one of facilitating debate enroute to a planning solution that is as equitable as it is optimal. Planning will be sought to provide a combination of "packaged" knowledge and "experience" knowledge to the decision-making process as a means of enhancing the chances for plan implementation.

Planning will be more rather than less active. It will be more rather than less political. Planners will be sought as advocates in causes that they have a stake or believe in. The expert witnesses in the rent control issue are a prime example. Although they allege unbiased neutrality in the production and analysis of data, they are sought by clients and prefer working for clients whose values parallel their own.

Although at times we seem far from a national energy policy, a national transportation policy, a national land use law, these are the scope of activities that some planners seem now to be concerned with.

And although retreats are frequent and compromises many, this scope of activity is probably essential to meaningful control.

Who Planners Are, How They Are Prepared

Reviewing the field of planning from 1909 to 1957—a span of time when formal university planning education evolved from adjunct courses in architecture and engineering to separate schools and departments, granting graduate degrees characterized by ever-broadening curricula—Harvey S. Perloff discerns the set of successive additions to the conception as well as the practice of planning [626:12]:

> From (1) an early stress on planning as concerned chiefly with esthetics, planning came to be conceived also in terms of (2) the efficient functioning of the city—in both the engineering and economic sense; then (3) as a means of controlling the uses of land as a technique for developing a sound land-use pattern; then (4) as a key element in efficient government procedures; later (5) as involving welfare considerations and stressing the human element; and, more recently, (6) planning has come to be viewed as encompassing many socio-economic and political, as well as physical elements that help to guide the functioning and development of the urban community.

The broadening domain was largely the consequence of the demands of the encompassing societal environment, which experienced the rapid urbanization and industrialization of the early 20th century, the Great Depression, World War II, and rapid postwar suburbanization during the half century under scrutiny by Perloff. Moreover, this constantly widening perspective of the planning field was also reflected in the education of planners—"of gradual assimilation of social science, regional aspects, and research into planning curricula—but always with considerable lag" [626:18-19]. A major expression of this development, circa the late 1950s, was Perloff's view of the planner as a "generalist with a specialty," with education centered about a unique planning "core", as well as specialized training. The concept of "core", which is still troublesome in present day discussions, was raised by the University of Chicago experiment, which "used planning as a generic term to refer broadly to the ways in which men and women, acting through organized entities, endeavor to guide developments so as to solve the pressing problems around them and approximate the vision of the future that they hold" [626:141-142]. The educational manifestation was the attempt to isolate those principles unique to planning-in-general, raising the question of the academic validity of a discipline unless it can develop a unique core curriculum capturing the basic principles and approach of the field.

While the Chicago experiment was terminated in an atmosphere of financial retrenchment at the University of Chicago—an event which may be of increasing relevance in the coming decade—its ideas had lasting influence. But through the 1950s, the old myth of the "all purpose planner" persisted, and the physical aspect of field bound whatever common core existed.

The 1960s brought what Lawrence D. Mann terms "a quiet revolution" in planning education [611:251]. The generalist notion succumbed to increasing numbers of specialty tracks or options. The extension of the broadening tendency noted by Perloff continued, undoubtedly a consequence of the social turmoil of the decade, but the general "common core" aspect lagged in evolution. As Mann asserted [611:255]:

> Planning has simply become a very broad and sometimes leaky umbrella. It shelters many different kinds of people, with different kinds of skills and approaches. Nor need we assume that any kind of mythical "planning team" is implied by the kinds of people who are being trained to call themselves planners. The outlook is considerably more anarchistic with the model of "each doing his own thing" probably a more accurate description than any alternative.

With the "war on poverty", the number of new professional roles also burgeoned, many with seemingly little commonality with traditional planning activities. And the gap of both and formal education tended to widen. With increasing specialization, the traditional planning approach became "little more than residual to some of the avant-garde options" [611:255]. And there was considerable question about the abilities of planning schools in training people to participate in social change. So by 1970, it was possible to suggest that the centripetal tendency of planning discerned by Perloff for the first half century—of planning drawing in adjacent competences centered about a physical oriented common core —had been challenged by a centrifugal counter-force, with specialization and fragmentation gaining increased momentum.

More recent history is somewhat more difficult to grasp effectively. Certainly the societal events are easy to recite: the worst recession since World War II, the demise of the "war on poverty", the ascendency of environment, "limits to growth", and the energy crisis. But within the academy, the differentiation between momentary abberrants and longer term tendencies is still unclear. Has a new "vocationalism" challenged the students' concern with social and economic change? Has the expansion into the urban domain by adjacent disciplines rendered the planning specializations less unique? And with regard to the latter, has a common core appeared that is central to the discipline and the profession?

Roles for Planners and Requisite Education: In Change

The role of planners, the gap between the professional and the academic, and the corresponding crevice between planning education and the realities of the world of practical application have been subjects of virtually continual discourse for the past two decades. The dialogues of the papers of this section span a host of lingering concerns, ranging from the question of what makes planning unique to the adequacy of preparation of planners for their professional tasks. Not surprising, a number of different conclusions are drawn, but yet several commonalities exist.

THEORY AND THE PROFESSIONAL

John Dyckman surveys the paradoxes which have continually afflicted planning and isolates the crises which have eminated from them.

1) Reflecting the shifting place of the profession in society as it evolves fully into the post industrial era, American planning is, according to Dyckman, beset by paradoxes which torment the practitioners of the art:

   a) There is an important American ambivalence about public planning itself—planners are unsure of the degree of national commitment to their work.

   b) The machinery of planning at the disposal of politicians is treated as confirmatory and symbolic, not as relevant to the actual decisions made, which depend upon political sensitivity.

---

* Quotes secured from the papers in this section are not directly referenced to page numbers, nor are comments taken from the initial conference transcripts.

c) As the functions of planning become more institutionalized in the American scene, the powers of planning seem to decline, since their institutionalization is at those levels of the American Federal system that are least influential—state and local governments.

2) As a more or less consequence, American planning faces three crises. The first of these settles around the growing incongruity of planning education and planning practice.

a) There is imperfect communication between academic planning study and the practice of planning. We are burdened with an unfortunately deep distinction between "professionalism" and "theory."

b) The university requires the construction of generalizations and ultimately of theoretical systems of explanation. The academic focuses on substantive rationality.

c) In contrast, professionalization has grown within a framework of the bureaucratization of planning which demands formal or "procedural" rationality. Substantive rationality, or what planning is about, takes second place to procedural efficiency in this environment.

3) The second "crisis" which Dyckman addresses is the development of planning theories and the crisis of planning education.

a) With a need to be "intellectually defensible" within the university context, planning education created a demand for planning theory. In the institutional environment of the university, pressures for generality, explanation and rigorous argument are paramount!

b) Moreover, theory is an important organizing function in the face of the rapid growth of planning curricula. There is a desire to "bound" the field, so that it is not preempted by other disciplines and so that it is not so diluted as to lose respectability.

c) As theory began to be developed in the academy, it encountered demands for explanatory power and rigor. But it must have application to the work of men of affairs if it is designed to affect the conduct of the planning profession. Efforts at developing the former were achieved, if at all, only at the expense of relevance (the latter).

d) The tensions and gap between the two partly result from the difficulty of classifying the professional practice to which the theory is supposed to relate. A profession is characterized by the exclusive possession of competence in a specified area and by the acceptance of a common ethic.

e) The "technical arts" or substantive areas of planning are shared by a host of other disciplines. What is distinctive about the planning profession is a common culture with a core of shared ideology.

In short, the core has a set of procedures, an attitude towards the use of information, and above all, a commitment to rationality. Further, the "ethic", or normative guidance of planning is the ethic of rational action.

f)   However, rational decisionmaking has been a troublesome element in the development of planning theory particularly its relation to the modern state and/or societal system. This leads to the third crisis of American planning.

4)   This third crisis concerns the relations of American planning to the American state.

a)   The condition of planning *vis-a-vis* the state in which it is to be located is not confused so much as it is insentient.

b)   Planning is an instrument of the State and cannot be separated from the environment of the State; but nonetheless, is an independent creation.   In this context, it is remarkable that it has largely ignored the organization of the State.

c)   But planning can draw on the independence of its intellectual resources to mount a major criticism of the modern State. Only by performing this critical function can it achieve ultimate substantive rationality and be true to its intellectual charge.

THE PROFESSIONAL'S ROLE

George Sternlieb tends to define the profession by what it does—the measurement of its effectiveness and its social utility much more a function of the results of its activity than the avowed theory or credentialization which may serve as veneer. Eschewing the normative dimension of the profession, Sternlieb's observations explore seven basic dilemmas inherent to the professional experience.

1)   *Defining virtue:* The virtue of competing interests are to be judged by elected officials. The role of the planner is to provide some semblance of neutral ground.

2)   *Numbers Do Not Read Themselves:* In pursuing the neutral ground of the technician, the data for analysis may fail to provide definitive insight. Nonetheless, the assemblage of numbers is our unique area of responsibility, and the reporting of ambiguity, rather than the invention of results where they do not exist, is a crucial element of it.

3)   *Have Regression—Will Travel:* There is great temptation to give our unique possession—numbers—greater authority through statistical routines and the computer, as well as blatantly moving from associative correlations to causality and policy.

4) *How High the Silhouette:* Whether the analysis is definitive or obscure, the difficulties of merchandizing—of getting the public and its leaders to agree on a path of conduct—can often be a harsh and disillusioning process.

5) *A World I Never Made:* Strict limits to execution are attached to the society in which those plans are to be brought to consummation. The capacity of stopping initiative in America has never been greater; the capacity for "through-put" never so frustrating.

6) *The Sick Man of the Metropolitan Region:* The failure to isolate what is happening—because we don't want it to happen—is an ever present danger. Undesirable changes such as irreversible urban decline must be acknowledged, with optimization predicated within a constricted sphere of action.

7) *In the Good Old Bye and Bye:* One of the more popular approaches to avoiding the crunch of hard realities, of resource limitations, of popular electorates that refuse to acknowledge eternal verity—and the enthusiasts' proposals—is to advocate the world as it should be rather than the world as it is.

THE PROFESSIONAL'S TOOLS

Shifting to a more technical subset of planning education and planning practice, Donald A. Krueckeberg examines the changing role of analytical methods as one of the urban planner's areas of competence. Methods are broadly defined as the array of analytical tools and skills, primarily quantitative—or at least analytically rigorous—that are used in the practical work of urban planners.

1) Despite the continuous advances of methods development in the academy the past 20 years or so, there is empirical evidence that suggests a seeming stability in topical interest in planning practice, and relative importance of problems (George Raymond's paper of Section I may well reinforce this suggestion).

2) The expected evolution toward social and economic planning of the last decade appears not to have materialized. Yet methods skills are relatively prominent in surveys ranking the importance of planning skills.

3) Some gaps are present between the educational and professional domains. Principal among these are the foci of economic base and input-output analyses, stressed by the former, with market analysis and cost-revenue skills preferred by the profession.

4) Krueckeberg provides a model framework which suggests three stages through which methods in planning are passing:

    a) The first stage, before 1950, saw models of analysis, as they applied to specific substantive concerns, all imbedded in the formal courses teaching these subjects.

b)   In the second stage of development, the ensuing period, the methods of analysis imbedded in each of the substantive areas were pulled out of these courses and centralized in methods courses. This centralization is probably general to the social sciences at large.

c)   The model implies a third stage—the elevated level of quantitative skills will afford the opportunity to integrate quantitative methods back into the substantive subjects of the planning curriculum.

5)   A parallel development in practice may be expected, with the centralized modelling function—prevalent in the survey reviews—dispersing throughout agencies.

THE EDUCATION OF THE PROFESSIONAL

Despite the transition and states that Krueckeberg has documented, William G. Grigsby expresses doubt whether academic planning programs are fully responding to the challenge—however defined—either in the education they provide or in the research their facilities undertake.

1)   While the content of planning curricula continues to be more and more rigorous, there persists troubling old questions about planning education.

a)   The first pertains to the myth of "the planner"; products of planning schools are rarely those who determine directions of urban growth and development.

b)   The second, related to first, concerns the fundamental attribute of those drawn to planning schools—they wish to devote their professional life to improvement and reform. But they are not provided with adequate training for reform goals or for implementation.

c)   The changing environment of universities provides another question: urban problems have been certified as valid concerns for other disciplines, rendering planning schools less unique in their competences.

2)   The latter problem has added to severity to planning's long term identity crisis, which manifests itself in a fear of takeover by alien forces, and the continuous debate over a number of overlapping planning dimensions.

3)   Where is the field heading and/or where should it go? While knowledge of substantive concerns has improved greatly, we don't know their impact on the urban environment. But ultimately questions of turf and the conflicting rights of citizens and groups are involved. Central to planning education's response is the recognition of this phenomenon.

Planning Education: A Search for Future Directions

The future of planning education and the role of the planner will continue to be shaped by the changes in the broader societal context. As the age structure shifts of the nation's population continue—when the "baby bust" generation ages into its graduate school years—America's institutions of higher education will be confronted by a marked shrinkage in clientele. The stage will be set for a clash of not insignificant proportions between the outward movements of planning's specializations and the thrusts of traditional disciplines into urban concerns. Will the increasing sophistication of the specialty tracks, as manifested by Krueckeberg's methods scenario, enable planning to remain competitive with other overlapping disciplines, which may be more competent in specialized concerns?

The need for planning to remain educationally defensible within the university setting will be an ever-pressing concern. As Dyckman has pointed out, the justification of a discipline is its possession of unique area of competence. Will a "common core" eventually come into fruition, so as to avoid the fate of the Chicago experiment if an era of financial retrenchment materializes?

The "leaky umbrella" picture of planning sheltering a variety of people and approaches may be completely inappropriate in the new environment facing universities. A clearer resolution of the professional role of planning and the linkage of the professional and educational systems may be concerns of a relevance heretofore unprecedented in planning annals.

Section I
Physical Planning in Change —
The Role of Environmental Planning

The Role of the Physical Urban Planner

George M. Raymond

My assigned topic is the role of the physical planner, and I want to say at the outset that I think physical planners have gotten a bum rap in the past ten or fifteen years.

There is the story of the Miami builder who, when asked whether he had sustained a lot of damage from a certain hurricane, replied: "I'm O.K. My buildings stood up well, only the architecture blew off." It is understandable that, in the storms of the 1960's many were quite ready to write off physical planning in the same way.

Those so inclined were mainly the idealistic, highly learned youths—social science Ph.D.'s—who invaded the field of planning in the last twenty years believing that the world responds predictably to buttons and levers, and that they really knew which buttons to push and which levers to shift. Not surprisingly, these educated youths were appalled when they closed the classroom doors behind them and experienced reality with all its unpredictability and contrariness. And so, in their deep disillusionment, they wrote cynically of the failure of planning because it did not eliminate poverty and racial discrimination in one fell swoop, and because they felt that no other objectives were even worth the effort.

Unfortunately, the world's view of physical planning has been influenced way out of proportion by the writings that came out of their naiveté, and the intensity of their attack even confused a lot of experienced practitioners who should have known better.

Before I go on to discuss what I believe physical planning is, what its objectives should be, and how we can best use it in furtherance of important societal objectives, I want it understood that, in my book, a true physical planner is one who understands the socio-economic-political context in which he operates and who is concerned with the socio-economic-political implications of physical planning objectives. A true planner, by definition, is one who works towards his objectives with a deep sense of responsibility for all of the consequences of the course of action he recommends. This belief underlies everything I will say in the remainder of this paper.

1

Planning Objectives, Historical and Current

Let me try to clarify the proper objectives of physical planning by dipping a little bit into history. In this country widespread physical planning started as a "city beautiful" movement, with purely aesthetic objectives. Are those objectives still valid? I say yes, remembering, of course, that just as taste in painting and sculpture has evolved, so has taste in environmental aesthetics. While we still appreciate formal boulevards and axial views, we prefer informal arrangements replete with space and greenery. As to dense urban areas, we seem to prefer forms that yield visual surprises, more like those that were characteristic of medieval cities than those of the Renaissance or Baroque periods.

From the "city beautiful" movement in the thirties, physical planning moved into a "city efficient" phase, dominated by the civil engineer with his slide rule. During this phase, planning attempted to assure that the scarce public dollar was spent to greatest advantage, and that urban populations would be supported by a solid foundation of service facilities and systems. Are these objectives still valid? Of course they are.

From the "city efficient", physical planning proceeded into broad-scale land use arrangements on the theory that land use patterning determines many other physical and functional characteristics. To a greater or lesser degree, land use determines air quality, transportation patterns and energy consumption, community character, environmental amenities and aesthetics, the convenience with which people can reach frequently used facilities, and their privacy, peace, quiet, and so on. Besides, the juxtaposition of incompatible land uses is still as harmful as it always was. (As our tastes and lifestyles have changed over the years, so has the list of uses that are considered to be incompatible. No matter—the important thing is that there are still uses that are incompatible!) Is the rational distribution of land uses still a valid objective? Except perhaps for Jane Jacobs and a few of her more extreme acolytes, I haven't found very many people who do not think that it is.

It was during this "land use planning" phase that the nation's suburbs exploded. Thousands of suburban communities that now house more than 50 percent of the nation's population were shaped by the system of planning and control that evolved up to that point. This system may have been far from perfect, but to say that the suburbs it created are by and large not what the public wants is sheer fantasy. In the 1960's, there were some who decried the sterility and heartlessness of suburban towns, but I have yet to see a stampede away from them. On the contrary, the stampede away from the cities and into the suburbs is accelerating, and among those who are stampeding, I might say, are many who, when they were younger, thought that the suburbs were terrible.

Not very long ago, a very enlightened governor asked his planners to recommend a statewide planning policy. And they labored diligently and in time presented him with a carefully prepared proposal. The principal objective of the recommended policy, an eminent member of the planning team kept saying, is to prevent more "urban sprawl." "Urban sprawl," finally asked the governor, "what's that?" So the planner patiently explained that it was all those awful, sterile suburbs that were submerging fields and hills, that were. . . . "Wait a minute," said the governor. "What you are talking about is all those communities in which most of the people of the state now live, bring up their children, and are ready to defend practically with their lives!" That, of course, was the last that was ever heard of a statewide land use policy in that state.

All of this is not to say that the physical manifestation of post World War II suburban explosion could not have been improved upon. Quite the contrary: had that development wave followed the basic principles long advocated by physical planners, Earth Day might have created much less stir in 1970. But more about that later.

It was in the 1960's that—having discovered on the one hand that the world is imperfect, biased, inequitable, and irrational; and, on the other, that physical planning could not solve all those problems—the huge new crop of social science Ph.D.'s struck out for the high ground of societal perfection. The culmination of their thrust was the McGovern debacle. Without faulting the new idealists for being concerned with the continued presence of deep-seated problems in our society, one can question their logic in sacrificing physical planning objectives on the altar of social utopias. It is my contention that stemming physical deterioration, preserving neighborhood values, restoring dwindling tax bases, achieving safety, beauty, and convenience, and other similar objectives are important and not beneath the dignity of the planning profession, including its theoreticians.

Earth Day, 1970, brought the environment into the foreground of planning, and with it a sharpened awareness of the broad implications of development patterns on the macro-scale. As for the micro-scale, with which physical planning is mainly concerned, let me suggest again that, while the rhetoric is new, there is little in the environmental movement's text addressed to planners that you won't find in "Nothing Gained by Overcrowding"—Sir Raymond Unwin's sermon on sound development principals written sixty years ago. Was not Radburn the first practical demonstration of how to preserve critical environmental areas, including flood plains, by clustering? What else is new?

The real problem today is that we seem to have become unable to talk to one another. As the planning profession grew, it emulated that other structure that men set out to build without limits in Biblical times:

those who were building it began to speak in tongues and soon no one knew what anyone else was saying.

Thus, the history of planning teaches us that, while the techniques of physical planning must change in response to new knowledge, we cannot achieve a satisfactory physical enviornment without it. We must get off the kick that the planning process is the thing; whatever "muddling through" a la Charles Lindblom may be, it is not planning. My concept of planning is based on two premises: first, that regardless of difficulties, it is better to try to be rational than to give up, because giving up is irresponsible; and second, that there is a great deal to be gained from trying to follow an overall plan even if it has to be changed frequently in response to changed objectives brought on by unforeseen circumstances.

At this point, someone is sure to ask: "But how do you know whether your planning is pointed in the right direction at the outset?". The answer is that I don't, but that the formulation of a plan is, in my view, the most important part of the process of making that determination. With a plan, one can talk about something concrete, and one can know that all those involved in the process, whether they are primarily interested in social, economic, political, or physical objectives, are talking about the same thing. Without a plan, it is impossible—and I stress this word, *impossible*—to be certain what it is that those who discuss community objectives are talking about, and whether, in their evaluation of the consequences of various alternatives, they have even considered their impact on physical forms. In fact, in the absence of a plan, one cannot even be certain of one's own ability to put alternatives into a form permitting a meaningful weighing of the various trade-offs.

Improving the Effectiveness of Physical Planning at the Local Level

Having established my feeling that physical planning objectives are still vital and that the best way in which they can be articulated is by means of a plan, I am prepared to admit that physical planning is not very effective. The reason that physical planning is ineffective is because local governing bodies can ignore it. And the reason why it can be ignored is that, in almost all states, plans are not developed by, or under the aegis of, local governing bodies. Even though plans are prepared at public expense, the governing bodies are not required to enact them as official policies. And the reason for that may be that local government officials cherish their freedom to respond to pressures for land use changes. They cherish it so much that they would rather not give their communities the advantage of guided growth in accordance with a carefully developed plan. And so, carefully prepared plans gather dust and go out of date.

There is another problem too: the courts don't often give full credence to plans that, under our present laws, are required to be adopted by planning boards. The courts quite properly feel unable to allow the planning board—an appointed advisory body—to preempt the legislative function of the elected governing body by adopting a plan of its own. And remember that, since the law gives the planning board exclusive jurisdiction over the development of the plan, it is entirely possible for the legislators to have no idea of what that plan contains, and why.

As long as the present situation is allowed to continue, planning will continue to lose credibility. I believe that we must have a legal requirement that plans be adopted by the local governing bodies: if they're not officially adopted, they wouldn't be official plans. And if they *are* officially adopted it can be expected that the local governing bodies would be sufficiently committed to them to make sure that they were kept up to date and properly administered.

If the law required plans to be adopted, not by planning boards, but by governing bodies, the contents of plans would probably change also: they would be more realistic and less likely to parcel out ideal land use objectives. This would be salutary, for ultimate land use patterning is not a very meaningful activity anyway.

Let me illustrate this point through two examples—one of a developed, but changing area, and one of an undeveloped area. First, let us consider a declining built-up neighborhood with small, old homes on small lots. Generally, in such circumstances, letting in non-residential uses—stores, home-businesses, machine shops—hastens the neighborhood's deterioration. In this situation, the zoning ordinance usually attempts to prolong the life of the neighborhood by prohibiting non-residential uses. A long-range land use plan, on the other hand, usually sets forth the desired ultimate use of the area. That's O.K. if the land use plan is backed up by a plan for the redevelopment of the area, because then it can actually be achieved through the use of eminent domain. But if publicly-sponsored redevelopment is not in the cards, the ultimate use envisioned in the plan cannot occur, since it would be prohibited by the zoning ordinance.

Even changing the zoning ordinance would not bring about the desired ultimate land use. Let us assume that the desired use is industrial. Rezoning the neighborhood for industry would only attract small, scattered marginal uses. Substantial industries would require the assembly of many parcels from different owners—and that takes too much time and, in a built-up area, is very expensive as well. For these reasons, such assembly is very unlikely if acceptable vacant land is available elsewhere. Under the circumstances, the real outcome of zoning the neighborhood for industry would be a long-lasting area of mixed uses—not a good environment for either homes or industry, and certainly not what was contemplated in the land use plan.

Second, let us consider an undeveloped area. A land use plan for such an area usually shows various types of uses, not in specific locations, but rather by indicating that such uses would be appropriate somewhere in the area, sometime in the future. The zoning ordinance probably places all the vacant land in a low-density residential or agricultural "holding" classification on the theory that it will be changed later when demand for the preferred uses materializes. This pairing of a holding zone with a vague, highly generalized land use plan gives the governing body complete freedom to accept or reject any land use proposal. It is almost the same as having no plan at all.

Another problem is that holding zones often become "real" zones. People who own land in holding zones frequently develop it in accordance with existing regulations. This creates a specific physical, social, and economic environment with which any future changes must be compatible. A holding zone thus becomes a zone like any other. This has happened in many suburbs where low-density holding zones spawned low-density subdivisions whose residents now resist whatever may have been originally contemplated to replace such zones.

A "definitive" plan showing future shopping centers, apartment concentrations, and industry in specific locations would be no better; and it would be arbitrary because it would increase the value of some of a possibly large supply of vacant land that is equally suited for more intensive use. This type of planning would also be largely meaningless since paradoxically, developers tend to shun lands whose value has been appreciated by the plan and request the rezoning of cheaper lands—cheaper because the plan shows them as intended for low-density residential use. Nor does the locality have much choice—if it wants the taxes from the proposed use, it must agree to rezone.

Let us assume that planning enabling acts have been amended to require the local governing body to enact a comprehensive plan. What form should the plan take? As I envision it, this plan would consist of two mandated elements: a land development plan and a public facilities plan. Such a plan should allow every landowner to make a reasonable use of his property as of right, not in the distant future, but immediately. If the locality chooses to make such reasonable use conditional upon the provision of the necessary infrastructure, the public facilities plan should show what this infrastructure will be and when it is proposed to be provided. This would end the present vicious cycle where, on the one hand, the local governing body can deny a rezoning request on the grounds that facilities are inadequate and, on the other hand, it can refuse to provide the facilities on the grounds that they are not yet needed!

A comprehensive plan along these lines would establish a unitary planning and regulatory system. In part, it would have the attributes of a zoning ordinance and map, but its total form would be unlike anything we now have and would have to be carefully crafted from scratch. One thing that this kind of plan should not, and would not, have to do is to designate future land uses with precision, far in advance of actual development pressures. A unitary land development plan would establish a balance between total residential capacity, on the one hand, and environmental constraints and an achievable system of facilities and services, on the other.

The plan would begin by identifying precisely the flood plains and open spaces that the locality would like to preserve, either through acquisition or clustering. It would then establish, on an areawide basis, a desired residential density, *i.e.*, that which would achieve the total appropriate use intensity over the entire area available for such development. This would permit the clustering of development within the overall capacity envelope, at the option of the developer but subject to detailed site plan approvals and environmental impact analyses to assure compatibility with surrounding developments. This would also permit trade-offs: if a given tract within such an area were to be developed at lower than the average permitted density to satisfy a market for large homes on large lots, a corresponding increase in density could be authorized elsewhere.

Since a plan can only be effective if it is actually used to guide the development process, a plan adopted by the governing body should be binding on all agencies of the municipality and govern all their actions. At any time that the governing body finds that the plan interferes with some action that, in its opinion, would further the public interest, rather than ignoring the plan, as is so frequently done now, it should formally amend it. This should be done by following the procedures prescribed for its original adoption and by giving all those affected full opportunity to participate in the debate. If, for example, the municipality wishes to amend the plan so as to increase the permitted overall capacity envelope, it should be required to show how, and when, the capacity of the supporting systems would be increased and how the proposed action would preserve essential environmental values.

All of this would assure that proposed land use changes and public facility decisions would be examined through a disciplined process, open to public scrutiny and debate. This would strengthen local planning by increasing its responsiveness to the public interest and would thus revive public confidence in its efficacy. It would also relieve the planning process of the need to continue to justify legislative actions as being "in accordance with" some vague land use plan that probably could never come to pass because it is insufficiently grounded in the realities with which the legislative process must deal.

If it is not clear already, I want to make it very clear that what I have outlined is emphatically neither an argument in favor of "end-state" or any other rigid-for-all-time kind of plan, nor an argument against planning studies of alternatives. It is clearly desirable that planning agencies explore alternative directions in searching for the best possible future for the community. Local governing bodies would undoubtedly continue to base their policymaking decision on these studies. I suggest, however, that plans that are not sufficiently precise to be enacted are merely hypotheses and should be treated as such, certainly in law. Preferably, they should not even be labeled "plans" but "planning studies." The speculative part of the planning process would be thus relegated to a fitting status, while the mandate for plan adoption would end that case with which such plans as do exist can be ignored, changed, or forgotten that is at the root of the ineffectiveness of physical planning at the local level. If local planning were a continuing, disciplined, and accountable process, in time it would also educate the general public so that public participation could become as meaningful in practice as planning theory suggests that it should be.

Planning at Higher-than-Local Levels

Localities, which must be guided by their own self-interest, because their decisions are made by elected officials, are inevitably forced into fiscal zoning, exclusionary zoning, or both. For these reasons, as well as for the obvious additional one that localities can seldom understand and relate to areawide objectives, some land use decisions should be made at higher-than-local levels. But then, many kinds of planning decisions are already made at higher-than-local levels. The state highway system is not planned piece by piece by individual local governments in the hope that all roads will meet at their boundaries. Major airports are not located at the whim of every village. The Port Authority of New York and New Jersey was established more than fifty years ago as an institutional framework for solving the highly complex transportation problems of the New York Metropolitan Area on a basis that involved not only many localities, but two states. There are countless examples of regional sewer and water systems and of regionally conceived and operated airports, park systems, and so on.

There are really only two major issues that are intimately involved with physical planning that we have *not* been able to resolve on a regional basis almost anywhere in the country. These two issues are the regulation of land use and the equitable and rational distribution of the working population.

The Model Land Development Code, developed by the American Law Institute, in introducing the concept of state jurisdiction over developments of regional impact or regional benefit, laid the groundwork for a possible framework within which some of the conflicts related to these two issues might be resolved. In seeking solutions, however, I believe that we would be wise to accept as a fact that the social problems that are now concentrated in the cities cannot be solved by means of physical planning. Those problems must be addressed by national social and fiscal policies.

Maybe, given present realities, our areawide land use planning goals should be limited for the time being to the achievement of the obvious environmental objectives (*e.g.*, preservation of critical areas), the equitable distribution of economic activities or tax revenues, and the distribution of various housing types so that workers can travel to their jobs at a reasonable cost in time and money. If we did no more than that, it would be a great deal, even if it fell short of perfection. More decisions modeled on the New Jersey Supreme Court's Mount Laurel, and more Metropolitan Tax Disparities Acts, such as the one in effect in Minnesota's Twin Cities Region, while representative of forms of public intervention that are certainly less than apocalyptic, could make major contributions to orderly development and growth. This would be particularly so if they were backed up by cash—enough to build, in advance, the public facilities that actually shape development.

As for the work of regional planning agencies, frustrated as they are by the almost universal resistance to area-wide plans, most of them have turned into publicly-funded, planning, consulting organizations which devote much of their time to local planning assistance. In doing this, they have allowed themselves to become tied into their local constituencies to a point which renders them incapable of developing plans that, in furthering important area-wide objectives, must run contrary to local aspirations. As a result, almost without exceptions, true regional planning does not exist in this country, and the illusion that it tries to give that the public's very real area-wide concerns are being addressed in a meaningful way, works against the chances of this early institutionalization.

So What Do We Do Today?

Where does all this leave the physical urban planner? It all depends on where we want to go. As Justice Frankfurter once said, "The history of liberty has largely been the history of the observance of procedural safeguards." This dictum applies equally to all major purposes that can only be achieved through governmental intervention. If the proper use of land—whatever one may wish to subsume under the adjective "proper"—is an important public purpose, we must safeguard it with carefully formulated procedures.

Today, the process of zoning—of determining the use of land—is well-nigh irresponsible. Worse, it is fraught with opportunities for corruption and for the exercise of tyranny by the majority. It is my contention that the only solution is to adopt as a basic principle that the future use of land should be made the subject of open covenants, openly arrived at, between the local legislatures and the people. If these local decisions are unsatisfactory from the point of view of the regional, statewide, or national interest, let legislation be enacted, whether voluntarily or under court compulsion, that would establish standards and constraints intended to safeguard other than local interests.

Pending improvement of the framework in which he is called upon to work to the point of enabling him to affect land use patterns in a fundamental way, the physical urban planner must continue to try to be as effective as he can. In doing so, he need not feel apologetic. In fact, I believe that it is time for physical planners to point out with pride their contributions towards an improved human environment. They didn't achieve perfection, but the world would have been a sorrier place without them.

How Do You Educate a Physical Planner?

I've talked about what I think planning ought to be, and now I'd like to say a few words about the type of education that can produce good technical planners. I emphasize the word "technical" since there is a fundamental difference between that type of planner and a planning administrator. A planning administrator may—usually has—some area of technical planning competence in his background, but this is not essential. Consider Edward J. Logue, former Development Coordinator for the City of Boston: the Planning Department was under his jurisdiction, and so was the Boston Redevelopment Agency. Whether or not one agreed with his planning policies, one could not deny that he was a most competent planning administrator. Yet, his education was in law, and before becoming a planner, he was a generalist in government.

What makes a good planning administrator is not his specific education, but the person, his experience, and opportunity. The same could be said about a good planning technician, *except* that he must be an expert in his field.

What is the expertise of a physical planner? Or, to put it another way, what are the essentials of a physical planning education? Like a good education in any field, a good planning education teaches the student how to figure out what he needs to know and where to go to get that knowledge, and gives him enough technical background so that he can understand what he reads or hears. Beyond that, a physical planner must develop a thorough understanding of land: what makes land developable and what creates special problems, both for the developer and the locality. He must also learn the meaning of various development forms, their interaction with the environment, community character, costs, and convenience.

Second, physical planners must understand real estate market realities: why land is marketable for certain uses in certain locations and not in others; land value dynamics; and the physical and economic expectations of potential users.

Third, physical planners should understand the financial imperatives of the development industry: the motivation for various types of development and the limits of possible compromise; the order of magnitude of costs of various elements of development; sources and costs of financing; the impact of time delays on costs; tax laws as they affect development; and so on.

Fourth, the school must make every student try his hand at designing different types of developments. Someone who has never tried cannot understand what those who do it for a living are talking about. As Socrates put it, "Human nature cannot know the mystery of an art without experience."

Fifth, physical planners must understand the legal framework within which they operate, including the courts' basic interpretation of the 14th Amendment: that land use regulation is in derogation of property rights; that specific regulations should be determined in the interest of achieving important societal goals, rather than in furtherance of color symmetry or orderly patterning on maps. The planner must, in fact, have a thorough grounding in the fundamentals of the American federal system of government; the basic statutory and fiscal constraints and requirements affecting each level of government; and the historical and political context within which officials and planners operate.

Sixth, the school should give students an understanding of cities and regions: the functional interrelationships of the various parts of the city and of the region; of circulation and transportation systems and of their cost determinants; and of the roles that each subsystem plays in the whole. The student must also understand the effects of age, obsolescence, deterioration, and disinvestment; the relationship between tax base and quality of life; the inevitable, and frequently painful, trade-offs that must be considered in the formulation of policies regarding change; the interrelationships of people, incomes, behavioral patterns, neighborhood stability, and city survival; and programs, subsidies, and social and political imperatives that determine the outer limits of public intervention.

And, above all, the schools must teach the student to see the world as it is rather than as the instructor would like it to be. As an example, many planning students of the late 1960's and early 1970's complain that their schools taught them no zoning. Their instructors, who were training armies to fight the War on Poverty, were not interested in the intricacies of zoning variance procedures! Yet, while the War on Poverty was being mounted, fought—and lost—the world went on being governed by zoning ordinances and boards of appeals.

I suggest that, equipped with these basics—and, of course, with the necessary technical skills such as statistics and computers—a physical planner can probably be very useful to society—and to his employer as well. Thus equipped, the physical planner may not be able to make a perfect world—but he'll have some skills that can help improve its physical environment. After all, ultimately, providing everyone with an environment suitable for his or her needs is what physical planning is all about—as that great declaration of national policy so clearly and eloquently said it in the preamble to the Housing Act of 1949.

Ecological Planning: The Planner as Catalyst

Ian McHarg

By and large the virtues of the planning I was taught were orderliness and convenience, efficiency and economy. The first set contains minor virtues, and the second set contains less than noble ones. These virtues have little to do with survival or success of plants, animals and men in evolutionary time.

A fallacy is that planners plan for people. Actually this is not an asumption at all; it is a presumption. The planner who comes from out of town and is prepared to solve problems is a menace.

I prefer to think of planners as catalysts. The planner supresses his own ego and becomes an agent for outlining available options. He offers predictability that science gives him about the consequences of different courses of action. He helps the community make its values explicit. He identifies alternative solutions with attendant costs and benefits. These vary with different constituencies as do their needs and values.

This sort of planning might be called ecological. It is based on an understanding of both biophysical and social systems. Ecological planners operate within the framework of a biophysical culture.

Ecological planning addresses itself to the selection of environments. Ecological planners help institutions and individuals adapt these and themselves to achieve fitness.

For example, when I prepare a planning study, I insist that scientists of the environment study the region in terms of the processes which produce the phenomena constituting the region. They describe the phenomena of the region as an interacting biophysical model. Such a model can then be seen to have intrinsic opportunities and constraints to all existing and prospective users. Fitness is defined as the presence of all or most propitious attributes with none or few detrimental areas.

This notion of planning stems from two fundamental characteristics of natural processes: creativity and fitness. Creativity provides the dynamics that govern the universe. There is a tendency for all matter to degrade to entropy, but in certain energetic transactions there is a process by which some matter is transformed to a higher level or order. All of biology subscribes to this law: entropy increases but a local syntropy can be achieved. It is seen in both energetic transactions, in the evolution of matter, life and man. This biological "creativity" enables us to explain the rich and diverse world of life today, as opposed to the sterile world of yesterday.

The second concept—fitness—stems partially from Darwinian notions about how organisms adapt and survive. Equally important is the thought that the surviving organisms are fit for the environment. The world provides an abundance of environmental opportunity. This teaches us that the world is environmentally variable offering variable fitness. This results from the most basic elements—hydrogen, nitrogen, oxygen and carbon—the earth itself provides environmental opportunity.

All systems are required to seek out the environment that is most fit, to adapt these and themselves, continuously. This is a requirement for survival. This is called adaptation. It is an imperative of all life, it has been, and it always will be. Fitness can best be described as finding an environment—physical, biological or social—in which the largest part of the work of survival is done by the environment itself. There is then an energetic imperative for evolutionary success. Systems which are "fit" are evolutionary successes; they are maximum success solutions to fitness.

Planning, of course, is more than understanding environments and explaining why they are what they are, and where they are going. It is also explaining why people are where they are, doing what they are doing. An ecological planner would look at this over time, through an ethnographic history: Where did the first people who occupied a given place come from? Why did they leave? Why did they choose the environment they did? What adaptive skills determined their location? What adaptive skills did they practice? What modifications did they make to the environment? What institutions did they develop? What plans?

The social value of a given environment is an amalgam of the place, the people, and their technology. People in a given place with opportunities afforded by the environment for practicing a means of production, will develop characteristic perceptions and institutions. These institutions will have perceptions and values that feed back to an understanding of the environment—both national and social—and that have a modification of technology. Thus, I believe, we have a continuous model, which emanates from the physical and biological, and extends to the cultural.

The most critical factor is the value system, for it determines the planning solution. I strongly object to much of the current planning philosophy as it is emerging in both teaching and practice, for it assumes that the planner imposes values and exercises for the good of the people. I resist this. Given a set of data, the planning solutions will vary, not with respect to the set, but with respect to the value systems of the people who seek to solve the problem. Most of the important values are particular and there is no substitute for eliciting them from the constituents themselves. These values themselves become the data, whether it be for describing rocks, soils, animals, people or institutions. Planners must elicit this data from their client if they are going to help solve the problems posed by the particular system within which the client functions. This, in fact, is the planner's most important role. After he has done it, he should step aside, and the resolution of the problem of the explicit system will be found through the political process, and ultimately, in some cases, through the courts.

In sum, the planner is a catalyst and a resource. He determines what skills and branches of knowledge are appropriate to solutions, and what institutions. He helps to describe the interactions of systems. He describes probable alternative courses of action and assists his constituents in making their value system explicit. The planner then helps his clients understand what the consequences of applying that value system are in terms of their costs and benefits. He participates with them in negotiations among different constituencies over the relaxation or change of values in order to come to some agreement about the allocation of resources.

If the process is successful the constituencies will select the fittest environments, adapting these and themselves to achieve a creative fitting. As health can be described as the ability of persons, families or institutions to seek and solve problems, so planning is, not only a measure of the health of a group or institution, but, is health-giving to such agents.

It could make planning more fitting, perhaps even healthier.

Planners as Architects of the
Built Environment—or Vice Versa

Morton Hoppenfeld

Is planning or architecture each as a process and producer of urban pattern, separately or even together sufficient to the development of the good city? This is a good question from which to begin. By choice of words, it establishes two of the key issues.

First, it is not unreasonable to relate the word architecture to its most common association—building/buildings, i.e., a project, a contained fragment of a larger environment typically viewed by architect, client and critic as a sufficient entity and reflective of the piecemeal, haphazard way we add to our cities. I would contend that no conglomeration of such singularly designed "entities" is likely to be sufficient to make a good urban environment, nor is the "project" way of thinking likely to lead in that direction.

Our society is too complex, too motivated by private material acquisition, too inhabited by desensitized peoples, illiterate in matters concerning their own environmental well being to produce cities which are more rather than less, satisfying and salubrious.

Second, is the question of who, if anyone, *is* responsible for the quality of the built environment. Architects have in fact advertised a desire for that stewardship but certainly a reasonable answer need be more inclusive. Where are the decisions made? By people involved in real estate, development maintenance and sales: the owners, their lawyers, the engineers, public officials, planners, architects and the public user, each has a share of responsibility.

In a meeting among and about planners, it is necessary to admit that we, too, in our occasional moments of influence, advisement and participation in urban decisions, are partly, and typically wish we were more, responsible. The word "Architect" as used in the title ° of this paper, however, is not useful enough to satisfy our needs.

Nor in fact is the word "planner" any more helpful. While not many would consider themselves to be architects, many do consider themselves to be planners. More important is that those of us who consider ourselves "professional planners" are really only a special kind of planner, a specialist among many. If one accepts the obvious fact of enormity and complexity in building the city then how audacious to suggest that there is a specie "planner" with knowledge and ability to do it all. By suggesting it in the title we ask only for derision when we inevitably fail. We fail by definition, as would any other specialist working at a piece (likely not even a critical piece) and suggesting ability to affect the whole.

It would be very useful to acknowledge the largeness of the task of city planning and development, and to specify our respective areas of expertise and concomitant limitations. Such a posture might invite colleagues to join to help create the teams necessary and to eliminate the need for any of us to be "perfect" at the task.

With this in mind let us focus then on a facet of the planning-design-ing-building task. It is the one I practice and know best. It is the hybrid field called "urban design" and it bridges the space between traditional architecture and traditional physical planning.

Urban design is a useful terminology because it is sufficiently descrip-tive. It suggests that while all of the millions of pieces of artifacts that make up the built environment are, in fact, "designed" for some purpose, they are not necessarily and, in fact, seldom are consciously designed for their "urban role" to connect with others and to add up to a good city. It is the concept of the whole, the urban system; the relationship among the pieces; the public interest and concern for the detail/quality of the public environment which is typically missing from other activities.

Are there any who would argue with the observation that our built environment is not good enough; that, in particular, the urban manifes-tation of our public wealth has been dissipated; that among the highly developed countries of the world, American cities appear the least beauti-ful and salubrious and finally, that the direction of our predominantly laissez-faire approach to urban growth and change has, for the most part, served only to encourage growth, but at the unnecessary expense of many other humane qualities.

The attainment of those humane qualities in the perceptible city must certainly be the special responsibility of the genus planner; specie, urban designer.

For the purposes of this paper, I must set forth some definitions that we can share, since the language we use is painfully imprecise. With some simple definitions to establish the who and the what of which we talk, I will explore a few of the questions about roles, purpose and po-tentials which we face today.

Asserting that as planners at large we have as part of our professional purpose and stated values, to work toward the best possible socio-physical environments for specified groups of people—our clients, our constituency, then—we must ask, how do these changes/trends affect the potential quality of cities. The answer is evident in:

—the decline of public encouragement and support for large scale development projects as promised in Title VII and Urban Renewal programs;
—the growth in PUD's and neighborhood preservation programs;
—the reduced ability of public bodies or private investors to pay for new, large, capital facilities and amentities;
—the general loss of confidence in long range and large scale plans.

Given all of the above, what is the future role of urban design in urban planning? In these new roles, what are the skills needed to be effective? Who are the likely new clients?

First, let's agree to some definitions, or at least understand mine.

By *urban planning,* I mean the processes of stating goals, objectives, articulating issues, conflicts, opportunities for value creation and conditions for resource allocation in both physical phenomena such as the land, the capital improvements we associate with urbanization, the buildings and the array of public services identified with urban life. Following such goals or problem statements, urban planning then identifies policies and designs programs for resource allocation and activities aimed at achieving goals or ameliorating problems. Together with social programs, planning gives physical definition to places by establishing kind, intensity, and location of land uses, movement systems, the urban infrastructure, and the natural environment. Planners do these things with and for their clients, in both the public and private sector. Most large scale urban planning is done in the public sector, most small or project scale, in the private sector.

In the private sector, a program for project development is generally limited to the internal aspects of the problem, the private or client interests; i.e., so much floor space, so many units at such a price range and density, etc. To complete this kind of program, the unstated, but significant interests of the public community in all its manifestations need to be identified as a balance to the special interest of a given landowner. To many, a program is simply a statement of physical and functional objectives; in reality, and more significantly, a program does, in fact, describe a "life style." All of these planning activities are highly political and value laden. As a result, planners representing different interests will conflict with each other.

Planning and programming for development is the first and often the most important act of *urban design.* Programs are derived by many means. They should, in fact, evolve through the interaction of many of the specialists involved in the urban planning, building, and service delivery process.

Among these should be the *"urban designer"* who will identify the formal implications of what others suggest, and the human implications of what might be a formal proposal or a formal imperative to a given site and symbolic situation. The designer should be part and parcel of the planning program-making process—always in at the formative stages, less design decisions be, in fact, created by those with no adequate concept of an end environment, with limited realization of the physical impact of their work.

Program plan formulation must be a feedback process, with "design feasibility" as a critical mark.

Urban design then is the deliberate process (as opposed to accidental incrementalism) of giving perceptible (visible) shape to a community (a city, a place) in creating its physical environment in response to stated social, economic and esthetic objectives, ultimately, to every last detail. Designing the environment is not something that is done after many previous planning development decisions are made.

Levels of design input are often required in the earliest stages of concept development, program definition and general planning in order to assure project feasibility. These activities should not be thought of as sequential, but interactive and continuing throughout the development stages of a community.

In essence, urban designing is a way of solving those problems which have physical manifestations and components. In community development, the design problems lie in resolving the sets of complex, often competing requirements placed on the limited physical environment in order that all of the physical and social pieces which make up a community can best function.

To design is to analyze the problem, to identify its respective components and their interrelationships and to synthesize the components into a harmonious, working whole (acknowledging that any "whole" is always but a "fragment" of a larger, changing phenomenon). While design decisions are made continually by countless designers, it is the phenomenon of relatedness to each other and to a whole which is the critical and public interest and it is that urge and knowledge of how to relate that distinguishes the urban designer.

The media of community design are the important buildings and places, the circulation and other basic systems connecting them, the paraphernalia of the landscape (trees, signs, lights, benches, etc.), the natural setting and the sets of housing, and other repeated building types.

Why Is Good Urban Design Important?

One of the most significant attributes of any designer is the ability to imagine an object-environment before it does, in fact, exist. Thus, the designer will simulate a future reality, cast in the many possible media of plans, perspective drawings, three-dimensional models, verbal qualitative descriptions, capable of being tested for economic, social feasibility, or esthetic and symbolic desirability.

An environment which works well for its people will inevitably evoke love and loyalty. Feeling good about a place can add dimensions to a person's life, away from anomie and toward belonging. Good environments can encourage social interaction and the workings of a communal life.

In the most measurable terms, good design can conserve land and minimize and/or optimize infrastructure and costs in general. While they can effect first costs, good design decisions can also help keep project life costs down by proper detailing and use of materials.

The other side of social and economic benefit is cost. Poor design can make life's activities difficult, costly, and unpleasant.

Thus, the urban designer is not an architect drawn large; architects are trained and experienced mostly in the realm of building design. Much more is required. Size does, indeed, tend to change things in kind. To suggest, as some poetic designers have, that the "city is a house and the house a city" is a pleasant euphemism, but dangerous as an idea. The oversimplification of urban design process by the analogy to the house can only lead to bad design.

Urban design is not a function of project scale, but is in the most real sense an attitude of mind. The range of urban design concern extends through no less a spectrum than from city tree to city sector to metropolitan area. As the project changes in size, from the neighborhood to the urban region, the design elements change in kind, from the tree to the watershed, from the width of street to the mode of travel, and with these changes in elements, there must come a corresponding change in the designer's knowledge and abilities. This is not to suggest that the specie selection and placement of a tree is as significant an act of urban design as the selection and placement of an employment center.

In earlier pre-industrial times, in the natural "undesigned" city building process, the shape evolved slowly to reflect and satisfy the organic content of the city. The nature of urban form in kind and quality was an expression of the values of the people involved, many of whom were artisans with developed sensibilities and pride in work. The occasional "grand plan" of the past always found a special designer—it was by today's criteria a relatively simple task anyway. The differences between the past and the present are fundamental: few artisans are left; over recent generations esthetic and social sensibilities as they are manifest in the public environment have been dulled; leadership in pursuit of quality is wanting; single-mindedness in quest of profit or efficiency will carry the day.

The Designer Needs a Client

The environmental "problems" that design must solve are typically identified by many parties, and it is not uncommon to have divergent interests manifest in a single physical place. But the ultimate recognition
and statement of "what is to be done" must come from those who will be
responsible for building and/or using the place, the community. They
are the rightful "client" of the designer. In this sense, the designer's
responsibility is "limited." It is important in the urban design process
that this distinction between roles be kept clear. The designer must
have the proper frame of mind, viewing himself as a servant to and participant with client groups, being responsive to their needs and interests.

Participation in Design Process by Non-Designers

The word participation is a relatively new one for designers. Many jokes
revolve around the concept of committees in the design process. Fact is
that designers are at best insufficient to the multitude of tasks involved
in community design. Were that recognition not enough, practicing in
a democratic society today requires real participation in environmental
development procedures—people will no longer tolerate the "elitist-ex-
pert" approach to having it done for them. This kind of participation
can often furnish insight, feedback, and creative energy to willing designers.

Urban Design as a Function of Local Government

Acknowledging the ubiquitous nature of urban design actions, the most
critical part of professional urban design practice should logically be
done as a function of local government. The most essential elements of
the urban scene, which are the essence of the urban designer's media,
are such things as circulation systems ranging from freeway to walkway,
sewers, curbcuts, zoning ordinances, etc. Managing these is a public
mandate paid for with public funds and is the responsibility of public
officials, responsible ultimately to an electorate. Only when the designer
is in touch with these elements of the city and the institutions where all
of these are brought together, and where the various interests involved
can sit at one table, can the best planning/design process begin to be
effective.

So far I have attempted to establish the need for planner/designers
in the city building process. I ended by stating the importance of their
role in the public sector to insure the public interest. The facts have
been that compared to need, relatively few such planner/designers have

been schooled and experienced in the last thirty years and of these, only the smallest number have been attracted to the low paying, typically unvalued positions in public offices. So what else is new?

I have dwelled so long on the meaning of urban design and the role of urban planning-designers to establish their value in the planning-building process and to clarify the bias from which the questions asked will be addressed.

What about large versus small scale projects; the planning and building of new towns, renewed city sectors versus planned unit developments and neighborhood renewal?

Why must we choose between necessities? The argument about scale is not unlike the previous one about location. Need one be against planning and designing of new towns (expanded villages, etc.) in the suburbs in order to be for the continued rebuilding of the older inner cities?

To acknowledge that good planning/design processes can enhance the renewal of existing urban environments and then to deny the benefit of such processes to new suburban development seems destined only to make the new rapidly old, or more accurately, less than it might have been. The real argument is one of allocation. Given limited funds and human resources, where do we apply them?

In response to such a strategic question, I might opt for those places which are most in need of public intervention—assistance and subsidy.

Does the same concept of greatest need resulting in applied resource apply to the question of scale? I doubt it. Here, I believe the issue to be simply one of survival strategies for employed professionals. Planners/designers and local, public and private policymakers might be opting for small versus large enterprises for the simple reason that a choice among them does not currently exist. Long before national economic conditions of inflation and depression bound up the real estate "industry," the Nixon-Ford administration had decided in principle against public assistance in the urban development process. It would seem as a matter of national policy that the concept of planning for the public interest by the public sector was thought "bad;" individual, private, or "local" government initiative thought "good" and by definition, anything of a large scale requiring public participation in any form was to be discouraged. Hence, the demise of Title VII and Urban Renewal, with little regard for original objectives or for the real reasons behind apparent program "failures."

Let me state briefly some of the dilemmas in regard to large and small scale planning and development.

Important social goals in communities are attainable only if the scale and scope of proposed projects are sufficient in several ways: to capture the imagination of the people, i.e., if the land area and prospective populations are large enough to provide for a full range of human activity, wherein everyone can find some positive value and reason to participate or at a minimum to let it happen.

Land use and physical development must be based on facilitating the work of social institutions and systems such as learning, health, recreation, etc. This relationship establishes a fundamental integrity in the plans and development process. Thus, the physical development process can properly and creatively be used as a lever for social and institutional change and development, which is one of the essential activities of a healthy democratic society.

Community development goals should be made public—people buy and hold on to concepts as tenaciously as to real estate. Ownership of community goals must eventually be shared by developer, citizens and local government. It takes a degree of "largeness" to do these things.

One of the most exciting outcomes of the new city, Columbia, Maryland is the fact of racial integration. I am convinced that the only reason racial integration was possible in this new community was because everyone in their traditional, conservative, real estate mind was convinced at the outset that this integration would take place over a sufficiently large area; namely, the whole city of upwards of a hundred thousand people, and that their particular neighborhood would not be subject to ghettoization. This promise can only be made if the area is large enough. Hence, everyone was willing to move into and invest in an integrated neighborhood because they didn't have the fear that their particular residential enclave would become an island of segregation for some racial or ethnic minority. So that reality is there.

In addition to the potential benefits of influencing social systems, fostering activity mix, optimizing facility and program choice, perhaps most important is the potential for racial and economic mix of populations. Large scale development has also been proven to be extremely cost effective in expenditures for infrastructure. Add to all these the ultimate potential for attaining ecological goals in open space or historic preservation and the enhanced probability of finally achieving esthetic objectives because of greater available dollar resources, human talents, and leverages to condition design review and community participation.

In many ways, communities themselves really do demand the setting forth of long term goals and holistic plans, however general. This comprehensive long-term aproach is a requirement based on the need to have a "general plan" for land use and other development criteria legally adopted by the local government in order to participate in many federal programs and to assure equity in particular decisions. It is also an essential requirement for the comfort of long-term financial investors asked to invest millions of dollars in front-end costs and insisting on reasonable guarantees as to the ultimate nature and intensity of development, resultant value and potential profit.

Another requirement for the holistic long-term view of community development comes from the marketplace. Few people are comfortable with uncertainties, particularly when these might effect the value of their homes or businesses, most often representing their single most important financial asset. Therefore, the comfort apparent in clearly stated development goals and a planned framework for their attainment is an unquestionable attraction to most every non-speculative investor in real estate.

In the face of this desire for long-term plans is the opposite desire for small projects. The constancy of change, the unpredictability of money and market, the fickleness of all external conditions effecting community development mitigates in favor of small bites and minimum risks for private developers. Not the least among current external obstacles to large scale is the "Environmental Impact Analysis" which so clearly favors small versus big, regardless of potential benefits.

The promised large profits of large projects never had a chance to show here in the United States, as externalities got in the way—certainly our optimism about the economy was ill-founded.

In the face of all these development problems, what are the chances for large-scale planning and development?

First, let me express the deeply felt bias that planning undertaken without the reality or anticipation of pursuant development is a questionable activity; interest in it will wane as the activity proves academic or unrelated to decisionmaking. Therefore we are necessarily linking large-scale planning with large-scale development, or at least the relatedness of small projects to add up to the impact of large-scale development.

Small projects require less front end money, fewer highly skilled persons (including urban designers), less time, less energy, less commitment. There is ample precedent and everyone knows "how to do it." So, who's arguing?

The question remains, *do all the small projects add up to the potential benefits suggested above?* This will seldom be the case, unless there is a strong public interest at work in the larger planning-development process to identify the range of social needs and opportunities, to ensure that the pieces fit and "spaces between" are filled. There is too little precedent for such a public role and performance.

In short, the demise of public and private interest and support of large-scale projects is likely to reduce substantially the potential for improved urban environments.

The role of the urban designer in project design is well known; it is a scale at which the architect and landscape architect can excel. A lack of opportunity to plan and design at community or "urban" scale will simply reduce the ranks of urban designers and often planners working in the public interest.

We are in a socio-economic slump but the job to be done in the built environment is still there, even more so if we could seize the opportunity. Londoners were planning and designing for their future while in the bomb shelters of 1943. Surely we should be so wise.

The roles of urban designers described and alluded to above are by now pretty well known in the schools and professional world. Unfortunately, reduced development activity makes these roles academic. I can only wish that they survive the current conditions and refine in ability to perform when called upon in the future, to work with public-private partnerships in the building of better cities, both new and old.

I want to close with a wishful proposal for a truly new, and I would say, essential role for some urban designers to aspire to. It means new skills—working with a new clientele, skill as colleague to those in more traditional roles.

The Neighborhood Designer/Teacher

Part of the problem of not valuing "good design" process and environment is the fact of an undemanding, unsophisticated clientele. City folk are reared by our educational milieu and the public schools in particular to be blind to the visual qualities of the environment, to be generally inexperienced and not confident in the use of personal creative activity in the plastic and graphic arts. In addition, we grow up generally ignorant of the socio-economic and physical processes by which the city lives, changes, and dramatically effects the quality of our individual lives. Only with inroads into the educational processes will young people become first sensitized, then educated, and ultimately demanding of a better urban environment. It is a vicious circle for bad and a symbiotic relationship for good.

Imagine this scenario: Cities politically organized by "neighborhoods" (population 5,000-15,000); an electoral process which leads to representation by neighborhood in essential governing bodies; the school(s) as focal point of neighborhood governance and communal activity; central government viewed as coordinator, resource allocator, enabler and mitigator of conflicting local-regional interests.

The school (primary and/or secondary) has a curriculum which uses the city and urban process from which to teach other subjects, the urban environment is a learning place, planning/design process, a learning activity. All things are subject to change within the urban schools, within the community, by design, through publicly known planning-design-development processes.

A neighborhood urban designer-educator is housed in the school. Each neighborhood has one. The job is conceived as half time paid teacher and half time paid community planning-designer.

In school she/he works with teachers and students on curriculum and their learning environment. In the community, she/he helps to manage socio-physical change—design review—plans for the future—advocate to the central office.

In such a new role, the planner-designer becomes most critically a teacher. The results: a sophisticated, demanding citizenry—a contemporary analogue to the artisan of pre-industrial society. Whatever the cost, the pay-off would be significant in physical and social terms—the quality of urban life would have to benefit.

Make No Big Plans . . .
Planning in Cleveland in the 1970's

Norman Krumholz, Janice Cogger, John Linner

City planning is both in a state of flux and quite static. We are all familiar with the manifestations of change. While most planners used to be generalists in the area of land use and zoning, the profession is becoming broader and, at the same time, more specialized. One is no longer simply a city planner but a housing planner, land use planner, or transportation planner. A myriad of new specialties are emerging—historic preservation, economic development, water quality management, energy conservation—in areas that were formerly outside the planner's domain. At the same time, old specialties such as urban renewal fade away.

Just as the job titles of planners have changed, so too have the publications emanating from city and regional planning agencies. The traditional land use, transportation, and public facility plans are now being supplanted by reports which speak the arcane language of social policy.

To some members of the profession, these may serve as signals of fundamental changes in the role of city planning, changes that will have a permanent influence on the planning profession. When viewed from a larger perspective, however, the latest upheavals in planning may appear as but one of a series of identity crises precipitated by shifts in federal programs, budgets and the public's consciousness. During the late 1960's and early 1970's, both the news media and national political leaders discussed the "urban crisis" constantly. Now, concern for the environment has displaced the urban crisis in the popular imagination. In a sense, we consume issues in the same way that we consume new styles in cars, clothing and popular culture. After a couple of years of worrying about one problem, the novelty wears off, and we search for something new to worry about. Our priorities shift; our laws and regulations change; new acronyms enrich our professional jargon.

Despite the state of flux that planning appears to be in, it remains unchanged in many fundamental ways. Planners have traditionally lacked access to the political decisionmaking process, and consequently, have had little impact on important public policy issues. Has that changed? With some rare exceptions, planners have generally avoided conflict, especially public conflict with individuals and institutions who they perceive as being more powerful. Has that changed? Planners have tended to be technique oriented rather than goal oriented. By and large, they have seen themselves not as people who decide what to do but as people who decide how to do it. They have been technicians or facilitators, helping to build highways, subways, or urban renewal projects without questioning the goals to be served. Has that really changed?

I must conclude that the changes which appear from time to time to ripple the surface of the profession are superficial and transient. Just as federal programs flit from fad to fad, changes in city planning practice are more changes of style than substance, more a replacement of goals than their fulfillment. To be more useful and effective—particularly in the context of central city planning—more fundamental changes are needed. Let me try to suggest the characteristics of a more useful approach by drawing from my own experience in the City of Cleveland.

In 1969 I joined the Administration of then Mayor Carl B. Stokes, intent on producing a new general land use, transportation and public facilities plan for the City of Cleveland. An earlier plan had been published in 1949, and a new plan seemed in order. However, after a few short months of actually looking at the City and its people, it became obvious to me and to my staff that this traditional planning exercise would be irrelevant.

Cleveland has been losing population and employment for many years. Its property tax base has been shrinking. Much of the City's public and private physical plant is approaching obsolescence. Public service costs are high and rising while the quality of public services is becoming more and more questionable. Disinvestment and abandonment are well underway in many parts of the City. Cleveland does not need an elaborate plan for controlling growth. The City is not growing; it is declining.

The City's most serious problems are social and economic in nature and bear most heavily on the least advantaged citizens of the Celeveland region—the poor, racial minorities, the elderly. Hence, my staff and I have decided to direct our activities to serving one simple overriding goal—to promote a wider range of choices for those Cleveland residents who have few, if any choices. This decision has both an ethical and a practical base. Ethically, it represents a commitment to helping those who need help the most. To emphasize this objective is to be in accord with the social values of our society and our perceptions of proper planning practice. While nearly all planners would endorse the idea of working in behalf of the poor, a much smaller group would assign it a higher priority than boosting downtown, managing growth, or building rapid transit systems. On a more pragmatic level, this decision is an acceptance of the fact that until the social and economic problems of the poor are abated, central cities are not going to attract much new investment or development.

In these opening remarks, I have tried to establish the concern for the people of Cleveland—and especially the poor—which guides the day-to-day activities of the Cleveland Planning Commission. But putting goal statements down on paper is relatively simple; it is much more difficult to move from statement to reality. Let me relate two examples of our work over the past few years and try to describe where our goal has taken us.

My first example concerns a proposal for new downtown development.

In the winter of 1974, a local real estate developer approached the City with plans to construct a major downtown commercial complex called Tower City. The developer claimed that the total cost of planned construction would reach $350 million. The media, the business community, and the City's political leadership hailed the proposal as a bold step toward revitalizing Cleveland.

The Planning Commission staff reviewed the proposal and found several disturbing aspects. The developer was asking the City to pass legislation drafted by his attorneys. In this legislation, the City would waive rights it held to the development site, agree to make several million dollars of repairs to bridges on the site and assume full liability for any accident that occurred before the repairs were completed. Our investigation revealed that the City was not responsible for the bridge repairs and that the cost of the repairs would probably exceed the developer's estimate by seven to twelve million dollars. Further, it appeared that the developer would request property tax abatements for twenty years on his development.

In our judgment, the City had little to gain from Tower City. A recently completed staff study of Cleveland's downtown urban renewal project indicated that nearly all of the new office space built through renewal was occupied by tenants who had relocated from other downtown buildings. New development did not increase demand; it simply resulted in a kind of "musical chairs" among existing users of downtown space. Hence the impact of more construction would likely be rising vacancy rates and declining tax valuations in older office buildings. We could see no compelling reason to encourage this through public subsidies.

Following the staff's recommendation, the Planning Commission refused to approve the legislation unless several amendments were made and the developer agreed to pay full property taxes on the project. These conditions were not acceptable to the developer.

Very quickly, the Planning Commission's position came under fire from City Council and the newspapers. We were accused of obstructing progress and being anti-development. We explained that we did not oppose development per se, only development that imposed unfair burdens on the City without the assurance of net increases in tax revenue for the City or new jobs for City residents.

Attacks on the Planning Commission and its staff grew stronger and more personal throughout the City Council committee hearings. Eventually, Council overrode the Planning Commission's disapproval and passed the legislation.

On this particular issue, we lost badly, but we succeeded in raising some important issues. We pointed out that the money to subsidize this project would come at the expense of high priority capital improvements in the City's working class and poor neighborhoods. We asked to what extent the City should go to underwrite the risk of private development. We introduced the idea that the City should expect something in return for its public subsidies, a startling concept to some people.

Our approach does not always cast us in the role of obstructionists or place us in losing positions. Very often we are fighting for our own solutions to the City's problems, and occasionally we win. Our involvement in mass transit is a good example.

Urban transportation problems have traditionally been defined in terms of auto access and traffic congestion. During the 1950's and early 1960's the standard response was to call for the expansion of arterial systems and the development of intra-urban highways. As freeway construction has met increasing opposition, and as energy conservation, pollution and the environment have become popular issues, emphasis has been shifted from accommodating the automobile to encouraging increased reliance upon mass transit. Implicit in the decision to support mass transit for energy and environmental reasons is a commitment to making service more accessible and more attractive to those who have automobiles.

Our goal has led us to a different definition of Cleveland's transportation problem and a different notion of transit priorities. In 1970, 32 percent (78,000) of all households in the City of Cleveland did not have a car. While the increasing availability of the automobile and massive public expenditures on highways have vastly expanded the mobility of the majority of the population, the mobility of those who cannot drive or cannot afford an automobile has been greatly reduced. We believe that Cleveland's highest transit priority should be to restore some of the mobility lost by the poor and the elderly as a result of the national decision to opt for an automotive society.

This policy position reflects not only our sense of equity but also our understanding of what can and cannot be achieved through transit improvements. In the Cleveland area, it is unrealistic to expect that transit will lure large numbers of drivers out of their cars or have any significant impact upon regional development patterns. However, in the City of

Cleveland, it is realistic to expect that improved transit can provide more mobility for those who have no alternative means of transportation.

We first became involved in the transit issue through the Cleveland area's Five-County Transit Study which began in 1970. The City-owned Cleveland Transit System (CTS), at that time the largest system in the world to be operating exclusively from fare-box revenues, was rapidly approaching financial disaster. The Five-County planning process was seen locally as providing the impetus and framework for a regional transit system.

I asked to represent Mayor Stokes and later Mayor Perk on the Transit Study's Executive Committee. In that capacity I argued long and hard that expanded mobility for the transit-dependent population should be acknowledged as the Study's highest priority objective; that a project manager and prime contractor should be selected who appeared to be sensitive to the needs of the transit-dependent population; and that adequate funding should be provided for the transit-dependent element of the analysis. I won on each of these points. But such victories are fleeting things. The project's staff quickly identified its interests in terms of responding to and even anticipating political pressures, and a wide gap developed between the goals stated in the Study and the final recommendations.

The Study's final recommendations called for the expenditure of more than a billion dollars over the next ten years on expanded rail facilities. Based upon a careful review of the analysis supporting this recommendation, my staff and I concluded that such a rail system would provide few benefits to anyone except those involved in its construction and financing. Moreover, it threatened to draw resources away from those service improvements offering the greatest potential benefits to the transit dependent. In the eighteen-month interim between the publication of the Five-County Transit Study and the initiation of negotiations over formation of a regional authority, we worked quietly but consistently to discredit the rail expansion plan locally, at the regional level and at UMTA.

By the end of 1974, CTS could no longer continue to operate without drastically increasing fares and reducing service. In mid-December, Cleveland decisionmakers began the serious business of forming the Greater Cleveland Regional Transit Authority (RTA). In spite of our having specialized knowledge of the transit issue, the planning staff was not invited to the first meetings.

The negotiations centered around one issue—what the City would receive in return for transferring CTS to the new regional authority. Initially, the City's political leaders did not have a clear idea of what to ask for, so they simply demanded a majority of the appointments to the RTA Board. The Planning Commission staff felt that this was insufficient and that the City should be bargaining for fare reductions and service improvements for City residents. We took elements of the Five-County Study, translated them into terms which decisionmakers could relate to, and presented them to the Mayor and City Council. When the City's political leaders realized that abstract concepts such as "route-spacing guides" and "service headways" could mean tangible improvements for their constituents, they quickly shifted the focus of their demands. Our recommendations provided us entry into the discussions and served as the foundation for more than five months of negotiations.

Throughout these negotiations, the City's Law Director and I argued for fare and service guarantees for the City, while our opposition argued for "flexibility" for RTA. The opposition included the Cuyahoga County Commissioners, suburban mayors, the staff of our regional planning agency, the Growth Association (Cleveland's Chamber of Commerce), and even the management of the City's own CTS. This was the same alliance of powers which had strongly promoted the rail development portion of the Five-County Plan. Since we had succeeded in convincing Cleveland's Mayor and City Council that rail expansion might divert massive resources away from those transit improvements most needed by City residents, rail plans were rarely mentioned during the negotiations. However, when the transit operators, regional planners, and downtown boosters spoke in terms of "flexibility" for RTA, rail expansion was clearly one of the issues on their minds. Thus, while our opposition fought to keep the City's guarantees as meaningless as possible, we fought to insure that RTA would be legally committed to reducing fares and improving service for Cleveland residents.

During the protracted negotiations we were forced to make a number of concessions, but when agreement was finally reached, it was clear that we had made substantial progress toward insuring that RTA would be responsive to the needs of the transit-dependent population. In the final agreement the City was guaranteed:

1. that a twenty-five cent fare would be maintained for at least three years;
2. that senior citizens and the handicapped would ride free during non-peak periods (twenty hours daily) and pay only half fare at peak;
3. that service frequencies and route coverage within the City would be improved;
4. that Community Responsive Transit, originally envisioned as supplementary Dial-A-Ride or pre-scheduled service would be initiated. Moreover, early in the negotiations, City Council accepted my suggestion that RTA be prohibited from spending funds on planning or developing a downtown subway or elevated system for at least five years.

Our involvement in transit issues did not end with the creation of RTA. Despite the fact that RTA was legally committed to instituting Community Responsive Transit within the City, its management opposed assuming responsibility for the existing Dial-A-Bus service for the elderly and handicapped. Three months of intensive bargaining was required before the RTA Board reluctantly agreed to spending a million dollars in 1976 on such supplementary transit service. And despite the fact that RTA is prohibited from planning, constructing or operating a downtown subway or elevated system, an application was recently submitted to UMTA for a Downtown People Mover demonstration project.

I must conclude that we have won some important skirmishes in the area of transit policy during the last seven years, but the war is far from over. Fare-cuts and service improvements which benefit the transit dependent are in effect, but management's devotion to these elements is tenuous, at best. One million dollars for CRT, out of a sixty million dollar budget, is not a great deal, but it is a foot in the door. The legislation prohibiting development of a downtown distribution system may be amended, but as it now stands, it is an impediment to investment in rail expansion. Efforts to change public policy result in few clear-cut and final victories. It is a continuous process of pushing at margins, of creating opportunities and sometimes creating obstacles.

What do these two examples indicate about the responsibilities of planners in the declining central city?

First, one of the primary responsibilities of a planner in a declining central city is simply to fight off wasteful or counter-productive proposals for using public money. Proposals to use public money merely for urban decoration abound, as do proposals for the public to absorb all the risk in otherwise private enterprises. When a planner discerns that a proposal to subsidize a new private office building may produce nothing in the way of additional tax revenues for the city or more employment for its residents—especially the unemployed—his obligation is to publicly oppose the proposal or attempt to re-shape it in a more useful direction. When a local transit authority proposes a massive capital program that will provide yet another transportation option for affluent suburbanites at the expense of improvements for the transit-dependent population, the central city planner should forcefully spell out the consequences and fight the proposal.

A corollary is the planner's obligation to point out what is possible and what is probably impossible to accomplish in the declining city. Many local decisionmakers still believe (or say they believe) that present trends can be reversed. They seek to restore the aging central city to what it was thirty years ago. This would require substantial changes in social tastes along with huge sums of new capital. A more realistic approach would be for local leaders to concentrate on preserving the city's remaining assets, which in many cases, are still quite substantial. Instead of promoting expensive schemes to lure people back from the suburbs, most older cities should try to improve conditions for their present residents. Instead of trying to stimulate new housing construction, they should be trying to maintain their existing housing stock. This seems like a fairly modest goal, but given the realities of demographic and economic decline in the central city, even it may be very difficult to achieve. It may be heresy of the highest order, but for those of us who labor in central cities, it might be appropriate to reinscribe the motto on the escutcheon of our profession to read: "Make No Big Plans . . ."

Another primary responsibility of the planner in a declining central city is to address the most pressing problems of its residents—poverty, unemployment, inadequate mobility, deteriorating neighborhoods, and declining municipal services. These social and economic ills are at the heart of the much discussed "urban crisis" and the greatest obstacles to making our cities attractive places to live and work.

We should note that the problems identified above are not the problems of the public at large. The majority of Americans who live in metropolitan areas make a good living and can afford decent homes in neighborhoods with good schools and little crime. The victims of our urban "crisis" are mostly the poor and working class residents of our central cities. To solve urban problems, we must give priority attention to their needs, perhaps at the expense of other needs. For example, we may decide—as we have decided in Cleveland—that it is more important for mass transit to serve individuals who cannot drive or afford a car than to induce suburban commuters away from their automobiles. We may decide—as we have decided in Cleveland—that while making downtown a more attractive place is a worthy goal, it is not as urgent as slowing the rate of deterioration in the city's neighborhoods.

This, however, means abandoning one of the planning profession's most cherished myths—that the planner is an apolitical technician, promoting goals that are widely accepted through the use of professional standards that are objectively correct. This fanciful notion has helped planners justify highways, urban renewal projects and other public actions that have devastated poor and working class neighborhoods and have left central cities worse off than before. In fact, all public actions have political implications. They serve different interests and different values. Ultimately, each planner must decide which values and which interests he or she will serve.

In Cleveland we have focused upon advocating the interests of the City's low- and moderate-income residents. This goal was not given to us; we chose it for ourselves. Those planners who, in the tradition of our profession, look to political leaders for clear statements of goals or objectives will be eternally frustrated. The political process is a decision process, not a process of goal formulation. Elected officials usually avoid clearly identifying goals and objectives.

While the political process demands that goals remain ambiguous, the planning process requires that they be clearly defined. Unless planners are prepared to select goals for themselves, they will flounder aimlessly in search of direction or serve as rationalizers and expediters for the narrow and shifting interests of others.

The selection of a goal is only the first of many initiatives required of planners who desire to influence public policy. Most planners have been taught that theirs is a passive profession. The typical planning agency waits for matters to be referred to it and then offers its recommendations. While a city charter or federal regulations may require that certain proposals be submitted to planners for their review, neither law, nor custom, nor political instinct will send many decisionmakers in search of the planner's "wisdom" on key policy issues. If planners are to have any significant impact on policy, they must seize upon important issues, formulate their own positions, and then forcefully bring their work to the attention of decisionmakers. If you will recall in the transit example, we were not even invited to the first meetings establishing RTA. We simply developed a series of policy recommendations and convinced the Mayor and City Council to adopt them as the City's bargaining position. Simply stated, planners must become more innovative, more entrepreneurial and more aggressive than they have been in the past. They must become "activists."

Our experience indicates that there are ample opportunities for planners to expand their role within city government. The bureaucratic structure of the city is more porous than is generally imagined. Broad areas of public policy are viewed as being outside the domain of any specific agency of city government. For example, in Cleveland, no city department is specifically responsible for the development of city policy regarding interstate highways, mass transit or regional planning policy. In such areas, an activist planning agency with objectives, competence and the willingness to seize responsibility can become recognized as the city's "expert."

An activist agency can also influence the policies pursued by other city agencies. Planning organizations differ from most city departments in that they enjoy the leisure needed to analyze problems, research policy alternatives and formulate recommendations for program changes. City agencies which are encumbered with day-to-day responsibilities for administering service programs can be encouraged to look to the city's planners for suggestions about the re-orientation or restructuring of their

activities. We are currently serving in this type of consulting capacity
to Cleveland's Department of Community Development, the agency which
administers the Community Development Block Grant. The Department
initially sought our help only in dealing with management issues and data
requirements. But information shaped by a policy orientation is potential
power; we are now helping the Department prepare the City's housing
assistance plan and redesign its neighborhood rehabilitation strategy.

There are many avenues through which policy can be influenced: the
range of potential clients for the planner's work is almost unlimited. Local
politicians and administrators must deal with increasingly complex problems without adequate information, a long-range perspective, or even a
clear idea of what they wish to achieve. The desire of decisionmakers
for more information and better analysis to which they can relate presents
great opportunities to a planning agency which can meet such demands.
Moreover, individuals and organizations outside the formal decisionmaking structure can be important allies in efforts to influence policy.
We have found that the news media and community organizations can
often use the information and analyses which we generate in a far more
dramatic and effective way than we can. In the transit negotiations, the
informed support and omnipresence of organizations representing the
interests of the elderly and of poorer neighborhoods was absolutely essential to the achievement of our objectives.

However, if planners are going to aggressively attempt to influence policy, they must accept the fact that they will find themselves in conflict
situations. Not surprisingly, if their efforts are directed toward serving
the needs of the poor and the powerless, they may frequently find themselves in conflict with the rich and the powerful. For example, at one of
the final transit negotiating sessions, the Chairman of the Growth Association angrily ordered me to "get out" and take my "spy" (a staff person)
with me. He is a partner in one of Cleveland's most prestigious law
firms and a formidable power in the Cleveland Establishment. Our current relations are, I believe, quite good. Again, during the Tower City
controversy, the President of Cleveland City Council referred to the Commission as "a bunch of baboons," publicly questioned my competence and
called for my resignation.

One does not take such attacks very personally or very seriously. They
are generally a manifestation of that large part of government which is,
in fact, theatre or an attempt to whip the opposition into line on a specific
issue. Shortly after the Council President had called for my resignation,
he was seeking my advice on transit issues, and we remain on good terms.
Within city government alliances are constantly shifting. Those who
oppose you on one issue are often allies on the next. The risks associated
with challenging powerful interests and developing countervailing positions are real, but they are not nearly so great as they may appear to be.

All of this calls for changes in the way planners are trained and educated. Planners today are much better versed in such things as linear scaling, computer modeling, and factor analysis than they were ten years ago, yet few elaborate statistical techniques are very helpful as tools in local government. With rare exceptions, politicians do not understand or trust them. Adequate data are rarely available, and seldom do you have enough time to use such techniques. More often than not the final product of technical exercises is increased confusion. It would be much better for planning schools to focus on teaching students how to think clearly and communicate effectively. Much of the "conventional wisdom" in urban affairs is an accumulation of half-truths, outdated information, and rhetoric. Central cities need people who can see through this to the heart of the problem.

Much more attention should be given to helping would-be planners understand how decisions are made in urban government. This is one area in which planning schools have definitely failed. A great many students enter the profession believing that public policy decisions are made within an orderly, rational context that hinges heavily on planners' recommendations. Nothing could be further from the truth. The public decisionmaking process in big cities is generally irrational (in our terms) and chaotic and always highly politicized. The institutional role of planners is almost inconsequential. Politicians ultimately make the decisions, and if planners wish to influence those decisions, they should be able to formulate issues within a framework that politicians understand and can relate to. The exact mechanics of the decisionmaking process cannot be taught, since they vary from city to city. At the very least, however, planning students should learn that local government rarely meets the high standards set forth in textbooks and that planners must adapt their style (but not necessarily their objectives) to suit the politicians. It would also be useful to convey to the student that decisionmaking in government is not an act but a process. If the planner hopes to shape policy, his protracted participation in this process is essential.

Planning educators should impress upon their students the fact that there *are* many opportunities to influence the resolution of important issues, there *are* opportunities to help shape the future but that most of these opportunities do not emerge from a planning agency's normal day-to-day operations. Planners must seek them out and occasionally take some risks to be effective. It is not clear whether planning education can make risk-takers out of non-risk-takers, but it is worth a try.

Ironically, one of the greatest obstacles to restructuring planning education and the role of city planners is the noble history of the profession itself. City planners must acknowledge that confronting the most urgent problems of our cities is more important than preserving the planner's traditional image. Otherwise, they will have admitted that city planning has little to contribute to solving the most critical problems of our older cities and their people and perhaps, students who are interested in helping resolve our cities' problems should be counseled to look to other professions for their training.

But, if planners are willing to shift their focus, if they are willing to work seriously within the context I have described, if they are willing to interact with other public officials and accept their share of responsibility and risk in the day-to-day decision process, then the planning profession may indeed play a pre-eminent role in the future of our cities.

Section II
Social Planning in Change —
Practical Applications of Social Sensitivity

Social Planning and Social Science: Historical Continuities and Comparative Discontinuities

Irving Louis Horowitz

The Political Context of Social Planning

The antecedents to the planning model have strangely contradictory histories within socialist and capitalist nations. Planning became the essential touchstone of the Soviet revolution. The ability to predict the future and organize the present to reach specific goals was viewed as a fundamental law of socialist society distinguishing it from capitalist society. Some critics refer to the Soviet Union as the epitome of an over-managed society (Etzioni, 1969:37).

> The productive forces of socialism differ basically from the productive forces of capitalism in their social form, although they have much in common with the latter from the material and technical standpoint. The new social system has opened up for them great additional possibilities and advantages; a planned and rational use of productive capacities, greater efficiency in the organization of production, balanced development, higher rates of economic growth, unlimited overall technical progress, new incentives for labour, and the creation of a new man (Zvorykin, 1966:16-17).

For a considerable amount of time, planning on a national scale, certainly as it relates to industrialism, was viewed within Anglo-American culture as a veritable harbinger of the communist menace, an example of what happens to a society lacking in freedom. A powerful anti-planning and anti-utopian literature sprang up and quickly took hold, even before World War Two came to an end. In Friedrich von Hayek's words (1944), planning represented the "road to serfdom," while for Karl Popper (1945), planning incorporated the worst features of social engineering and led to a "closed society." Even a hint, as in the work of Barbara Wootton (1945), that there could be "freedom under planning" was met by a barrage of denunciations. Milton Friedman (1962:11) put the matter in blunt economic words: "Collectivist economic planning has interfered with individual freedom"; while more recently, Robert Nisbet (1975:227) made the same point in sophisticated sociological terms:

Large-scale government, with its passion for egalitarian uniformity, has prepared our minds for uses of power, for invasions of individual privacy, and for the whole bureaucratization of spirit that Max Weber so prophetically identified as the disease of modernity.

While laissez-faire European and American conservatives were denouncing the planning ideal, American planners, often quite conservative in their economic and political values, went about their business oblivious to and unconcerned with the ongoing ideological ballast. Within an Anglo-American context, planning was institutionalized, not via Marxism, but rather via Keynesanism. Planning in America became at least as extensive, if not as intensive, as planning in the Soviet Union. If the Soviets were primarily concerned with planning in the industrial sector, in the United States planning was employed in urbanization, education, transportation, neighborhoods, and almost all areas outside the world of industrialism (cf. Frieden and Morris, 1968). "Free enterprise" and the "market economy" were allowed to flourish unhampered, exactly in those areas where Soviet planning was most intensive, the factory and the industrial work setting. Thus, a peculiarly distorted vision of planning prevailed in both worlds, each protecting a charade of freedom—be it "democratic centralism" or "free enterprise"—which, in fact, assumed that industrialization and modernization necessitate guidance and forecasting of needs and performances.

The specific mechanism that brought planning to the fore in the United States was the New Deal, followed by the Second World War, and in rapid succession, the Marshall Plan and the War on Poverty. Each of these efforts used planning almost as an afterthought, to deliver on political promises. The goals were announced, the policies enumerated, and the plans followed in helter-skelter fashion. Planning in the United States was never ideological imperative as in the Soviet Union, but a functional imperative, situationally determined.

Lepawsky (1976:17) in his recent "vignette" of the New Deal, indicates how policy formulators, program administrators, and planners coalesced in the Roosevelt Administration, never again to be parted:

Despite devastating criticism from the opposition, planning burgeoned and virtually became a national policy in its own right during the New Deal. Often in disarray, but always dynamic, this system of policy planning and program planning embodied the aims and brains of the Roosevelt administration. It was this powerhouse of intellect and interest, experience and experiment, which, by 1939 when the New Deal stood at its midpassage, constituted the core of the planning apparatus. Reciprocally the planning apparatus had by 1939 virtually become the cortex of the Brain Trust.

So firmly embedded had planning become by the end of the 1930's that the movement from welfare to warfare was accomplished with hardly a bureaucratic ripple. The continuum between HEW and DOD continued into the postwar ear—cemented by the planning factor.

Coming into the rebellious decade of the 1960's, the profession of planning, which arose in connection with accounting, engineering, and finance, operated within a bureaucratic context. Planners had as their essential task delivering on the long-range rational goals of a society. In the United States, at least, planning, far from being an ideological imperative demonstrating the superiority of the free enterprise system, was in fact an essential handmaiden of the industrial and urban complex. If ever a demonstration were required that practice has its own imperatives, the example of planning would surely rank high. Planning resources depended on the inexorable complexities of urban industrial life far more than upon the rhetoric of liberalism or radicalism. Whatever else planning is, few can doubt its essential place as the centerpiece of twentieth century bureaucratic administration.

Postwar planners came to recognize the risks involved in a highly aggregated definition of the public interest. Planning was often seen in opposition to community welfare. The very rationality of the planning syndrome was said to involve irrationalities at the level of implementation.

> Our concepts of optimality, our focus on an abstract welfare function, and our concern for an illusory greater good (or "public interest") is brought into serious question. Planning is being challenged more and more, not on its service to an overall public, but rather on the differential and distributional aspects of its results affecting particular publics (Bolan, 1969:308).

By the 1970's, it became part of the new conservatism to suggest that communities, rather than regions or nations, should be viewed as the basic systems unit, directing greater attention to the needs of the local community.

> One way to do this might be to recognize *communities* as the fundamental systems units, and attempt to build up regional service systems from community-based modules supplying urban services. By thus inverting the planning strategy, it may become possible to adequately represent not only processed knowledge, but, along with it, the personal knowledge of community and neighborhood impacts in urban system planning (Hudson et al., 1974:264).

The difficulty is that even with a more expansive vision of constituencies, the planner seems unable to get beyond an interest-group model into any kind of general theory that would in fact entitle planning to be considered a social science.

What makes "liberation planning" or "participating planning" (Kravitz, 1970:240-267) difficult, if not impossible to achieve is the constituency planning agencies serve. Market values have their own laws, and planners serve economics, not aesthetics.

> As long as discount value dominates economic calculations in resource allocation decisions, it appears difficult indeed to opt for wildlife protection or aesthetic urban design—unless, and only unless, those can be rendered in favorable quantitative terms within a context of discounted value. We must show, in that case, sufficient near-future, if not immediate, quantifiable pay-offs for keeping the fish and birds at that hypothetical pond. The birds and fish must be valuable for killing insects which bother people or for providing recreational sport, or some such utilitarian benefit. This view decrees that if the wildlife cannot serve man some way, it has to go. And wildlife has been going, as ponds and meadows are filled, streams are polluted, and ecosystems are disrupted. Seldom, though, can discount calculations justify otherwise (Moffitt, 1974:402).

It has been argued that the social sciences also service the marketplace. But one might note that this breakdown of autonomy represents a failure of social science, not its success and certainly not its core definition.

The degree of restraint one encounters in present-day planning literature contrasts markedly with the euphoria characteristic of planning literature during the sixties. The themes of "brave new world," "progress" and "change" were so overwhelming, that one text insisted that "we are beyond debating the inevitability of change." The notion of planned change was considered so central that "no one will deny its importance" (Bennis, Benne, Chin, 1969:2-3). Amidst the heady wine of movement and rebellion, of new demands for racial, ethnic, and sexual equity, one can well appreciate such a sense of confidence. Under such circumstances, there seemed no question that social planners, policy makers, and social scientists would come together in a grand assault against the establishment. In the move toward planning, neoconservative attacks were dismissed for having so wide a set of assumptions about tradition, as to betray the very variety of the authoritative traditions to which they appeal (Benne, Bennis, and Chin, 1969:28-32). Why a similar argument could not be adduced against pluralistic liberalism and its multiplicity of theories of change is not made clear. Yet, it is clear from the perspective of only a decade, that the much heralded unity of social planning and social science has not taken place. Their shared participation in the glories of policymaking have likewise not materialized. Why these anticipated outcomes have not occurred is, in large part, the subject of this paper.

On the Relationship Between
Social Planning and Social Science

The basic premise of this paper is simple enough: social planning and social science, far from being "handmaidens" in a common concert, are in fact exceedingly different and for the most part profoundly antithetical in their missions. The commonsense of planning rests on maximum utilization of resources and perfect equilibrium of economies. The commonsense of social science rests on maximum equity and liberty, and that entails producing an excess of supplies to satisfy demands. The bugaboos of planning—waste, unused resources, and inefficient organization—may be seen by social scientists as precondtions for a decent society, serving the public interest.

This observation is not intended to dissuade people from seeking careers in planning or to negate the obvious fact that as new legal measures arise—new safety standards for industry, environmental protection agency standards, stiffer building codes with respect to zoning ordinances, etc.—a wide new area for physical planners has opened up. But it is of dubious worth to recite these new opportunities. More to the point, it is important to show that the essential dialectic, or if one prefers, the dialogue for the immediate future, is between social planner and social scientist. The planner more often than not functions as a technocrat urging the completion of practical tasks in the shortest possible time and with least expenditure of funds. The social scientist functions as ombudsman, indicating the risks of a purely planning perspective and the human worth of building a high error factor into all calculations concerning the proximate future.

There is a considerable body of literature informing us that social planning is in transition, crisis, disarray, transformation, etc., but precious few planners have paused to give us a workable definition of planning. About the closest thing to a definition to be found in a basic text on the subject of urban planning is that planning represents an "action-producing activity which combines investigation, thought, design, communication, and other components. But in another sense, planning is a special kind of pre-action action" (Fagin, 1970:133). It is by no means unkind to note that this valiant effort at definition is viewed even by its progenitor as "two steps removed from an actual environment-shaping activity," and is at best "an efficient substitute for trial and error regarding the relations of wholes and parts" (Fagin, 1970:134). This strongly subjective definition of planning in terms of a process of feeling, knowing, and acting, invites grave doubts as to its structural status, or placement within a social science cosmos. Yet, even the most rigorous social planners characteristically define the field in highly operational terms, clearly dependent for implementation upon constituencies rather than concepts, doers rather than demographers, and systems without structures.

Despite the noteworthy efforts of some to create a "linking process" between physical planning and social planning (Perloff, 1968:346-359), it is evident that as definitions of a "decent home and suitable environment" came to signify moving to suburbs and high income areas rather than systematic urban redevelopment, the linkages became more apparent than real, and old ideological hostilities reappeared. Demands were made that the "inequalities and pathologies of the urban low-income population must be eliminated before the attractive, efficient, and slumless city for which physical planners are striving is realized (Gans, 1968:75). Further, just as terms like "slums" and "ghettos" were subject to a labelling process that magically transformed these into "communities" and "neighborhoods," so too did the distinction between physical and social planning become highly subjective. Whether uniform building codes based on performance standards are actually a function of physical or social planning very much depends on who is establishing the codes and standards, and negotiating them to what purpose. Again, the larger issue is a remarkable absence of simple guidelines for the concept of planning in general.

The essentials of planning appear simple enough. Planning has to do with charting future developments in terms of present tendencies and trends, which, adjusting for changes in technology and the economy, can predict lifestyles, industrial growth, and real wealth for a future population. To extrapolate further from the literature: planning can be either short range or long range. It can be concerned with planning a menu for tomorrow, or planning soft landings on Mars ten years hence. Planning, in short, at some level is forecasting; presumably, the better the forecast, the more accurate the plan, and in this sense, it is more like engineering than science. (Maruyama, 1973:346). One might further add that it is more like art than engineering.

Deriving indicators or benchmarks for proving or disproving the worth of a plan becomes the essential task of social accounting, which in turn relies upon social indicators for its information. Planning involves maximizing rationality. It presumes that targeting goals is eminently feasible, even necessary, and probably desirable, whatever idiosyncracies may appear in human behavior in the first instance, economic systems in the second, and technological innovations in the third. This may not be a completely orthodox view of planning, and certainly it is open to challenge, but it seems fair to say that for most people in the business of planning, most, if not all of the foregoing is considered a precondition for success.

Even those statements by planners that recognize the need for precision, for "forced choices" employing the gaming and scaling techniques of the social sciences, make easy the identification of social planning with the public interest. Even when this public interest dissolves into a higher level of cacophony, planners are urged to strengthen the ability of the political leadership to respond (cf. Wheaton and Wheaton, 1970:152-164). But this reverses causal dilemmas: the political leadership is already powerful. It is the social planning field which finds itself under assault and in a weakened position. To raise the cry of public interest or betterment of professional standards in a shrinking market does not address itself to the dilemmas faced by social planners. Advocacy of what, and planning for whom, remain issues buried beneath the rhetoric of the public interest.

In a sense, the central political role of planners made them unlikely candidates as social science performers. As Rabinovitz (1969:79-117) indicated, apart from forces beyond their control, planners do assume various political guises: the roles of technician, broker, and mobilizer, being paramount. In addition, the planner must sometimes initiate and at other times veto political directives. But these multiple roles, brought to fruition in an authoritarian context, represent far less (or more) than a scientific appraisal of circumstances of situations.

Planning remains a process far different than what planners describe. In point of fact, planners only rarely define the planning situation. The planning context is defined by the political system and hence the goals set are very often outside those indicated by the planners themselves. Without getting into the literature on the struggle between bureaucrats and politicians, it should be evident that planning involves a huge mobilization process. To set goals is the task of the political system; to implement these goals is the task of the planning community. However, the political system sets its plans in terms of parameters having little to do either with the available technology or the available bureaucracy. Political life depends upon industrial events external to planners. When Stalin declared, in 1931, that Soviet industrialism would have to reach the level of the West in ten years or face utter defeat in another world war, he was accurately assessing the international situation. It then became the task of planners to realize Soviet industrial goals. It also became the task of the police and the secret police, to make sure that those goals were achieved in accord with the plans, whatever the human costs.

The success of Soviet industrialism almost, but not quite, blocks out the human costs involved in its realization. In situations where police functions are minimal, the same planning results cannot be guaranteed. Thus, despite Fidel Castro's announcement of a ten-million ton sugar harvest, the net yield was only six-million tons. The police force never operated quite maximally, and the political leadership was embarrassed. One might conceivably argue that the New Deal planning system worked in much the same way and came to a dead halt by 1939. This might easily have led to the demise of the New Deal, but for the divine intervention of the Second World War, which provided new tasks for planners and new aims for the political leadership. This is not intended as a cynical mini-review of history, but simply to indicate that planning is not simply a technical chore performed by technically competent personnel, but is in fact a janitorial mission in the service of the political system, with mobilization being the lynchpin of the process.

There is implicit in the planning function a political morality. Whether it be stated in terms of a new society, a new man, or a new deal, the moral foundation of planning is absolute rationality. Without such rationality forecasting clearly becomes an odd game. Hence the planner makes a strong investment in rationalizing human behavior, not because of any propensity toward rational concepts of the world, but because irrational behavior becomes a mode of destroying the realization of the plan. As a result, within a Western context, things like strikes, work stoppages, slowdowns and sick leaves, become vicious attacks on the plan; downright irrational forms of behavior. One would think that the purpose of the strike is to thwart the planner rather than to gain better wages, better working conditions, or better working hours. Of course, in the Soviet context, this was stated more bluntly, in terms of those who would wreck the plans of the state, saboteurs, all appellations given to those who would strike or slow down, in short, those who refused to receive the benefits of the plan by refusing to implement the costs of the plan.

The foundation of planning and the planning ethic, far from providing a basis for radical behavior, in fact was a source of a new conservatism: an industrial conservatism, whether of a capitalist or socialist variety, which saw all shortfalls with respect to achieving plans as illustrations of the miserable nature of human behavior, of the willful, spiteful and hateful character of people, of an irrationality that had to be destroyed. Thus it is that what started out as a new economic mobilization leading to a new society and a new man, in fact became the captive of the oldest political network of all, dictatorship and rule from the top down. Never has the road to hell been paved with more honorable intentions.

As an effort to cope with this monster in the machine, the planners began to realize both by themselves and through the criticism they received from the social science community, that planning is not all of one piece; or better, if it is of one piece it is terribly dangerous. One could conceive of planning in various ways.

To begin with, there is private planning versus public sector planning. The problem here is that public sector planning has many options available to it that private sector planning does not. The public sector can lower taxes and provide rebate incentives, intensify inflation, or create new jobs. About the most the private sector can do is move the profit margin up and down as a means of inducement and enticement to buy or to sell. Hence it becomes evident that planning in a public sector is of necessity quite different than planning in the private sector and has more possibilities for realization as well as more possibilities for abuse. As Weidenbaum (1976a:35) points out:

> There are fundamental differences between business and Government planning. Essentially, we are dealing with the difference between (1) forecasting and reacting to the future and (2) trying to regulate it. Corporate planning of necessity is based on the principle of trade—attempting to persuade the rest of society that they ought to purchase the goods and services produced by a given firm; the controls that may accompany the plan are internally oriented. In striking contrast, the Government is sovereign and its planning ultimately involves coercion, the use of its power to achieve the results that it desires. Its controls are thus externally oriented, extending their sway over the entire society.

Planning takes place at various levels: local, regional, national, and even international. Clearly, the question of planning at international levels is more problematical than planning at local levels. It is frought with many more possibilities of failure since many uncontrollable variables are involved, not the least of which are the ubiquitous character of international law and international conflict. Thus, as one moves from local planning, which has a maximum possibility of forecasting, to national and international planning, one also moves from a more successful to a less successful source of planning.

Furthermore, there is the question of long-range and short-range planning. Here it might be the case that short-range planning since it involves, again, a fewer number of selected variables, has higher propensities to precision and exactitude than long-range planning. The five-day plan should theoretically be easier to realize than a five-month plan, which in turn should be easier to realize than a five-year plan. On the other hand, the length of time may work the other way around since failures in one year may in fact be made up in a following year, whereas with a short-range plan, the possibility of make-up or correction becomes exceedingly difficult, if not impossible.

A still more advanced consideration is planning from the top down versus the bottom up. By "bottom up," I have in mind a kind of planned self-management characteristic of Yugoslavia and parts of Italian industry, in which the actual plans are made by factory workers. Likewise, bottom-up planning can be the sorts of recommendations made by condominium developers who determine for themselves what the wages and salaries of management ought to be, what improvements can be made, and under what forms of supervision. Top-down management is so well known it

requires little illustration. But here too, there may be a problem of
a priorism. It may well be that top-down management is superior to
bottom-up management because of the waste involved in self-management
and the conflict set off by everyone having their say.

There are residual and large-scale questions of increase in equity versus
increase in profitability. This may involve issues ranging from environmental controls to housing startups. Compliance with all of the rules
and regulations of the Environmental Protection Agency might so reduce
profitability for either a housing or industrial unit, that the increase in
equity, which is the ostensible goal of such an agency, is itself frustrated
by the absence of growth per se.

These types of planning problems—dilemmas between private sector
and public sector, regional versus national, top-down versus bottom-up
administration, long range versus short range forecasting, environmental
orientation versus profitability orientation, are in fact empirical problems
that can only be analyzed within a context of social research.

The planning field provides data for a rather interesting fourfold table.
Among the radicals, some conceive of planning as the very touchstone of
American democracy, while others argue that social planning is little
more than a statist-inspired, self-serving instrument for maintaining class
and race differentiation. Among the conservatives, some see planning as
blurring the hard and firm need to respond to the economic marketplace,
while others see planning as a final barrier to anarchism in our times,
and a necessary component to law and order. Hence, those in search
of neat correlations between planning and ideology are likely to come
upon serious frustrations. For this reason, a functional, rather than ideological account of the relationship between social planning and social
science is required.

Given the fact that relatively few planners are either trained in, or
make their living through the social sciences, it is hard to accept the
well-intentioned belief that "of all the client-serving professions, planning
is among those which call on the greatest depth and diversity of social
science disciplines," and equally difficult to view "the planner as social
scientist turned practitioner in the arena of public policy" (Marcuse,
1976:269). Beyond the demographic distinctions is the central fact that
any social science must be more than a profession; it further requires a
critique of its own practice, as well as public policy.

The rhetoric and professional identity of planning has increasingly
moved in the direction of social science. A study of M.I.T. graduates,
for example, indicates that in the early 1960's the source of planning
personnel was largely engineering, whereas by the end of the decade,
and continuing into the 1970's, architecture and the social sciences were
most often mentioned as the undergraduate major of prospective planners

(Schon et al., 1976:200). This report indicates that less than 20 percent of planners have the university as their primary job location. Less than 20 percent combine the categories of academic researcher and teacher as their primary role identity (Schon, 1976:196). Another recent study of state planning directors reveals even more emphatically the gulf between the profession of planning and the various sciences of society.

> Certain attributes of state planning directors—their background and their office—are correlated with the relevant performance of state planning activities. Their level of education appears to be irrelevant; the type of education is only slightly related; but their career background is highly significant, especially in terms of prior work in management, political experience, and mobility. And the closer the relationship of the director and the governor, the more likely is the agency to be performing activities. These conclusions do not enhance the prospect of seeing state planning become a science which can be learned in school. They suggest an art which must be learned by experience (Beyle, Seligson, Wright, 1970:34).

What this and similar data suggest, is not simply the craft-like nature of planning, but the political context that makes any impulse for autonomy and self-criticism a special responsibility of social scientists, not so much by empirical design as by *fiat*.

The increasing number of reports on social science advances and planning applications, each in its own way underscores the gap that remains between social science and social planning (cf. Friedmann and Hudson, 1974: Mann, 1972; Deutsch, Platt, and Senghaas, 1971). But these reports proceed only in relation to "positive" criteria, i.e., methodological, theoretical and institutional breakthroughs that are incorporated into planning practice. It is a measure of planning myopia that breakthroughs from operations research systems analysis to cost-benefit analysis are considered only in terms of stepping-stone growth. The dynamic of social science discovery, the interpenetration of research and criticism, and the consequent emergence of new paradigms, tend to be ignored, even suppressed in the mechanistic rendering of social science innovation by the planning community.

In the various summaries of the impact of the social sciences on planning, there is an underlying conflict between those who are in search of formal, generalized models of planning, and those who view this effort as mechanistic and pernicious. Only recently the search for social science antecedents has turned away from the customary sources to the contributions made by phenomenology, the new philosophy of language, and symbolic interactionism within sociology: a very different set of antecedents than what one customarily finds in the planning literature. But this in itself would indicate both the dubiousness of a general theory of planning, and of equal importance; how the literature of planning remains firmly linked to theoretical and methodological developments within the social sciences. (cf. Krieger, 1974:156, 163).

The recent forum on making planning more responsive to a "public philosophy" illustrates the critical difference between a planning and a scientific standpoint. Friedmann quite persuasively argues that the reform movement within planning ended by a statement of the public interest that was little else than the interests of the planners themselves. He seeks to remedy this situation by relabelling the public interest as the public good, and by changing the equity emphasis from opportunity networks to results (Friedmann, 1973:2-7). But both the "conservative" sociologist, Robert Nisbet, and the "liberal" sociologist, Herbert J. Gans, indicate the critical edge in social science analysis. Nisbet indicates that "there is no likelihood of our achieving cultural or social pluralism, of genuine and creative localism, of regionalism, so long as present tendencies toward centralization of power, administration, and function go on and on (Nisbet, 1973:9). And Gans, while sharing Friedmann's political goals, nonetheless must conclude by stating that "even if all planners agreed to be in the public interest, it would still have to be achieved through political struggle" (Gans, 1973:12).

A less attractive, but equally devastating critique of the idea that planning somehow represents a unitary community interest, or an objective social science, is contained in Frances Fox Piven's blunt statement on planning and social class.

> Planners were committed to the values of growth and development, and to the economic and political interests in the city that prospered through growth and development. Planners did indeed take sides, and they took sides with the powerful, with the city builders. It was also not true that planners played a large role in the decisions that shaped the form of our cities. To say that city planners served the city builders is not to say that they made the city building decisions, or even that the plans they prepared were of significant influence. The key decisions, the decisions that accounted first for the huge concentrated agglomerations of our older industrial cities, and then for the subsequent evisceration of these cities as capital moved to the outlying rings and to the new cities of the south and west based on oil, autos, electronics, and aerospace, were never decisions embodied in any plans made by planners. Compared with the formative influence of capital investment decisions, planners and their plans were mere shadow play. At most, planners only struggled to service the cities built by private capital with the support of public capital (Piven, 1975:308).

Again, the point is not to castigate planners for doing their job; indeed, even severe critics hold out the prospects of a different kind of planning based on the new urban constituencies of poor whites, ethnics, and blacks. Nonetheless, it would be folly of a misanthropic type to assert an isomorphism between planners and social scientists, given existential conditions which clearly point in an opposite direction.

Social Science as the Measurement of Success and Failure in Planning

What we require is not yet another statement of planning principles, but an identification of those aspects of social science that can demonstrate, in specific contexts, the superiority or inferiority of one or another type of planning strategy. My assumption is that the planner per se has neither the political stamina nor the intellectual autonomy to carry out a solution to these dilemmas outside the context of social science. Hence, what the social scientist can provide is a sense of the limits and capacities of planners, in effect, indicating the limits beyond which planning cannot go without incurring certain risks or without inviting sure tragedies.

There is a powerful tendency to think of social planning and social science in strictly cumulative and interactive terms. John Friedmann characterizes basic discoveries that are implemented by planners, and Lawrence Mann discusses the same subject in terms of the constant shortening of lag-time in implementation of social science findings (theoretical, methodological and institutional) into the planning process. But this consensual view assumes the purely cumulative, aggregative nature of social science, dropping out its critical functions. Beyond that, there is a grave doubt that the basic breakthroughs are really as stated. It is problematic whether "think tank" approaches represent an institutional breakthrough, or a clear waste of public resources. Those who have studied this matter have pointed out that think tanks work in areas where a clear consensus exists (i.e., racial equity in housing and education) and fail miserably when addressed to areas in which a wide dissensus exists (civil action to counter guerrilla movements, or as in the *Pentagon Papers*, studies addressed to the conduct of an unpopular war). Admittedly, it is flattering for social scientists to read that planners are shortening a lag in literature absorption; it legitimizes the distinction between an applied craft and a scientific profession. But it fails to address the degree to which issues in planning are absorbed, if at all, by social scientists; and, more pointedly, whether the absorptive process, to the extent to which it operates, may serve to weaken the critical resolve of social researchers.

A considerable amount of planning, especially urban planning, has to do with developing appropriate models and identifying suitable criteria. Hence the research burden shifts from goals to instrumentalities. The burden is on information systems, data processing, how planners can locate manufacturing supplies, proprietary software, federal agency sponsored software, accept and deliver data in a variety of forms, improve and implement existing data files, adopt standardized data collection procedures, develop administrative records as new data sources, and collate data collection of dates and time intervals (Stuart, 1976:284, 292). While this is a perfectly accepted procedure for an applied discipline, it still represents little more than a model. The critical experimental tests remains the implementation of such modular approaches within the intrusive complexities of the ordinary world, rather than the initially delicate and protected trial period.

The commitment to formal, experimental protocols and models unfortunately fades at precisely this implementation phase. As a result, there is little effort made to determine whether a plan worked or did not work, and if it did not, whether this was due to the selection of goals, the mix of strategies, or specifically, the configuration of tactics (Mendelbaum, 1975:188-89). Examining the planning literature, one is struck by how little effort is expended on the questions of what went wrong, and how much is model construction despite the general recognition that much does go wrong when plans are implemented in real-world terms.

Social science must point out that planning involves planners. To carry this beyond the level of tautology, social science must include an analysis of social planners: problems of occupation, income, and stratification. How this occupational group relates to each other becomes a central factor in the success or failure of a planning mechanism. The social scientist can provide a self consciousness, or perhaps a consciousness of self, that the planner so often lacks. For example, one sociologist has pointed out how the gulf between master planners and advocacy planners came about. "The master planners were advocates for themselves, for the city's business interests, and for the upper and upper middle-class residents of the community. Indeed, modern advocacy planning, which seeks to represent the interest of the poor and the black community in the planning process, has developed precisely because comprehensive planning has largely ignored their problems, goals, or needs (Gans, 1970:242). Without prejudicing the merits of such an approach, it clearly places the planner in a context of stratification and demographic information. For example, what are the background variables of the planners; from whence do they derive? Unless one believes that background variables have no relationship to behavior, this would become exceedingly vital information, first in distinguishing the planning community from the social science community, and next, in separating out the planning community from the political establishment, itself a vital undertaking which social research can perform for social planning.

Because of the essentially dependent role of planners and their lack of scientific autonomy, they perform the same sorts of service roles in socialist countries as they do under capitalist nations. In the rush for industrialization, the kind of polluted environment socialist planners thought was a result of aggressive capitalist development, resulted in socialist nations as well. Thus, it is not merely service to the market that becomes a problem, but service to the state. Which economic system is the harsher taskmaster, can be left to the imagination of those familiar with comparative economic systems (cf. Abrams and Francaviglia, 1975:268). Under socialist planning, the very survival of an independent social science is threatened in the rush to convert the chaotic present into an orderly future. Criticism becomes suspect and constructivism becomes the marching order of the day (Horowitz, 1976:11-28).

Aaron Wildavsky (1975:257-259) has summed up the dilemmas of planners with unusual clarity. Once planning is placed within a perspective of society, and society itself is considered as a system of power, then the actual relationships of planning, budgeting, and reform become quite clear.

> Where disagreement over social goals or policies exists, as it must, there can be no planning without the ability to make other people act differently than they otherwise might. There would be no need to plan if people were going to do spontaneously what the plan insisted they do authoritatively. Planning assumes power. Planning requires the power to maintain the preeminence of the future in the present. The nation's rulers must be able to commit existing resources to accomplishing future objectives. If new rulers make drastic changes in objectives, the original plan is finished. . . . Planners are spenders. Their raison d'etre is economic growth. Typically they underestimate spending and overestimate revenues to leave room for investments they believe are necessary for accomplishing the goals they wish to achieve. Planners are natural allies for large spending departments whose projects planners believe desirable for securing economic growth. For the same reasons, planners are natural enemies of financial controllers who want to limit expenditure. If planning could not control budgeting, budgeting might yet become a form of planning. By expanding budgeting to include planning, the same goals could be achieved from a different direction. The idea is marvelous; if planners suffer a power deficit, they balance their books by becoming budgeters, who have a power surplus. Budgeters are powerful but ignorant; planners are knowledgeable but powerless; what could be more desirable, thought the proponents of PPBS, than combining the virtues of both classes by making budgeters into planners.

The dilemma is that planners no longer like the idea of seeing themselves as bookkeepers or accountants. This is where the problem of planning as a social science is joined. But it is evident in the work of people like Wildavsky that the analysis of planning is itself open to social research, whereas the very nature of the planning process limits that self-awareness, or even the possibility of self criticism. Planning is connected to power, and science to knowledge. To see the requisites of planning simply in terms of knowledge is to doom planning itself.

The most precise way to underscore the difference between social planning and social science is by example. The planner must assume optimum rationality. This is interpreted as optimum usage of a facility. However, economic theory, if not always directed toward the public interest per se, might assume that the functions involved in this kind of planning optimality, for example, the constant queuing to get service, whether it be a retail facility, the cinema, or a bathhouse, may make the very notion of planning dysfunctional from the point of view of encouraging incentives and hence economic growth. This is exactly what the great Soviet economist, Yevsei Lieberman, pointed out in relation to Soviet planning. In a delightful essay entitled: "Waiting for a Bath—and Just Waiting," the essential difference between planning and science is made plainfully evident (Lieberman, 1971:596-97).

> Why must we, for example, stand in queues for hours to buy railroad tickets, particularly during the vacation season? Frequently we do this not because the capacity of our railways is insufficient but because of the hidden workings of the theory of so-called "full capacity." It is considered profitable to have a railway timetable in which not one single seat remains empty. And the bath—excuse my frankness—what's it like to visit a public bath on Friday or Saturday? First you must stand in a queue, because the "washings per person" are planned on the basis of "full bath benches and tubs." From the standpoint of public interest, such unoccupied "optimum" facilities are also suitable to movie houses, on trains, in post offices—briefly, in all public-service establishments. There is no other possible solution. If there is to be no queuing, then supply must everywhere exceed demand. Only in this way can we provide high quality products and conscientious service.

Following through for a moment on the Soviet situation, there has been a rising crescendo of criticism concerning State Planning Commissions and the Supreme Council of the National Economy. During that remarkable period of ideological thaw in the early sixties, a host of criticisms were made of planners. Their essential thrust is that although they provided for the opening and closing of the plan, planners failed to address themselves to the placing of orders for equipment for construction projects; construction costs had to be revised upward for almost half the projects, despite the fact that many of the designs had been rated of high quality. Wildavsky's charge about American planning is doubly true for the Soviet system. There is a strong tendency to equate maximizing results with minimizing costs.   Deputy G. I. Popov (1971:170-71) of Leningrad, makes this point strikingly evident.

> In recent years the construction workers of Leningrad and other provinces of the country have repeatedly proposed the introduction of a method of financial accounts for fully completed projects, without intermediate payments.   Such a practice stimulates better work on the part of the construction organizations and contributes to the quicker opening of new structures.   The government has approved this initiative, but through the fault of USSR State Planning Committee this completely progressive method of financing construction work has not yet been introduced.

This was followed by another report summarizing the shortcomings of Soviet planning (Kachalov, 1971:1717).

> In our opinion, the chief shortcoming is the unscientific, arbitrary planning that has taken root in many cases.   Departmentalism and local allegiances lead to the fact that the construction of more and more new projects is launched while at the same time already built production premises and units are being poorly utilised and technological processes are not completely operational.   This occurs because there is inadequate responsibility for the working out of the technological part of the designs for enterprises.   Moreover, the compilation of the plans for capital construction is delayed until the end of the year.   Furthermore, at the outset the plans are inflated, and then they begin to reduce and tighten them.   Therefore decisions on inclusions in or exclusions from the draft plan are frequently made hastily.   Where now is your meticulous economic verification of the designs and your genuinely scientific planning!

This is a time for planners to take seriously the unitary nature of the strengths, weaknesses and prospects of planning.   One way to do so is to carefully examine their colleagues in the Soviet Union to see what the major outcomes have been of nearly sixty years of a planned society.   It is crucial also to outline the constraints on socialist planning in terms of the breakdown of innovation and its inroads on efficiency.   In the Soviet model at least, the greater the degree of planning, the lower the degree of innovative capacity; and the higher the degree of efficiency, the less the degree of total planning.   In recognition of this, the Soviet bloc has introduced market mechanisms such as incentive systems, differential pay structures, the attenuation of discrimination against private sectors, and the reintroduction of notions of profitability and a market network.   The limits of planning are nowhere made plainer than within the Soviet framework, the result of which is a borrowing of foreign technology and the intervention of foreign firms in order to overcome the breakdown of internal innovation.   The strains between party absolutism and economy relativism are such as to make impulses toward efficiency and innovation subject to communist politics and ideology (Marczewski, 1974:227-243). Under such stress conditions, purchasing overseas research and development permits weaknesses in centralized planning to be papered over.

Precisely the structural deficits of the master plan and of centralized planning has led to a drastic breakdown of Soviet innovation and efficiency at crucial industrial points; especially in areas of older industries where the fulfillment of plans does not depend upon technological breakthroughs. Berliner summarizes the situation of planning and innovation very neatly in terms of the transformation of capitalism and the "invisible hand" into socialism and the "invisible foot" (Berliner, 1976:528).

> Adam Smith taught us to think of competition as an "invisible hand" that guides production into the socially desirable channels. By a curious ideological confluence both Adam Smith and the designers of the Soviet economic structure had in mind the smooth allocation of resources under a basically unchanging technology. Central planning may be regarded simply as a visible form of the same guiding hand that operates invisibly in capitalism. But if Adam Smith had taken as his point of departure not the coordinating mechanism but the innovative mechanism of capitalism, he may well have designated competition not as an invisible hand but as an invisible foot. For the effect of competiton on innovation is not only to motivate profit-seeking entrepreneurs to seek yet more profit but to jolt conservative enterprises into the adoption of new technology and the search for improved processes and products. From the point of view of the static efficiency of resource allocation, the evil of monopoly is that it prevents resources from flowing into those lines of production in which their social value would be greatest. But from the point of view of innovation, the evil of monopoly is that it enables producers to enjoy high rates of profit without having to undertake the exacting and risky activities associated with technological change. A world of monopolies, socialist or capitalist, would be a world with very little technological change.

In adopting central planning, the Soviets achieved the benefits of the invisible hand, but they lost the advantages of innovation. Worse, they were not able to back away from mistakes, i.e., not properly adjusting for inflationary rates or breakdowns in shipments and supplies, since error factors were not built into the planning network itself. Thus, under capitalism, even large-scale errors, let us say in the automobile industry, or in the chemical industry, development and promotional costs can be absorbed by more efficient sectors far more readily than in the Soviet system where the organizational structure protects producers against losses from both their own unsuccessful innovations and the successful innovation of others. Thus, the planning synapse may itself become a major obstacle to innovation. Again, the central point, in terms of our own task, is to show how clearly and distinctively the process of planning differs from the process of social science. For only a science of economics could make these points about planning without fear of either contradiction or destruction.

Nor should this be viewed as simply a Soviet problem. In point of fact, if one turns to urban planning in the United States, the same kind of optimum rationality produces a similar kind of public inequity, and at times results in anti-federalist "pathologies." Herbert Gans indicates that the upper-class origin of planning in America made such lower class pathologies inevitable (Gans, 1968:78, 75).

> City planning grew up as a movement of upper-middle-class-eastern reformers who were upset by the arrival of the European immigrants and the squalor of their existence in urban slums and the threat which these immigrants, and urban-industrial society generally, represented to the social, cultural, and political dominance the reformers had enjoyed in small-town agrarian America. As reform groups and businessmen gave city planning increasing support, it became a profession. Its physical emphasis naturally attracted architects, landscape architects, and engineers; these developed planning tools that were based to a considerable extent on the beliefs which the movement had accepted. The inequalities and pathologies of the urban low-income population must therefore be eliminated before the attractive, efficient, and slum-less city for which physical planners are striving is to be realized. When the latter can be persuaded to the validity of this concept, it may be possible to achieve a synthesis of the so-called social and physical planning approaches to create a city-planning profession which uses rational programming to bring about real improvements, not only in the lives of city residents but also in the condition of the cities themselves.

The same fears about planning are now being voiced in an American context across the stratification axis—specifically in terms of weaknesses in federal regulation as a whole, rather than planning mechanisms in particular. The isomorphism between Soviet and American social science concerns can hardly be more clear than in the following description of the costs of federal regulation (Weidenbaum, 1976:2-3).

> Federal regulation adversely affects the prospects for economic growth and productivity by laying claim to a rising share of new capital for-mation. This is most evident in the environmental and safety areas. It is revealing to examine the flow of capital spending by American manufacturing companies just prior to the recent recession. In 1969, the total new investment in plant and equipment in the entire manu-facturing sector of the American economy came to $25 billion. The annual totals rose in the following years, to be sure. But when the effect of inflation is eliminated, it can be seen that four years later, in 1973, total capital spending by U.S. manufacturing companies was

no higher. In "real terms," it was approximately $26 billion both in 1969 and 1973. The direct cost of government regulation, a topic rarely studied, is substantial. The number and size of the agencies carrying out federal regulations are expanding rapidly. The administrative cost of this veritable army of enforcers is large and growing. The expenditures of the major federal regulatory agencies came to almost $1.9 billion in the fiscal year 1974. A 48 percent increase is budgeted over the next two years, with the total federal costs of these regulatory activities rising to $2.8 billion in fiscal 1976. The costs of government regulation are rising far more rapidly than the sales of the companies being regulated. Regulation literally is becoming one of the major growth industries in the country. But this represents only the tip of the iceberg. It is the costs imposed on the private sector that are really huge, the added expenses of business firms which must comply with government directives, and which inevitably pass on these costs to their customers.

The central contribution of social science in relation to the world of planning has to do with levels of planning. It might well be that the social indicators approach, or the ecological movement generally, contains within itself a certain rebellion against the content of planning. It might also be that a revolution of falling expectations that comes about through a world-wide redistribution of the sources of wealth, will serve as a limiting device to national planning. The scientist also lives in a world of interests rather than a world of production. These interests may have a sharply limiting effect on the viability of planning, even if the plan is entirely rational and empirically feasible on fiscal grounds. There might be a question of interests that have been overlooked: racial, class, ethnic, sexual—or just plain interests in preservation instead of development.

The evaluation of the plan cannot be left to the planners any more than it can be left to the politicians. If left to the politicians, all planners would be shot for failure. If left to the planners, all politicians would be eliminated for placing unreasonable economic goals upon their modest skills. In such a context, the social scientist is uniquely capable, if not destined, to discuss and decide upon the efficacy of specific plans. We need merely turn to several instances from the world of Soviet planning and its failures, to the world of American planning and its failures, to indicate how essential is the role of social science as honest broker in this tension-filled context of planning and politics.

Toward Social Science Checks and Social Planning Balances

To examine the literature on planning, whether it be local, regional, or national, whether it be Marxian or Keynesian, or American or Russian, one notes a strange desire to solve the problem of planning within a planning context. Yet, those who contrast populism to planning often hold out few alternatives. It is as if elliptical slogans such as "power to the people," one abstraction, will overcome the "power of the planners," another abstraction. The search for anarchic resolutions might be premature if not downright destructive. Although they start from different philosophic premises, anarchism and conservatism each carry with them penalties for large sectors of the American population. In such a context, it behooves the social scientist not to become captive to anti-statist ideologies any more than to state authority.

An impressive paper on the relationship of justice and planning (Berry and Steiker, 1974:414-420) indicates by means of a "claims matrix" that the choice for the planner is rationally uni-dimensional, that in fact, in a hypothetical situation of clean water and employment, the needs and wants of the environmental party might be quite different than the needs and wants of the trade-union party, if we can call it that. To have water clean enough for swimming may signify a level of unemployment that is unacceptable, whereas to have water clean enough for boating, but not for fishing or swimming, may involve zero unemployment, but on the other hand, not satisfy the advocates of clean water. Berry and Steiker properly point out that:

> When the claims of two or more groups conflict, efficiency or net benefits are less relevant criteria. In such a situation, maximizing net benefits will not prevent, and in fact may require, having certain groups subsidizing others and perhaps suffering severe and damaging losses. The key consideration in these issues then becomes the distribution of costs among the different groups.

One notes even in this sophisticated study, that decisionmaking under such circumstances is really not a matter of the planner. They refer to it as a Sisyphean task, and again appeal to that mythical "general good," in this case called the "publicly argued and the publicly decided," which in point of fact indicates the pragmatic limits of a planning effort. In other words, the fairness doctrine is really outside the purview of the planning mechanisms. Interestingly, in this environment/economy takeoff the situation is so structured that any new employment opportunities created by firm ecological standards is not entertained; nor is the possibility of solving the zero-sum game by building a swimming pool and leaving the lakeside alone, discussed. Yet, the very effort to get beyond reification and polarization is central to the task of social scientific analysis.

Still another illustration of the special problem the planner has with social contradictions is the area of planning as it effects geographic and demographic changes. One recent report (Greenbie, 1974:81) simply notes that:

Wherever mass migrations occur, the interests of two opposing parties must be considered, and constructively provided for; the cultural integrity of the incoming people and the territorial integrity of the proprietary group. The law and its institutions can provide a structure for appropriate compromise, but the negotiation and arbitration will have to be personal and particular in each case. Because modern society requires cross-cultural communication and cooperation on an *intellectual* basis, spaces and social mechanisms for this must be created.

Here too the problem is simply that the author, rather than seek to adjudicate these contradictions, creates another phrase called "conceptual territories" which presumably will provide emotional security based on the native culture. But, of course, the problem here becomes that the native culture at some point stands in the way of all change, and hence itself must be viewed as an interest group rather than a resolution of cultural and territorial integrities. It might indeed be wise to add the notion of the "folk" to those of culture and geography, but this add-on feature hardly resolves the question of planning and justice.

There is altogether too much concern for synthetic solutions. Within an American context, it is the absorption of social science within social planning; within a Soviet context, it is the absorption of social planning within social science. I am suggesting that neither represents a higher solution, and that both leave intact and unchecked the relative powers of the political apparatus. In this sense, social science has the unique advantage of providing a critical role, critical in the sense of criticism, and in this way, counterbalancing the positivist and constructivist limits of a social planning approach. Clearly, planners should learn from social scientists, and vice versa. But such a learning process should not be viewed as an absorption process.

A profession is not a science, and a science may at times resist and even reject professionalism. In a democratic society there are plural mechanisms in expressions of wants and desires. There are Constitutional safeguards provided by a system of checks and balances. No one really expects the legislative and executive branches to be identical, even though executives are chosen from the legislative branch, and likewise, executives may go into legislative activity. The same sorts of interaction might be encouraged in the areas of planning and social science: first, that systems of checks and balances rather than mutual commissions be established; and second, that there be arenas and forums of interaction and discussion without necessarily liquidating one discipline at the expense of the other through processes of either destruction or cooptation.

A revolution of falling expectations, or at least a sense of proportion, is coming to dominate American thinking: the greedy legislation of the planning decades of the fifties and sixties have come to an end. The work on *The Urban Predicament*, by Gorham and Glazer, is indicative of this new sense of modesty, in part, forced upon the planning community by the social scientists. The word "planning" itself is even used more cautiously. The authors (Gorham and Glazer, 1976:31) indicate that:

> We know that many things will not work: a simple expansion of expenditure, under which the greater share must inevitably go to the professionals in the fields of employment, crime, education, and housing, may offer little improvement in the quality of life or opportunity in declining neighborhoods; the creation of new community organizations through the infusion of outside funds seems to hold little promise at this point in history; the imposition of a *great plan* from the outside cannot, it seems, be responsive to the complex, interlinked problems that are dragging these neighborhoods down.

Nor is it merely a few researchers who hold to this point of view. Social scientists have noted that in their areas as well, planning has its limits within a democratic context. In the worlds of transportation, for example, it might not be reasonable or even worthy to have everyone take public transportation. There may be aspects endemic to private automobile travel that are so superior that all one can really do is to assume a basic continuing dependency on the private car, but then work toward the scenario of the redesign of that private car. Hence, in the world of transportation, new voices are heard about "signals from the marketplace," and consensus about what they are willing to adjust to, and minimizing political risk for legislators. This indicates how profound the social science impact on planning and transportation has been.

In the area of education, alternative models to achieving equity within the school systems are introduced; and more, whether it is even worthwhile to push for involuntary desegregation if these result simply in the loss of one race from the central city school system. This is not to claim that these social scientists are necessarily correct; merely that these voices of concern serve to arrest a planning impulse that oftentimes does enormous violence to the sense and sensibilities of the ordinary citizenry—including the presumed victims of inequalities.

In the world of crime, social scientists are less likely to argue the case for bigger and better police forces, instead directing attention to methodological problems and statistical estimates, pointing out that differences in crime rates that are absorbed across jurisdictions may not represent differences in criminal behavior as much as differences in the proportions of victims who report crimes to the police, or differences in the methods and skills with which local police departments report and record crimes. Again, the role of social science is clearly not to limit crime fighting, but to indicate the kinds of issues that one might look at more carefully than planners have in the past.

In the field of housing, the earlier euphoria with model cities, new towns, cash grants to households, and other programs designed to achieve perfect housing equity, have not realized these goals. Again, the social scientist tends to look at the problems somewhat differently, with a greater sense that the problem may be one of public administration rather than housing units or startups:

> An argument against a comprehensive program of cash grants to households, on the other hand, is that they could have unintended consequences for property owners. One can readily imagine a substantial wave of household relocations as recipients try to improve their housing-neighborhood situations. Thus, owners of properties in undesirable neighborhoods, or even of properties into which recipients move, in neighborhoods where socio-economic conditions were superior before the program was implemented—all could suffer significant capital losses. Others would enjoy windfall profits. Supplier targeted subsidies may not be the answer in this instance either; still, such side effects need to be considered in assessing cash transfers.
>
> Model Cities which are designed to improve the general conditions in neighborhoods, to created a heightened sense of community, and hence to help stabilize housing and families, are not generally viewed as having achieved their goals. If one removes the impediment of poverty or at least attains adequate structural housing for those who presently are slum residents, greater success will still be debatable unless some greater stability is achieved. The major stabilizing forces have already been noted, but it is possible to improve the condition of streets, parks, and lighting and other public services—trash collection, street cleaning, and so on—to produce a positive effect on the attitudes of residents and producers of housing services (Gorham and Glazer, 1976:172-73).

This is illustrative of what the social scientist might do within a national context on behalf of the planning community. This is not to argue that there is a struggle between the rationality of planners and the irrationality of social scientists, but rather to indicate the dynamic ongoing within the social system, which extends far beyond the specific planning mechanism. The sense of the whole, perhaps better called the sense of the higher rationality, can help overcome the "crackpot" rationality which is so often characteristic of planning on a limited scale.

It might well be that social science shall become a repository for a kind of wisdom that is in direct conflict with social planning. Social planners, for their part, may be charged with defining areas of society and culture that are best left unplanned, unlegislated, and where simple market mechanisms or personal social preferences be held as final arbiter of what is and what is not to be done. But whatever the specific relationships between these two groups, they are clearly not the same as each other.

Let me conclude with a warning made by an outstanding representative of the democratic temper a quarter century ago, Karl Mannheim (1950:29). His warning on the gravity of the risks involved in bifurcating planning from its imagined publics still stands.

> Our task is to build a social system by planning, but planning of a special kind: it must be planning for freedom, subjected to democratic control; planning, but not restrictionist so as to favor group monopolies either of entrepreneurs or workers' associations, but "planning for plenty," i.e., full employment and full exploitation of resources; planning for social justice rather than absolute equality, with differentiation of rewards and status on the basis of genuine equality rather than privilege; planning not for a classless society but for one that abolishes the extremes of wealth and poverty; planning for cultural standards without "leveling down"—a planned transition making for progress without discarding what is valuable in tradition; planning that counteracts the dangers of a mass society by coordination of the means of social control but interfering only in cases of institutional or moral deterioration defined by collective criteria; planning for balance between centralization and dispersion of power; planning for gradual transformation of society in order to encourage the growth of personality; in short, planning but not regimentation.

Mannheim's words remain as urgent today as when they were written. In the rush to professionalism, planners could ignore such social science warnings with impunity. And given the fact that professional planning identity has been largely achieved in the absence of a critical social science standpoint, it becomes even less likely that the warnings and premonitions introduced by Mannheim will be easily taken seriously. But until the basis for rapprochement is worked out between social planning and social science, let those differences which exist continue to form the basis for intellectual discourse and practical checks and balances.

REFERENCES

Irwin Abrams and Richard Francaviglia, "Urban Planning in Poland Today," *Journal of the American Institute of Planners*, 41, 4 (July 1975): 258-269.

Kenneth D. Benne, Warren G. Bennis and Robert Chin, eds., "Planned Change in America," *The Planning of Change* (New York: Holt, Rhinehart and Winston, 1969).

Warren G. Bennis, Kenneth D. Benne and Robert Chin, eds., *The Planning of Change*, (New York. Holt, Rinehart and Winston, 1969).

Joseph S. Berliner, *The Innovation Decision in Soviet Industry* (Cambridge, Massachusetts: The MIT Press, 1976).

David Berry and Gene Steiker, "The Concept of Justice in Regional Planning: Justice as Fairness," *Journal of the American Institute of Planners*, 40, 6 (November 1974): 414-421.

Thad L. Beyle, Sureva Seligson and Deil S. Wright, "New Directions in State Planning," *Planning and Politics: Uneasy Partnership*, ed. Thad L. Beyle and George T. Lathrop (New York: The Odyssey Press, 1970): 14-34.

Robert S. Bolane, "Community Decision Behavior: The Culture of Planning, " *Journal of the American Institute of Planners*, 35, 5 (September 1969): 308-314.

Karl W. Deutsch, John R. Platt and Dieter Senghass, "Conditions Favoring Major Advances in the Social Sciences, " *Science* 171 (February 5, 1971): 450-459.

Amitai Etzioni, " Toward a Theory of Societal Guidance, " *Societal Guidances A New Approach to Social Problems*, ed. Sarajane Heidi and Amitai Etzione (New York: Thomas Crowell, 1969).

Henry Fagin, "Advancing the 'State of the Art,' " *Urban Planning in Transition*, ed. Ernest Erber (New York: Grossman Publishers, 1970).

Bernard J. Frieden and Robert Morris, eds., *Urban Planning and Social Policy* (New York: Basic Books, 1968).

Milton Friedman, *Capitalism and Freedom* (Chicago: The University of Chicago Press, 1962).

John Friedmann and Barclay Hudson, "Knowledge and Action: A Guide to Planning Theory, " *Journal of the American Institute of Planners*, 40, 1 (Jan. 1974): 2-16.

John Friedmann, "The Public Interest and Community Participation: Toward a Reconstruction of Public Philosophy, " *Journal of the American Institute of Planners*, 39, 1 (Jan. 1973): 2-7.

Herbert J. Gans, "City Planning in America: A Sociological Analysis," *People and Plans: Essays on Urban Problems and Solutions* (New York: Basic Books, 1968).

Herbert J. Gans, "The Need for Planners Trained in Policy Formation, " *Urban Planning in Transition*, ed. Ernest Erber (New York: Grossman Publishers, 1970).

Herbert J. Gans, "The Public Interest and Community Participation: Commentary, " *Journal of the American Institute of Planners*, 39, 1 (Jan. 1973): 3, 10-12.

William Gorham and Nathan Glazer, *The Urban Predicament* (Washington, D.C.: The Urban Institute, 1976).

Barrie B. Greenbie, "Social Territory, Community Health and Urban Planning," *Journal of the American Institute of Planners*, 40, 2 (Mar. 1974): 74-82.

Irving Louis Horowitz, "National Realities and Universal Ambitions in the Practice of Sociology," *Sociological Praxis: Current Roles and Sellings*, eds. Elisabeth Crawford and Stein Rokkan, (London and New York: Sage Publications, 1796): 11-28.

Barclay M. Hudson, Martin Wachs and Joseph L. Schofer, "Local Impact Evaluation in the Design of Large-Scale Urban Systems," *Journal of the American Institute of Planners* 40, 4 (July 1974): 255-265.

N. N. Kachalov, "Speech on the Soviet State and Budget, " *Politics and Society in the USSR*, ed. David Lane (New York: Random House, 1971).

Alan S. Kravitz, "Mandarinism: Planning as Handmaiden to Conservative Politics, " *Planning and Politics*, eds. Thad L. Beyle and George T. Lathrop (New York: The Odyssey Press, 1970).

Martin H. Krieger, "Some New Directions for Planning Theories," *Journal of the American Institute of Planners*, 40, 3 (May 1974): 156-163.

Albert Lepawsky, "The Planning Apparatus: A Vignette of the New Deal" *Journal of the American Institute of Planners*, 42, 1 (Jan. 1976): 16-32.

Seymour J. Mandelbaum, "On Not Doing One's Best: The Uses and Problems of Experimentation in Planning," *Journal of the American Institute of Planners,* 41, 3 (May 1975): 184-190.

Lawrence D. Mann, "Social Science Advances and Planning Applications: 1900-1965," *Journal of the American Institute of Planners,* 38, 6 (Nov. 1972): 346-358.

Karl Mannheim, *Freedom, Power, and Democratic Planning* (New York: Oxford University Press, 1950).

Peter Marcuse, "Professional Ethics and Beyond: Values in Planning," *Journal of the American Institute of Planners,* 42, 3 (July, 1976): 274-82.

Yevsei G. Liberman, "Waiting for a Bath—And Just Waiting," *Economic Analysis and Policy,* eds. Myron L. Joseph, Norton C. Seeber and George L. Bach (Englewood Cliffs: Prentice-Hall, Inc., 1971).

Jan Marczewski, *Crisis in Socialist Plannings Eastern Europe and the USSR* (New York: Praeger Publishers, 1974).

Magoroh Maruyama, "Human Futuristics and Urban Planning," *Journal of the American Institute of Planners,* 39, 5 (Sept. 1973): 346-357.

Leonard C. Moffitt, "Values Implications for Public Planning: Some Thoughts and Questions," *Journal of the American Institute of Planners,* 41, 6 (Nov. 1975): 397-405.

Robert Nisbet, "The Public Interest and Community Participation: Commentary," *Journal of the American Institute of Planners,* 39, 1 (Jan. 1973): 3, 8-9.

Robert Nisbet, *Twilight of Authority* (New York: Oxford University Press, 1975).

Harvey S. Perloff, "Common Goals and the Linking of Physical and Social Planning," *Urban Planning and Social Policy,* eds. Bernard J. Frieden and Robert Morris (New York: Basic Books, 1968).

Frances Fox Piven, "Planning and Class Interests," *Journal of the American Institute of Planners,* 41, 5 (Sept. 1975): 308-310.

G. I. Popov, "Speech on the Soviet State and Budget," *Politics and Society in the USSR,* ed. David Lane (New York: Random House, 1971).

Karl R. Popper, *The Open Society and Its Enemies* (London: Routledge and Kegan Paul, Ltd., 1945).

Francine F. Rabinovitz, *City Politics and Planning* (New York: Atherton Press, 1969).

Donald A. Schon, Nancy S. Cremer, Paul Osterman, and Charles Perry, "Planners in Transition: Report on a Survey of Alumni of M.I.T.'s Department of Urban Studies, 1960-71," *Journal of the American Institute of Planners,* 42, 2 (April 1976): 193-202.

Darwin G. Stuart, *Systematic Urban Planning* (New York: Praeger Publishers, 1976).

Friedrich A. von Hayek, *The Road to Serfdom* (London: Routledge and Kegan Paul Ltd., 1944).

Murray L. Weidenbaum, "Government versus Business Planning," *Monthly Labor Review,* 99, 5 (May 1976): 35.

Murray L. Weidenbaum, "Reforming Government Regulation of Business," *Imprimus* 5, 6 (June 1976): 1-6.

William L. C. Wheaton and Margaret F. Wheaton, "Identifying the Public Interest: Values and Goals," *Urban Planning in Transition,* ed. Ernest Erber (1970).

Aaron Wildavsky, *Budgeting: A Comparative Theory of Budgetary Processes* (Boston: Little Brown and Company, 1975).

Barbara Wootton, *Freedom Under Planning* (Chapel Hill, North Carolina: The University of North Carolina Press, 1945).

A. A. Zvorykin, "The Development of the Productive Forces in the Soviet Union," *Industry and Labor in the USSR*, ed. G. V. Osipov (London: Tavistock Publishers, 1966).

The Redistributive Function in Planning: Creating Greater Equity Among Citizens of Communities

Paul Davidoff

This conference is one of the first occasions on which the redistributive function in planning has been recognized as a major direction in planning. Surely there is no better means of establishing reality than that of receiving a university's recognition.

The redistributive function—recognized as such—is just taking root in planning. I am speaking about a way of conceptualizing planning activity and thought. There are pockets of planning where redistributive norms are established standards for planning. And one of the strongest Norms operating is Norm Krumholz. His agency, the Cleveland Department of City Planning, has adopted a plan for Cleveland that is explicitly redistributive.

The redistributive function in planning is aimed at reducing negative social conditions caused by great disparities in the possession, by classes of the population, of important resources resulting from public or private action. It aims to create conditions of greater justice, equality, or fairness —which is usually termed equity. In some cases, the redistributive goal is substantive, as in the number of years of education received or the quality of a living environment. In other cases, it relates to process, that is, is a system of decisionmaking open to all—is adequate notice provided, is the hearing process meaningful?

I heard an Englishman say once that the important question to be asked of another person for determining whether or not they were engaged in meaningful work was, "Are you a redistributionalist?" I agree. That question may in fact be the crucial determinant. Are you for maintaining the distribution of goods, services, opportunities, and processes as they are, or do you favor a redistribution so that those who now have the least will receive considerably more and thus the gap will be reduced?

If a planner is not working directly for the objective of eradicating poverty and racial and sexual discrimination, then she or he is counterproductive. If the work is not specific in its redistributive aims, then it is at best inefficient. If the work is not aimed at redistribution, then a presumption stands that it is amoral. These are strong words. They must be. So long as poverty and racism exist in our society, there is an ethical imperative for a single direction in planning.

Redistribution is a political and an ethical issue. The difficult problem for those of us who are trying to alter significantly the present system of distribution is that the profession and the schools that educate planners refuse to accept and act as if that were the case. Even the most advanced schools of planning, advanced in terms of their commitment to a curriculum that educates students for a world of decisionmaking about the distribution of resources (and I think of Peter Marcuse's program at Columbia as being most specific about this goal) fail to teach a system focussing sharply on distributional analysis.

Planners should know who gets what out of a proposed plan—by class, by race, by sex, by age, by ethnic group. How much do they receive, and what does that do to them relative to what they had before and what they have relative to others? Planners should know whether the aim of a program is to equalize the opportunities of all to receive equally, to participate equally, or to produce equally. And they should know over what time period the system aims to bring about a condition of equity or equality.

Most planners know the acres in a square mile and the color of a residential zone. But few know the amount of income received annually by income fifths of the population. Too few know the median income of non-whites and blacks and fewer still know the proportion of non-whites or blacks or Puerto Ricans whose income places them in each of the income fifths of the population as a whole. Knowledge of the distribution of internal living space or of the time, condition, or cost relative to income of commuting is lacking. We must begin to understand these things, for as planners we affect them by our work.

These are examples of questions we have not yet learned, as a profession, to ask. Planning schools and the profession should begin asking them. But first, those of us who are proponents of an active redistributive function in planning must assume a more forceful role in raising these questions and in developing answers. Chester Hartman's Network Newsletter is a form of communication among the people who are posing the questions and searching for ways to answer them.

In the preparation of the annual application of Community Development Block Grant funds, is the list of requests derived from an analysis that aims to have specific effect on the distribution of goods, services, opportunities? In most instances the answer to this question is that the analysis is not done that way. It is not conceived of as a question of relative shares. Further, even if the planners wish to do some or all of the analyses in a distributional manner, the political system, it is said, would not allow it. Is that the case? About 50 percent of the constituency of big cities have income which place them within the bottom 40 percent of income earners in the nation or in their metropolitan region. Majorities, or close to majorities, of city populations are non-white and Hispanic. Why does it not make sense politically to think explicitly in redistributive terms in the preparation of plans to serve this constituency? If it doesn't make sense, perhaps we need to promote the idea more affirmatively.

Despite the fact of the high proportion of those who have least residing in the cities, common knowledge of political power assumes that power rests with that small number in possession of the majority of wealth. True. But it is also true that a coalition of between 70 and 75 percent of the income earners, measuring from the bottom of the barrel in income terms, up—possess a majority of the votes. Effective redistributive political coalitions must be built to that point at which there exists a majority of voters, understanding that among lower income groups there is a sharp falloff of voting. Thus the necessity for a three-quarters coalition in order to garner a majority of voters. That same majority of voters—say 75 percent of the population—receives about half of the income, and far less of other wealth in the urban economy. In other words, a redistributive policy aimed at advantaging 75 percent of the population does not make such bad politics for a mayor or city council.

Who is involved in the redistributive function in planning? Many planners are engaged in expanding opportunities for racial and economic minorities and for women.

In many ways the redistributive outlook that is growing today in planning is only an expansion of the advocacy movements that were common to many professions in the 60's. Those movements still have some life, despite the fact that they have been institutionalized and accepted as routine in many planning departments, and despite the federal abandonment of its 60's commitment to "maximum feasible participation of the poor." A year ago, when I offered a course in advocacy planning, I observed at the outset that it was a course in nostalgia. I was wrong. The string of executive vetoes and Supreme Court decisions in the recent past had produced an excess of pessimism. Many are still actively engaged in community planning projects aiming to create power and wealth where it should, but does not now, exist. Certainly it is true that those planning for equal opportunities run into far more open resistance than in the late 60's.

It is important to recognize that the organization of professional planners, the A.I.P., has adopted as a part of its Code of Professional Ethics, a strong affirmation of the duty of planners to act in a redistributive manner. The Code calls for planners, in all their actions, to aim to expand the opportunities of the disadvantaged and to take action against policies that work against that goal. This brief statement, as well as the book published by the AIP on the social responsibility of planners, is a powerful professional statement. But what are we to make of it? It is an unenforceable exhortation. Not unimportant, just unenforceable. Probably all planners are in violation of it most of the time. In other words, if it could be enforced, and were, the AIP would not only be out of funds, it would be without a membership.

But the statement is still an important reminder that at the end of the days of the Great Society, the AIP recognized that omission to act can be as ethical or unethical an act as commission and so it ceased its neutrality regarding the central issues of the time and joined the War on Poverty and the battle for civil rights. While its present stance reflects a national disinterest in these problems (as evidence read the decreasing lineage devoted to minority issues in the statements of candidates for AIP office over the past five years, I believe that the AIP's Board affirms its Social Responsibility code, and would, if pressed, take action to support further education of the profession to act in accord with its high standards of redistributional justice.

As one who has been associated with a social action agency which considers its program to be redistributive, I think it is most important to observe the obvious: it is damned difficult to find the resources to support redistributional activities. But I am optimistic. There are foundations that have been strong backers of redistributional programs. And there are a few state and local agencies which are supportive. And perhaps we shall find in a few months that the federal government is ready once again to tackle the social issues of poverty and race. For radical critics of liberalism and gradualism, it should be noted that the Census reports indicating median nonwhite income as a percent of white in the years since World War II showed a steady horizontal curve at a few points above 50 percent from 1948 to 1964, when for the first time the proportion went to the upper 50 percentiles; in 1970 it reached its peak at 64 percent of white median income, and since then has declined. If a new commitment to eradicating poverty and racial discrimination materializes in November, redistributionalists should be prepared with their program for a national urban growth policy. And, perhaps then there will be an Administration in the White House, HUD, and elsewhere that will devote the funds required to enable the advocates of redistribution both within and outside government to have the resources required to promote and implement the plans urgently needed.

All planning issues have a distributive impact. There is no neutral turf on which one can stand to avoid enlarging, maintaining, or redistributing the relative shares of a good possessed by different population sectors. And regardless of our political disposition, as supporters of open, nonarbitrary planning, we should all agree that planners, as a part of their responsibility to the public, should provide the reasons behind the distributional choices they make.

Social Planning and the Political Planner

Chester W. Hartman

As those of you familiar with my work may know, I believe all planning is inherently and deeply political. Different planners and planning work are characterized by differing levels of explicitness and self-awareness as to the political thrust involved. But the work we all do is never free of values, ideas about good and bad social orders, and explicit or implicit strategies about how we move from our present state to the state we are trying to plan for (or against)—or in some cases, how we insure maximum stability for the status quo.

In recent years I have been defining myself increasingly as a socialist activist, and hence my work—writings and doings—derive directly and consciously from the analysis I make of the present society, my vision of socialist democracy, and the ways in which we must act to bring about that goal. It is in that context that I want to address the topic of social planning, the evolving role of the public sector, the needs of working-class people in our cities, and what role can and ought to be played by a planner who shares those values.

I believe the overriding, central fact of urban life in the immediate future is what it loosely referred to as "the urban crisis," which sometimes goes by the more specific recent title, "the urban fiscal crisis." That set of conditions will define the distribution of costs and benefits in our cities, the problems we are called upon to deal with, and the kinds of solutions that are possible and desirable.

The elements of this crisis are:

> —An increasing proportion of poor and Third World people in our large cities, a substantial number of whom are unemployed (and under the present economic system, unemployable), and are in need of a wide range of support services.
> —The continuing departure of the cities' traditional economic base: taxpaying middle- and upper-income families and businesses.
> —The rising cost of running municipal governments and providing services for those who live and work in cities.
> —The growing size of the municipal workforce and growing strength of the unions to which they belong.
> —The increasing problem of crime, as it affects property and people.
> —The deterioration of the cities' physical plant (particularly the older rental housing stock) and the level of municipal services—most notably, mass transit, hospitals and clinics, schools, libraries, parks.

While the poor have been victims of this urban decline for many years (they have no place to run to), the problem has been regarded as more acute in the past year or two, and certainly has received far more publicity, because of its fiscal dimensions: the fact that a good many of our large cities are on the verge of bankruptcy (the financial variety). As *Business Week* recently noted (June 14, 1976): "By 1980 every one of the 30 cities in the U.S. with a population of more than 1 million will be in financial distress to some degree. These big cities are all in decline." Budget needs rise, revenue sources decline, the banks refuse to buy municipal bonds or will do so only at usurious interest rates, and the fiscal crisis is upon us.

The recommended and actual response to this crisis has been: cutting back on services; job freezes and firing municipal workers; lowering worker pay scales; speedups; raising taxes. The victims of these responses have been by and large the poor, white and Third World, for whom many of these services (income support payments, health care, childcare, transportation) are literally vital; municipal workers, who lose jobs, job opportunities and pay increases necessary to keep pace with inflation, and who suffer the discomforts and dangers of work speedups; and those who bear the burden of increased taxes, usually of the regressive kind (sales and property). More progressive forms of taxation—higher corporation taxes, a more steeply progressive (in fact as well as theory) personal income tax, taxing away wealth—or massive shifts in the national budget, most notably, gouging deeply into the $100 billion "defense" allocation—are rejected by those who direct the government and the economy.

The attempts to manage and alleviate the urban fiscal crisis are producing severe strains and conflict within our cities. Municipal workers demanding decent pay and working conditions and pay raises commensurate with inflationary cost of living increases are thrown into conflict with homeowners and renters who have to pick up the tab via property tax increases. Those who rely on urban services come into conflict with the providers of these services, who, due to job freezes and work speedups, are unable to provide them at adequate levels. The unemployed fight each other for scarce job openings. And so on. Rifts of this type will only increase as attempts to manage the urban fiscal crisis take more stringent forms. The bitter, 5½-week municipal workers' strike in San Francisco last spring, coming a year after the police and firefighters' strike, and intermeshed with a bevy of retaliatory ballot propositions and supervisorial actions limiting city workers' collective bargaining rights and pay levels, reflect the kind of conflict that can be expected in city after city.

The dilemma this presents for the ruling class in the United States is profound. The *Business Week* editorial cited above ended with the ominous words: "The cities of the U.S. cannot be allowed to continue their financial deteroriation. The result could be violent social and political upheaval." But the conflict engendered by steps undertaken to improve the financial condition of cities may produce the same kind of social and political upheaval. Reduced job opportunities and pay scales, elimination or reduction of needed services and mobility opportuniites, increased taxation of the poor (through their rents and purchases) can only exacerbate the urban crisis, in social and political if not in fiscal dimensions. As noted in a recent study of urban development:

> The question of the 1970's is no longer whether, but instead *what forms* social revolt will take in the cities. Will the ghetto-riots of the 1960's recur, where blacks successfully destroyed their own neighborhoods only to have to continue living in them? Will street crime escalate further—where disorganized elements of the oppressed inflict their frustrations on one another, thus creating a cruel double jeopardy? . . . Or, alternatively, will the crushing tensions of the urban milieu break open along class lines thrusting the oppressed together as allies in a common fight to overthrow the capitalist class and the state forces of repression? And in this struggle will they transform the class system which lies at the roots of their powerlessness with a social system based on workers' self-management and a planned economy in transition to a humane socialist society?" [1]

It is that kind of conflict and those options that are the setting for the coming period of activity for planners and everyone else involved in urban policies and strategies. The sides we take in this conflict and the ways in which our work serves the antagonistic social and political forces in the city is the most important social planning issue we must grapple with. These are the terms in which we must consciously begin to judge our work. Internally, the urban crisis, and externally, revolutionary movements in the Third World (plus nationalist movements in the Middle East and competition from Western European and Japanese corporations) are creating a crisis of unprecedented proportions for U.S. capitalism. It is a system that has proved itself incapable of providing all its people with a decent standard of living, meaningful work and leisure-time activities, or democratic control of their lives, government and productive apparatus. In its attempts to manage the urban crisis, the economic and political leaders will try to shift the burdens onto those without wealth or power. (The *Business Week* editorial I have cited, referring to New York City's crisis, concludes: ". . . the only options are reducing services and making massive layoffs.")

I would define the work of social planning over the coming years, for those who share my view of class conflict and the system's intrinsic defects, as:

—Support of defensive struggles that seek to prevent loss of needed services and facilities to lower income urban residents.

—Support of offensive struggles that seek to improve services and facilities available to lower income urban residents.

—Support or organizing activities among city workers and consumers of city services, and of attempts to unify struggles and concerns of the two groups.

—Development of mechanisms that provide for more democratic popular control of economic and governmental activities.

—Development of alternative proposals for financing local government.

—Development of strategies to counter tendencies that split the working class along lines such as "productive" (defined as those with jobs, and increasingly as those with jobs in the private sector) and "nonproductive" (those without jobs or with jobs in the public sector). In particular, the racism and sexism that have traditionally been used to divide the working class must be countered via organizing activities to unify the class in common struggle against its enemies.

What the specific content of this work will be will depend on individual cities and situations, and the fact that much of the struggle is new means that we will be travelling in relatively uncharted waters. And while there is much to learn from other struggles in other cities, we should not attempt thoughtlessly to copy what has worked elsewhere, for under altered conditions what works in Boston may be totally unworkable in Seattle. Let me try to lay out some illustrative specifics of what is to be done, drawing to a large extent from my home base, San Francisco.

The pitting of various elements of the working class against one another around the urban fiscal crisis in large part is attributable, as noted above, to the ways in which city governments are financed. The property tax is far and away the largest source of municipal revenue, and as the residual means of balancing the budget it bears the brunt of any shortfall between expenditures and other revenue sources. For the city worker to obtain a decent salary takes directly from the pockets of his or her fellow workers who owns or rents housing in the city. Achieving an adequate level of municipal services involves the same conflict. If the fiscal crisis is not to result in further oppression and internal conflicts among the working class, there must be a more widespread understanding of the operation of the present tax system, what forces created it and keep it in existence, and the changes needed to provide adequate revenue for cities under conditions of social equity.

The inherent regressivity of the tax—whereby a standard rate is applied to something all people consume, so that tax takes a far higher proportion of one's income the lower one's income is—must be fully realized. (Seemingly minor steps could help unmask the impact of the property tax: for example, requiring landlords to itemize that portion of the rent bill that goes toward payment of property taxes—in the way utility companies itemize taxes separately—and ending the practice of folding property tax payments into mortgage payments.) Similarly, assessment practices in many cities, which underassess commercial properties relative to residential properties, single-family homes relative to multifamily structures, lower income and non-white areas relative to middle and upper income white areas, new areas relative to older areas, areas of rising property values relative to areas with stable or declining values, all must be documented and publicized. Disproportionate use of assessment appeals mechanisms by large commercial property owners, who can afford expensive technical assistance from assessors and attorneys and who have political influence, must be documented and exposed. The history of the property tax is also instructive: the original California constitution, for example, drafted by populist-minded legislators, taxed intangible as well as real property and hence reached wealth holdings; subsequent amendments pushed through by financial and corporate interests limited the tax almost exclusively to land and buildings.

Specific alternatives must be proposed and explained, so that working people begin to understand there is a way to have improved urban services and pay public employees decently without having to foot the bill themselves. Superficially attractive but illusory solutions, such as "federal aid to the cities," must be exposed and resisted, as long as the federal income tax system is not truly and steeply progressive, and as long as such proposals do not involve wholesale shifts in the way the federal budget is not allocated. Developing proposals for more progressive forms of property tax (graded according to income or property holdings, taxing commercial property at higher rates than residential property, taxing intangible property and wealth holdings steeply) and for introducing progressive local (possibly metropolitan or statewide) personal and corporate taxes are the positive steps. Actual introduction of proposals and legislation of this sort will also clearly reveal the sources of opposition. Work of this type can place the "urban fiscal crisis" in its proper political perspective, help identify clearly the nature of class interests involved, and begin building a unified working-class movement for radical change.

Many of the urban struggles of the past two decades have been around turf, and we can expect that as the urban crisis intensifies such struggles will grow in intensity, and possibly in number as well. Increasingly, there will be demands to "improve the business climate," as a way out of the fiscal crisis; making "underproductive" land available for "higher and better uses" will continue to be seen as a necessary step. Working-class residents and users of such sites will find themselves increasingly under attack. Two of the better known single-building struggles going in San Francisco now are the International Hotel and the Goodman Building. Each goes back many years, and they present an interesting pair because one involves the power of the state directly, through the San Francisco Redevelopment Agency while the other is a purely private venture.

The Goodman Building is a living and working space for two dozen artists, and a community arts center. It has the bad fortune to be located within the Redevelopment Agency's Western Addition A-2 project area, and thus since 1970, through harassment, legal and illegal moves, the Agency has been trying to force the residents out, tear down their 107-year old building, and replace it with yet another shiny highrise. The International Hotel is a low-rent semi-communal home for about one hundred elderly Chinese and Filipinos. Its bad fortune is that it sits on the wrong side of Kearny Street, the border between Chinatown-Manilatown and the downtown office district. Profit-hungry developers, who have bought the hotel and several surrounding properties, have been trying since 1969 to evict the tenants, demolish their building, and create a "higher and better use."

In both instances, community struggle, with widespread support, has kept the bulldozers at bay—although the current situation is ominous for the Hotel. The Goodman Building's residents have employed rent strikes (using the money to correct code violations), historical preservation (they convinced the State Historical Preservation Commission to include their architecturally important, extremely attractive building in the National Register of Historic Places), aggressive use of the Building's five store front spaces for community arts productions, successful application to the National Endowment for the Arts for a $10,000 grant to study the feasibility of rehabilitating the building, and have put together an offer to purchase the building back from the Redevelopment Agency. The I-Hotel residents raised sufficient protest around a 1969 attempt to evict them by the owner, one of the city's political bigwigs, that he agreed to let them sign a three-year lease. The residents and those supporting them have carried out extensive repairs on the structure to remove code violations and otherwise upgrade their living conditions. Their counterattack has also included a financially viable plan to purchase the Hotel for permanent use as low-cost cooperative housing, development of an ordinance to require private redevelopers to provide adequate relocation housing for those they displace, and a legal fight against eviction, plus a countersuit against the new owner for damages. Their long, well publicized fight against eviction resulted in a hung jury and a directed verdict for the landlord by the judge. Following a brief stay of eviction, the appeals court turned down the tenants' appeal, but the California Supreme Court has just issued another temporary stay, pending its decision on whether to hear an appeal. The sheriff's office has twice been on the verge of posting the order to vacate, and should the tenants finally lose in court, he is ready to move on the Hotel. What will now happen is anyone's guess, regardless of the outcome of the appeal. The fight to save the I-Hotel has become a symbolic struggle of human rights vs. property rights, one regarded with great interest by many groups in the city (a recent benefit dinner for the Hotel drew 500 people), and there are hundreds ready to put their bodies on the line to prevent eviction from being carried out. The sheriff is a widely known liberal figure, with some national reputation, who is caught between wanting to protect his image (plus whatever personal feelings of support for the tenants he might have) and his role-imposed duty to carry out court eviction orders. The tenants are proposing that the city (through the Housing Authority, Redevelopment Agency or Real Estate Department) either buy the Hotel or take it by eminent domain and convey it to the tenants for the price the new owner paid for it ($850,000). This would be an extraordinary step—one without precedent in this country, to my knowledge: intervention by a public agency to forestall a profit-oriented private development in order to maintain low-rent housing (traditional urban renewal stood on its head, you might call it). The mayor has actually gone before the Housing Authority to propose that that agency (borrowing Community Development funds for the purpose) undertake the purchase, rehabilitation and sale of the Hotel to the tenants. All of this is the direct result of militant struggle, backed by supportive social planning activities.

In both the Goodman Building and International Hotel struggles, significant roles have been played by social planners. In the case of the former, these include:

—The development of material and support for the politically significant designation of the building as a historical landmark.

—Development of a detailed financial plan for purchase of the building, and negotiations around that plan with the Redevelopment Agency.

—Preparation of the National Endowment for the Arts proposal and carrying out the feasibility study, legitimizing plans to renovate the building as a community arts center.

In the case of the Hotel, these activities include:

—Development of the supportive ordinance prohibiting the granting of a demolition permit to a private developer unless he provides adequate relocation housing. The eight-month process of redrafting the ordinance (the final version was the eleventh draft), lobbying for it with city agencies and among the Supervisors, and organizing community support turned the proposed law—and the problem it highlighted—into a major public issue, the subject of (unfortunately negative) newspaper and t.v./radio editorials and active counter-lobbying on the part of the city's downtown and real estate interests. Although the Supervisors rejected the proposed ordinance, 7-4, the class-based nature of the issue and its proponents and opponents were revealed in a clear and well publicized way.

—Preparation of a detailed financing plan for purchase of the Hotel,
and securing initial financial commitments to make the plan feasible
and credible.

To develop plans for public enterprises within the city, the Mayor of
San Francisco has appointed a Select Committee to replan Yerba Buena
Center, the 87-acre downtown urban renewal project that has been stalled
by controversy and litigation for a decade. One of the principal ideas
being considered for the Central Blocks (on which the previous plan had
a $225 million convention center, which would have absorbed all of the $11
million annual property tax increment from the rest of the project, plus $6
million from other sources, to repay the bond issue) is a 20-acre Tivoli
Gardens type amusement-cultural-recreational park. Apart from its social
value to the city, it would be a big money-maker: low development costs
and high revenues (from a small admission charge and concessions) give
it a projected $6-10 million annual profit. Now that the idea has attained
some currency, some of the planners on the Mayor's Committee are pushing
the idea of public ownership rather than have the area developed by a
private entrepreneur, with the city's financial gain limited to rental charges,
taxes and a small percentage of profits. Advocates are working out detailed
comparison charts of the benefits to the city under public and private
ownership, suggesting specific uses for the city revenue (such as subsidizing
replacement housing in the area or providing community medical and
daycare facilities). Apart from its intrinsic merits, the public ownership
campaign has considerable educational value in showing the public how
alternative development possibilities could benefit them instead of private
entrepreneurs, as well as revealing the forces for and against such a shift
in plans and the interconnections between the public decisionmakers and
the private profit sector. Options for meeting the city's fiscal problems by
bringing profitable enterprises under public ownership are thus made
credible.

A parallel effort has been made in the field of utilities ownership. For
several years, a campaign has been underway to municipalize gas and
electricity services in San Francisco (backed by some legal and historical
considerations unique to that city.) Planning studies illustrating the long-
term benefits of public ownership have done a great deal to develop support
for the idea (which has not yet succeeded, in large part because of the
vast sums—of our money—Pacific Gas & Electric spends in mounting op-
positional publicity campaigns). The Cleveland City Planning Commission
staff, in defining its function as advocates of "equity," has undertaken
similar supportive studies.[2]

A campaign currently underway in San Francisco is to change the way
the city's governing Board of Supervisors is elected, from city-wide to

district representation. An initial petition carrying 37, 500 signatures has just been filed, and the measure will appear on the November ballot, where it has an excellent chance of passage. The present eleven Supervisors live almost exclusively in the city's upper income areas and represent its ruling class interests. The complementary occupations of these part-time governors of the city are in such fields as law, real estate, business and investment counselling. The allegiances and orientations of those members who by background and training do not stem from the middle and upper class are effectively purchased via the realities of campaign financing, the necessity to raise up to $100,000 for a successful city-wide campaign (for this $9, 500 a year post). The locked-in nature of this electoral system is well illustrated by the fact that non-incumbents stand virtually no chance of being elected to the Board (turnover generally occurs only when a member resigns and the mayor appoints his or her successor—who invariably runs and wins at the next election); and in a city with nearly half Third World population, no non-white Supervisor ever has gained his post originally via the election route.

San Francisco is a city of strong, well defined neighborhoods, and the current campaign is an attempt to make city government representative of that make-up, by dividing the city into eleven districts; candidates from each district would have to be residents of that district, and only residents of a given district would vote for that district's seat. On one level the effort is being undertaken to give various neighborhoods of the city more direct, responsive representation in city government. But the thrust is also to clarify and bring into strong relief the various and conflicting class interests in the city. Policies pursued by the Board of Supervisors in past years—high-rise development downtown, reduction in public transit service, opposition to daycare centers, ignoring the needs of Third World neighborhoods—have had a clearly unequal distribution of costs and benefits by social class. District representation, and the vastly reduced financial needs for running such campaigns—changing from a reliance on money to a reliance on neighborhood-based organization—can lay the basis for drawing out the class implications of city policies and actions, and building organization and struggle based on that analysis. District representation of course is not in itself a guarantee this kind of change will occur (*vide* Chicago), but in tandem with strong, democratically based local organizations it provides a structure that facilitates movement of this type. The reasons for and proposed solutions to the urban fiscal crisis can be made far more evident, in class terms, under this form of representation.[3]

Skills needed to mount and run such a campaign, and to make use of the new structure if the initiative passes, are:

—Assistance in drawing district boundary lines, through presentation of data that suggest natural and politically sensible divisions or groupings. This is a process that should be done with maximum public input through work committees and public hearings, but reliable and relevant information makes a sound decision easier and more likely.

—Analysis and critique of the performance of Supervisors under the at-large system, how their actions have affected different areas and classes within the city.

—Development of neighborhood improvement plans, and assistance in integrating such plans with one another, in light of city-wide considerations.

These, then, illustrate the kind of social planning tasks needed for the coming period, from this planner's (political) perspective. Many are not traditional city planning skills—but I don't think that zoning, master planning and physical design are where it's at in the 1970's. My outline also suggests that the line between "professional" and "non-professional,'" "political organizer" and "community" ought to be a very thin and easily traversable one. Social planning skills and activities must be put at the disposal of communities, organizers and political activists, and the social planner ideally should see him/herself as part of that organizing process and change movement.[4] The challenge and task is not how to do social planning without adequate funding. The task is how to use our skills to help bring about the changes that insure that all our human needs are adequately funded. There's no question the country has the wealth, resources and talent to achieve that end. Things just have to be reorganized somewhat, so that those resources are distributed according to everyone's needs, and so that we create work and living environments designed by and for the mass of working people in this country.

NOTES

1. Graham Barker, Jennifer Penney and Wally Seccombe, *Highrise and Superprofits* (Kitchener, Ontario: Dumont Press Graphix, 1973), pp. 137-138. I am indebted to Jim Shoch's unpublished paper "Toward an Urban Urban Organization" for some of the references and material in the first part of this article.

2. See Norman Krumholz, Janice M. Cogger and John H. Linner, "The Cleveland Policy Planning Report," *Journal of the American Institute of Planners,* September, 1975, p. 303.

3. In the November, 1976 elections the district election of supervisors proposition won by 11,000 votes, getting 53% of the total vote. In November, 1977, all eleven of the supervisorial seats will be filled via the process outlined above.

4. In an effort to exchange information and create a sense of community among social planners with that vision of society and their own role in it, I organized, a year ago, a communications/action Network for radical urbanists. Persons interested in becoming part of that Network should contact me, giving some background information, at 360 Elizabeth St., San Francisco, Cal. 94114.

Politics, Planning, and Categories
Bridging the Gap

Lisa R. Peattie

The subject proposed for this paper was something like what happens to "advocacy planning" when it loses its constituency? In thinking about this, I found myself thinking not only about the way the constituencies of planning have changed since the sixties, but also about the kinds of issues community groups are organizing around, and the relation between these issues and 'planning' as commonly understood. Finally, I tried to confront in the process my own growing interest in the categories of economics, and to understand how *that* evolution in my own mind connected with my interest, in the sixties, in the movement we called "advocacy planning."

The outcome of all this has been less a description of what radical or reform-minded planners are up to now, or a set of predictions as to the future, than it is some comments on the processes by which planning, politics, and ideas change over time in interrelationship.

Planning and politics are components or aspects of the processes by which social purposes are forwarded. Purposes have both conceptual and social aspects; a purpose implies some person or group for whom it is the channel of desirable action, and it also implies a conception of the nature of the problem to be solved and of the processes by which solution would be arrived at. Where the interests in a situation are relatively stabilized, there may appear to be agreement on the nature of the problems; in this case, planning appears as the technical analysis of means to specific ends. Politics also appears as mobilization around ends the character of which is, in some sense, taken for granted. When new interest groups come into being, their purposes are shaped, both practically and intellectually, by the existence of those already formed; we get the politics of confrontation, and counter-planning. Advocacy planning came into existence in the sixties out of such a situation.

In the sixties we learned to say that "all planning is politics." We meant that it performs the classic task of politics: it decides who gets what, when, where and how. It was important to make that point because planning decisions, treated as "technical" and the proper province of "experts," got made in a realm where many people couldn't get at them, and in which the interests of particular groups or even the general run of ordinary people could easily sink out of sight under tables of figures or be papered-over by handsome maps and renderings said to represent the general welfare.

But we recognized planning as a very special way of dealing with the agenda of politics. In this sense, planning and politics may be contrasted as modes of pursuing human purposes.

Planning tries to achieve purposes by rationalizing them. The planner uses devices like cost-benefit analysis to provide what at least seems to be reasonable justification for pursuing the purpose; he goes on to show feasibility and encourage action by presenting a program and scheduling of the activities and resources required to get from here to there. (This, too, may be something less than perfectly realistic, but as Albert O. Hirschman points out in his hilarious essay on "the Hiding Hand,"[1] the kind of map which makes us think, however falsely, we have no major obstacle in the way, is often necessary to give us the confidence to commit resources and begin). The planning document should have a few paragraphs of gung-ho-ism, but it convinces by its tone of dispassionateness, its columns of figures, and its graphics, so nicely executed, that they were obviously done by a steady hand backed by ample resources—in brief, reasonable people.

Politics, on the other hand, operates in a more emotional and more directly coercive vein. It tries to achieve purposes by building support for the purpose and mobilizing the supporters to push the scheme forward. It thus deals in personalities, deals, rallies, slogans, banners, struggles and confrontations—the activities which build commitment to collectivities and collective purposes. (Even our not very passionate national parties have all that strange behavior at the conventions.)

These two modes, as described, are of course ideal types. Many public programs have elements of both; indeed, one of the things which seems to have happened in the last ten years is a marked diminution in the activity of classic plan-making, and a prevalance of "programs" with components both of social mobilization and rationalizing analysis.

And even when the two modes are sharply differentiated, planning and politics turn out to be very closely connected. Each depends for its vitality on the other. Planning without a political force behind it becomes a paper exercise and politics without planning becomes a politics of symbols or personalities: we say that this candidate or that movement lacks a program. In addition, the planning and politics or a period are linked conceptually; they both define and express the "idea in good currency" of the period.

When in the sixties our group called Urban Planning Aid was doing advocacy planning, the work always had a peculiar tension between planning and politics. The two met in an uneasy tandem. When a citizens' group in Cambridge asked us to help them to stop the Inner Belt highway which was going to be routed through their neighborhood, wiping out many of their homes, we began, planner-ishly, to study alternate routes. But since we felt uncomfortable about wiping out other neighborhoods too;

since planners are trained to look at transportation systems; and since, unlike the original Inner Belt planners, our political base—such as it was—had no commitment to a road at all, we went on to analyze the whole process of transportation planning in Boston. We looked at it through our politics, and perceiving, as planners, that it had a bias towards highways as against mass transit, we saw it as having an inherent class bias between suburban automobile owners and central-city users of mass transit. This was a planner-analysis, but it also served two political needs. On the one hand, it gave the protests of the tiny neighborhood group rational justification; they could be seen as not simply a bunch of petty-minded cranks, but as contenders in a reasonable cause, to which people like Harvard and MIT professors might reasonably lend their support. On the other hand, it presented an image of the issues through which the neighborhood group might see their problem in a broader context; to use the standard phrase, it might help to raise their consciousness.

But the Save Our Cities organization of Cambridge was still a very local group with parochial interests (literally—for the Church, as so often happens, was active in the struggle to save the neighborhood). The members' consciousness was not a point, nor was the group's political muscle of a dimension to take up our newly-defined, wider issue. We had started with a client, but a locally-defined issue; now we had a broadly-defined issue, but no client.

At this point, Jim Morey, of Urban Planning Aid, made a political innovation; he built a client around the issue. He got together all the little neighborhood groups in Boston which were engaged in highway struggles analagous to that of our client and formed them into a confederation. The Greater Boston Committee on the Transportation Crisis was a front organization if there ever was one; it met in the Urban Planning Aid Office. But it stuck and it worked. In time it became independent and went off on its own.

Here the mode of action around the issue became frankly political. We had come to understand by then that it was not possible to move systems by planning alone; the plan had to have political muscle behind it.

We learned this partly by experience with another client of ours, a citizen group in the South End urban renewal area. Our report on the renewal program there was not a bad job, and in its red binder, looked like a professional document; it took the noisy invasion of a parking lot by South End residents to stop clearance under the renewal program; what were we doing fooling around with red binders?

Also, we were by now feeling less guilty about being negative. At the start, academic people, we had twinges when people said that advocacy planning seemed to be purely negative, a vetoing operation; we felt we should do counter-planning, develop a "positive alternative." When one of our members who, amazingly, managed to be a Redevelopment Authority planner and an Urban Planning Aid Board member simultaneously, argued that this was silly, I remember being shocked. "We haven't the staff or the resources to compete with the BRA," he said. "Its more efficient to position the agency so that it is forced to do the technical work on alternatives." He was right.

Now it was perfectly clear that we did not have the resources, even if we had had the mandate, to re-study and re-program the development of a transportation system for the Greater Boston area. We helped the citizen groups to organize rallies, demonstrations, petitions around the general position to stop highway building until the system could be re-studied. This was what happened.

But one thing we were never able to do, even though in many hours of meetings we tried to do it. This was to develop a completely articulated positive program for transportation in our political framework, to spell out what would be a radical program for transportation. Urban Planning Aid was able to move from a definition of the issue as "Beat the Belt" to one of less highway-building and better mass transit, and to help get that issue established in the political framework and moved into the planning process. We could not take it further than that. The Greater Boston Committee on the Transportation Crisis became absorbed in the citizen input to the Boston Transportation re-study. The Department of Transportation is funding studies of new strategies in urban transportation. Jim Morey is now in a steel mill in the Midwest, trying to develop issues and build membership as a shop floor organizer.

I now think that our long, agonizing meetings on the particularities of a radical perspective on urban transportation showed our innocence in both planning and politics. We were trying to short-cut, to telescope into a few evenings of small-group discussion, what would actually need a long process of joint evolution in politics, planning and technology.

We have cities built around the most individualizing and most expensive of transportation systems, the private automobile. Very important and generalized economic and political interests are built around the automobile. The shape of our cities is determined by the availability of the automobile. Central cultural values are centered on the automobile. There is no simple device, in such cities, for giving equal access to all. Neither "freeway fighting" nor "mass transit" comprises a radical transportation policy; the re-appraisal of the Bay Area Rapid Transit system as serving primarily the more affluent, and citizen protest in Los Angeles over special lanes for pooled automotive transit have underscored that. The issue was too complex, required for its solution too many interdependent social and technical changes, to be 'solved' at one point in time.

One could form purposes and organize groups around ameliorating the situation or pieces of the situation, but not around transforming it. Transformation, if it were to take place, would be a long process of many steps, including technical inventions, spatial reorganizations, value changes, changes in conceptualizations of the issue, in which the political evolution and the technical evolution would be interdependently linked. Nobody creates this by a one-time act of planning"

There are good reasons why advocacy planning was defensive, negative, a vetoing operation, and why it focused on amelioration of the existing system, rather than proposing new positive alternatives. The objectives of even radical planners always hover around what is, and its prevailing structure is necessarily critical.

Radical planning is dependent on radical politics both for efficacy and legitimacy, for without a constituency the radical planner not only lacks means for influencing outcomes, but also has difficulty in substantiating a claim to represent any important social interest.

But it also needs radical politics for an equally basic function: for the categories and concepts which define its purpose. The planner can move beyond the categories and concepts given at any one moment in the political process, as Urban Planning Aid moved to re-define the transportation issue from one of the damage done to low-income neighborhoods by highways to the class bias in the transportation system. But he cannot freely invent "issues." He starts with some sense of problem on the part of some group of people. The radical planner, like any other planner, moves within the groups, the interest, the purposes, given by his or her times.

Organizing is most easily brought about "when threats are" immediate, concrete, spatially localized. When the issue becomes more generalized, it tends to become diffused. Mancur Olson has pointed out,[2] that rather paradoxically, the wider the potential constituency, the harder it may be to develop organization around the issue. Furthermore, it is harder to organize around a threat which is essentially invisible. It is not such a great trick to organize the population living in the area to be cleared against the federal bulldozers; it is harder to organize against the policies of the Federal Reserve Board.

One might think that the best way to escape the presuppositions of the existing system, the perpetual sense of fighting on the terms set by the opposition, would be to move into the generation of "positive alternatives." This is simply not so. A practicable alternative is a modification of the existing system, or a variant of an existing institution—or perhaps a "counter-cultural" experiment on a very small scale. Beyond, one soon moves into the realm of the Utopian—fine stuff for clarifying the issue, at least for some of the radicals, but extremely difficult stuff around which to build organization.

In the case of transportation, for example, one could organize to re-route highways, to stop highways, to lower (or at least stabilize) mass-transit fares, to improve services. But how to create an efficient and egalitarian system of transportation for a city the whole layout of which presupposes the automobile? As the Vermonter is supposed to have told the visitor inquiring his way to some small hamlet: "I wouldn't start from here." A different system could only happen through a set of consecutive and cumulative modifications in both the political and technical order, each opening up new constituencies, new possibilities, new ideas and new purposes, each building on previous developments.

Among the people who, in the sixties, called themselves "advocate planners," there was current certainly more than one model of social change. Thus it is natural for the "advocacy planning" of the sixties to have transformed itself or have been transformed into more than one sort of activity.

In one view, desirable processes of changes are arrived at by a more inclusively pluralistic political process which incorporates into decision-making and invention the ideas and interests of the broadest social spectrum of people concerned. The "advocate planner," in this view, is an instrument of interests which might otherwise lack representation; he serves both to cast these interests into coherent form and to push to see that they are dealt with in the planning process. The legacy of this strain is not only current efforts at "advocacy planning" in this classic model, but the many institutional arrangements for "citizen participation" in public programs which came out of the turbulence of the sixties.

In another view, whatever desirable modifications of the system may emerge from the activities of the "advocate planner," these are not the real output of his work; the real output is the growth of radical consciousness and organizational competence in his constituency, and these will have their payoff when they go into making the revolution. Indeed, the advocacy planner does not want to be *too* successful in gaining his clients' demands; if he were, his followers might well run out of steam. In any case, he feels, these small gains and systems modifications are only relevant to the existing system. They are not particularly useful cues to the design of the future after-the-revolution system which, starting from a different base of power, will flow from totally different premises. This kind of "advocacy planning" becomes classic radical political organizing.

A third version sees radical political change in the base of power in society as necessary but not sufficient; the revolution, in this view, does not obviate the need for the long march through the institutions; the transformation of urban neighborhoods, housing policy, the family, schooling, the workplace; the invention of new "convivial" technologies; the re-organization of society along new lines. These re-organizations are seen as, in some sense, almost independent of shifts in the social basis of power; they can begin now, within the shell of the old society, and they will have to be worked through with attention and effort even after the revolution comes— if it does. "Advocate planners" in this stream of thinking find themselves in food coops and communes, the women's health centers, the centers for the study of policy alternatives.

This third version is clearly the closest to my own. I have less confidence than some appear to have in a change of management, and more of a preoccupation with some problems of institutional structure which seem to recur within a variety of different political systems. However, there was in the advocacy planning of the sixties two strains which I miss in some of the "counter-cultural" "alternatives" cited above: a continual interaction with and responsibility to the concerns of working-class people on the one hand, and, on the other, an attempt to place local organization within the structural context of large-scale policy.

Advocacy planning came into existence in the sixties because at that time change was relatively rapid in the sense of organized groups coming into existence and issues being re-defined. People who wanted to alter the system according to any one of these models of change found advocacy for the emerging constituencies a ready handle for change. To defend those in the path of an urban renewal project, for example, was to give the planning process a more pluralistic character and to redress, to a degree, the inequality of access to that process by different social classes. It was also a way of developing, among the participants in such struggles, a heightened radical consciousness. It could also be thought of as a way of developing new sorts of competences among the "community group" members which would, in time, evolve into new, more democratic and decentralized kinds.

The seventies have a different quality. Now even the locally-based more limited forms of advocacy planning seem to be in some retrenchment. The American system adjusted to the conflicts of the sixties by withdrawing from circulation a number of the programs—most conspiciously, urban renewal—which had proved to be sure-fire ways of stirring up the population, and by incorporating citizen participation into a number of the others. It would be hard to claim that these modifications rendered American society egalitarian or the American people happy. I believe there is a general agreement that American society is currently characterized by a widespread sense of times-out-of-joint. But this does not mean it is easy to form purposes with reference to the difficulties

We seem to lack the kind of politics which sharply defines the issues of planning. When such movements exist, planning (and counter-planning) centers around the purposes these embody. The political groupings aggregate purposes into programs and projects. These enterprises come to stand out very sharply as the field of "planning" against a field of less aggregated purposes thought of as "the system."

In the absence of the kind of politics we had in the sixties, none of this happens. Purposes seem disaggregated. We talk on the one hand of issues—as for example "environmental ones"—at a scale so large that the constituency of an "advocate planner" may be hard to locate, and recognize on the other hand a trend to the privatization of policy in the form of the contracting-out of "public" services and of using public funds to subsidize individual market transactions as in Sec. 8 and Medicare. In the absence of the great federal programs of the sixties, "planning" as a specific field of action and focus of controversy seems to evaporate.

With all this goes a curiously unsatisfactory politics. The general retrenchment of the Left might be seen as victory for the status quo were it not that the national parties no longer seem to carry a great deal of credibility as managers of our national life. We all seem to be struggling in our various ways in a system which is neither "natural" nor under anyone's management and control, and in which public and private are no longer seen as distinct categories.

It is in this context that I have been thinking about the categories of economics. In trying to understand why this seemed to me appropriate now, I think it is more than simply the accident of a train of thought set off by a particular research, though it is that; I was doing fieldwork among the street vendors and tiny shopkeepers of Bogota, and came to be troubled by the categories with which economists evaluate such activities. However, I think it has a link to the character of our times as well. I think that for me the conceptual exploration is an attempt to locate new purposes. The link between planning and politics is, as we found in Urban Planning Aid, not simply one of mutual need to get things done. Planning and politics are also linked by the conceptualization of problems. One way to try to feel out where new purposes are coming into being, at a time when the political process sends mixed messages, is to see where the loose ends are in our ideas, the points at which the concepts no longer capture felt need.

It is easy enough to see that the issues which are coming into being, which require more adequate formulation, and constituencies which will press them, are ones surrounding the flow of resources—to whom? for what purposes?—and the distribution of what society produces. But these flows are not so easy to chart among the complex institutions of corporate capitalism; the potential issues with respect to the way our institutions manage the system are not so transparent as were the turf issues of urban renewal and the struggles over program control of the sixties, and the evaluations of outcome are not always self-evident.

With extraordinary acumen and organizing energy Michael Ansara and his "Fair Share" group in Boston have been getting the folks into the streets on the issue of electric power rates, so we see that intelligence and energy will find a way even in this boggy terrain. But it can be argued that in some respects the way this issue has been conceptualized is an over-simplification and will turn out to have been a first approximation. In such issues, the potential for manipulation by the "advocate planner," always an issue in the movement ten years ago, is even more acute. It will take advocates of energy, unusual organizing capacity, analytic skill, and a high degree of patient willingness to work interactively with their constituencies to make this kind of thing function over the long haul to build democratic controls into our sort of society.

The skills relevant to this new arena are clearly the skills of economic analysis. And here I want to make a last, perhaps peripheral, but nevertheless strongly-felt suggestion. It is that it will not be enough for reform-minded planners to learn to do economics according to the text; there are also going to have to be some changes made in the conceptual apparatus. As the constituencies re-form around emergent issues, new categories of analysis emerge as well. Now ways of defining the issues also contribute to the emergence of new purposes and new constituencies.

Like any set of categories, those of economics exist in order to focus on the elements we find important, and to get done what we want done. Economics as a way of thinking about how to manage the system has some very great advantages; for example, the advantage that "public" and "private" are not important distinctions, as they are in the language of politics, but it has some huge disadvantages. It has a very large evaluative-ideological component which is peculiarly difficult to disentangle because of the deductive and mathematical form in which its propositions are rendered.

I will note briefly some issues of economic thinking which seem particularly relevant to the up-coming issues in planning.

The *concept of productivity* is the central evaluative concept in economics; there are a number of versions in use, and all subject to question. The mainline neoclassical types seem to take earnings as the measure of productivity and hence, in some sense, of social worth; this is a bit hard on the rating of all the earners and enterprises that just haven't got a very good grab on the system such that would enable them to turn the earnings their way. The Marxists, on the other hand, have a whole set of rather moralistic judgments on various kinds of activities which place (to me) unreasonably high value on the production of physical goods—surely we have enough schlock already?—compared to services.

If you think about it, you will see there is no "right" answer to this issue; we want to measure what we want to measure. It is a political-intellectual problem to work out what we want to measure.

Concepts of ownership and of capital resources need to be re-thought in the context of the twentieth century economy. As Charles Reich has pointed out, there is a large and important body of "new property," closely tied to actions of the state, which consists not of cash or bonds or material goods but of licenses, entitlements, pensions, and other regularized claims on a steady flow of income. Until we get this incorporated into the body of practice in economic analysis, we'll miss major issues of policy.

The tendency of economists to focus only on the monetized aspects of the system makes for terrible confusion in handling the issues of the women's movement, and probably of men's life, too.

Finally, and most generally, as demands for reform move beyond the bread-and-butter issues to issues of the quality of life—bread and roses too—we will certainly have to do something to stretch the conceptual framework of economics to get it all in and do it all justice. Economists are beginning to push at their discipline in this way, responding, I believe, to a general sense of dissatisfaction with the capacity of traditional economic accounting to measure what makes life good. E. F. Schumacher writes about a "Buddhist economics" which tries to "obtain the maximum of well-being with the minimum of consumption." [3] Kenneth Boulding urges a push not to economic growth, but to a "steady state economics." [4] S. B. Linder writes about how the choice of goods as against time creates the "harried leisure class." [5] And most delightfully of all, a hitherto conservative welfare economist named Tibor Scitovsky has just published a book on pleasure [6] designed to show that an economy can produce a high level of comfort without being very much fun.

You may say these are all issues for the elite to worry about, and the reformers and radicals should stick with income inequality. I don't think so. I believe everyone should be entitled to elite issues.

Neither neo-Keynesian economics nor reformulations of Marxist theory are perfectly adapted to articulating the plights and problems of people in the United States of the seventies. If we simply try to fit what people tell us of their trouble into those categories, we'll lose it, politically and intellectually. We have to keep the point of the exercise in mind: we want to help bring about a society more agreeable, just, and viable in the long run than the one we have. It's our job as planners, as intellectuals, to find out how to say what's needed in reasonable language. But that process of planning, and the language which it uses, has to be the outcome of a political process in which what people really want out of life gets expressed. The institutions, the politically organized interests, and the concepts have to change in interaction.

Planning touches on all aspects of that process: It forwards purposes implying both ends and appropriate means, linked by ideas as to the nature of problems. "Advocacy planning," thought of as the forwarding of the purposes of groups at the margins of representation in the processes of social management, has a particularly complex task. Groups which are not represented tend not to be well organized; their purposes tend to be implicit, not clearly formulated because people rarely spend energy striving for what seems unattainable. The task of advocacy planning thus has to go: from transplanting plight into problem, problem into purpose, purpose into programmatic action or planning—and building a political framework in which the outcomes of such a process can themselves be further modified by the people affected in a cumulative process of social change.

NOTES

1. Albert O. Hirschman, "The Principle of the Hiding Hand" in *Development Projects Observed* (Washington, D.C.: The Brookings Institute, 1967).

2. Mancur Olson, *The Logic of Collective Action: Public Goods and the Theory of Groups* (Cambridge, Mass.: Harvard University Press, 1965).

3. E. F. Schumacher, *Small is Beautiful: Economics as if People Mattered* (N.Y.: Harper and Row, 1973).

4. Kenneth Boulding, "The Economics of Spaceship Earth," *Collected Papers,* Colorado University Press, Vol. II (1971).

See also Herman E. Daly, ed., *Toward a Steady-State Economy* (San Francisco: W. H. Freeman, 1973).

5. Stegan Burenstam Linder, *The Harried Leisure Class* (N.Y.: Columbia University Press, 1970).

6. Tibor Scitovsky, *The Joyless Economy: An Inquiry into Human Satisfaction and Consumer Dissatisfaction* (N.Y.: Oxford University Press, 1976.

Social Planning and the Mentally and Physically Handicapped: The Growing "Special Service" Populations

Julian Wolpert

When the urban planner in one of our large northeastern cities looks at the social, demographic and household characteristics of the client population for whom he is expected to plan, he will count up the total of elderly people in nursing homes, ex-mental patients in SRO hotels and boarding houses, the ex-alcoholic and drug addicts in group homes, the juvenile offenders in community residential facilities and the adult offenders. He may legitimately ask where are those upwardly mobile working class people, and solid middle class citizens for whom planning was supposedly intended. These "left-over" people will never have the purchasing power to afford the fruits of a traditional urban renewal of the center city. Their income maintenance funds and service payments in-kind from medicare and other urban care services will insure subsistence but no more. They are drawn to the center city or placed there because housing is cheaper, and services are concentrated there, and no local outcry prevents their infusion.[1] They share the center city with other groups—the single parent households, the unskilled and the elderly needy who live alone.

The center city is one of our warehouses, where people and land can be stored until the land can be reutilized. Physical renewal cannot take place until the center city handicapped population is integrated and dispersed and given a stake in conformity. Then how shall the area, land use, and social planners occupy themselves while waiting for suburbanites and affluent singles and couples to make their home in the city where "they belong?" The model of urban revival assumes that income transfers and housing allowances provide residential mobility to the elderly, needy, and the mentally and physically handicapped groups. The model also assumes that human services are able to restore their clients to a state of health and well-being so that integration or at least pseudo-integration into "normal" communities is possible. Substantial evidence reveals relative stability in the concentration of handicapped people in the center cities and suggests a highly significant new role for the urban planner.[2]

The Provision of Social Services to the Handicapped

The handicapped population of which we speak are the groups who require a lifetime of support. Their handicaps are permanent and not easily mitigated. They include the large numbers of long hospitalized, returning mental patients, mildly and moderately retarded adults, physically handicapped, the elderly infirm—people who are not now and are not likely to become full labor force participants. These are the groups whose surrogate for employment are human services. Their surrogate for the "journey to work" is the trip to the service facility. For the largest majority, commercial entertainment is unaffordable. They are powerless. They have nothing to bargain with.

The income of disabled people is much less than that of the non-disabled work force. The disabled population is older, disproportionately non-white, has a lower educational achievement level and is likely to have no other sources of income but public income maintenance. Disabled people are twice as likely as the general population to use medical care services. One in six is likely to be hospitalized during a given year. Disabled people are more likely to be separated or divorced than the general population. The model disabled individual in the urban area lives alone in a hotel, boarding house or modest apartment. His income maintenance and other earnings place him in the middle of the poverty category. He is highly reliant upon public sector medical and social services. His disability is permanent. His income in the future will, at best, keep pace with the inflationary rate.

Handicapped people often require advocacy intervention merely to establish eligibility requirements for statutory assistance, or attention by social service agencies. They are the most vulnerable potential victims of consumer fraud, property and personal crime. Their mobility is not increased by social welfare programs which lift only a small minority above the poverty level.[3]

The welfare system seems to work in a rather perverse manner in the center city. It increases the cash flow to elderly and disabled people in comparison with single parents with dependent children. At the same time, it funds human services more generously for single parents than the disabled group. This process denies residential mobility, through access to service facilities. Human service provision is a significant contributor to the quality of life of the aged, needy and handicapped groups because substitute or surrogate services are not normally produced by the private sector, even if personal income is substantial. Ties to home, a familiar neighborhood and a proven method of coping with problems of shopping and other local trips all combine to reinforce residential stability.

A more satisfactory welfare system would permit families with young children the mobility which would place them in good school systems.

This is exactly the reason that such mobility is not provided. Fringe and suburban communities more readily accept elderly and disabled people than poor families with children. The mobility bottleneck has rendered the two groups joint but non-complementary occupiers of center city land use, an outcome which is harmful for both.

SOCIAL SERVICE ALTERNATIVES

One human service approach assumes that economic, cultural and social systems have casualties and victims. It is easier to redress through public programs the gaps in the market basket of the handicapped and the needy than to create a human support system which has no casualties. In this perspective, the handicapped make a claim upon the majority society for its persistence in pursuing an economic, social, and cultural system which is matched to the attributes of a healthy, well-functioning youthful society. The norms of the most advanced societies, whether they are capitalist or collectivist, assume a work role following a training period in the education sector which is based upon high ability and energy and an absence of impediments or other handicaps to hinder work, family development and socialization to community mores and values. In a mechanical fashion, one can enumerate the impediments which the physically and mentally handicapped have which hinder their ability to take part in the activities of the "healthy society". In this framework the handicapped strive to approximate normalization. The role of public sector programs, and the volunteer sector as well, is to facilitate the route toward normalization or at least a moderate level of pseudo-integration. Handicapped people are assumed to have a stake in pursuing conformity.

Another social model assumes that progress in creating open and accepting societies requires a stage of labeling and even stereotyping its casualties so that corrective actions can be taken. This approach assumes that the labeling and the accompanying segregation of the handicapped permits conspicuous attention to be focused upon imperfections in our society. Social "motion" in a large, diverse and complex society ignores victims who are dispersed and hidden. The examples are the residents of mental hospitals, prisons, and the remote facilities which house mentally retarded people. This model of social process requires wide pendulum swings which have now yielded a return of formerly institutionalized people into our very midst where they cannot be ignored. This process also has its costs in the lag of public responsiveness. The outcome, though delayed, evolves to a broader and more inclusive society.

Both models, and others as well, can find validation in the social service delivery systems for handicapped people in our urban areas. The efforts of the social service system are uncoordinated, diffuse and insufficient. In the aggregate, the provision of social services is uncontrollable and illogical. The helping role seems to make sense on the individual level but no sense whatever on the macrolevel. The programs are divided between public, private and volunteer agencies. Monitoring and evaluation seem not to be feasible. Much of the human service provision is inappropriate or irrelevent. The market model of service provision which would seemingly drive out the "bad" service providers in favor of the "good" service providers does not operate. The chaos of the system invites the intervention of management and systems experts, but their duration of interest and their impact is short-lived. It is easy to dismiss the importance of individual helping roles, however, by focusing exclusively on the floundering of the aggregate system.

The planner who assumes that his intervention at the macro service level will have pervasive impact is as likely to be disappointed as the microplanner who feels that a well functioning program in one area can be replicated on an area wide basis. The planner who assumes that a pervasive national problem with respect to the quality of life of handicapped people can find a local solution is also a good candidate for disappointment, as is the believer in a broad new federal initiative which will provide an immediate solution. No dramatic changes are expected and this means that the handicapped populations will continue generally to be concentrated where housing costs are least and where the service facilities are concentrated. They will live in areas of capital disinvestment, where land use markets are soft and where service facilities can find sites in the shrinking retail and commercial structures.

THE CLIENT POPULATIONS AND THEIR PRIORITIES

The mental hospital population has declined from 550,000 in 1955 to a present level of 200,000.[5] If the experience of states which have reduced their institutionalized population most rapidly is a proper example, then an additional 130,000 will be released by 1985 and resident populations will stabilize at a national level of 70,000. Much of the catching up will occur in the states of Connecticut, Massachusetts, New York, New Jersey, and Pennsylvania which have lagged behind the more progressive Midwest and West Coast states. In these northeastern states, the rate of institutionalization is three times that of Oregon, Washington, Iowa, and Wisconsin. The northeast is also slowest in releasing its retarded people and adult and juvenile correctional offenders into alternative community settings. A massive bottleneck in community placements hinders the release process. More than half of the attempts in the recent years to site group homes have resulted in failure. Anti "groupie" zoning legislation adds to the housing cost factor in limiting the opportunities for community placement. The consequence has been severe competition between handicapped people and other poverty groups in the same low cost housing market in the center city areas. Opportunities are found occasionally in transitional zones to purchase large houses for conversion into group homes. Conformance to local regulations and life and safety codes usually insure, however, that the group home alternative results in an expensive institutional-like community building. Housing and access to medical and other services, rather than employment sites, are the locational anchors which determine where the elderly and handicapped must live. Human service hubs evolve to serve the handicapped groups and their presence serves to attract more clients. A projection of this trend would yield a facsimile of the total institutions in the center city. In this scenario, normalization would consist of a new mutant form of community institutionalization, comprising the alliance of the service dependent and their caretakers.[6]

Why are the handicapped more deserving of the planners' attention than other groups in need? Where should they rank in our scheme of priorities? What are the implications of their need for a *permanent* support system rather than short-term and remedial help? What can we learn about the persistence, longevity and ubiquitousness of skid rows for the "down and outers" which have outlived the efforts of a whole generation of social workers and planners? The failure to provide sufficient attention to income, housing and neighborhood needs has required that service provision to address social necessities must be managed by professional helpers in an institutionalized service sector. By concentrating handicapped people with others in need, the dilemma of competitive priorities arises because community needs far surpass internal resources.

The priority position of the elderly and the handicapped over other needy groups has a complex basis which is apparently deeply rooted in our own as well as most other cultures. The elderly and handicapped are excused from the need to be self-sustaining or their work is sheltered. Their disability is permanent so that programs need not be devised to bring them back into the labor force and thereby diminish their consumption of human services. We can afford to be more generous in our programs for disabled people because they are assumed to be liabilities in the work force; so much so, in fact, that firms are subsidized to hire handicapped people. The exclusion from work generates a search for surrogate jobs or other activities that can be used to consume the daylight hours when normal and healthy people are working.

Our society does devote a disproportionate share of its income transfers and services to the elderly and handicapped groups rather than to single parents. Disabilities are more uniformly distributed among the population than is unwed motherhood. Important and powerful people have handicapped relatives or elderly parents. Handicaps attract the attention of private philanthropy and the volunteer associations. Disabled people are not to blame for their handicap and we give of ourselves because we are active and strong. We do not worry about handicapped welfare cheaters.

PLANNING FUNCTIONS

The planner obsessed with notions of cosmetic neighborhood improvement is a detriment in the helping role because he diverts attention and resources away from vital social functions. His efforts lead to a reduction in the stock of low-cost housing, neighborhood shops and community-based service facilities. The infusion of funds provided for income maintenance and human service provision can clearly not sustain private sector capital investment. Neither do efforts at attracting industry and jobs assist this sector of the population. On the other hand, the social planner who understands how to deinstitutionalize center city life for the handicapped population has the requisite skills for intervention.

The most common set of residential solutions for the handicapped require a range of housing alternatives, each associated with a package of services to constitute a human support system. Depending upon the degree of reliance on human services or income support, the assistance package determines the residential solution. The range could cover the gamut from skilled nursing care to half-way houses, board and care homes, placement with families and independent apartment living. The human support system should supplement the residential solution by providing access to medical and social service needs.

Some degree of clustering of the handicapped is unavoidable but neighborhood saturation is probably harmful to both the handicapped and the community. Suburban sprawl is a bad environment for most handicapped people, as is a high crime inner city zone. The best sites seem to be in blue collar and lower middle class social areas which contain a community focus of shops, services and mass transit, and strong community institutions. These are the areas that can absorb reasonable numbers of handicapped people without tipping. In a number of cities, San Francisco, Milwaukee and White Plains for example, planners have coordinated their redrafting of zoning definitions of group homes with safeguards to insure against over-clustering of the group homes in single blocks and neighborhoods. In White Plains, a single planning group, CRISP, has responsibility for the siting of the group homes of all local agencies. This group has succeeded in renting or purchasing homes according to a systematic pattern of community opposition and there have been no significant negative spillover effects in any one area. The advantages, of course, of dispersing handicapped people into stable residential communities is that much of the social support can come from the communities themselves rather than only from professional targeted services. It seems clear, for example, that the elderly needy who are living alone like breakfast and lunch programs and lecture series at the Y's or in libraries, and have little use for therapy or nutrition services. Returning mental patients do not seek mental health services but instead are drawn to daytime community centers.

The habits, preferences and behavior of the needy, aged and disabled suggest strategies for planning intervention which will permit these groups to remain in center city sites. One solution which parallels a present HUD initiative favors subsidized middle class center city housing which allocates a share of apartments to elderly and handicapped people. The implication is clear that the welfare of elderly and disabled people requires not only low-cost housing and services, but the presence of compatible and stable neighbors and active community institutions. This left-behind group needs to be rejoined by its cohorts who are also attracted by urban amenities and services. This scenario pictures the integration of elderly and handicapped people in an adult-oriented center city, housed in individual apartments or group facilities and within close access to shops and service facilities targeted to their needs.

This description of the habits and requirements of handicapped groups must sound very familiar because it must bring back memories of the functioning of the traditional community of the "gemeinschaft" variety. Handicapped people seem to fare best when their numbers and representation in communities are no greater than consistent with the normal incidence rate of disabled people in a community. That is, the removal, extrusion and labeling of handicapped people in itself results in "unnatural" clusters of healthy young adults. The normalization process is symmetrical in that communities become normalized and humanized by the return of their handicapped members, much as those who return become resocialized to community living. The rather simple message which can be inferred from this process is that if strong communities can develop, we need not plan specifically for the handicapped. The converse statement is that, planning for the specialized needs of the handicapped requires outside intervention because such strong communities do not exist. The concentrations of the handicapped and the elderly needy are indicators of the manner in which our society had defined its left-over marginal people.

Common and Targeted Services [7]

The great temptation for the community-based planner is to assume that he can function within a framework of other professionals who also serve the needy, aged and handicapped groups. This model allocates discretion according to the specialized area of expertise. The model seems to make little sense, however, to the service recipients or even the community at large. Professional helpers diagnose problems and suggest remedies which are consistent with their frame of reference for the diagnosis.

One of the major consequences of this process is a proliferation of targeted services which are justified by their specialized attention to major problem areas of the handicapped population. The sheltered group home for ex-mental patients, for example, requires a sheltered workshop, and a sheltered recreation center. Separate sets of all of these facilities are needed for white, black, Spanish-speaking and other various ethnic groups. The same decentralized pattern is repeated for facilities for the elderly, mentally retarded, alcoholics, drug addicts, and probationers and parolees. The helpers, professional and volunteer, the consultants, the evaluators and monitors and the advocates together outnumber the clients and far exceed the representation of stable families in these communities. The service facilities, their clients and staff outnumber the retail stores and their customers and the commercial establishments and their employees. These findings are based upon a survey of service representation within the older industrial towns within the Philadelphia to New York corridor.

The first empirical study was conducted in New Brunswick, New Jersey, in a somewhat more comprehensive analysis of service facility representation than has been carried out in other sample communities. In all, 152 service facilities were identified in New Brunswick, including all three types of facilities: common, administrative and targeted services (Exhibit 2). Of the total common facilities, 52 are churches, 11 schools, 2 hospitals, 9 social and fraternal organizations and 3 labor union locals. The remainder represent a wide variety of service types well distributed over the United Way service classification. The aggregate of 152 facilities include 86 classified as common, 21 are administrative and 45 are targeted.

New Brunswick's common and administrative services were established earlier than the targeted ones. In fact, during the past two years, the targeted services have been augmented by one-third while other types of facilities have only held their own.

The targeted facilities have fewer personnel and see fewer clients than the other kinds of facilities. They utilize para-professionals and volunteers relatively as frequently but their facilities are smaller and oriented to more intensive visits with fewer clients.

In all, the 61 direct service provision facilities accounted for a staff of 3,200, of whom roughly one-quarter are professionals and one-third are unpaid volunteers. Client members also total about 3,200. This aggregate one-to-one ratio of staff to clients appears quite consistent with previous studies especially if para-professionals and volunteers are included within the staff category. Staff-to-client ratios are lowest in the largest agencies. This tendency would appear to indicate some scale economies regarding support staff. Two-thirds of the facilities do meet with 30 or more clients a day.

Sponsorship and funding for the services are very substantially derived from government. Federal sources predominate followed by state, county, and municipality levels. The remaining portions of the budgets are derived principally from United Way allocations, the Urban League, private charities and service fees.

Almost half of the common facilities are located alongside residential structures (Exhibit 3). Another 25 percent can be found in commercial areas. The siting of targeted facilities reveals quite a different pattern. These facilities are relatively more prominent in institutional clusters and commercial districts and relatively less common in residential areas (Exhibit 4).

The physical appearance of targeted facilities is generally somewhat better than surrounding structures but the headquarters and common facilities are in even better physical condition (Exhibit 5). The targeted services share their facilities with other services and non-services to a considerably greater extent than the other types of facilities (Exhibit 6). The targeted services are considerably less conspicuous physically than are the common type of facilities (Exhibit 7). The targeted facilities are less clustered than the administrative service facilities and their pattern coincides much more regularly with the location of population which is low income, black and Spanish-speaking (Exhibits 8, 10).

The facility distribution pattern for New Brunswick conforms closely to expectations. The targeted services are smaller in scale and serve fewer clients. They tend to be located in converted structures which they share with other services and non-services (Exhibit 9). They are relatively more recent in origin and their pattern conforms very well to the distribution of client population and existing clients (Exhibit 11). They are easiest to reach through public transportation and are accessible to the CBD work places and commercial remnants. The targeted services obtain a good deal of financial assistance from governmental sources with a supplement provided by private agencies. The individual siting decisions for the facilities appear quite reasonable if accessibility is the major criterion. Furthermore, they are able to occupy sites which otherwise would remain vacant. Their rents are low and minimal renovations are needed for the building to be serviceable for staff and clients. The targeted facilities do make use of volunteers, whose members exceed professional staff on the average, and para-professionals are used extensively as well. The small-scale facilities have maintained relatively low staff-to-client ratios.

A number of unanswered questions remain which relate to community and client satisfaction with service provision. Data are not available to indicate if clients receive adequate attention, care and treatment in the facilities. Data are also not available to tell us what high priority needs of the city's residents are not being met. The 61 sampled facilities attract

EXHIBIT 2

Service Facility Classification: New Brunswick

Services	Income & Economic Opportunity		Environmental & Material Needs		Health		Knowledge & Skills		Social Adjustment		Social Instrumentalities		Total	
	#	%	#	%	#	%	#	%	#	%	#	%	#	%
Common	0	0	3	3	4	5	13	15	66	77	0	0	86	100
Administrative	7	33	4	19	3	14	2	10	2	10	3	14	21	100
Targeted	5	11	10	22	7	16	5	11	16	36	2	4	45	100
Total	12	8	17	11	14	9	20	13	84	55	5	3	152	100

EXHIBIT 3

Neighboring Land Use of Service Facilities: New Brunswick
(Right and Left Neighbors)

Services	Institutional		Office		Commercial		Industrial		Residential		Vacant		Lot		Total	
	#	%	#	%	#	%	#	%	#	%	#	%	#	%	#	%
Common	18	10	6	3	44	26	2	1	84	49	15	9	3	2	172	100
Administrative	5	12	5	12	11	27	3	7	9	21	9	21	0	0	42	100
Targeted	19	21	6	7	25	28	0	0	27	30	11	12	2	2	90	100
Total	42	14	17	6	80	26	5	2	120	39	35	11	5	2	304	100

EXHIBIT 4

ZONING CLASSIFICATION OF SERVICE FACILITIES: NEW BRUNSWICK

Services	Residential		Retail		Professional		Industrial		Educational		Special		Total	
	#	%	#	%	#	%	#	%	#	%	#	%	#	%
Common	44	51	25	29	14	16	0	0	3	4	0	0	86	100
Administrative	5	24	5	24	10	48	1	4	0	0	0	0	21	100
Targeted	16	35	12	27	12	27	0	0	4	9	1	2	45	100
Total	65	43	42	27	37	24	1	1	7	4	1	1	152	100

EXHIBIT 5

PHYSICAL CONDITION OF SERVICE FACILITY RELATIVE TO SURROUNDING STRUCTURES: NEW BRUNSWICK

Services	Much Better		Better		Same		Worse		Much Worse		Total	
	#	%	#	%	#	%	#	%	#	%	#	%
Common	10	12	17	20	51	59	8	9	0	0	86	100
Administrative	6	29	0	0	15	71	0	0	0	0	21	100
Targeted	3	7	9	20	29	64	4	9	0	0	45	100
Total	19	13	26	17	95	62	12	8	0	0	152	100

EXHIBIT 6

BUILDING OCCUPANCY CHARACTERISTICS OF SERVICE FACILITIES: NEW BRUNSWICK

Services	Exclusive		Shares with Other Services		Shares with Other Nonservices		Shares with Services and Nonservices		Total	
	#	%	#	%	#	%	#	%	#	%
Common	56	65	13	15	16	19	1	1	86	100
Administrative	7	33	4	19	7	33	3	15	21	100
Targeted	14	31	14	31	13	29	4	9	45	100
Total	77	51	31	20	36	24	8	5	152	100

EXHIBIT 7

SERVICE FACILITY CONSPICUOUSNESS: NEW BRUNSWICK

Services	Inconspicuous				Neutral				Very Conspicuous		Total	
	#	%	#	%	#	%	#	%	#	%	#	%
Common	2	2	13	15	16	19	12	14	43	50	86	100
Administrative	6	29	6	29	2	9	4	19	3	14	21	100
Targeted	10	22	9	20	10	22	11	25	5	11	45	100
Total	18	12	28	18	28	18	27	18	51	34	152	100

EXHIBIT 8

Census Tract Location of Service Facilities: New Brunswick

Services	51		52		53		54		55		56		57		58		59		60		Total	
	#	%	#	%	#	%	#	%	#	%	#	%	#	%	#	%	#	%	#	%	#	%
Common	6	7	9	10	12	14	20	23	2	2	11	13	4	5	10	12	10	12	2	2	86	100
Administrative	0	0	0	0	2	9	12	57	1	5	2	9	1	5	1	5	2	10	0	0	21	100
Targeted	4	9	0	0	2	4	18	40	3	7	4	9	0	0	6	13	6	14	2	4	45	100
Total	10	7	9	6	16	10	50	33	6	4	17	11	5	3	17	11	18	12	4	3	152	100

EXHIBIT 9

Building Type for Service Facilities: New Brunswick

Services	Converted Residential		Store Front		Office Building		Institutional Building		Total	
	#	%	#	%	#	%	#	%	#	%
Common	7	8	20	23	0	0	59	69	86	100
Administrative	4	19	3	14	8	38	6	29	21	100
Targeted	13	29	3	7	9	20	20	44	45	100
Total	24	16	26	17	17	11	85	56	152	100

EXHIBIT 10

SELECTED SOCIAL AND ECONOMIC CHARACTERISTICS OF NEW BRUNSWICK
(Census Tract Numbers)

	5100	5200	5300	5400	5500	5600	5700	5800	5900	6000
Total Population	4656	4642	2911	3364	4698	4852	2342	4000	4625	5795
% Black	2	2	12	19	40	17	38	44	46	14
# over 65 (Male & female)	409	719	413	219	396	720	224	369	279	334
# in group quarters	2046	54	69	1809	19	32	0	24	1282	1040
# primary individuals	445	561	357	269	348	585	195	399	419	364
% children w/female	14	9	25	23	30	14	17	25	36	10
# persons of Spanish language	86	162	537	265	225	168	92	286	161	150
% 16-21 not in or grads of H.S.	1	4	26	7	26	6	12	14	7	4
Median school years	12.9	10.6	9.0	9.0	10.6	11.8	10.8	10.5	10.5	12.4
Residence 1965—same as 1970	1268	2817	1581	487	2013	2969	1432	1580	1527	2333
Males 16 or over inmates of inst.	22	0	81	0	0	0	0	0	0	38
Median family income 1969	13640	10162	7486	7075	7979	10670	9677	8603	6310	12852
Median unrelated ind. income 1969	1405	2566	3400	1302	2790	3775	3670	2000	1085	1091
% families below poverty level	3	8	16	23	11	6	6	11	24	2
% families below poverty level with public assistance income	0	8	28	23	58	16	59	42	40	0
Median housing value ($)	20500	20800	16200	17200	16100	20100	18000	17700	17500	22000
# owner occupied units	315	806	389	60	516	817	353	518	149	667
# renter occupied units	799	971	676	511	1014	974	454	790	988	974
Median contract rent ($)	159	99	97	85	118	110	119	111	106	138

SOURCE: U.S. Census 1970.

a total of 6,400 people to the city's core each day, a number which surpasses the daily shoppers in the CBD and surpasses as well, the number who are employed in the CBD's private sector of commerce, industry and services. Yet gaps in service provision may still be felt. Will attention to these further needs, once elaborated, lead to further clustering of service facilities within the CBD? The zoning pattern and process would appear to reinforce the degree of clustering. The stable and middle income areas of New Brunswick would be difficult targets indeed for any planned attempt at deconcentration of facilities.

Captured by the unsupported rhetoric of the "half-way house," the "group home" and the "sheltered workshop," a new form of community based institutionalization has evolved which limits the provision of service to handicapped people to an abnormal and synthetic community setting. The aggregation of professional expertise which is reasonable at the micro-level leads to unreasonable consequences at the community level. Attention to the other motto of "the least restrictive environment" would be more suitable for the planner who is a community advocate. The planner should be able to ask why the group home or half-way house is regarded as essential if many of the residents could manage in individual or shared apartments? Why is a sheltered workshop proposed by the experts when "sheltered work" is feasible and preferable? These statements are not to imply any belittlement of professional helpers, but to point to some of the disbenefits of their specialized focus on treatment sectors. This focus omits attention to two major issues which are the responsibility of the community based planner: the support system of the individual within the community; and the community as a viable unit.

The planner should keep in mind the severe bottleneck in community placements which prevent the return of additional people to community life. He should also recall the bases for the present trend toward decentralization of service provision and the justifications for advocacy in the human service sector. Furthermore, the professionalization of service provision through the public and voluntary sectors implies a growth of public commitment to disabled and handicapped people. Similar evidence is provided by the growth of recruitment into the helping professions. All of these factors add up to better resource prospects which can be brought to bear at community levels. The planner can help to insure that these additional resources are applied in a manner which is best supportive of stable communities; that communities provide a fair share to take care of their own; and that communities exercise control over service coordination.

One very specific role for the social planner is to assist the common services to develop complementary programs to the targeted services. The common services, the schools, churches, libraries, fire and police stations, and recreation facilities are more uniformly distributed and more inte-

grated within their community than are the targeted services. We understand that the targeted services were initiated because specialized programs, funding and advocacy were deemed necessary at the time of their
origination. At this point in time, however, it may be useful again to
foster the integration of service provision which could more easily occur
through expansion of the functions of the common service facilities. The
common services are not only more dispersed in their location but they
serve a wider spectrum of the population in a non-stigmatizing way. The
planner becomes an advocate for service universality and for removal of
service eligibility criteria. He uses the carrot to induce dispersal of the
handicapped people to all residential neighborhoods by agreeing to abide
by local codes against group living arrangements. He uses the power of
regulation to insure that each residential neighborhood accepts some quota
of handicapped people into its midst. The dispersal of handicapped people need not isolate them if a compensatory social support system is developed to insure their integration. In this framework, the planner is an
advocate for the least restrictive environment for handicapped people. He
is also an advocate for a community based support system.

Conclusion

The community-oriented social planner is rather poorly equipped to intervene on behalf of the concentrations of aged, needy and handicapped
people. He does not have command over resources that will make any
substantial difference in their lives. The communities in which these people are concentrated are overwhelmed by the competing and conflicting
needs of the separate groups. The dumping and the segregation and the
supervision of their care by professional helpers does not add up to community-based care or normalization. The planner can assume that the
presence of these groups in center cities is reasonably permanent and he
can assist in developing programs for housing and service support that is
atuned to the long term needs of this kind of segregated community. Alternatively, he may direct his efforts to metropolitan-wide programs which
encompass the planned dispersal of these groups according to some long-
term, equity-based quota system. Either program should be directed to
the goal of a least restrictive environment and to the integration of handicapped people within community-based support systems. The decentralization to community-based treatment and support requires that the planner exercise a different set of skills than has been in his traditional bag of
tools. The evacuation of employment and commerce from the center city
has been supplanted by a considerable infusion of public support through
income transfers and service payments-in-kind. These resources, if man-

ipulated skillfully by planners, can improve, if only modestly, the quality of life of the handicapped while simultaneous efforts at dispersal and integration are taking place.

NOTES

1. See, for example: J. Wolpert, M. Dear and R. Crawford, "Satellite Mental Health Facilities," *Annals,* Association of American Geography 65 (1975): 24-35.

2. See, H. R. Lamb, *Community Survival for Long-Term Patients* (San Francisco: Jossey-Bass, 1976).

3. See the discussion in Richard Perlman, *Consumers and Social Services* (New York: Wiley, 1975).

4. See M. Aiken, et al., *Coordinating Human Services* (San Francisco: Jossey-Bass, 1975).

5. See J. & E. Wolpert, "The Relocation of Released Mental Hospital Patients into Residential Communities," *Antipode* 6, 3 (1974).

6. See J. & E. Wolpert, "From Asylum to Ghetto," *Antipode* 6, 3 (1974).

7. *Common* facilities divide the community into catchment areas; *targeted* facilities are clustered in low-income areas; *administrative* facilities appear in the center city core.

Section III

Public Policy Planning in Change—

Macro-Planning Versus Local Control

Planning Behavior and Professional Policymaking Activity

Lawrence D. Mann

The question of whether or not "planning" is a distinct "professional" activity has elicited a remarkable amount of nonsense over recent decades. Polemic has been the mode on either side, almost incredible semantic games have been played, and there have been no generally acceptable answers. The question persists. My discussion here seeks only to apply a bit of common sense to the matter.

It is clear enough that, when a very narrow definition of "professional" is applied to a very broad concept of "planning," the "planning profession" can be shown not to exist. But the opposite is also true. Any of several quite specific definitions of planning, when examined against a very broad concept of the professional, provide an overwhelmingly strong case for the existence of professional planning activity. And some of the standard trappings of a profession are there. The interesting discussion, then, lies between the extremes for each concept.

Some kinds of planning are impossible to fit into any concept of "professional." There is "amateur" planning much as there is no end of amateur medical diagnosis, prognosis, and cellblock lawyering. But, beyond this, some things that are called "planning" are simply not specific enough to be arguably professional activities. The key question is whether some of the identifiably specific kinds of planning fit, or promise to fit in the future, a reasonably precise definition of professional activity. That is, if we can agree that some (broadly) professional planning exists, that much planning is not very professional, and that little planning is (very narrowly) professional, what kind or kinds of planning are or may become (sensible) professional activity? This complex question should become clearer below.

Problems of a Contemporary Discussion of the Question

Fifteen or twenty years ago, the question of "professional planning" might have been discussed in a more straightforward manner than is possible today. The contemporary era exhibits some attributes of hostility toward both "planning" and "professionalism," at least in important quarters of the academic wing of society. (Indeed, the convening of this conference and the commissioning of this paper must be viewed as a counter-cyclical initiative.) It will be useful to examine some of the elements of this intellectual climate before going much further.

THE RISE OF THE POLICY FIELDS

A generation ago, and in decades immediately preceding, some of the best minds of the social sciences and of public administration were concerned with "planning" questions. It was a controversial topic, involving the disentangling of ideology from rationality, of calculation from control, of the latter from market and political processes, and of communications dynamics in governmental and other bureaucracies. These interests, as well as some new ones, now are concentrated in programs called "policy science," "public policy," "policy analysis," "policy development," etc. The idea of "planning" is largely ignored, and in some cases it is aggressively attacked. In at least one current approach, "planning with a small P" is treated as tolerable but trivial usage while "planning with a big P" [1] is to be rejected out of hand. The transition between the usages is fairly clear in the writing of Yzekiel Dror and John Friedmann, where quite clear concepts of planning have given way to cursory treatments or even total avoidance of the concept.[2] The older careful distinctions between planning and other kinds of administrative decision-making or social practice have disappeared.

The content of the new "policy" fields is far from homogeneous. In some places it is little more than a version of applied political science, modifying an older body of public administration doctrine. More often, however, there is a strong infusion of economics of one kind or another. In some cases this becomes markedly econometric, with much more attention to quantitative techniques than to content.

Particularly instructive are those instances where new "policy" fields are being developed aggressively alongside existing "planning" programs of a certain legitimated stature—as has occurred in some universities. The two programs become competitive but distinguishable from each other only by the most imaginative hair-splitting on matters of style. (That most of the "planning" programs are nominally concerned with urban and regional questions is little help; for they may be actually concerned with questions more at a national than a local level, and there is nothing to keep the "policy" field from moving into the local and urban sphere in response to opportunities.) * It may well be that time will arbitrate this curious overlap between "planning" and "policy" in institutional settings. But it would seem preferable to think through these two concepts and

---

*Regardless of what suspicions may come to mind, I do not have any one particular situation in mind: There are at least three to which this discussion applies equally well.

fields. Though complex, the relationship should be possible to clarify. It is clear enough that neither mutual scorn nor unilateral subordination is appropriate.

Clearly, policy is the source of most kinds of planning. Planning provides the strategy and sometimes the tactics for broad policy guidelines. This is the main distinction, surely. However, very broad planning (the strategy of even broader policy) may provide the basis for more specific policies. None of this is novel, and it is the usage we shall follow below, even though this much explicit attention to planning is slightly out of fashion currently.

INTERNAL ANTI-PROFESSIONALISM

Another problem with discussing the selected question is the thinly-masked anti-professionalism of a number of leading intellectuals and academics internal to the planning movement—notably my own area of urban and regional planning. How this has come about is fairly clear. When, after World War II, a number of social scientists moved into this field, they were confronted with a thrust toward a narrow physical planning professionalization drawing upon architecture, engineering, and the law. The highly impactful University of Chicago interdisciplinary doctoral program in planning resisted both physicalism and localism and thus opposed the professional thrust of the day. Planning-qua-planning, moreover, was a vast and exciting intellectual enterprise that could only be hindered by the characteristic strictures of professionalization. (There were some who thought that, at some time in the future, this pervasive kind of planning would have sufficient knowledge, principles, and techniques to become a profession—at least that seems implicit in Tugwell's "Fourth Power" concept and in some work of the period by Perloff, Banfield, and Meyerson. But that was for later.)

The anti-professional strain became characteristic of many of the leading university centers of planning during the ensuing years and decades: University of Pennsylvania (since the mid-1950s), Harvard (variably since 1957), Berkeley (since the mid-1960's), MIT (since the later-1960's), and many other centers. Even after all pretense at narrow physical planning professionalization was dropped by the profession in the mid-1960s, the anti-professional trend continued.[3] Nor was there any strong and sustained effort to discover much fundamental knowledge about planning, its overriding principles, and techniques consistent with these. Effort rather turned to the study of the city, sectors of activity, the "in" specialties, and the almost blind aping of techniques from economics, quantitative geography, and engineering. Not many "planning" academics are prepared even to discuss any kind of professional planning today. On those occasions when the matter is even raised, it is greeted by reactions ranging from quiet embarrassment to protests that any professionalization of the field would be an infringement on academic freedom! Only the pressure from newly career-oriented students and from some university officials has been able to stimulate some ventures in return to the question of professional education and research. (If planning isn't a profession, for purposes of its location in a university, then what is it?) But the basic anti-professionalism of many planning academics will persist for some time to come, making such discussions as the present one a difficult form of communication.

Compounding the difficulties of overt anti-professionalism is the recent increase of a more invidious form that might be called "perverse nominal professionalism." This has been the response of some anti-professional-ists to current pressures. The trick is to call it "professional" education, incorporate some of the surface trappings of a professional approach, but to avoid any of the critical commitments of real professional activity. This has worked well so far, but there is always the possibility that countervailing tendencies will develop.

"TROJAN HORSE" PROFESSIONALISM

Quite a different kind of difficulty for the present discussion is the long-standing pattern of established professions being incorporated into the field. As mentioned, in traditional urban and regional planning the main professions were architecture, engineering, and the law. Similar patterns have been evident in other kinds of planning—even medicine in the emergent field of health planning. During times when this absorp-tion is relatively gradual, there is no great problem; for the members of the established professions may become more committed to planning than to their profession of origin. During periods of rather rapid growth, however, large numbers of unassimilated "other" professionals accumulate. Having their prime loyalty to their established profession, they have little interest in professional development of the new field. They are quite content to let planning remain what I have called elsewhere an "umbrella" field.[4]

With the increased intellectualization of planning during recent decades, disciplines that behave like professions demonstrate the same tendencies within planning. Most notable here is economics. While very clubbish about who is "really an economist," they tend to be, understandably enough, quite resistant to any attempts to be precise about who is a planner—and thus intolerant of efforts toward our meaningful profes-sional development. Since economics and economists have come to dominate urban planning overwhelmingly of late, the problem of "trojan horse professionalism" from that quarter will become more serious, until economists tire of planning or planners are able to put forward a convincing line of thought more central to planning.

The above tendencies have made, and still make, serious discussion of planning behavior problematic, particularly where professional development is touched upon. Indeed, if one were to rely on these major currents of the North American public policy and urban and regional planning body of thought, one might expect that serious discussion of "planning" is on its way out. However, there is plenty of healthy thinking about planning in some other quarters.

Where Vital Discussion of Planning Thrives

Thinking about planning is alive and well in at least three loci outside the traditional strongholds of political science, economics, and their synthetic public sector application. The first of these is in the study of group and organizational processes, based on group social psychology. A second is in corporate and other organizational planning, which is related but distinct. And the third is in public sector planning in Britain and other European countries, at various levels and in various sectors. This is not the place to summarize all of this discussion, but a glimpse of each body of thought should be provided.

THE SOCIAL PLANNING PROCESS SOURCE

The behavioral aspect of planning has often been neglected for varying reasons. But an increasingly insistent body of thought has developed in this area in recent years, providing important nourishment to what discussion persists in the traditional bastions of planning.

The initial concern of applying small group psychology to planning seems to have come in the search for understanding the problems of one person "planning" for another in a "helping" relationship. A dynamic of planned change was analyzed.[5] The same kind of thinking soon became applied to whole communities and then, more concretely, to organizations within them.[6] Here there was the intersection with a vast body of group psychology applied to the problems of business organizations for a much longer period.

Similar ideas came to be applied to planning for national social policy and, by extension, to the consideration of all kinds of centrally planned change.[7] There was some intersection here with writers on planning who were interested in the same subject from a different vantage point.[8] But much of the really original thinking came from the behavioral science side.

Similarly, the applied behavioral sciences were highly important in articulating long range, almost futurist, social planning.[9] (The "hard" social
sciences are practically worthless for such purposes, it seems.) The best
of this discussion centers around the concept of "learning" to plan so that
society can learn to adapt to the inevitable fundamental changes that
lie ahead.

A more exhaustive treatment of this social planning thought, based on
the behavioral sciences, would take far more time and space than we
can give it here. But much of it has already worked itself into at least
the margins of mainstream planning thought, through the work of some
social planners of the traditional mainstream. One final point on this
body of thinking should be made, however. The original impetus for
it was the unblushing profession of social work. And, for all the amor-
phousness, ambiguity and incomplete coherence of this social planning
thought, it remains a vivid arena for discussing planning with *professional*
applicability.

CORPORATE PLANNING

The explosion of high-quality discussion of planning in the private
sector may come as a surprise to those who have not followed it closely.
At least one major commentator has been so impressed by the concentration of planning expertise in the large corporations as to call it "the planning sector" of American society.[10] It is ironic that the private sector and
its ideologues in economics were so instrumental in deprecating "planning" to such an extent that public policy people avoid the concept, and
then proceeded to develop planning in the private corporate sector. But
the private sector has been a good location to work out some of the
problems of planning thought.

Corporate planning thought has become abundant, variegated, and technically sophisticated without losing close touch with concrete examples.
The mark of its present maturity is that several serious popularizations
of the subject have been written.[11] There seems to be a remarkable
degree of consensus about the main issues in corporate planning.

While, again, space and time limits preclude any exhaustive treatment
of corporate planning here, we may identify several main points in this
body of thought that have implications for the present discussion. These
are as follows:

1. The best corporate planning discussion rests on behavioral science
insights into group processes and organizational dynamics, often using
systems-theoretic perspectives, as well as approaches more traditional in
administrative and economics frameworks.[12]

2. Corporate planning thought is quite clear on the distinction between "planning" and other kinds of "management." "Planning" is almost always reserved for decision-making when there is a major organizational change in prospect—either because of a change in the organization's environment or due to an internal change of fundamental importance, or a mix of both. "Management" refers to administration between such changes, when used separately from "planning." Of course some "planning capability" is maintained at all times to be able to cope with major future changes, and this ongoing planning activity is a branch of current management. And it is possible to think of even the major planning phases as "change management." Thus while the relationship is subtle and complex, it is clear enough to avoid major confusion.[13]

3. There is generally a clear recognition of two levels of corporate planning: (a) pervasive and high-level planning in the sense that the chief executive officer is the chief planner and that planning must take place throughout the organization if it is to be effective; and (b) a more specific kind of planning that may be lodged in an administrative entitity of that name and which backstops the more pervasive and high-level sense of planning. It is also understood that this latter planning agency must be more than just a technical research bureau if it is to function well in organizational planning.[14]

4. Much of the supportive technical work for corporate planning consists of quite elaborate quantitative analysis. But there is plenty of indication that this can be easily overdone unless great care is taken to communicate the sense of methods and of conclusions to others who cannot follow the details of such analyses. Moreover, there is a clear thrust toward developing techniques that are specific to the kinds of change situations of concern, rather than relying on the existing kit of tools of economics and engineering.[15]

5. Corporate planning thought is very much open to outside discussions. One of the first major books on corporate planning was written by an urban and regional planner, and one of the better of the recent books on the subject cites approvingly the literature of both urban planning and of social planning.[16] It is difficult to account for the lack of reciprocity to date, for there would seem to be important lessons from corporate planning developments for other kinds of planning.

BRITISH AND EUROPEAN PUBLIC PLANNING

The reticence and even antipathy of the American policy fields toward planning has had little counterpart in most other nations. For years the developing countries have been a focus for multi-level public planning (and for Americans who were serious about these matters). There have also been important initiatives in some West European countries, not to mention the pervasive planning systems of the socialist countries. In countries such as Sweden and France where urban planning was pretty firmly in the hands of the architects, much of the interest was at the national and regional levels. Developments in France in recent years have made the discussion of public planning at several levels much more coherent, and that thought has been well engaged. This is true to some degree in Italy, Holland and several other countries. But the most dramatic development of planning in public policy has undoubtedly been in Britain.

Fifteen years ago, Britain would have seemed an unlikely setting for the development of vital discussion of planning issues. The inspiration for "muddling through" at the national level, with alternating administrations undercutting any beginnings of sustained planning, the country had a regional policy that was notoriously ineffective and near incomprehensible. There was a strong body of town planning statutory authority and a clearcut profession to go with it, but all this seemed to add up to such a narrow, closed system that any fresh thinking about planning seemed quite impossible. Certainly this was much the picture that American planners came away with at that time.[17]

What happened to British planning thought on the way to the 1970's is undoubtedly complex, but a good part of it was that British planners and public officials took their American critics seriously in a way that was almost without precedent. Moreover, they picked up the whole conceptual, theoretical, and technical baggage of the largely ignored public planning thought in the United States, incorporated whole chunks of it into their own approach, and adapted and took further still other parts. The result is a remarkable body of planning thought with some of the following characteristics.

1. The systems approach is generally accepted as the basis for planning thought in Britain. This implies varying degrees of complexity in what is being planned, ranging from interaction of elements in an urban environment to fairly sophisticated information-theoretic hypotheses about planning processes themselves.[18]

2. There is a great willingness to experiment with analytic frameworks and quantitative techniques of various kinds, some of them highly speculative formulations by American academics. The failure rate is high, but the failures are faced up to; and there seems to be some progress toward concentrating on more promising lines of "new planning" technology.[19]

3. There is some considerable attention to issues of public involvement and participation in various kinds of planning processes.[20]

4. British planning is clearly anchored at the urban planning level, but it is stretched therefrom to concerns at regional and national levels, par-

ticularly in matters of resource allocation issues and of income distribution changes.[21]

5. There is some general acceptance of a basic three-fold classification of kinds of planning:
   a. Policy development
   b. Analysis
   c. Design[22]

The first two are of course of general applicability while the third is limited to local physical planning, at least in most usage.

6. There remains a clear view of planning as a profession moving out from concerns of traditional urban physical planning into broader responsibilities in scope and scale. It is recognized to be an imperfect and an incomplete profession, and it is understood that the broader reaches of some "structure" plans and all "policy" plans will be shared with other professions.[23]

7. The development of local corporate planning processes is perhaps the most interesting development in British planning thought and practice. This began with "strategic choice" approaches to solving a wide range of local governmental problems, but it has now proved itself in the political process and seems to be catching on rapidly under central government impetus. This is the area of "policy planning," including, and sometimes directed by, the traditional urban planning professionals. The flavor of advanced analytic frameworks and methods of quantitative analysis are characteristic, and there is plenty of evidence that some of the main ideas of private sector corporate planning have been ignored. But accommodation to the political process has already taught some important lessons, and more are sure to follow.[24]

8. There is solid thinking about what present planners would have to do and to learn how to do to be able to participate more broadly in the changing reality of such broad planning, as well as other changes in British society. This is also reflected in thought about planning education, where some solid proposals are starting to be implemented.[25]

9. British planning thought exhibits a strong sense of responsibility for developing international comparisons of planning of various kinds and at various levels. The British are also concerned about where they get their planning ideas and how their own planning ideas will be used in other countries—including both Middle Eastern countries and the United States. In view of this attitude, it is not surprising that British planners have taken the lead in developing a remarkable comparative study of national, regional, and urban planning in Britain, France, and Italy.[26]

We have seen in this part of the paper that vital planning discussion is going on in the social planning/behavioral science area, in private sector corporate planning, and in British and some European public planning. With some exposure to these somewhat surprising sources of high-quality thought on planning, as well as to the communications problems due to "planning" and professional concerns being presently out of vogue in some sectors, we may turn to a restatement of the key concern of this paper.

The Question Revisited

Let us now look more closely at the behavior that is planning and at what may be called "professional activity" related to policymaking. Each may be taken in turn.

MICRO-PLANNING BEHAVIOR

The reluctance of the policy fields to treat "planning" seriously has not prevented the production of a huge amount of writing on the subject in the U.S. public sphere. Except for the areas of behavioral science-based social planning and intracorporate planning just discussed, however, most of this writing has the flavor of a subordinate body of thought—alternately grandiose and defensive. (I include here much of the writing by urban and regional planning academics, not excluding some of my own.) This is nowhere clearer than in the failure to come to grips with the essence of planning behavior. The basic defect, I believe, has been to treat this key matter too superficially and from a macro perspective. (The macro perspectives of much of economics, political science and sociology make writers from these sources quite clumsy at the individual and group behavioral level; and pre-Liebenstein microeconomists are scarcely better.) [27]

For purposes of any professional considerations, it is most critical to understand the behavior of individual practitioners. And this is best understood at the behavioral-science microlevel, rather than from facile generalizations drawn from national societal guidance systems or even of "organizations" viewed from the top down. I would like to develop here the beginnings of such an approach to essential planning behavior.

THE ESSENCE OF PLANNING

Planning is one kind of human behavior and thus involves the activities of individual human beings, often in groups or organizations. That planning is more specific than behavior itself should be clear enough to thoughtful people. Purely emotional or capricious behavior, totally reflexive or habitual behavior, and completely traditional behavior are all quite distinct from planning behavior.[28]

Planning behavior involves some degree of calculation for the purpose of governing future sequences of actions. In this, it resembles "decision-making" behavior, on the one hand, and "management" behavior, on the other.[29] Yet it is distinguishable from both.

The behavior that may properly be called "planning" explicitly draws upon a value-structured "memory" or "record" for the criteria by which to evaluate prospective action-sequences.[30] It is rational only in the psychological sense. Decision-making behavior, on the other hand, takes goals as given from outside and adheres to a standard of rationality which is tantamount to economic efficiency.[31]

The idea of "management behavior" is broad so that, for organizations, planning should be thought of as a specific function, or method, or style within it. What differentiates planning from management behavior in general is that planning concentrates on (a) non-immediate futures;[32] and (b) action sequences (chains of actions and consequences typically with a minimum of three iterations) rather than the more typical management action-consequence unit.[33] It can be argued, on the other hand, that planning is even more separable from management behavior. This argument is sometimes made at the level of governments, from municipal to national, where the significance of political variables makes "management" take on a very reduced meaning.[34] (Indeed, even the term is used for whole governments only at the municipal level.) But the separability of planning from management is even clearer at the level of individual behavior and in group behavior, where the use of the idea of management would be "reaching." Individual planning and group planning, however, do very clearly exist.[35]

PERSONAL PLANNING

It is at the level of the individual that the essence of planning ought to be first understood, for all planning (just as all behavior) is by individuals in the first instance. It may be at this level that our understanding of planning behavior is most complete, and there are in any case sound reasons for beginning the discussion at this level.[36]

Individual planning is a conscious, cerebral process, directed at governing sequences of activity.[37] Such planning is based on value-structured information and knowledge available to the individual. This means that the "why" of intended activity-sequences is consciously explicit. "Subconscious planning" would be a contradiction in terms; and, because of the crucial importance of memory, no victim of amnesia could conceivably plan until at least partial recovery. The memory, organized and structured by learned values, combines with current experiences to form a series of views of likely futures.[38] Many of these future-views are matters of indifference to the individual; but some are highly regarded (potential opportunities) and others are of serious concern (potential problems). It is these latter, particularly the potential problems, that provide the basis for criteria to govern activity sequences. These criteria become tests against which operational activities will be compared.[39] As Kenneth Boulding has written:

> The human condition can almost be summed up in the observation that, whereas all experiences are of the past, all decisions are about the future. . . . The image of the future is the key to all choice-oriented behavior. . . . The individual's image of the future is . . . the most significant determinant of his personal behavior.[40]

Individual planning is "rational" in the psychological rather than the economic sense of that term. The future-images are recognized and evaluated consciously and they include some possible options for the individual's action-sequences. Moreover, some of the probable consequence-chains of these action-sequences will be in the individual's memory. And there will be a "comfortable" process of partial calculation and choice about which of the main options to select. But only in the most extreme circumstances would even the rarest of individuals ever approach the kind of "economic rationality" that is utility-maximization and optimization.[41]

Planning is cybernetic in nature, as is behavior itself. As mentioned, it moves experimentally against general criteria provided by value-structured knowledge. Behavioral effort is amplified or dampened, or simply continued, until a "fit" is confirmed by test—or else the individual tires of trying with a plan in effect and abandons this for a new plan. It is in this sense that planning is learning behavior. Accordingly, the planning that survives and thrives in the individual will be most dependably that which is positively rewarded. Plans that fail, in the sense of producing very negative consequences, will not have a symmetrical tendency to reduce planning in general, or even very similar kinds of planning. Rather the individual will learn to *avoid the negative consequences* next time such planning is undertaken. Or he may avoid the particular context, or plan anxiously.[42]

Individual planning is hierarchical, in two different senses. First, there is a general structure of planning that begins with a "plan for planning," to more intermediate frameworks for planning of certain kinds and for certain times and situations, to more specific plans themselves. Secondly, each plan has its own internal structure. The terminology of the successively smaller components of a plan is not important, but one nomenclature is as follows: "Programs" make up a plan and are in turn made up of "projects," which are made up of "project components." "Strategy" is the sequencing of programs, while 'tactics" is the sequencing of projects, and "action" is the carrying-out of project components.[43]

Individual planning is often only in rough outline form: a general sequence of intended program strategies, project tactics, and actions. Detailed activity sequences are often left to later planning or to opportunistic decision. The degree of completeness of the outlines depends on the situation, the tastes of the individual, and his skills.

DIMENSIONS OF PERSONAL PLANNING

Personal planning varies according to individual abilities and individual definitions of specific situations. One of the matters on which planning varies is the *source of plans*. While plans are mostly borrowed with some adaptations from past experience, some individuals always borrow with practically no adaptation while others adapt very extensively.

Least frequent but most impressive is true invention of plans, with only minor borrowing. More usually, individuals adjust the amounts of borrowing and adaptation to the situation as they understand it.[44] Environmental pressure encourages inventiveness.

Another dimension of variation in individual planning is the *time span*. It is well known that most people can plan with only relatively short periods. However, some are capable of very short spans, while others plan easily for quite extensive periods. Again, this often varies according to the situation and the way it is viewed. Pressure for long-range planning comes only with a combination of clear long-range crisis and short-range leisure.

A third dimension of variability in planning is the extent to which plans are *internally consistent*. Typically, human individual planning is far from perfect on this score, yet still quite impressive. People learn to become more careful about the consistency of their plans in more stressful situations—up to crisis points, beyond which there is rapid breakdown. Related to this is the dimension of the *relative rigidity* or flexibility of plans. People with rigid plans must pay more attention to internal consistency, whereas those who plan more flexibly (rough outline form) may be able to tolerate slightly greater "looseness" in the relative consistency of plans. This is because flexible plans allow for later, incremental plans to correct any "bugs" that may be in the initial outline. Both the relative consistency and the relative flexibility are, again, partly matters of skill and partly matters of learned adaptation to situation.

Even more closely related to skill is the *speed* at which individual planning takes place. And this, in turn, is related to the *information retrieval* aspects of the planning. That is, planning that requires very little information retrieval during the action sequences intended may be much more rapidly accomplished. This is not always the case, however, for some people are quite skillful in planning rapidly for sequences that will require a great deal of information retrieval at various stages, while others are very slow at achieving plans with relatively little information content.

The final dimension of planning skill and situation adaptation is that of *perseverance vs. "stop orders."* That is, some individual planning is characterized by persistence in a planning pattern with no apparent reinforcement through reward, while other individuals rapidly give up on a plan if no accomplishment is quickly experienced. Some clearly give up too soon. The most skillful personal planners are those who vary the degree of perseverance according to situation, not giving up too soon but not staying with a hopeless plan. And, in general, humans do learn how to stay or quit pretty well; for perseverance is mainly a matter of learning.[45]

EXTENDING MICROPLANNING BEHAVIOR

In the above paragraphs, I have tried to outline some main understanding of the essential nature of planning by examining it closely at the level of individual behavior. There is certainly much more to be worked out on this level, but the treatment of it just covered will have to be sufficient for now. Even if we had complete understanding of individual human planning, however, there would be no automatic extension of it to group and organizational levels—much less to communities and nations.

The General Systems Approach—One possible way of extending individual planning behavior to groups, organizations, etc. is suggested by general systems theory. All of these may be thought of as "open systems" in Bertalanffy's terms; and, by logical homologies, what holds at the level of a subsystem may be argued to hold for an inclusive system. Indeed, it was Bertalanffy himself, in a little remarked passage, who opened the door to the discussion of planning in open system terms. He says that the most complex kind of "finality" is "planning intelligence," going beyond the mere "equifinality" that is characteristic of all open systems. "Planning intelligence," in those particular open systems where it is found, is based on the phenomenon that the future end is already present in thought and directs present action.[46]

The prototype open system in which planning intelligence occurs is, as we have just seen, the human individual. The only problem for extension, then, is to work through the logical homologies from the human individual to those other open systems, the human group, the human organization, the human community, and the human nation. This is precisely what Richard Meier attempted,[47] but the result is not totally convincing. Too many problems of acceptance remain for general systems theory to be used quite in this way as yet.

The main problems with general systems theory for bridging micro- to macro- are twofold. The first is that it will mask the central importance of individual humans in planning activity by abstracting to "actors" who may be one or more individuals—or even whole organizations. While this is certainly convenient for some purposes, it is not appropriate for a discussion of possible professional activity. Secondly, as mentioned, much of general systems theory remains "counter-intuitive." This is not bad in itself, of course, but it does put the burden of demonstrating overwhelmingly powerful conclusions that convince people that an approach, though not understood, must be right. General systems theory has not yet achieved such powerful conclusions and would therefore provide a weak bridge for our purposes.

Microaggregation Approach—A second approach to bridging from individual planning to group and organizational planning would be aggregation, as in economic utility theory. Thus planning at the group level would be the aggregation of the various planning behaviors, with due allowance for conflicting planning. In this approach, planning could be thought of as "future concern", a vector of more specific planning behaviors (the dimensions just discussed), to be integrated with the more general vector of "constraint concern." From this point, planning behavior would aggregate quite straight-forwardly into group, firm, and by extension into organizations, communities and nations—indeed everywhere that microeconomics is arguably applicable.[48]

It does seem probable that some such aggregation approach will be the way to move from individual planning to group, organizational, and community and national planning. However, there is one particular conceptual clarification that will be necessary for sensible discussion of planning at these other levels.

Planner-Performer Levels of Behavior—The most important single difference between individual planning and planning at higher levels is the *separation of the planner from the performer*. An individual planner is his own implementation agent. Can this be true of other levels of planning behavior?

At the level of a small group, if there is very strong consensus on learned values and if the experiences are largely shared, it is possible for this collectivity to behave much as an individual planner: the planning is done collectively, and the action sequences are carried out collectively.

For more heterogeneous groups, larger groups, and organizations, however, it is not possible to expect full consensus on values, full sharing of experiences, or collective carrying out of action sequences in plans. Moreover, in such groups and organizations there is specialization of function such that those who work through the plans are almost never the same people who carry out the main activity sequences. Before going any further, therefore, it will be well to specify the main kinds of planning by "planner" and "performer."

It has become rather usual to refer to the abstract "actor" in group and organizational analysis. For our purposes, however, it matters very much whether an "actor" presumes or is presumed to "plan" or not. Thus we make the distinction between "planning actor" and "performing actor", or, more briefly, "planner" and "performer."

If it is of the very nature of planning at levels other than the individual that the performer is often not the planner, the specification of who plans and who carries out the behavioral sequences is crucial. Indeed, this may be the most important variable in specifying the kinds and levels of planning behavior.[49]   An attempt to work through the implications of this specification is presented in Table I.

It will be evident that we have given central importance to the "performer" in identifying the main levels of planning. For example, for group planning, we ask, "Who plans?" While the group may, as a unit, plan for itself, as discussed above, it will be more typical for it to *delegate* some planning—or have it *applied* or *imposed* from another group or a high organization. And it is necessary to know the planner-performer breakdown inside a group, or the extent of outside planning, before planning behavior can be well understood at that level. The potential payoff from a fuller understanding of group planning is considerable. Since we are building up planning behavior in a manner quite parallel to Leibenstein's approach,[50] results of similar importance may be expected. For instance, Leibenstein's theory of selective rationality produces "bands of insensitivity" to pressure which result in "inert areas, " where an individual will not alter behavior in response to increased pressure. At the group level, these "inert areas" act as a "lubricant" between members even when there is a high degree of required interdependence. But, the higher the required interdependence, the more difficult it is for individuals who are highly "sensitive" to changes in outside pressure.   From this is inferred the need for some internal delegation or outside consultation to remove or decrease the intragroup pressure on highly sensitive members.[51] This becomes the simplest kind of a "social planning" phenomenon. And it is almost certain that other kinds of specialized planning behavior, delegated or consultant, arise in very much the same way.

Group size is also important as it effects the kind of planning behavior that will occur. Leibenstein is able to show that, the larger the group, the larger will be the group "inert area" and the more inflexible will be the group as to changes in its "group effort position." The dif-

TABLE I
TYPES OF PLANNING BY "PLANNING ACTOR" AND "PERFORMING ACTOR"

Planner	Performer	Individual	Group	Organization "Corporate"	Community	Nation/State
Individual	Primary	Personal	Group (Member-Delegated)	Organization (Member-Delegated)	Community (Member-Delegated)	National/State (Member-Delegated)
	Other	Individual (Delegated, Applied, or Imposed)	Group (Consultant-Delegated)	Organization (Consultant-Delegated)	Community (Consultant-Delegated)	National/State (Consultant-Delegated)
Group	Primary	Individual (Group-Applied)	Group-Auto	Organization (Constituent Group-Delegated)	Community (Constituent Group-Delegated)	National/State (Constituent Group-Delegated)
	Other	Individual (Group-Imposed)	Group (Consultant-Group-Delegated or Imposed)	Organization (Consultant-Group-Delegated)	Community (Consultant Group-Delegated)	National/State (Consultant-Group-Delegated)
Organization	Primary	Individual (Organization-Applied)	Group (Organization-Applied)	Organization-Auto "Corporate"	Community (Constituent-Organization Delegated)	National/State (Member Organization Delegated)
	Other	Individual (Organization-Imposed)	Group (Organization-Imposed)	Organization (Consultant Organization-Delegated or Imposed)	Community (Consultant Organization-Delegated, or Imposed)	National/State (Consultant-Delegated, or Nonmember Organization-Imposed)

ficulties in introducing such changes imply, when planning and performing behavior are distinguished as I do, that the planning effort will
increase with group size—if the group is to survive in the face of environmental change. It is known that another way to increase flexibility
in large groups is to split up into a hierarchy of smaller groups—
which requires considerable planning. But such a break-down of large
groups almost inevitably involves the creation of a human organization,
without which the communication between units would become impossible.[52]

On planning behavior at the level of the complex human organization, we have had some substantial understanding for some years.
Some of this has come, as indicated earlier, from corporate planning
where it intersects with organizational planning. Ruth Mack's recent
synthesis of much of the understanding of organizational planning
behavior and its relation to decisionmaking has coined the term
"DOSRAP" to clarify the nature of planning at this level—in both the
public and private sectors.[53] The letters stand for "deliberative, ongoing, sequential, recursive, administrative process." And this concept,
of course, is remarkably consistent with the nature of planning discussed
below at the individual level. From these findings, a number of remarkable guidelines to deal with problems of uncertainty can be developed.[54]
From the present approach, we would expect these to vary according
to who is doing the planning for the organization.

It will be rare that an organization delegates to one individual all the
planning for its activity sequences, over any period of time, and over
any substantial range of questions. Such total delegation is conceivable
only as a limiting case. Consultants will be used frequently, but normally
for specific matters over short time spans. More usual will be to delegate
organizational or corporate planning to a group within. (External consultant groups, again, will be for a narrow range of matters, and briefly.)
An organization may be said to "plan for itself" to the extent that the
broad range of membership is involved substantively over an appreciable
period of time. This will be rare but quite effective in "situation change"
planning efforts. More day-to-day preparatory planning will be largely
delegated. At times an outside organization may act as a consultant,
or, in some circumstance, impose its planning on another organization.
There are enough examples of this to make it worthy of serious treatment
in a discussion of organizational or corporate planning.

A human community may be treated as one kind of an "organization",
but it has enough particular characteristics to merit its being treated
as a special category. Certainly where, as in urban planning, the community is a localized one which includes a variety of organizations, it
deserves separate treatment. Communities have in the past delegated

important planning to individuals, usually consultants, or to groups, typically, planning boards. But, more recently, there has been a tendency to delegate a combination of internal organizations, planning departments in local government, and outside consulting organizations. Yet much of the planning that governs local community activity sequences is applied by organizations of higher governmental levels. And more than is well-recognized is imposed by private corporations with an interest in what happens in a given local community.[55] It is important to recall, however, than even if an "organization" does the planning, individual planners within the organization are the fundamental planning actors.

At the national or state level, similarly, delegation of planning to individuals or even to groups may be expected to be so limited in time and subject matter as to be practically trivial. Planning behavior at these levels is primarily done by organizations, through which individual planners and planning groups work. Again, in our approach, we know the planning is going on because of the nature of the activity sequences. It thus becomes important to specify who is doing the planning, how, and with what kind of direct or indirect results.

Evolutionary Learning-Planning—Edgar Dunn has worked out quite carefully the way organizational planning is tied to social learning at the level of the national society.[56] Social and economic development is seen as an evolutionary process of social learning. The predictions of planners become sub-processes of hypothesis exploration and development (though not formal testing) in successively unique situations. Planning itself becomes a form of experimental design, based upon the developmental hypotheses and the new modes of behavior these include. In this approach, planning will often fail (much as mutations in biological evolution often do not pass the environmental test). But where planning yields recognized improvement in a system, it will be reinforced and endure.

Prediction and planning in Dunn's framework have two main modes. The first of these is a normal, ongoing practice of gradual system improvement according to accepted system goals. But, from time to time, this normal-state planning reveals problems with the ongoing stream of change (or new knowledge may fundamentally change the way the situation is seen). At such points, the "Image" of the system entity and of its ends are themselves subject to revision. Prediction becomes a developmental hypothesis that a fundamentally new "game" for a markedly different system would yield appreciably superior results. And essential planning behavior consequently becomes the preparation of an experimental design for a fundamentally new situation, in which the system itself and its rules may become changed. Michael [57] and others have followed Dunn's lead in thinking at this national-society level.

This kind of evolutionary learning, of course, is quite consistent with thinking at the organizational level. The work of Herbert Simon and associates has pointed in this direction for years.[58] Ruth Mack's work is consistent with both Simon and Dunn and becomes quite concrete in applications to learning in planning at the organizational level. And much of the corporate planning thought we have reviewed follows much the same lines.

At the level of individual planning, the work by Miller and others is also consistent with this experimental learning view. Even more explicit on the subject is Skinner,[59] who is quite eloquent on the way the combined social and physical environments select out behavior in the process of individual learning.

What we have, then, are a remarkable series of parallels in essential planning behavior as we move from individual, to groups and organizations, to local national community, "regional" and national society, and back down. It is on this basis that planning behavior can be understood, I am convinced, for purposes of developing a coherent body of thought for professional activity.

The Nature of Professional Activity

We have all been told a great deal about professionalism. For forty years and more we have been made aware of the increasing professionalization of modern society. We are told that business has become professionalized; and so have the military, politics, and even labor. While these descriptions and interpretations have often been presented as objective analyses, the subtle message of intellectuals is that the negative consequences of increased professional activity are greater than the positive. Careful specifications of the nature of professional activity have been quite rare, however, and other conclusions are possible.

According to Alfred North Whitehead's famous distinction between craft activity and professional activity, craft behavior is based on custom and trial and error of individual practice; but professional activity is based on theoretical analysis and is modified by conclusions from such analysis.[60] Other writers have stressed the importance of professional services being based on knowledge not accessible to clients, or real or claimed special skills, of particular objectivity on the subject matter, of the demand for client trust, of close solidarity internal to a profession, of intra-professional codes of ethics and policing, and symbolic rewards—as well as the related matter of responsibility, for individual professional actions.[61]

Some writers have attempted to take these criteria to their logical extreme, to distill them to their essence, and arrive at an "ideal type" of profession with which to compare supposed ones in the real world. Goode has produced the most notable of these analyses.[62] He speaks of the "generating traits" of professional activity, and he finds it possible to reduce these to two or three—though each of considerable complexity.

Goode's first "generating trait" of professional activity is *professional knowledge*. Ideally, this is abstract and organized into a *codified body of principles*, while at the same time supposedly *applicable to concrete problems* of living. Key members of a society should believe that the applied *knowledge can actually solve a set of problems*, and they should accept that it is *appropriate to delegate* these problems to some occupational group posessing applicable *knowledge not generally held* in the population. The resulting *profession* itself *should have a role in* creating, organizing, and transmitting the *knowledge and related skills*. This, in part assures that the knowledge and related skills will be substantial enough, and hard enough to acquire, as to provide them with *some effective degree of "mystique"* on the part of clients. This knowledge is also related to the *professional organization* having an important *voice in arbitrating any disputes* of validity of technical solutions within the area of the profession's supposed competence.

The second "generating trait" that Goode identifies is the *service ideal*. This implies that *technical solutions* proposed by the professional should be *based on client needs*, which may not be in the best material interest of the professional himself—or indeed for the society at large. Yet it is the *professional* who, after thorough consultation with the client, *decides what is in the best interest of the client* in the matter at hand. ("The more the client dominates the judgment, the less professional is the relationship.") Yet *real sacrifice is demanded of professionals* (as an ideal, and occasionally, in fact). Some of this "sacrifice" is nothing more than the cost of *acquiring professional knowledge*, but there is the further demand of *defending unpopular truths* implied by professional knowledge. Moreover, the profession undertakes to *speed obsolescence of its own members* by (a) contributing to the generation of new knowledge of the profession's subject and (b) recruiting new and talented younger professionals. It is essential that outsiders believe that these *ideals are given more than lip service* by the professionals. A key way of accomplishing this is for the profession to have a *system of visible rewards and punishments* such that *the practitioner who conspicuously lives by the service ideal appears as more successful than another who overtly does not.*[63]

A third trait, *autonomy*, in part crosscuts these other two. Goode sees it being derived from knowledge and service:

"Occupations, like people, claim the right of autonomy and usually fail to get it. Professional autonomy—in a bureaucratic era, this means having one's behavior judged by colleague peers, not outsiders—is a derivative trait and is based on both the mastery of a knowledge field and commitment to the ideal of service."

It is not surprising that Goode's analysis of actual and would-be professions, yielded a fairly clear-cut ranking. At the top are the "four great persons professions": medicine, the psychotherapies, the confessional clergy, and the law. After this come university teaching and architecture (for private clients) and, perhaps, the military and accounting. (The accountants have achieved professional status only during the most recent generation.) Other recently-arrived professions are dentistry, electronic engineering, aeronautical engineering, cyrogenics, and very few in addition. (Note that engineering is not one profession but several in this analysis and the more traditional mechanical and civil are in doubt.) Goode cautiously predicts that social work, marital counseling, and, perhaps, city planning, will achieve true professional standing during the coming generation. On the other hand, various kinds of managerial occupations are classed as either unlikely or certain to fail in achieving professional status in the coming generation.

These conclusions are at least partly based on a view of the natural history of professional development put forward by Wilensky [64] earlier. (Goode does not consider the sequence necessary and objects to a lack of theoretical basis but otherwise cites Wilensky with approval.) The basic temporal criteria of professional development are these:

1. Full-time activity at the task.
2. Establishment of university training.
3. National professional association.
4. Redefinition of the core task; giving "dirty work" to non-professional subordinates.
5. Conflict between the old-timers and the newcomers who seek to upgrade the job.
6. Competition between the new occupation and neighboring ones.
7. Political agitation to gain legal protection.
8. Establishing a meaningful code of ethics.

It is remarkable how well the approaches of Goode and Wilensky fit with common sense. Nearly twenty years ago, a representative of one of the undisputed top-prestige professions addressed a group of planners who were much exercised about the meaning of "profession" as it applied to them.[65] He noted that planners were missing a few key points in arguing about the criterion of full professional accountability of that of full power to control implementation. Both of these criteria, he said, are actually quite relative in the older professions. More important than these, he had found in the study of his own and other professions, were these:

(A.) Ability of *operate in concrete situations on the basis of principles,* but with full sensitivity to the novelty of situations. This means that steady reference must be made to the *kinds of principles that imply and include potential variations,* so that the professional learns from *the interaction of principles and experience.*

(B.) Use of *technical means to solve problems,* but *avoidance of domination by any one particular technique* or narrow range of techniques.

(C.) Acting in *direct ways for human well-being and service.*

(D.) Behavior according to *a pattern of personal and professional self-limitation* consistent with a professional ethic. Knowing where are the limits of one's own professional activity, when a related professional should be called in, is an important part of this self-limitation.

(E.) Operating, not only individually, but also in *conscious representation of his or her profession.* Professional responsibility is definitionally exercised individually, but the *behavior is based on the professional entity* supporting, correcting, and transcending the individual practitioner.

Professional Planning Behavior

Having looked at the essential behavior of planning at some length, and about professional activity a bit, what can be made of "professional planning behavior?" It is clear enough that there exists a kind of behavior, frequent in organizations and groups, which may be defensibly called "planning." We can say quite a lot about this behavior in individual humans, and it is possible to build up rather systematically from there.

This planning behavior is, at the local community level and related thereto at other levels, characteristic of an emerging profession—urban planning. The fit between essential planning behavior and what urban planners do is not perfect, but it is reasonably close. One of the main shortcomings urban planning has as a potential profession is a lack of coherent knowledge base, distinct enough from that of other fields and would-be professions. Both the (a) lack and (b) potential are probably greatest on the matter of planning behavior itself.

Urban planning could complete its transition to full professional status with no more than modest developments on the knowledge and other fronts. But to take these steps would require rather extensive consensus on the part of urban planners and those most closely related to their movement. Some practicing urban planners are not decided on the advisability of becoming full-fledged professionals. The ambiguity of quasi-professional status avoids some risks. Moreover, the academic wing of urban planning has elements who are strongly anti-professional and who would resist further moves in this direction with much subtle covertness and some overt eloquence. Yet the pressures of the late 1970's and the 1980's are almost certainly going to push urban planning toward a decision for full professionalization. And I am convinced that the core of the resulting professional definition will center around *planning behavior* far more than about *urban places* themselves. (Many specialists may claim knowledge expertise about how local, urban communities work; fewer, presumably, will claim to "plan" them in any substantive sense.)

During the time that all this plays itself out, there will be great and agonizing discussions about the nature of planning behavior and of professionalism on the part of planners. The preview has probably been given us by McLoughlin[66] with reference to British local planning. His discussion, which draws on an impressive amount of British thinking about the professions,[67] may well describe what North American urban planning will go through as adventures such as "spatial planning" go out of fashion and something more like a "strategic community corporate planning" begins to take hold.[68]

If this indeed is the thrust of development of planning professions in countries such as Britain and the United States (and probably in a number of other countries as well), the nature of professional criteria will undoubtedly change. McLoughlin has gone almost to the point of predicting that planning in Britain will evolve from a traditional technical profession (column 1 below) to a more intellectualized and totally "open profession" (column 2 below).[69] Since I believe this represents the kind of academic fervor that goes too far yet not far enough, I am taking the liberty of suggesting a more likely mode of professional development (column 3 below).

If I am correct in my prognosis, urban planning is going to develop as a "mature-emergent" profession with these characteristics. It will never be one of the "personal service" professions, for individuals, groups, and even small organizations will be below threshold scale.[70] There will be more limited entry to the profession than at present, but precluding entry only to those with clearcut incompetence or documented irrelevance in training and background.

At least some kinds of urban planning will be regulated by law. This will cover "community corporate" planning as well as local land use planning, as well as several specialties. There will be sanctions on professional conduct, partly codified in law and partly in regulations of the professional organization or organizations. The market position of an incompetent or an unethical professional urban planner will be adversely impacted. (But we cannot expect these sanctions to be more effective in urban planning than they are in medicine, law, architecture or engineering—which is to say, not very effective.) Criteria for the malpractice of planning will develop but will probably cover the worst kinds of incompetent or offensive practice, and only those on which very substantial consensus can be attained.* Where evidence of conflict of interest is found, the offense will be doubly serious.

Preparation for the planning profession will move beyond the present largely "remedial liberal arts" approach to more serious professional education, fusing solid planning behavioral principles** with practice-linked training. (As in Britain, education in social science and other theory, as well as mathematics, logic, and statistics will increasingly be matters of undergraduate educational pre-requisites.)[71] Accordingly, the content of education will increasingly come to be recognized as the affair of leadership of all branches of the profession, not only of academics. This newly-mature mode of professionalism will also impact the nature of the research content of planning. Rather than attempting to ape a succession of "in" social sciences, serious attention will be given to using the theory of planning behavior and the central concerns of the profession to develop a coherent body of research. The canons of method of the scholarly and scientific disciplines will be respected, but the first priority will be the applicability of the research to real problems.

PROFESSIONAL ORGANIZATIONAL (CORPORATE) PLANNING

The outlook of professional urban planning seems fairly clear. The prospect for the emergence of fully professional corporate or organiza-

---

*One scenario of professional planning accountability follows: (a) A planner in a planning organization recommends action-sequences to a client organization; (b) The client organization carries out important parts of the action-sequences with seriously disadvantageous results, or otherwise becomes aware that another professionally-known alternative would have, in all probability and in professional consensus, yielded sharply more advantageous results; (c) the client organization challenges the planner and the planning organization in proceedings of civil law and before the professional organization; both the planner and the planning organization are found guilty of damaging malpractice by the court, and the individual planner is additionally punished by the professional organization with temporary or permanent exclusion.

**At the heart of these "planning behavioral principles," I am convinced will be the dimensions of planning skill and adaptation outlined above. These are (1) inventiveness, (2) time-span adjustment, (3) internal plan consistency, (4) rigidity-flexibility adjustment, (5) planning speed, (6) information retrieval, and (7) appropriate perseverance. It is my expectation that categories such as these will become the bases of aptitude for planning professionals as well as the criteria for measuring their skill and competency. The crude estimations of planning aptitude and skill today, from the quasi-IQ measures of the GRE to various estimations of interpersonal skill or traditional technique mastery can hardly survive any serious professional development in this field.

TABLE II

ALTERNATIVE MODES OF PROFESSIONAL DEVELOPMENT

	Traditional Craft-professions:	Intellectualized-Emergent, Quasi-professions:	Mature-Emergent Professions:
Dominant Employment	Dominated by independent practitioners	Mainly public-plural groups, some firms	Balanced mixture of public and private organizations
Clients	Individual (private)	Plural groups	Mainly organizations
Entry	Severely restricted	Relatively free	Moderately limited
Thrust	Skill/technique dominated	Interest/attitude or problem dominated	Problem-knowledge-skill dominated
Regulation of Practice	Statutory regulation of practice	None	Specific aspects regulated by law
Sanctions over Prof. conduct	Institutional	Job market only	Moderated mix of institutional and market
Malpractice	Clearly defined criteria	No criteria	Complex criteria at most negative extreme
Preparation for Entry	Apprenticeship training dominant	Academic education overwhelmingly dominant	Mixture of academic and practical education
Control of Education Content	Determined by professional institution	Determined by academics exclusively	Determined by mix of academic and professional institution inputs
Research	Little or none	Ambitious, based on academic criteria and considerations almost exclusively	Based on professional problems and knowledge, roughly consistent with criteria of academic disciplines

tional planning is a separate question. Certainly, the two are going to be related conceptually and functionally, for further development of the knowledge areas of organizational planning must be a necessity for the advances in urban planning just discussed. The evolution and contemporary situation of corporate planning is thus central to a reasonable gauging of this outlook.

Ansoff and associates[72] have traced "long range planning" in corporations at least back to the early 1950's. Following this, they show how the more narrowly analytical "strategic planning" evolved out of a new set of business problems. But, in fifteen years of attempted application of this more technological approach to planning, serious resistances have developed in many corporations. Efforts to solve this problem through direct coercion by top management have worked only temporarily and have sometimes produced merely "a disembodied set of documents." The "total system" approach of PPBS produced its own "resistance to planning" in these organizations.

The root causes of this imperfect development in organizational planning, according to Ansoff and his associates, are to be found in fuller understanding of (a) the relations between an organization and its environment, and (b) the failure so far to integrate planning into the broader aspects of organizational management, in a mode of combined competitive-entrepreneurial behavior. Dealing with these shortcomings will involve transforming both an organization's external linkages and its internal management capability. The process is called "strategic posture transformation," and strategic planning is just one element of it. Out of such strategic posture transformation, however, emerges a new and broader methodology of planning: "planned learning," which balances the "inefficient extremes" or narrowly rational planning, on the one hand, and the organization's loosely evolutionary socio-psychological and political processes, on the other. In practice, this broader "planned learning" will involve and be involved in management to integrate competitive and entrepreneurial behavior modes appropriately within organizations, as well as to modify relations with the environment.

The "professional planners" in corporate planning to date have been the rather general long-range planners and the highly rationalistic and technological "strategic planners." Both groups are well recognized in writing as "professionals," even though they lack some of the trappings of professionalism. It is evident that some synthesis of these two types of professional corporate planners with a new breed, humbled by more understanding of the intricacies of evolving organizational behavior (but still with a decisive cutting edge) is in prospect. This fusion will probably produce the professional organizational planner of the future.[73]

LIKELY LINKS BETWEEN URBAN AND ORGANIZATIONAL PLANNERS

It is clearer and clearer that urban planners and corporate and other organizational planners are going to become more and more alike in very important ways. The main thrust of their professional knowledge will have to do with how organizations work and how to make things happen in them for the benefit of specific client organizations. The issues of technological vs. behavioral approaches will be quite similar. The issues of traditional content will be parallel. The relations to broader management will be practically identical.

The question is then posed: Will the emerging-mature urban planning profession and the emerging-mature organizational planning profession become a single profession? I believe that may well come about a few decades hence. In the shorter run, I doubt it. The traditions of public sector progressive reform and confusion of planning with social criticism may remain too strong for the urban planners to make decisive movement in that direction. And the subject matter of concern to the corporate planner may seem to that branch too self-contained to work through the parallels between organization and community. Yet there will undoubtedly be some increased movement across the line between the two professions very soon. Some urban planners are essentially operating as organizational planners at present, more or less competently. And, depending on how policy moves, in both the private and the public sectors, we may see more people trained and experienced in corporate planning —hopefully of the newly-fused mode—working at least for a time in urban community planning.

Professional Policymaking Activity

Having examined the emerging-mature professions of urban planning and corporate planning, we may return to public policymaking activity. Are the various emerging policy studies programs tending toward a similar kind of professional development?

There is clear evidence of a thrust toward professionalization of policymaking activity, in the broad sense that political life itself is professionalized. Clearly there is great interest in participating in political life while resting upon professional principle. Many who were entering public service after college or after law school a generation ago are finding their replacements trained in public policy programs.

The development of the policy schools seems to promise the emergence of a body of knowledge, principles, and skills. And many of the elements of the public service ideal appear to be present, if only latently. A kind of professional association exists, if certain battles are won against the traditional approach to public administration.

The critical question may be whether or not the body of knowledge and technique is too diffuse, and variable from center to center, to make it sensible to talk of a profession in this whole area. Perhaps this is partly why Goode is so pessimistic about this kind of management achieving professional standing. (It is tempting to suggest that, if public policy is everything, maybe it cannot be a profession.) Moreover, a very considerable amount of the knowledge and skills displayed are those of research in the academic disciplines. (In at least one policy center, practically all of the graduates are going into university teaching and research, often in departments of economics or of political science.) Staffing the research and analysis departments of the public sector will not lead to the development of a profession. Most importantly, many of the graduates have little interest in becoming part of any profession, old or new. They fear professional restrictions more than planners do. Professional policymaking activity in general, then, is doubtful at best.

Specific kinds of policymaking activity, however, could much more easily become professional. One clear example is that of accounting, which is of recognized importance in business policymaking and may well take on added significance with the maturation of public policy programs. Military policy is mainly in the hands of unabashed professionals. The same applies to some degree for a number of other sectoral specialties.

It is even possible that, if a coherent body of knowledge and definition of appropriate behavior were developed, planning could become a clear-cut professional activity within the broad policy field. That may be quite distant as a general phenomenon. But specific *sectoral* kinds of planning at both the Federal and state levels seem not inconceivable. Moreover, several kinds of multi-sectoral planning at the state level are within reach. And both multi-sectoral and sectoral planning at the urban scale is practically at hand as a professional activity.

The return of serious attention to planning in public policy in this country will almost certainly come from a belated imitation of the private sector. Hopefully, the lag will not be too great and it will be possible to "catch up" to the new "planned learning" approach.

Professional Planning Activity in Urban Policymaking

At the urban policy level we are likely to develop a federation of linked planning professions, having some common core around ideas of planning behavior. The core knowledge and skills for each of these professions would consist of a fusion of knowledge and skills about planning behavioral processes with that of a sectoral or other subject-matter areas. Hopefully there would not be too many of these and the core on the planning behavior side would enable planners in one area to move into another with only a reasonable amount of retooling. What seems in store is something like the pattern in engineering, which operates as a single profession for some purposes and as several distinct professions for others.

The main focus of the planning profession will probably be urban policy planning, with specialties, a variation on the pattern of British local corporate planning. The core of the planning behavior knowledge area, I believe, will be much as outlined above including stress on major-change planning, as in U.S. corporate planning, and with important inputs of the group-process aspects, (that is, management in the mode just discussed, sustained by a flow of real services to political and economic leaders in an urban area). These were suggested nearly two decades ago and still are something of an agenda for the development of urban planning in a mixed economy:

1. Market analyses for housing, new plant investment, consumer income and spending, land and building costs, etc.

2. Pulse-taking over a wide range of local social, economic, demographic, and physical indicators to provide early warning on problems.

3. Generation and pre-evaluation of alternative policies, programs and projects to deal with identified problems or to achieve positive improvements.

4. Integrated five-year development plans centering on the budgetary process.

5. Review and evaluation of the effects of policies and plans that have been carried out.[74]

Conclusion

Planning may be said to be a fairly unique activity in policymaking, if one is careful to maintain some precision in what is meant by "planning." This is clearest at the urban scale. Policymaking in general is not a very professional activity, but planning, when linked to fairly specific subject matter, is professional according to most definitions we would want to use. Again, the strongest case for the existence of a profession is at the urban and organizational levels. In one sense, it is most accurate to talk of a professional federation of planning each member of which has a functional or topical specialty that makes concrete the general principles of planning behavior. It is in this framework that some kinds of planning behavior are, or are rapidly becoming, distinct kinds of professional activity, both inside and outside of public policymaking.

NOTES

1. I owe this insight to my politically-astute, sometime colleague, Richard Neustadt.

2. For examples of this change see Yzekiel Dror, "The Dimensions of Planning," *Public Policy* (Harvard University, 1956) and his "The Planning Process: A Facet Design," *International Review of Administrative Sciences* (1963) vs. his treatment of planning in *Public Policymaking Re-Examined* and *Design for the Policy Sciences* (New York: American Elsevier, 1970 and 1971, respectively, Also see John Friedmann, "Introduction," to a special issue on "The Study and Practice of Planning," *International Social Science Journal* (1955) or even

his "Planning as a Vocation," *Plan* (Canada), (1967, in two parts) vs. his paper on "Social Practice," summarized in *Bulletin* of the Association of Collegiate Schools of Planning (1974).

3. For a deceptively low-keyed recent analysis of this and related problems in planning education, see Melvin R. Levin, "Why Johnny Can't Plan," *Planning* (ASPO), October, 1976. While the diagnosis of the problem is mainly accurate, Levin's prescriptions are both naive and shortsighted.

4. "The Fuzzy Future of Planning Education," in Erners Erber, ed., *Urban Planning in Transition* (New York: Grossman, 1970).

5. Ronald Lippitt, Jeanne Watson, and Bruce Westley, *The Dynamics of Planned Change* (New York: Harcourt Brace Jovanovich, 1958). Some key ideas from this work were taken further by George M. Beal, and others, *Social Action and Interaction in Program Planning* (Ames, Iowa: Iowa State University Press, 1966).

6. The main thrust in development of this body of thought is set down in two distinct collections: Warren G. Bennis, Kenneth D. Benne and Robert Chin, eds., *The Planning of Change* (New York: Holt, Reinhart and Winston, 1961 and, almost totally revised, 1969). For more focus on application of these ideas to community organization, see Murray Ross, *Community Organization—Theory and Principles* (New York: Harper and Row, 1955). Also Ralph M. Kramer and Harry Specht, eds., *Readings in Community Organization Practice* (Englewood Cliffs, N.J.: Prentice Hall, 1969 and 2nd rev. ed. 1975). For a sharply pointed overview of the implications for individual activity, see Lyle E. Schaller, *The Change Agents The Strategy of Innovative Leadership* (New York: Abington, 1972), especially Chapter 3, "The Process of Planned Change."

7. Robert Morris, ed., *Centrally Planned Change: Prospects and Concepts* (New York: National Association of Social Workers, 1964). Also Robert Mayer, Robert Moroney and Robert Morris, eds., *Centrally Planned Change: A Reexamination of Theory and Experience.* The earlier volume has the academically-oriented political science paper by James Q. Wilson, "An Overview of Theories of Planned Change," but other papers are of behavioral science orientation. A more diverse group, including some urban planning academics and economists, comprises the second volume; but the behavioral emphasis is still clear in the editorial portions of the book.

8. Richard Bolan's various writings are perhaps the best example. See his "Mapping the Planning Theory Terrain," in David Godchalk, ed., *Planning in America: Learning from Turbulence* (Washington: Americain Institute of Planners, 1974) and his own works cited there.

9. Donald Michael, *On Learning to Plan—and Planning to Learn* (San Francisco: Jossey Bass, 1973) and his earlier *The Unprepared Society* (New York: Basic Books, 1968). Many other sources could be cited here, but the one general book directly based on learning theory proper is B.F. Skinner, *Beyond Freedom and Dignity* (New York: Bantam, 1971). This thin volume may yet turn out to be a much more important source to planners of coming decades than most contemporaries are able to understand. For the way that futurists have so far had to turn to "soft" social science formulations, see Herman Kahn and A.J. Weiner, *The Year 2000: A Framework for Speculation on the Next Thirty-Three Years* (New York: Macmillan, 1967).

10. John Kenneth Galbraith, *Economics and the Public Purpose* (Boston: Houghton Mifflin, 1973), part III, passim, plus Chapters 26 and 31.

11. The best, I believe, are David W. Ewing, *The Human Side of Planning* (New York: Macmillan, 1969) and his *The Practice of Planning* (New York:

Harper & Row, 1968), as well as his evolving collection, *Long-Range Planning for Management* (New York: Harper & Row, 3rd. ed., 1972). A more systematic development of both systems theory and organization theory to planning for firms and other organizations is the remarkably lucid James C. Emery, *Organizational Planning and Control Systems* (New York: Macmillan, 1969). An earlier landmark in this literature was Melville Branch, *The Corporate Planning Process* (New York: American Management Association, 1962), and Branch remains one of the few urban planners to keep up with corporate planning thought. A number of bibliographies on this writing exist, but they are of such a variable quality that the reader is advised to spend several days working in a good library of business administration.

12. There are virtually scores of works that could be cited on this point. My choice for the best and clearest statement remains Emery, *op.cit.* More current is John Argenti, *Systematic Corporate Planning* (New York: Wiley, 1974). Better, but more dispersed in net message is H.I. Ansoff, R.P. Declerck, and R.L. Hayes, eds., *From Strategic Planning to Strategic Management* (New York: Wiley, 1976).

13. Ansoff, *et al.*, ibid, passim, but especially the introduction and the title article.

14. Ibid, but this is too widespread in this writing to require more explicit documentation.

15. Emery, *op.cit.*, is very good on this point. Some writers go much further in the mathematics of "strategic" corporate planning. See, for examples, Anthony L. Iannone, *Management Program Planning and Control* (Englewood Cliffs, N.J.: Prentice Hall, 1967), John L. Livingstone, *Management Planning and Control: Mathematical Models* (New York: McGraw Hill, 1970), Ernest C. Miller, *Advanced Techniques for Strategic Planning* (New York: American Management Association, 1967), and Akira Ishikawa, *Corporate Planning and Control Model System* (New York: N.Y.U. Press, 1975). *Ansoff, et al., op.cit.* strike a rather good balance on these techniques.

16. See Russell Ackoff, *A Concept of Corporate Planning* (New York: Wiley Interscience, 1970) for remarkable openness, but the tendency is quite widespread. Urban planning writings are frequently cited to illustrate points, particularly in the more general corporate planning books.

17. See, for example, Donald Foley, "British Planning: One Ideology or Three," *British Journal of Sociology* (1960) for a flavor of how it looked to one outsider then. Others of us then workng in Britain came to similar conclusions. See my *Housing, Planning and Social Relations in Urban Race Contact Areas* (Cambridge, Mass.: Harvard University Library, Doctoral Dissertation, 1961).

18. See especially George Chadwick, *A Systems View of Planning* (Oxford, England: Pergamon Press, 1971).

19. For a sampling, see A. G. Wilson, *Papers in Urban and Regional Analysis* (London: Pion, 1972). For an evaluation, see David Eversley, *The Planner in Society* (London: Faber and Faber, 1973).

20. See the discussion in Eversley, *op.cit.*, also Thomas Blair, *The Poverty of Planning* (London: MacDonald, 1973).

21. This very clear, for example, in the collection, Peter Cowan, ed., *The Future of Planning* (London: Heinemann, 1973) which includes papers by Christopher Foster on "Planning for the Market," David Donnison on "Planning and Government," Derek Senior on "Planning and the Public," Peter Willmott, on "The Tasks for Planning," and Alan Wilson on "How Planning Can Respond to New Issues," as well as "The Future of the Planning Profession" by Brian

McLoughlin and a thoughtful conclusion by Emrys Jones. It is also evident in Eversley, *op.cit.*

22. See discussion by Donnison and by McLoughlin in Cowan, ibid.

23. Donnison, ibid.

24. Tony Eddison, *Local Government: Management and Corporate Planning* (London: Leonard Hill, 1973). Also Donnison, in Cowan, ibid, and Mahlon Apgar IV, "Corporate Planning in British Local Government" plus A. Hicking and A. Sutton, "Planning as a Process of Strategic Choice," both in *Proceedings* of the International Federation of Housing and Planning (1975).

25. See various papers in Cowan, *op.cit.*, plus Eversley, *op.cit.*

26. Jack Hayward and Michael Watson, eds., *Planning, Politics, and Public Policy: The British, French and Italian Experience* (London: Cambridge University Press, 1975). This is an excellent comparative treatment of planning at national, regional, and local levels. For the expectation that British experience is directly applicable to the U.S. see various entries in Arnold Whittick, ed., *Encyclopedia of Urban Planning* (London and New York: McGraw-Hill, 1973); but this slant is widespread in both planning and publishing circles. On the applicability of British planning to developing areas, see: John L. Taylor, ed., *Planning for Urban Growth: British Perspectives on the Planning Process* (U.S. edition, New York: Praeger, 1972); and Robert J. Marshall, ed., *Spatial Design and Planning in the U.K.: Its Relevance to Developing Countries* (U.S. edition, New York: Praeger, 1974).

27. See Harvey Leibenstein, *Beyond Economic Man: A New Foundation for Microeconomics* (Cambridge: Harvard University Press, 1976). He is forced to invent a "micro-micro" level to get into meaningful discussion of individual and group, as opposed to firm, behavior.

28. Max Weber, "The Principal Types of Social Action." He distinguished these from simple and complex rationality. It is not necessary to accept his definitions of rationality in order to exclude various kinds of emotional and traditional behavior from our concept of planning.

29. Otherwise careful writers have sometimes failed to distinguish the behavior of planning from decisionmaking in general or from management. Herbert Simon has not always been careful on this point. See, for example, James G. March and Herbert A. Simon *Organizations,* (New York: Wiley, 1958).

30. George A. Miller, Eugene Galanter, and Karl H. Pribam, *Plans and the Structure of Behavior* (New York: Holt, 1960). They refer to the "Image" and liken it to the memory of a computer. My use of the term "memory" does not intend the analogy; I add the idea of a "record" to ease extending these concepts to organizations.

31. See Robert Dahl and Charles Lindblom, *Politics, Economics and Welfare* (New York: Harper, 1953) on the various kinds of delegation as aids to calculation at the macrolevel. One thrust of the decisionmaking literature is assembled in William L. Gore and J. W. Dyson, eds., *The Making of Decisions: A Reader in Administrative Behavior* (New York: Free Press, 1964). However, the "behaviorist" approach is the minority one in this field. The main thrust is clear in Ruth Mack's summary of "Choice by 'Rational' Man," in her *Planning on Uncertainty, op.cit.*

32. Quite a number of writers have made the point that planning is concerned with actions in the future, but then so is all management decisionmaking. If decisions are made in the present, with action following, then action must be in the future. My attempt is to clarify this somewhat by stipulating planning as concerned with actions in the non-immediate future.

33. Then management dealing with action-sequences rather than "single-loop" proposals should be called "planning."' I believe the distinction to be reasonable. Some nominal "planning" has failed to deal with action-sequences, but I consider that not central to the mainstream of planning behavior. My arbitrary criterion of three cycles as a minimum is simply to clarify further the distinction. I am not alone in finding the distinction meaningful. A number of management-oriented urban planners strongly believe that they are more sequential, working in paths of decisions and consequences, while most engineers, economists, and management experts tend to concentrate on single-cycle problem solving. Just how much truth will be found in this distinction is a matter for further study.

34. See James Q. Wilson, "An Overview of Theories of Planned Change," in Morris, ed., *op.cit.*

35. See Miller, *et al.*, *op.cit.*

36. See Leibenstein, *op.cit.*, especially Chapter 1 for a contrast of the merits of "atomistic" vs. "mollecular" approaches.

37. Much of what is known about this subject is developed from the classic study of Miller, *et al.*, *op.cit.* In terms of strict experimental psychology, which was their starting point, it remains impossible to prove that individual planning exists and that it and behavior generally have exactly the characteristics described. Yet it is convincing enough for our purposes, and the usage here is just as permissible as using the concepts of "perception" or "cognition"—neither of which can be proved to exist.

38. Miller, *et al.*, use the concept of "Image" for past, present, and future views of self and environment. In this they explicitly follow Kenneth Boulding, *The Image* (Ann Arbor: University of Michigan Press, 1956). As is made clear in Kenneth Boulding's "Foreword" and in Elise Boulding's "Translator's Preface" to Fred Polak, *The Image of the Future* (San Francisco: Jossey-Bass, 1973), there was an even broader and more philosophic inspiration to some of the terms and concepts. My use of "view" of the future rather than "image" is simply one of preference.

39. Miller, *et al.*, *op.cit.* Their terminology is "Test-Operate-Test-Exit" or "TOTE" behavioral sequence. They hold that all behavior is so organized. While this is certainly a cybernetic concept, they do not get into the more complex dampening or amplifying aspects of behavior. I add it here.

40. Kenneth Boulding in Polak, *op.cit.*

41. See the various writings of Herbert Simon, starting with *Administrative Behavior* (New York: Free Press, 1965, 2nd ed.). (1st ed. was published in 1947). He states these ideas most precisely in *Models of Man* (New York: Wiley, 1957), but his contribution is so widely known as not to require further citation. It is disappointing that Simon's message has had so little sustained influence on the main body of planning thought in the policy-related literature. However, with Leibenstein, *op.cit.* now going much further with this line of thought, within the discipline of economics, the wisdom of these basic ideas may become more widely appreciated and acted upon. Both Simon and Leibenstein attempt to bring psychological variables into, respectively, rigorous decisionmaking and microeconomics. Yet neither atuhor has any real mastery of the more rigorous body of psychological thought, experimental psychology. The result is something of an awkward mismatch, especially Leibenstein's use of psychoanalytic concepts (the id and the superego, but no ego) with microeconomics. The full integration of these two disciplines remains to be done.

42. Simon, Ibid.

43. These terms are fairly standard but taken from Miller, *et al.*, *op.cit.*

44. While these variables are presented here in a rather cursory manner, they are subject to more precise organization for more elaborate theoretic treatment. They parallel the variables in Leibenstein's "constraint concern." In this formulation, a series of behavioral variables are treated as a vector and then worked through a series of micro-economic theorems. The "planning skill" variables can be handled in much the same way.

45. The "stop order" terminology is from Miller, *et al., op.cit.*

46. The dimensions of planning skill and situation-adaptation are those found in Miller, *et al., op.cit.* What we have been doing here, as some readers will recognize, is to take some of the ideas from this classic work, build in somewhat more of a learning theory approach, and tie this to the kind of formulation that Leibenstein has recently put forward. The integration is still incomplete, but this will show the thrust.

47. Richard L. Meier, *Developmental Planning* (New York: McGraw-Hill, 1965), Chapter 3, "Open Systems for Growth and Development." See also Lawrence D. Mann and James Hughes, "Systems and Planning Theory," *Journal of the American Institute of Planners* (1969) or in Melville C. Branch, ed., *Urban Planning Theory* (Stroudsburg, Pa., 1975).

48. See Leibenstein, *op.cit.* This is the thrust of his whole book, for psychological variables. His method is made clearest in his appendix, "Toward a Mathematical Formalization of X-Efficiency Theory." We cannot take the space to demonstrate it here, but our substitution of experimental psychological theory for his psychotherapeutic and our insertion of planning or "future concern behavior" as distinct from but parallel to his "constraint concern" do nothing to weaken his powerful chain of theory. And of course, from our viewpoint, these innovations make the theory much more interesting.

49. Other dimensions are defined in Dror, *op.cit.*, (1957) and Dror, *op.cit.*, (1961). While he is not clear on the planner-performer dimension (since his is a macroapproach), it crosscuts several of his dimensions or factors.

50. Leibenstein, *op.cit.* He moves from individual, to group, to firm, and then shows the relevance of his theory at the level of aggregate national economic policy.

51. Ibid.

52. While Leibenstein (Ibid) stresses the interface with, and thus aggregation to, the firm, we move directly to the more general human complex, the organization.

53. Ruth Mack, *Planning on Uncertainty: Decision Making in Business and Government Administration* (New York: Wiley, 1971).

54. Ibid, and she has performed the extremely valuable service of working these out in sufficient detail so that more popular accounts can draw upon them for practical professional guidelines. This has not been done yet, however.

55. See my case study, *The Planning of 'America's Home Town'* (approximate title, forthcoming, late 1977).

56. Edgar S. Dunn, Jr., *Economic and Social Development: A Process of Social Learning* (Baltimore: Johns Hopkins Press, 1971).

57. Donald N. Michael, *On Learning to Plan—and Planning to Learn: The Social Psychology of Changing Toward Future-Responsive Societal Learning* (San Francisco: Jossey-Bass, 1973).

58. Herbert Simon, *op.cit.*, footnotes 29 and 41, above.

59. Works cited are those previously referred to.

60. Alfred North Whitehead, *Adventures of Ideas* (London: Pelican, 1948).

61. *Daedalus* (1963). Special issue on The *Professions* provides, in its various papers, both for general and for specific professions, what I take to be a fairly

complete catalogue of these supposed variables. This collection is notable for William Alonso's curiously tentative (and now dated) treatment of urban planning as a "profession." He saw the issues only as a transition from traditional design to the more analytic (regional science?) approaches; he did not anticipate the growing concern with social questions or with the bioenvironment—much less recent fiscal and energy concerns. Most seriously, the key questions of an urban planning profession were never faced up to. General intellectual concern with urban studies and broad policy were never clearly distinguished from the supposed future "profession" of urban planning.

62. William J. Goode, "The Theoretical Limits of Professionalization," in Amitai Etzioni, ed., *The Quasi-Professions* (New York: Free Press, 1969). But see also Howard Vollmer and Donald Mills, eds., *Professionalization* (Englewood Cliffs, N.J.: Prentice-Hall, 1966).

63. Ibid. I have modified these variables within each "generating train" only slightly for purposes of clarity and consistency with what I believe to be the main thrust of his argument.

64. Harold Wilensky, "The Professionalization of Everyone?," *American Journal of Sociology* (1964), and Goode, Ibid.

65. Steward Hiltner, "Planning as a Profession," *Proceedings*, Annual Meeting of the American Institute of Planners, 1957.

66. Brian McLoughlin, "The Future of the Planning Profession," in Cowan, *op.cit.*

67. He cites Millerson, *The Qualifying Associations* (London: Routledge and Kegan Paul, 1964), Prandy, *Professional Employees* (London: Faber and Faber, 1965), Bennion, *Professional Ethics: The Consultant Professions and their Code* (London: Knight, 1969), Great Britain, Monopolies Commission, *A Report on the General Effect on the Public Interest of Certain Restrictive Practices so far as they Prevail in Relation to the Supply of Professional Services* (London: H.M.S.O., 1970), as well as the classic A.M. Carr-Saunders and P.A. Wilson, *The Professions* (London: Cass, 2nd. ed., 1964). Only the last is well known in this country.

68. Eddison, *op.cit.*, It is notable that in Coventry, probably the most advanced locality in British municipal corporate planning, it was the "traditional" town planner who took the leadership, and still leads, this frontier effort.

69. McLoughlin, *op.cit.*

70. This is not to say that a profession for planning at these levels will not arise, for the social work profession has developed rather centrally about such planning. Urban planners who wish to do a great deal of planning for other individuals or for small groups as such, I believe, are advised to prepare themselves also for social work. In this, I suppose that I find myself in disagreement with Richard Bolan, who has on various occasions argued for planners to be specialists in the planning process at all levels. See note 8, above.

71. Peter Hall, "Manpower and Education," in Cowan, *op.cit.* He proposes, for example, that the intellectual skills be areas of undergraduate education, making graduate professional training more "vocational," preparing people for "junior management jobs with a large technical content." He also proposes a retread level of planning education for directors of major service departments in local authorities in "problems of large-scale coordination and strategic planning." The McLoughlin approach to an intellectualized profession, on the other hand, would practically make graduate education in planning a Ph.D. undertaking. The same debate, of course, is going on in this country.

72. Ansoff, *et al.*, *op.cit.*

73. Ibid. They are more interested in talking about managers in general, but there is nothing in what they say that would preclude the emergence of professional organizational planners within this management framework. I venture to predict this emergence on the basis of the demonstrated "staying power" of the long-range corporate planners. Indeed, the best writings of the 1950's (pre-strategic planning) sound very much like the best writings of the 1970's (post-strategic planning). There is evidently something very solid here, and I think it is a profession.

74. Martin Meyerson, "Building the Middle-Range Bridge to Comprehensive Planning," *Journal of the American Institute of Planners* (1956). See also Ira M. Robinson, "Beyond the Middle-Range Planning Bridge," Ibid (1965). Both articles are reprinted in Robinson's edited work, *Decision-Making in Urban Planning: An Introduction to the New Methodologies* (Beverly Hills and London: Sage, 1969). Meyerson has reminded us once again of this unfulfilled agenda for the planning profession by his most recent discussion of a closely-related subject. See his, "The Next Challenge for the Urban Planner: Linking Local and National Economic Planning," *Journal of the American Institute of Planners* (October, 1976).

A Difference Paradigm for Planning

Melvin M. Webber

Our host has invited us here, apparently hoping that this mix of minds will somehow generate some clues about next directions for the urban planning movement. I suspect we all share his desire for a new compass, for all of us must be eager to get out of the doldrum that displaced the optimism of the '60s. Images of New Frontiers and Great Societies have been tarnished by reforms that were to have changed the world and didn't, by imaginative programs that boomeranged to hurt the very people they were to have helped, and by formulas for betterment based on theories since abandoned. We worked through several styles of professional reform during those heady days of the Kennedy and Johnson administrations. We tested out quite a lot of the accumulated inventory of program plans. For a while there, many of us were pretty sure we knew how to solve the problems of the city and of the city's deprived people. By now that confidence is worn thin. Too many failures, or seeming failures, have been counted up, leaving planners rather shaken and discouraged.

Paradoxically, however, one outcome of the high promises and the frenetic activities of the '60s was widespread legitimation of planning practice in a country that had traditionally been hostile to the very idea of it. After decades of persuading and cajoling, planners finally in recent times have successfully created planning agencies in virtually all sectors of government, in Democratic and Republican administrations alike, and at just the time when planners themselves seem least confident of their own capabilities. But for the erosion of faith among the faithful, this might be the most propitious time for effective planning. It is certainly a propitious time for reappraisal. If we could just find out how and what to do, if we could just find out how to make planning work, institutionally the opportunities now may be greater than ever before.

The Eroding Myth of Scientific Planning

Despite the rising popularity and the new legitimacy of planning, the idea of planning remains ambiguous, however. I am aware of about two dozen rather different conceptions of planning, each of which is widely held. They range from management and control by central government, to polite discrimination, to precise scheduling, to being smart about the future, to controlling deviancy, to protecting consumers—and so on.

Although not universally so, two common threads tie these multiple conceptions into a rather coherent meaning that most people may attach to the name, "planning." They are the notions (1) that some kinds of collective rationality can be effectively substituted for private rationality, and (2) that social systems can be engineered to conform to some collectively willed future state of affairs.

I suppose that the seeds for those conceptions of perfectability were planted during the Enlightenment when ideas of Progress came into good currency. I suppose the images of a collective will were nurtured during the Progressive Era when reformers successfully implanted notions of the public interest as legitimate concerns of government. I suppose the prospects for social engineering have been husbanded by the several generations of scientific managers, by whatever name, who have believed that systematic application of formal knowledge can solve social problems. I suppose the most commonly accepted notion of planning is something like that—i.e., that organized societies can rationally and scientifically engineer future history, thus to guarantee Progress and to assure that the public interest will be served.

There have been any number of efforts to explain why the reforms of the '60s missed their targets. I incline to the proposition that both the reformers and their clients were taken in by the myths imbedded in that technocratic conception of planning. It is fundamentally fallacious, and so the expectations it has generated have been unrealizable. It is simply not possible to consign a set of social problems to any group of professional people, however skilled, and to then get a set of solutions delivered in turn.

The attractiveness of the idea of scientific planning has been hard to resist, for it has held out the promise of right answers, of revealing what we should want, and of saying what we need to do. It seduces with the prospect of certainty, and thus with the prospect of relief from the discomforts of ambiguity and of having to decide things in the face of conflicting evidence and competing wants.

But scientific planning is a mirage. Science has nothing to say about which valued ends ought to be sought, but that is of course the very stuff of planning. Selecting among alternative ends is among the toughest planning tasks we face, and yet there is nothing in the apparatus of science—or of engineering—that can make those valuative choices for us.

Science and planning are very different sorts of enterprises. As my colleague, Horst Rittel, has noted, because scientists seek to observe, describe, and explain, they have powerful incentives to leave that which they observe untouched. Planners are quite the opposite; their purposes are to change whatever it is they are confronting, preferably, of course, to improve it. Although planners, qua interveners, are fundamentally dependent upon scientifically acquired knowledge, they are users of that knowledge, not scientists themselves. Although some practising planners are *also* researchers and contributors to the body of scientific knowledge, their roles as planners are intrinsically distinct from their roles as scientists. Planners use measuring instruments, build models, work with theory, calculate, and in other ways employ the instruments and techniques that scientists also use. However, they direct their efforts to understanding and changing some particular situations, not to making generalized statements about classes of phenomena. White coats and test tubes are not the indicators of science, although they may signal technical skill.

I suggest that this simple-minded distinction between science and planning has evaded a great many planners. It has also evaded far too many public officials and laymen who have been led to believe that, through science, planners could tell them what is right and hence what to want. Of course, planners have been quick to accept the seer's role. It is almost a mark of the trade for planners to tell others what ought to be. However, these sorts of assertion are necessarily based in ideology, personal opinion, group interest, or, at best, in wisdom bred of the personal knowledge that comes with extensive experience. Unfortunately, neither planners nor anybody else has technical knowledge about what *should* happen, in the sense that scientists may have technical or theoretic bases for saying what *might* happen. Goals and objectives are extra-scientific kinds of statements.

Well then, if not scientific planning, might we claim something akin to social engineering? That is, if goal statements could be formulated outside the planning system and then presented to planners, might their role then be to devise the means for accomplishing whatever are the societal ends? This view has enjoyed the plausibility of analogy with the several branches of engineering which draw upon physics and chemistry for causal theory, then invent means that will transform problematic conditions into more desirable states. Thus, for example, a bridge engineer can responsibly say to a legislature, "*If you wish* to span that river with a highway, this is what you need to do." And he does indeed have enough accumulated instrumental knowledge at his command to show them how to build a bridge that will stand up.

It is quite true that the various types of planners are often placed in quite that role. Whenever they are also equipped with adequate theory, they may on occasion be able to create the social equivalent of that bridge. But, unfortunately, the state of social-change theory, even of urban-growth theory, is still far too primitive to satisfy any but the simplest demands. Although economists are sometimes able to make tenable recommendations about rediscount rates, spending rates, and so on (i.e., given consensus about economic stabilization goals), most of us are less well off than they. We have not been spectacularly successful in saying what needs to be done to increase the supply of low-cost housing, to reduce crime, to increase job skills, to control municipal budgetary inflation, to manage urban growth, to improve childrens' performance in school, to accelerate social mobility, to stem the growing apartheid afflicting our metropolitan areas, and so on. Each of you can add your own agenda of unsatisfied aspirations. The sad truth is that we simply do not yet know enough about the workings of social systems to be able to say what can be done to "engineer" them into more desired states. Only rarely can planners say with full confidence that if A is done, B will follow.

But even if we did know an awful lot more than we do, such that we could more readily play the roles that Technocracy, Inc. once predicted or that Systems Analysts now claim, a nest of other troublesome issues would immediately arise. First off, *who* is to formulate the goals that social engineers are to serve? The notion that "society" can formulate a purposive statement is peculiar at best and pernicious at worst. Only persons are equipped to do that, and so we are unavoidably led to ask *which* persons are to set the agenda. Is it the majority of voters? the legislatures? the more-powerful interest groups? individual consumers? professional planners? Obviously an old and persistently troubling question. But a terribly important one for the planner, because what he does might be consequential. What he proposes might matter. The ends he works for may be those some special interest groups seek, or they may be those his employers seek; but they may simultaneously be antithetical to other people's purposes. The specter of Eichmann is the constant companion of the wary planner.

A society as pluralistic as this one is unlikely ever to agree about anything except at rather high levels of generality. Pollsters may find virtual unanimity on issues of brotherhood, motherhood, and survival. The more specific the proposition, however, the more certain are the respondents to differ. So on questions of individuals' preferences for housing, busing and school integration, highway location, social services, or neighborhood social class composition, the disagreements are likely to be both wide and vociferous. Who is then to say which mix of policies and programs is the correct one? Which social engineer is to engineer which social situations for which social groups? And when the differences among persons are as heartfelt as these are likely to be, what is the technical expertise that will categorically assert which is right and which wrong?

The Rich Heritage of the 'Sixties

Most of us are far more sensitive about these matters than we were prior to the explosive events of the '60s. However unsatisfying we may have found experiences of the past decade-and-a-half, we have learned some important lessons well. Nowadays, almost reflexively, most of us instantaneously examine new program proposals for their potential redistributional consequences. Among the first questions asked is *who* will it help and *who* will it hurt? Back in the '50s those questions were seldom asked.

I hope it is accurate to say that planners have been learning how to trace potential repercussions of proposed actions—that, among their first questions, they ask: "What will be the likely chains of consequences of taking one action or another?" and, again, Which groups of persons will be affected in what ways by each of those consequences? This sort of repercussions analysis is being mandated by requirements for environmental impact reports, of course; but I suspect that, by now, the thoughtways are diffused well beyond legalistic requirements. I hope I am right about that, for, as I shall want to contend in a moment, this mode of thought is essential to the planning paradigm that may be guiding our work in the imminent future.

Recent efforts to apply the so-called systems approach have probably had some long-lasting and salutary effects. Many of us have learned to think in the language of complex systemic networks, rather than in the linear one-to-one links within the hierarchical structures we were told about in church and school. Inside complex systems, everything is indeed connected to everything else, such that actions taken anywhere reverberate throughout the whole system to affect changes in seemingly far-removed sectors. Moreover, since no condition and no event can be seen as isolated, every problem is but a symptom of some deeper problem imbedded in the next larger subsystem; and that perception compels of a depth of humility guaranteed to turn the most evangelical reformer into a cautious planner.

Systems analysis and PPBS may have had a further persisting influence upon current modes of thought, for the compulsion to assess the *outcomes* of programmatic activities has been powerful. It took a major conceptual shift to turn bureaucrats away from a preoccupation with efficiency to a concern for effectiveness and to turn instincts away from such input measures as levels of expenditure, man hours worked, and cases treated. I view it as something of an intellectual revolution when professionals in virtually the whole spectrum of social services struggled to rethink their program outputs in the language of human welfare. It turned out to be an uncommonly difficult task, of course; and by now most of them have abandoned the exercise. But the seeds of that revolution are still widely sown, and we can at least hold to the hope that the growing efforts to institutionalize evaluation of program effectiveness will extend the search for meaningful and socially relevant output measures.

One further heritage of the '60s may prove of lasting influence on the future evolution of planning. It is the huge social experiments—large-scale field trials of radical new programs, undertaken with the full apparatus of experimental controls, monitors, and formal evaluation. In some senses, these experiments in income maintenance, education vouchers, and rent subsidies more closely resemble formal science than almost anything tried before. The aim is to find out whether the objectives initially sought are actually attained—whether the hypothesized cause-effect relations seem tenable. Essentially the same questions are asked by evaluation researchers and by monitors who apply social indicators to check on outcomes of social programs.

Of course, the values these experiments and evaluation efforts are directed to promote are determined wholly outside the spheres of science. Although they are inherently political in character, they have commonly been arrived at through consensus among professionals, increasing numbers of whom are increasingly dubious about their prerogatives. In turn, that raises a central issue we need to address.

Toward the Next Paradigm for Planning

We learned a very great deal during the '60s about potentially effective approaches to social problems, and we learned that some interventional styles are ineffectual, and some unethical. Surely we are all less naive about the magic potions that would solve social problems in short order. Indeed, many of us are by now persuaded that social problems are never solved—that, at best, they are only resolved, over and over again. And so, we are increasingly dubious about the self-styled experts with large promises, those who will turn on their systems analyses and eradicate poverty, those who purport to discover optimum land use patterns, those who have just the right touch for turning lower-class kids into top-performing students. Too many quick-fix artists, too much snake oil, too many high promises that no one could deliver on—too much scientism has left a generation of skeptics in its wake.

As one result of the oversell, many are less certain than they used to be about the proprieties of anything like a fourth-power role for planning. Some of us are being increasingly disenchanted by any conception of planning that accords it the capacities of authoritative expertise. We are becoming convinced that a science of planning is impossible, that social engineering is intolerable, and that the concentration of goal-setting in any sort of planning agency, however benign, is politically unacceptable.

And so we are searching for a style of planning that might avoid these difficulties, while being sensitive to the diversity of goals that characterize the plural politics comprising American society. I expect that search will generate a paradigm of permissive planning, conceived as a subset of politics, its central function being to improve the processes of public debate and public decision.[1]

In the course of the search, I suspect the notion that there are right answers to be discovered or invented will be as difficult as any of our ideologic fixations to overcome. That fundamental doctrine has been so deeply woven into contemporary thoughtways as to have attained the status of a truism. It is nonetheless false.

Whenever people's belief systems and wants differ, there is no gainsaying who is right. Whenever governmental activities profit one person at the expense of another, there is no technical rationale that can alone supply sufficient warrants. Whenever alternative programs with divergent distributional outcomes are possible, there can be no one right way. Under virtually all the social circumstances in which planners work, the acceptable way is necessarily the outcome of political processes. That is to say, there are no scientifically or technically correct answers, only politically appropriate ones.

If that assertion be accepted, then it seems that many traits of traditional planning would be ill-suited to a syle of planning oriented to improving the qualities of political decision processes. City master plans, as one example, have presented unitary policy for entire cities, on the apparent assumption of community consensus. Urban renewal plans have been designed with the explicit purpose of serving whole-city interests. Large transportation systems have been designed and built, necessarily on an area-wide scale, again with the apparent objective of serving all who inhabit the area. But in each of these examples the presumption that everybody will be a winner is patently suspect. In the traditional mode, plans were drawn up by an elite group of some kind, put through formal hearing procedures, then adopted as though they reflected community-wide policy.

That routine of professionalized plan making has been undergoing some pretty dramatic changes in the years since 1960. Increasingly, citizen groups of various sorts have been voicing their objections to these plans and their outcomes. In turn, they have been finding ways of participating in civic deliberations, making their special wants known, negotiating for projects and outcomes they prefer, logrolling and bargaining in an increasingly populist debating forum. The new widespread participation of diverse publics is serving to expose the myth that there exists a metropolitan community, for as the many interest groups make their valued ends known, it is becoming apparent they really are in conflict and that all goals cannot be served simultaneously. In turn it is becoming apparent that unitary master plans purporting to serve "the whole community" are based on a fiction, hence are inherently flawed. Under those circumstances it is scarcely any wonder that the thousands of 701-sponsored plans have left the course of urbanization largely untouched.

The growing involvement of lay groups bodes well for the prospects of a politically responsive mode of planning. It suggests that an effective style of planning does not call for plans that present right answers, rather that it calls for procedures which might help plural politics reach decisions in acceptable ways. In that idiom, planning would become an integral aspect of governing, rather than a separate function of government. Its special task would then be to help assure that all parties' voices are heard; that available evidence, theory, and arguments are weighed; that potentially useful options are considered and evaluated; that latent consequences and their distributions among the many publics are identified and assessed.

A distinguishing mark of that conception of planning is the persisting question, "What if?" What if agent A does this and respondent B does that? What then? What chains of effects? What if X happens at time t, what'll we do then? What if at t+1? Who will be helped and who hurt? What if we want P instead of Q? What if we try program X? What if, instead, we try Y? What if the reactions to X are this instead of that? What do we do then? And if we do that, what does the other guy do in turn?

I suggest that the trait distinguishing planning modes of thought from others is that persisting analysis and evaluation of alternative actions, alternative ends, alternative outcomes, alternative redistributions, and, in turn, alternative reactions to prior actions. In this context, *planning is fundamentally a cognitive style,* not a substantive field, not a specialized departmentalized function in an organization, not a set of technical knowledge, certainly not an ideologically derived set of substantive goals about housing, economic development, human welfare, or anything else. In its generic essence, it is a special way of thinking about pluralities of individual and group wants and a special approach to satisfying those variously competing wants.

To suggest that planning is nonpartisan, being open to all sorts of arguments and group interests, is not to say that it is also value-neutral. Quite the opposite. The aim is to admit all manner of valued positions, and most especially those of minority interests whose voices are typically too muted to be heard. Nor is its openness to everyone's evidence and arguments to suggest that it seeks more closely to approach optimal solutions. As I've contended already, whenever group interests are less than perfectly aligned, which is probably always, there can be no optimal solutions. No. Its mark is neither value-neutrality nor efficiency, but rather a constant searching for equity.

The idealized style of planning I envision is fundamentally biased toward the defense of difference. Its aim, whenever possible, is to foster free exchange of dissimilar ideas and the open confrontation of divergent opinion, thus to encourage the generation of new ideas and innovation of all sorts. Where feasible, it promotes the production of differentiated goods and services and their consumption to accord with highly decentralized choices, thus permitting individual persons and subcultural groups more nearly to satisfy their wants. Being alert to the latent tyranny of majority rule, it is hypersensitive to the problems and preferences of minorities of all sorts. And so, it is constantly seeking to assure that their interests are ably represented and that they attain equal access to opportunities. It promotes deviancy as the medium of cultural experimentation, tolerates it as the prerogative of individuals, and defends it as the manifest trait of political freedom. It eschews standardized solutions to problems, and it is the enemy of regulatory standards that compel sameness.

Oriented to strengthening democratic processes of governing, permissive planning is predisposed to the *ways* decisions get made, rather than to specific preferred substantive content of those decisions. It takes its model from the U.S. Constitution whose genius lies in its orientation to processes of governing rather than to substantive statutory law. In that image, permissive planning seeks to formulate those minimal procedural rules that then permit and foster difference, being somewhat indifferent to the substance of those differences. Just as the First Amendment protects and encourages free thought, personal independence, and rights of protest, so too would the permissive style of planning foster open argumentation, seeking to find ways of joining latent conflict by creating the means for inducing debate and the media through which contending parties might effectively engage each other. Just as the Fifth and Fourteenth Amendments guarantee due process of law, so too would planners promoting the permissive style seek to frame the few warrantees assuring that all groups' interests are heard and the few rules governing processes of deliberation and argumentation.

Focused on improving processes of decision, permissive planning would not pursue "correct answers" to development issues or "correct solutions" to problems. It would be content to find procedurally acceptable resolutions. Accepting the essential political character of development issues and social problems, its test of a decision's goodness is whether it was arrived at through acceptable procedures. That is the judicial test of justice, and it has served us well. However often we may disagree with juries' decisions, most of us would agree that, if defendants are tried in the accepted manner, we are far more willing to accept jury decisions over other ways of assessing innocence or guilt. The essential test there is a procedural one, and it strikes me as a model worth emulating in the public policy arenas as well.

In the context I portray, the planner's role is as facilitator of debate, rather than as substantive expert. His contribution is initially as writer of constitutions, as formulator of the procedural rules that will foster more effective deliberation and argumentation. His skills are essentially cognitive. Perhaps in some modern sense they are Socratic; for he seeks to draw out implications, to provoke contention among potentially differing parties, to help all comers to explore potential consequences and their implications. His role may also be that of mediator, perhaps in the style of labor negotiators who help engage contest in accord with systematic procedures, then help resolve disputes by structuring negotiating and bargaining processes. In some senses he is teacher, who by example teaches others how to ask "What if?" in the planning idiom, then walks them through the creative processes that intelligent debate can generate. His role is necessarily also the inventor's. Employed full time to worry about questions that other participants can confront only avocationally, he is constantly called upon to think up better ways of confronting problems, resolving conflicts, or improving debate. As the cognitively skilled planner who reflexively searches for alternative actions and alternative outcomes, for redistributional repercussions, for feedbacks reactions, and for compatibilities of outcomes with goals, he is patently better equipped to think out the consequences of proposed actions than are most other participants. Moreover, having access to simulation models and other formal analytic procedures, he is inevitably better informed and so better equipped to formulate new objectives, new program plans, new compromises, new techniques for creating difference. In turn, he is in position to keep public debates fueled with a continuing supply of information, forecasts, analyses, arguments, and then the countervailing evidence and propositions that might reinforce opposing sides to disputes.

The permissive planner is literally a troublemaker. Finding persons or groups unconcerned about latent problems that will later affect them, he seeks to agitate those latent interests until they rise to the surface, then to find ways of involving those persons in pursuit of their self-interests. Finding dialogue lagging, he seeks to ignite conflict so that latent issues will become manifest. When decisions are about to be made that run counter to the wishes of some affected group, he feeds them with the evidence and arguments that might then keep the deliberations open a little longer.

I paint this permissive planner as something of an impartial and saintly soul, even though I know full well that few of us are capable of that sort of impartiality. Moreover, the planner worthy of our respect is a person who believes strongly about the issues he works on. Rather than the neutral eunuch, he is himself a strong partisan for some outcomes over some others, for the interests of some groups over others, for some styles of governance, for some conceptions of justice, some patterns of future development, and so on. I would hope, nonetheless, that the planner might also be capable of serving the interests of pluralism and diversity by aiding even those he opposes. And if that happy prospect should prove impossible, I am then led to the strategy of cultivating a plurality of planners, rather as Paul Davidoff suggested a decade ago, such that all groups might be represented by their own professional advocates. The possibilities for pluralism of either style need to be further explored; for, however it is to be accomplished, I suggest the goal is of overriding importance.

It should be apparent by now that permissive planning exploits quite different techniques from those that have been stock-in-trade for the professions. Regulatory standards that set minimum qualities for products have also made for standardized products, even as they have protected consumers from fraudulent and greedy suppliers. As one result, some minorities have been unable to get the kinds of goods or services they may prefer—or those they can afford. It is not self-evident that housing standards serve the interests of low-income persons who are thereby unable to buy new and low-cost housing. It is not self-evident that standardized school curricula best serve the diversity of pupils, as so many recent critics have made clear. And so, permissive planners are going to have to find some alternatives to these sorts of standards. Preferably they will be procedures that compel nonstandard outcomes—that foster differentiation of product lines that might then better serve diverse consuming publics.

Performance standards offer one promising approach to that end, and a lot of experimentation seems to be underway on these approaches now. Cash payments to consumers as alternatives to governmentally supplied services are being strongly advocated by commentators across the full political spectrum—from both the right and the left. Americans' peculiar objection to redundancy in government has made for monopoly-like service agencies, which inevitably supply standardized services, frequently barricaded behind complicated administrative screens. Perhaps privatization of some of these services will make for greater differentiation and hence for better service to consumers, but an income-supplements policy will obviously be a necessary counterpart strategy.

These approaches suggest that among the more radical techniques for fostering difference is the invention of market-like production-and-distribution systems for social services that are presently administered through central governmental agencies. Whether supplied by governments or by private corporations, the effort would encourage a diversity of suppliers to offer a variety of goods and services, thus to help assure that consumers can make choices on their own, rather than having to accept whatever styles and qualities might have been centrally determined to be right for them.

And that may be the essential mark of the permissive planning style. It would seek to open the processes of government to all parties. It would open choice making to consumers, open planning and decision processes to more and different arguments and values. In effect, permissive planning is aimed at further opening the society to the interests of minority groups, minority opinion, and minority wants. In a society becoming increasingly diverse, as this one is, the right style of planning is the one that champions difference.

NOTES

1. I first used the name in "Planning in an Environment of Change, Part II: Permissive Planning," *The Town Planning Review* (Liverpool), 39, 4 (Jan. 1969): 277-295.

Innovation, Flexible Response and Social Learning: A Problem in the Theory of Meta-Planning

John Friedmann

In theory, the practice of planning has always been closely linked to purposeful action. We say:
—architects prepare the plans for a house: they prepare blueprints;
—a general maps out a campaign against the enemy: he devises a strategy;
—economists specify a set of production targets: they lay out a production plan;
—physical planners design the future pattern of land uses: they draw up a land use or a master plan.

In all of these examples, forces are deployed, and resources or values are allocated. This enables us to label these activities as allocative planning.

Allocative planning is always central planning. It involves a central planner and/or political decisionmaker who will sometimes be the same and sometimes a different agency or person. Indifferently, I call them both the Central Planning Authority (CPA).

A main assumption underlying central planning is that a powerful authority is needed to direct and coordinate the movement of the many parts comprising an interlocking system of relations, and that a central plan is necessary for this purpose.

The implementor of a central plan, however, is always someone other than the CPA:
—blueprints are implemented by construction firms, contractors, and workmen;
—the strategy is implemented by subordinate officers and troops against an enemy;
—the production plan is carried out by managers, foremen, and workers;
—the land use plan is carried out by the market as well as by special regulators, such as the Zoning Commission or the City Council.

Despite the uncertainties introduced by shifting from the CPA to implementors and from an intended future in the head to projects on the ground, the phrase 'according to a plan . . . .' continues to signify a commitment to order, purposefulness, systematic procedure, a sense of proportion and measure, a design. And planning was and still is thought of as holistic, comprehensive, rational, and therefore, basically, as "good."

In this context, it has always been agreed and understood that, over time, the plan would have to be adjusted to specific circumstances as they changed, that it would gradually evolve—a 'rolling' plan—and so be useful primarily in guiding, rather than directing, social actions. Clearly, however, the plan could not evolve as rapidly as the actions themselves, for it would then become coterminous with them when, instead, it was supposed to stay ahead: planning was to be a form of decisionmaking in advance.

So constituted, a plan was understood to be a formal document, and its preparation was regarded as a task for skilled professionals.

"Very well," you will say, "It is agreed that this is so. But you have told us nothing new."

To discover what is new, we shall have to pay closer attention to the implicit assumptions on which this descriptive model of planning has been based. Earlier, I referred to 'guiding social actions' when the stronger term 'blueprinting' could have been evoked. In contrast to the latter, 'to guide' suggests a certain loss of efficiency (of energy, of information) between an original conception and its final execution. We might thus speak of the efficiency of a plan much as we speak of the efficiency of a steam engine.

This loss of efficiency is best illustrated by a curious paradox: when you have least need of planning because nothing changes, planning works best; it is 100 percent efficient. But when, because of rapid, universal change, planning is needed most, it does not work at all: its efficiency is zero.

The reason for this paradox is the uncertainty of planners' expectations. For what we need to know to achieve even a modicum of efficiency in planning is not merely the general shape of the future but the likelihood that some quite specific and particular events and situations will occur.

Any statement concerning the future must be cast into either the future tense or the conditional. We say: such and such 'will' or 'might' happen. But logic demands that in either case, the 'will' or 'might' has to be qualified with phrases such as 'I believe, I guess, I hope, I expect.' I shall not explore this question further. Yet it is clear that any quasi-historical statement that we might make about the future (and, indeed, about the present time as well, since planners' present is mostly a projection from data collected in the past), and regardless of how the statement was derived, will have implicitly attached to it a *coefficient of confidence*.

This coefficient is not usually expressed as a numerical value. It is a logically necessary qualification of any predictive statement about the future occurrence (or non-occurrence) of an event. The uncertainty with which we face the future and which lies at the root of all our actions derives from several sources, among which are uncertainties about the state of the environment for action, the future intentions of other actors, and the relative importance of diverse ends and interests and their inevitable modification in the course of the action. But whatever the source, uncertainty about the future must finally come down to this: how much we are prepared to wager on the predicted outcome.

Pointing to a map, the general will say: "Tomorow morning, the enemy will be deployed along the line," but silently add, "Of this I am quite certain." That is his 'coefficient of confidence.' His staff, his field officers, and his troops in frontline combat may each have somewhat different 'coefficients', however. And who can judge what the correct level of confidence should be? It remains a purely subjective judgment.

This subjectivity tends to be veiled from our scrutinizing eyes. Both in the army and in civilian life, the problem of different subjective judgments concerning future expectations is typically solved through the hierarchy of command. In such a hierarchy, the top official's judgment of the future counts for everything and the subordinate's, for nothing.

Bureaucracies appear to be designed to reassure us of the future, to create an illusion of institutional stability and infallible knowledge. But all they manage to do by invoking the epistemology of hierarchy is to suppress potential voices of dissent (Wilensky, 1969).

The illusion of infallibility created by bureaucratic hierarchies is only one way that we manage to confront uncertainty. In addition, central planners will attempt to enhance their confidence in the future by making the relevant environment for planning more predictable. For, in a completely predictable, that is, an unchanging environment, plans can actually be drawn up and carried out (except that nobody will need them).

The army general insists on the hierarchy of command and the principle of obedience to authority. Central planners, like the general, will attempt to totalize the system for which they are responsible.

To totalize a system means to subject all potentially significant variables to a hierarchy of command. It means to transform an institution into a total institution, and to transform the state into a total state. Closely related to this is system closure whereby the system to be totalized is cut off from contaminating outside influence. And just as in the army or an insane asylum, the extension of bureaucratic control, coupled with system closure, results in behavior that is often ludicrous and cruel.

But the hegemony of bureaus contains its own well-known contradictions: the insurmountable problem of coordination (the larger the bureaucracy, the more the need for coordination and the less ability to obtain it); rigidity of response where flexible and rapid actions are required; arbitrary discretion by powerful officials; widespread graft and

unequal access to power; byzantine factional struggles; the revolt of the
inmates; and numerous more (Downs, 1967). In short, bureaucratic control—the "ideal" of totalization—presents no solution at all.

These 'pathologies' of planning and bureaucratic control are only too
familiar. They have their root in the illusion that the future can be
tamed and made innocuous. Would that central planners knew this in
their bones! Instead, their normal answer to the steadily rising loss of
efficiency in planning is to impose still further controls and restrictions.
But, of course, this only increases the arbitrariness of bureaucratic procedure, and the process of planning becomes ever more inscrutable, not
only to its objects (which anyway, one might have reason to expect),
but to its subjects or practitioners as well. And with rising public ignorance, the mythology of planning has a chance to evolve. Belief in
the saving powers of planning tends to increase as its efficiency declines
(Friedmann, 1973).

Let me pause here to ask whether the ability to accurately predict the
future is, indeed, our most urgent need for making planning more efficient.[1]
If the "paradox of planning" is correctly formulated, this need would be
clearly established; alternatively, we would have to abandon the particular
conception of planning which underlies the paradox.

As I have used the term until now, and in accord with custom, planning stands for advance decisionmaking. This usage enabled me to
derive such related terms as order, control, predictability, blueprint, command, guidance, monitoring, goal achievement, and rationality. For this
traditional connotation, I shall now substitute the linking of knowledge
to action as the essential meaning of planning. In this formulation, planning is concerned with neither knowledge nor with action alone, but with
the mediation between them.

This definition has the advantage not only of broadening the scope of
planning but of rescuing us from the impossible and indeed repugnant
task of rendering the future more predictable. For as the linkage of
knowledge to action, planning can be instituted only in those social systems
that remain in a deep and fundamental sense open to the future and the
world. That world, by which I mean the totality of all forces that act
upon our lives, is continuously in flux. Such stabilities as we detect in it
are only relative, a slowing down of one component of the total flux.

Those changes that we are able to measure are typically linear in form
(e.g., the rate of urbanization). On the other hand, we can measure only
a few of the changes that actually occur and envelop our actions. And a
majority of them are not linear at all but coalesce to create what Emery
and Trist (1965) have called a turbulent environment. An environment
is turbulent when the impact of any action taken with respect to it will
yield an outcome that is unpredictable and, in addition, will produce a

significant threat to the actor himself. Whether a given environment is turbulent in fact, suggesting a high degree of entropy or loss of information, or merely extraordinarily complex but relatively stable, cannot be said with certainty. All we can say is that it appears to behave as if it were, in fact, entropic (Rittel and Webber, 1973).

I should like to give two examples of this. A classic instance of action in a turbulent environment was afforded by the unfolding of the Watergate drama. Bugging the national headquarters of the political opposition seemed such a small, easily controllable, and downright innocuous act (given prevailing standards of political morality), that it seemed scarcely worthy of attention by the President or his immediate collaborators. Yet, in a short time, it brought about the collapse of the Administration in a wholly spectacular and unexpected manner.

The second example is taken from computer science (Weizenbaum, 1972). It is a well-known fact that large-scale computerized models may take many months and even years to construct. The procedure followed is a process of trial and error. A group of programmers and subject experts will work together, adjusting and tinkering with their model, changing coefficients of relation, adding new variables, until in the opinion of the group a satisfactory result has been attained, until the model has become 'robust'. The process, as I said, is long and tedious. Some members of the group will therefore leave it in mid-course, and others newly join. It would be rare indeed to have the same team that began the work together at the finish of the program.

But now who guarantees the reliability of the model? Because the group that is working with it, simulating the future, is composed of members who are different from the group that built it, the only record that went into the construction of the model is the model itself. There is no way that anyone can check or verify the model now, except by its results, and these we are obliged to take on faith. The medium here has, in a very real sense, become the message. To understand the model, we should have to reconstruct it ourselves. But this would mean to build another model. The model that we have defies all efforts at further reduction. It is the Kantian thing-in-itself. It is, in the perspective of the user, as well a turbulent environment, a cipher, an enigma. Who knows what evil magic might not come from all the data and instructions that we command it to accept?

My claim is that in the realm of socioeconomic affairs, the environments we face are indeed turbulent. They have potentially dangerous properties of which we remain ignorant. Trapped within these environments, how shall we link knowledge to action? That is the problem in what Andreas Faludi (1973) has called the theory of meta-planning. It is a problem in the design of new institutional arrangements capable of guiding

us through turbulence and, therefore, capable of responding flexibly, with-
standing strain, and initiating wholly new sets of activity in response to
always new, unprecedented situations.

Let us agree that this is what we really need. Is it then possible to
design such institutions? What would they look like? And how would
they behave?

Before proceeding with an answer, I should like to reply to a possible
objection: even in turbulent environments, we are often forced to make
long-term commitments that cannot be reversed. Examples are large-scale
projects such as an irrigation dam or subway or nuclear power plant.[2] It
is true that building these facilities will introduce rigidities into the system
far beyond those which are imposed by the physical structures themselves.
in the long-run, those rigidities may well prove very costly to society. But
if an irreversible commitment must be made, then we should also be
prepared to deal with its results. *We shall have to develop a capacity for
handling the unexpected consequences of our actions as they occur and
become known to us* (Perloff and Flaming, 1976).

The principle involved here is as old as humankind itself. Albert Hirschman (1967) called it 'The Hiding Hand', because it hides from use the
knowledge of all the consequences that flow from our actions. If we had
perfect knowledge, Hirschman contends, we might not wish to act at all;
the costs would seem too great. It is our ignorance of the future that
gives us the confidence to act. It is a confidence we have, not in our
capacity to foretell the future, nor even to design it, *but to deal with it
in the very process of happening.*

This is another way of saying that, to live with turbulence, we need
to transform the social guidance system that we have (at the level of the
whole society) into an innovative social learning system. This new system
would have to correspond to at least three criteria.

The first criterion is derived from the common-sensical proposition that
innovations cannot be planned in advance but are emergents, unexpected
events that seemingly appear from nowhere (though they can often be
explained in retrospect). In that sense, emergents may be said to represent novel responses to novel challenges or crises. And, even though
organizational measures can ensure a heightened probability of innovation,
neither the specific form of innovations, nor the precise time when they
will appear, nor whether they will, indeed, appear at all, can in any
sense be guaranteed.

The first criterion then, simply asserts that social learning systems should
be structured so as to enhance the probability of innovation.

The second criterion for a social learning system is that its structure
should *increase the opportunity for social practice.* In social practice, learning arises from the interplay between knowing and doing. To do something

requires a set of values to which we wish to give expression, a theory of how the world is put together, and an explicit strategy for acting. These components constitute a single package and are subject to verification and revision in light of the consequences of the action itself. But the important point is this: in social practice, knower and doer are one and the same. The ancient separation of headwork from handwork is eliminated, and the conceptual foundation for the social division of labor is removed (Friedmann and Abonyi, 1976).

The third criterion is that the structure of a social learning system should *increase the opportunity for dialogue and face-to-face relations*. This derives from the proposition that innovative social practice (and therefore also social learning) best occurs in what I call 'experimental settings' (Friedmann and Abonyi, 1976). Experimental settings are social spaces that arise from the transactions among those who are engaged in an experiment to bring about a social change. Typically, they involve a small number of actors who stand to each other in a relation of dialogic encounter (Friedmann, 1973, 1976).

The familiar word 'experiment', however, has to be used with caution. In common usage, we are accustomed to distinguish sharply between experimenter and the object on which he operates; in social practice, on the other hand, we are drawn into an experiment as simultaneously a learning subject and an object exposed to the conditions of the experiment itself. This apparent contradiction (the experimenter as both the subject and object of his experiment) is resolved in the tensions that arise between them. Social learning is a dialectical as well as dialogic process, a process of *reflexive action*, that takes place in environments from which we learn in the very process of transforming them.

Our three criteria tell us what kind of social organization is appropriate for innovation and for social learning and, indeed, for a full life (Friedmann, 1976). The general solution to our problem would be this: *to build a heightened capacity for learning* and for doing into the living 'cells' of a society. Accordingly, the present form of central, allocative planning, with its single, thinking head and many servile limbs, would be replaced by a form of planning in which the limbs and head are brought together into a single unit of reflexive action, the units being multiplied until the entire social system stands transformed.

To the extent that the distinction between headwork and handwork is eliminated, each cell within a social system would become progressively despecialized, more centered upon itself, more self-reliant and autonomous. The despecialization that occurs when thinking and working are joined into a single unit can and ought to be extended further by despecializing work itself. In this way, the people that comprise each unit cell would gain a greater measure of responsibility and power over their livelihood.

And the intensity as well as the complexity of bonds that link each cell to the system of all cells would be reduced.

Where a system has become despecialized, it will also have become descaled. A descaled society is one in which apparent turbulence in the environment has been reduced, because many more problems can now be handled at the level of the cell (or by a group of associated cells) without affecting other units.

Of course, there will be problems that extend beyond the boundaries of single cells. Some of them may be adequately handled through coopera- tive, voluntary action involving two or more cells; others will require a more formal 'regionalization' of decisionmaking powers (or the formation of macrocells); and still others will call for appropriate collective action at the level of the system as a whole.

This 'reconstitution' of the social system from its despecialized parts, proceeding upward from single cell to systemwide coordination, corre- sponds to three general principles: (1) that all powers not specifically granted to higher units should be retained by lower ones—the principle of *federation;* (2) that decisions and actions should be taken at the organi- zational level where major effects can be internalized—the principle of *internalization;* and (3) that all cells should have direct voice and influence in the decisions and actions of higher, aggregated levels—the principle of *power at the base.* These principles seem to underlie all decentralized (or decentralizing) socialist systems, including Yugoslavia (Stefanovic, 1975; Zukin, 1975), Cuba (Cockburn, 1976), and China (Donnithorne, 1972, 1976; Lardy, 1976).

We must now turn to more specific questions in the application of these principles. Earlier, I spoke of cellular units as the basic elements of a learning society. How are these units to be organized? Two possibilities are given, relating to different bases of social integration. The first is *functional,* referring to vertically integrated structures whose elements are related to each other on a basis of dominance/subservience and the nexus of self-interest. Examples are corporate forms of organization, including bureaucratic structures, such as metropolitan transit authorities and De- partments of Transportation. The second is *territorial* and refers to hori- zontally integrated structures whose elements are related to each other on a basis of shared destiny and sentiment. Local neighborhood communities are integrated territorially; so are culturally defined regions, more prevalent perhaps in Europe than the United States, though even in this country they are not wholly absent; and, of course, the great majority of nations that occupy a bounded space.

Although both forms of social integration are present in all complex societies, they are rarely in harmonious balance with each other; their relationship is basically antagonistic. Corporate structures tend to have a weakening, disintegrative effect on the solidarity relations of territorial groups (at the same time that they open up the group to outside influence and stimulation), whereas a closing of territorial boundaries tends to place limits on the relentless expansion of corporate powers and to subordinate their growth to a collective will.

Function and territory constitute a "cosmic" *unity of opposites*. Necessary for each other, they are yet in contradiction with each other. The question that arises concerns the relative historical imbalance in the constitution of these forces.

The last two centuries have witnessed the progressive rise of functional organizations and the concommitant weakening of territorially organized communities, particularly below the level of nation. The bonds of neighborhood and region have been replaced by functional alignments; reciprocal relations of social solidarity have been replaced by functional criteria; a sense of place has yielded to an individual desire for material gain.

This growing imbalance in the relation of functional to territorial bases of social integration was accompanied by a steady upward drift of power from local communities (and other subnational territorial units) to national and even global levels of decision. It is this trend which rendered planning indispensible as a device for central allocation by the State. And yet, as we have slowly come to realize, the increasingly sophisticated machinery of central planning remains largely impotent in face of such effects of corporate growth as runaway inflation, unemployment, massive poverty, pollution, or the systematic destruction of irreplaceable resources —matters which are left for territorial governments to solve.

We have seen why this is so. The cognitive bases of central planning are inadequate to manage change in large-scale, "turbulent" environments. Instead, we have to constitute the social framework for an epistemology of social practice. *Social practice and the capacity for social learning must be directly graven onto the structure of society.*

The principles of social learning, I shall argue, must be applied, in the first instance, to territorial entities. This would lead to a relative strengthening of territorial powers, to the restructuring of territorial systems on a basis of descaled, despecialized, and territorial units, and so to a general restructuring of social guidance systems (Etzioni, 1968). Three specific reasons support this argument: first, existing imbalances in social integration excessively favor functional over territorial organizations; second, the application of social learning principles to corporate organizations will merely further their own growth at the expense of territorial power (most current work in organization development is of this sort; see Schon, 1971); and third, the corporate sector can be subordinated to a collective will only when the territorial power of communities is reinforced.

If territorial communities are strengthened, the tasks of central allocation will be vastly simplified and hence become more tractible. Most decisions will be taken and carried out close to the points of ultimate impact and in full awareness of the thousand particularities of local conditions. They will be taken by involving people from districts and neighborhoods—meeting in assemblies—in the active discussion of issues that vitally affect them, extending in all cases to residentiary but also to productive functions.

The following may serve as useful points of departure for thinking about how we might proceed to build an innovative, flexible response system, designed to further social learning.

1. In territorially organized social systems, such as a city, effective economic and political power should be vested in the smallest units having territorial integrity. These Districts, as they might be called, should be sufficiently large to sustain a significant measure of economic and cultural activity, yet small enough to involve substantial numbers of the population in the public affairs of the community.[3]

2. Effective communal control over basic resources is essential to a system of decentralized territorial power. Districts should retain the right to ensure development of land and other natural resources in accord with the long-run interests of the community as a territorial entity.

3. Both the legislative and executive powers of territorial communities should be exercised through a single Communal Assembly and its constituent Working Groups. Planning is integrated with the work of the Assembly.

4. Population groups that are likely to be affected by the potential actions of Communal Assemblies should be involved in the design of these actions and in the study of their consequences. This might be accomplished through a formal system of delegation, with delegates accountable to the units which have elected them. Relevant units would include subdistrict areas (neighborhoods, streets) as well as places of work and formally constituted interest groups (labor unions, environmentalists, commuters, youth organizations, etc.).

5. All members of the community should have equal and open access to all centers of public deliberation and decision, and the right to be heard.

6. Programs authorized by Communal Assemblies may be financed from rental charges levied on the occupance and use of public land; from taxes levied on incomes produced in the community; from public service and from user charges; from subsidies and other transfer payments made by higher units to equalize available resources; and from public borrowings.

7. A small number of hierarchical levels of reflexive action should be created so that actions whose consequences cannot be contained within a single District may be considered at the next higher, appropriate level. But the decisions of any higher level (or Assembly) should always be taken with the full knowledge, understanding, and participation of the Assemblies in all of the affected parts.

8. Communal Assemblies should retain all powers not specifically granted to higher units of reflexive action.

9. Assembly membership at levels higher than the District should be drawn at frequent intervals from Communal Assemblies within their relevant area.

Looking at this model of a society that is organized on principles of social learning, two questions spring to mind. Existing discrepancies between the designed and actual forms of social organization suggest a qualitative leap. To realize the complete design, or even an approximation of it, will require a vast effort. What gains might be expected from it? This is the first question we need to ask. And the second question is, assuming we agree that the expenditure of energy would be worthwhile, how might we then proceed to translate the design in our head into specific projects on the ground?

Turning to the relative merits of what has been proposed, let us recall how we arrived at our model. The argument was roughly this:

Central, allocative planning has become bankrupt. A major difficulty arises from our inability to know the future with any reasonable degree of certainty; it also stems from the apparent turbulence of the environment for public action. In their excessive pride to shape the future according to a preconceived design, planning authorities attempt to totalize the system for which they plan by the further extension of bureaucratic controls and command structures. However, because of the dynamics of bureaucracy, efforts in this direction are likely to be self-defeating. Expanding bureaucracy merely increases the turbulence.

Within the context of a broad definition that equated planning with the mediation between knowledge and action, the need to evolve a heightened capacity for innovation and for social learning was described as a task having the highest priority for the nation.

The task was treated as a problem in organization theory. The desired characteristics could be obtained, I argued, by the creation of multiple 'settings' in which innovation, social practice, and dialogue would be facilitated and encouraged. This formation led to the concept of a cellular structure of social relations in which the elementary units of a social system would have a heightened capacity for reflexive action (thinking and doing would be closely joined) and would become increasingly despecialized, descaled, autonomous, and centered upon themselves.[4]

Once the elementary units of the system had been identified and properly described, three principles were proposed for the reconstruction of a larger system out of these elementary particles or cells. This larger system was required in order to account for so-called externalities and spill-over effects. At the same time, it was essential to guard against the constant dangers of an upward drift of power and the unwitting reproduction of the present, crisis-ridden system. The principles for a process of reconstitution of a larger system from its parts were accordingly intended to ensure that the capacity for reflexive action at the base would not be harmed as 'cells' were reinserted into a more comprehensive form of governance.

Finally, the concepts of functional and territorial structures were introduced as a 'unity of opposites' that would be found in every complex social system. The present, imbalanced relationship between them has led to the hegemony of corporate structures and the progressive disarticulation of territorial communities. At the same time that the negative effects of corporate production—unemployment, inequality, and environmental degradation—have grown in severity, the ability of territorial communities to cope with them has been impaired. It was therefore argued that the principles of a learning society which had been previously described should be applied, in the first instance, to a strengthening of territorial bonds. It was this emphasis which led to a description of the local District as the basic cell of a reconstituted system of territorial governance.

But our model of this system is something more than merely a response to what might be described as a major crisis of knowing and control in advanced industrial societies. By advocating a reconstruction of territorial order, it points to a *human-scaled* society that, being open to the future, is self-transforming and experimental. We might describe it as an order in which we make our appearance as men and women engaged in social practice, in which the logical distinctions between subject and object have become attenuated, in which alienation is less than the problem that it used to be, and in which relations have become transparent.

And so the effort to achieve a human-scaled society would seem to be worthwhile. This brings me to the threshold of the second question; how might such a society actually be brought about? What strategy for action should we follow?

The distance that must be covered from where we are to where we want to be is great. But knowledge of the crisis is no longer the esoteric secret of a few; it has become the common knowledge of us all: the spectacle of New York, the second largest city in the world, crashing into insolvency; the sheer perversity of supersonic flight by which we subsidize the rich to wind their spiderweb of corporate power ever more tightly around us; the rapacious destruction of our natural wealth—the oceans of air and water that sustain us, the earth's resources that we turn into things we use—by interests that pay no heed to the survival of the race.

The situation is fluid and filled with possibilities of true emergents. Instinctively, we grope for answers, witness the widespread interest in zero growth (Meadows et al., 1972); the instantaneous popularity of 'small is beautiful' (Schumacher, 1973); the social movement for greater personal autonomy (Illich, 1973; Turner, 1976); the growing sense for the integrity of given places and environments (Kotler, 1960; Morris and Hess, 1975). There is thus receptivity, I think, for new proposals that promise to control the turbulence in which we live and to return to us a sense of purpose.

But what is to be done? I may venture some suggestions. In the first place, development must be refocussed on district neighborhoods in the range of from 30,000 to 50,000 inhabitants. Because many small towns are also of this size, their economic, cultural, and political revival should be regarded as a matter of national priority. This effort should be joined to a parallel effort to animate the wider regional economy of which they form a part by an intensive development of regional resources, with major benefits accruing to the population of the local area. Second, empowering legislation should be passed that will provide for self-governing structures at District and regional levels, closely articulating their relations with one another and with the national system of all regions. This legislation should designate the Districts as the primary territorial units of national life. It should also encourage and facilitate the equal access of all citizens to territorial power through a system of formal delegation. Third, this legislation will remain a hollow shell unless it comes as the culmination of a political movement that is rooted in actual experience with self-governance. Territoriality is not primarily a principle of administration; it is a felt reality, a sense of loyalty to place. And it arises as the natural result of a protracted struggle to refocus the economic, political, and cultural life of a people on the localities that are their rightful habitat.

What I am proposing is a beginning and not a destination. The course I have outlined implies a drastic change in the relationships of power and a political struggle to bring this change about that is likely to last for many decades. But every change begins from where we are.

ACKNOWLEDGMENTS

This essay was written while the author was on sabbatical leave from the University of California at Los Angeles and was supported by the Simon Guggenheim Foundation and the Centre for Environmental Studies, London, England. The help of all these institutions is deeply appreciated. In addition, I am extremely grateful to Professor Martin Wachs for his careful editing of this essay. Of course, as usual, all responsibility rests with the author.

NOTES

1. For a defense of future studies, albeit in a self-critical vein, see Dror (1975) and Fowles (1976). The anti-futurist position is argued in Friedmann (1973, 1976).

2. How wise such commitments are is another question. Recent mass transit proposals for Kuala Lumpur, Teheran, Bangkok, and Singapore have been estimated to cost, using these cities' population as a base, 82, 58, 50, and 38 per cent respectively of the Gross National Product per capita, a sum of money that relatively poor countries can ill afford (Peter Viola, unpublished data).

3. A population of between 30,000 and 50,000 would seem not inappropriate under a wide variety of conditions (Morris and Hess, 1975; Friedmann and Douglass, 1976).

4. John Galtung, one of Europe's leading sociologists, writes in this connection: "The policies of increased . . . national self-reliance in the rich world will have to be coupled with the policies of local self-reliance . . . at the subnational level. Generally, this will go together with increased 'nationalism' of local character, a phenomenon that has already been observed in the rich world for a long time. Thus, we would generally predict an escalating tendency for 'minorities', ethnically or territorially defined (or usually both) to assert themselves and to couple their demands for increased politcal autonomy to a local self-reliance that will have to be based on an alternative life style of the type mentioned. It is from such groups rather than from the Centre that initiatives for change are likely to come" (Galtung, 1976, p. 93).

REFERENCES

Cynthia Cockburn, *People's Power: The New Administrative System in Cuba* (London: Centre for Environmental Studies, 1976).

A. Donnithorne, *The Budget and the Plan in China: Central-Local Economic Relations.* Contemporary China Papers No. 3 (Canberra: Australian University Press, 1972).

A. Donnithorne, "Centralization and Decentralization in China's Fiscal Management," *The China Quarterly* 66 (1976): 328-339.

A. Downs, *Inside Bureaucracy* (Boston: Little, Brown and Co., 1967).

Y. Dror, "Some Fundamental Philosophical, Psychological and Intellectual Assumptions of Future Studies." In: *The Future as an Academic Discipline, Ciba Foundation Symposium 36, New Series* (North Holland: Elsevier/Excerpta Medica, 1975).

F. E. Emery and E. L. Trist, "The Causal Texture of Organizational Environments," *Human Relations* 18 (1965): 21-32.

A. Etzioni, *The Active Society* (New York: The Free Press, 1968).

Andreas Faludi, *Planning Theory* (Oxford: Pergamon Press, 1973).

J. Fowles, "An Overview of Social Forecasting Procedures," *Journal of the American Institute of Planners* 42, (1976): 253-263.

J. Friedmann, *Retracking America: A Theory of Transactive Planning* (Garden City: Doubleday/Anchor, 1973).

J. Friedmann, *The Good Society: A Primer of Its Social Practice* (Los Angeles: School of Architecture and Urban Planning, UCLA, 1976).

J. Friedmann and G. Abonyi, "Social Learning: A Model for Policy Research," *Environment and Planning* (1976).

J. Friedmann and M. Douglass, "Agropolitan Development: Towards a New Strategy for Regional Planning in Asia." In: United Nations Centre for Regional Development, *Growth Pole Strategy and Regional Development Planning in Asia* (UNCRD, 2-4-7, Marunouchi, Maka-ku, Nagoya 460, Japan, 1976): 333-389.

J. Galtung, "Alternative Life Styles in Rich Countries," *Development Dialogue* 1 (1976): 83-96.

A. Hirschman, *Development Projects Observed* (Washington, D.C.: The Brookings Institution, 1967).

I. Illich, *Tools for Conviviality* (New York: Harper and Row, 1973).

M. Kotler, *Neighborhood Government: The Local Foundations of Political Life* (Indianapolis: Bobbs-Merrill, 1960).

N. R. Lardy, Reply, *The China Quarterly* 66 (1976): 340-354.

D. M. Meadows, D. L. Meadows, J. Randers, and W. W. Behrens, III, *Limits to Growth* (New York: Universal Books, 1972).

D. Morris and K. Hess, *Neighborhood Power: The New Localism* (Boston: Beacon Press, 1975).

H. S. Perloff and D. J. Flaming, "Approaches to the Future in US Transportation Planning," *Transportation* 5, 2 (1976): 153-173.

H. W. J. Rittel and M. Webber, "Dilemmas in a General Theory of Planning," *Policy Sciences* 4, 2 (1973): 155-169.

D. U. Stefanovic, "Community Development and Popular Participation in Yugoslavia." *United Nations Conference on Human Settlements* (Vancouver, Canada, *Regional Preparatory Conferences*, A/Conf. 70/RPC/BP/10, 1975).

D. Schon, *Beyond the Stable State* (New York: Random House, 1971).

E. F. Schumacher, *Small Is Beautiful* (New York: Harper Torchbooks, 1973).

J. F. C. Turner, *Housing by People: Towards Autonomy in Building Environments* (London: Marion Boyars, 1976).

J. Weizenbaum, "On the Impact of the Computer on Society," *Science* (May 12, 1972): 609-614.

Harold L. Wilensky, *Organizational Intelligence: Knowledge and Policy in Government and Industry* (New York: Basic Books, 1969).

S. Zukin, *Beyond Marx and Tito: Theory and Practice in Yugoslav Socialism* (London: Cambridge University Press, 1975).

The Planner as Interventionist
in Public Policy Issues

Jerome L. Kaufman

American planners work in many more substantive areas today than twenty years ago when physical planning and urban renewal agencies were the principal employers of planning talent and land use, zoning, housing and transportation the principal fields of planning activity. Although more people educated as planners are finding employment outside of governmental planning circles today—e.g. in universities, private research firms, development firms, and community organizations—the planner's principal working habitat is still the governmental planning agency. What's different from the past is that more and more specialized planning agencies at all levels of government are taking their place beside the traditional, yet still predominant general-purpose city, county, regional, and state planning agencies. And although a sizable number of today's planners still specialize in some aspect of physical planning, increasingly other specializations have emerged, including health, energy, education, manpower, economic development, water quality, coastal zone management, and criminal justice planning. No doubt, the future will see the emergence of new planning specialties.

Despite the increasing diversification of planners, most planners who work in the government planning sector share a common interest—sometimes subdued, sometimes strong—in trying to influence the course public policy takes within their respective orbits. The health planner, for example, is not simply an analyst interested in better understanding the structure, functions, and dynamics of the health system. Going beyond analysis, the health planner tries to affect decisions made within the health system to realize some conception of an improved system state. The same holds true for land use, energy, manpower, and other type planners.

How successful are contemporary planners, regardless of their varied subject area interests at public policy and decision influencing? Little empirical data is available to answer this question, partly because the methodological problems involved in assessing the impact of a soft discipline like planning are hairy indeed. But informed opinion holds that, with some exceptions, the implementation record of planners is spotty and none too impressive. Planners, themselves, sometimes admit this. When city planning directors, for example, were asked in 1971 to assess their agencies' performance in twelve activity areas, they ranked their planning implementation performance quite low—third from the bottom (IMCA, 1971, Tables 5 and 6). So did regional planning agency directors in a 1973 survey. Of thirteen activities they were asked about, they ranked the plan implementation performance of their agencies fourth from the bottom (ACIR, 1973, p. 102). If similar surveys were conducted of planners working for more specialized planning bodies, they would probably respond in the same vein about the limited implementation successes of their agencies.

Unlike twenty years ago, when public scrutiny of planners was virtually nonexistent, a small but steadily growing stream of criticism is being directed at today's planners. While the criticisms come from different quarters and reflect different concerns, all, in some way, amount to questioning the planner's value as a public sector professional. One of these strands of criticism relates to the assumed difficulties planners have in influencing much in the way of public policies and decisions.[1]

As one who believes that planners have important contributions to make in furthering the public interest, I consider this criticism a tocsin that planners should heed. In large part, the effectiveness of American planning depends on the extent to which planners influence public policies and decisions for social betterment. And by virtue of their claim to be a profession, planners are obligated to continually seek to improve their effectiveness.

Planner Roles: The Advisor and Interventionist

How then do contemporary planners go about trying to affect the course of public policy within the environments in which they work? A commonly held view is that planners try to achieve influence by devoting much of their energies to performing as technical advisors to policy officials and decisionmakers, helping them solve both vexing and less troublesome problems by undertaking technical studies and analyses and proposing policy and programmatic recommendations for their consideration. Thus, in an institutional sense, the city planning department advises the mayor and city council, the health planning agency advises its policy board of consumers and health service providers, the state planning agency advises the governor, and so forth.

In this conception of planning, the planner attempts to introduce more rationality and objective thought into the decisionmaking process of the community or system being planned for by pursuing a rational planning approach. Whether the issue to be dealt with is simple or complex, the approach has consistency, proceeding sequentially from undertaking studies and analyses to developing policy alternatives, to evaluating the consequences of alternatives, to recommending a preferred alternative for the consideration of policy officials. If the approach succeeds, then the over-riding power of sound, intelligent technical analysis followed by prescription of sound, intelligent courses of action should eventually result in moving policy officials to accept the planner's advice. Consequently, as the theory goes, better decisions would be made in the public interest.

But there are two problems with this view. First, no assurance exists that public policies and decisions will indeed be substantially affected by planners if they energetically pursue the advisory-rational planning approach. Second, it is doubtful whether most contemporary planners follow such an approach anymore as their exclusive mode of operation.

Let me first address the notion that faithful pursuit of the advisory-rational planning approach by planners will result in their achieving significant policy and decision influence. To the contrary, it's likely that a rigid, excessive reliance on this approach may limit—at best, not appreciably enhance—the capacity of planners to impact decisions. Why? Because the approach is premised on the belief that decisionmakers will be favorably disposed towards and thereby influenced by a process that follows logical processes of analyses, development of alternatives, and evaluation of consequences. Would that it be so simple. Unfortunately, most decisionmakers rarely behave so responsively. As Edward Banfield bluntly contends, decisionmaking is more often the outcome of social choice—i.e., "the accidental by-product of the action of two or more actors who have no common intention and who make their selections competitively without regard to each other . . . it is an outcome which no one planned as a 'solution' to a 'problem'." (Banfield, 1961, pp. 326-7). So relying too heavily on the rational planning approach as a means of influencing decisionmakers, who often act on a social choice basis, may at best yield only marginal success. The real question for planners interested in achieving more decisionmaking influence then becomes: where do they go beyond just the advisor-rational planning approach?

The second notion is that contemporary planners essentially pursue the technical advisor-rational planning approach as their basic method of trying to impact public policy and decision outcomes. Having had fairly close contact with a wide variety of practicing planners and planning agencies in some twenty years of experience as a planner, I seriously doubt the validity of this contention.[2] While planners do act in the advisor-rationalist mode at times, the model insufficiently describes the reality of contemporary planning practice, specifically failing to capture the full range of behavior of planners as they go about trying to affect public policies and decisions.

Yet the neutral, technical service image of planners is one that continues to be widely promulgated—often by practicing planners themselves. Some project this image because they do in fact try to conduct themselves in this manner. But others, who behave in more overt and covert politicized ways, tend to project this image because it is a relatively safe and unthreatening one to convey. Following are a couple of representative planning agency statements designed for public consumption that reflect such an image:

> "In a recent policy decision the Commission declared that a high priority was to assist local governments by providing technical assistance, upon request . . . All plans produced by the regional planning commission are advisory and carry no authority." (From 1974 *Annual Report*, Bay-Lake Regional Planning Commission, Wisconsin, pp. 8-9).

> "The Regional Development Plan won't mean that all tomorrow's problems will be solved, but it gives us a framework to assess regional needs early and make allowances. Which is where you come in. *All the staff and technical work is about complete. It's up to the political process now.*" (underlining mine) (From *Action*, Atlanta Regional Commission, July 1975, Vol. 4, #7, last page).

Some planning educators also lend credence to the notion that the technical advisory role is the predominant one performed by planners. For instance:

> ". . . where planners once furnished end-state physical development plans to an appointed planning commission comprised of the civic and business elite, planners now function as decision aides to executive and administrative office holders in matters concerning both physical and socio-economic development." (Bergman and Malizia, 1975, p. 1).

Or, while bemoaning the planner's "historical obsession with planning as an advisory role to decision makers," the author of a recently published book on planning implies that the majority of planners do in fact perform in such a capacity—with conviction.

> "The quintessential element of planning as process, theory, technique, and profession in the American system of state and local government has been its advisory nature. Transformed into a role in the political process and life of state and local government, this has meant that the planner fulfills the role of advisor to the persons making the decisions . . . Periodically there have been suggestions from a surprising variety of sources that maybe the planner should do more than just advise . . . *Such notions have been steadfastly repulsed by planners* and politicians alike . . . (underlining mine) (Catanese, 1975, p. 126).

My own belief is that, despite protestations to the contrary, an increasing number of today's planners transcend the narrow behavior patterns prescribed by the advisor-rational planning approach in their efforts to influence public policy and decisions. The reality is that they act pur-

posefully at times as interventionists—exercising various degrees of politicized behavior—by injecting themselves into various policy issues to
try to influence the issue outcomes so that they more resemble their
agency's policy preferences.[3]   At such times, planners go beyond the objective neutralism implied in offering advice to public policy officials
through pursuit of a rational planning approach.   Indeed, their behavior
is not unlike the behavior of other self-interest groups who use a variety
of tactics of a persuasion, exchange, engagement, and sometimes even
pressure and threat nature to try to get their point of view incorporated
in decision outcomes.[4]   What is interesting, however, is that although many
contemporary planners and planning agencies engage in interventions, such
behavior is little acknowledged by planning practitioners or little discussed
in the published planning literature.[5]

The pull towards politicized intervention behavior on the part of planners is understandable in several respects.   Some years ago, Norton Long
wrote a particularly perceptive article in which he looked at a community
as a territory in which various actors played out a number of games:

> "Sharing a common territorial field and collaborating for different and
> particular ends in the achievement of overall social functions, the
> players in one game make use of the players in another and are, in
> turn, made use of by them.   Thus, the banker makes use of the news-
> paperman, the politician, the contractor, the ecclesiastic, the labor
> leader, the civic leader—all to further his success in the banking game."
> (Long, 1958, p. 254).

If a planning game exists—and I believe it does—whereby planners try
to impact decisions so these more closely resemble their agency's policy
preferences, then why shouldn't planners, like the banker in the above
example, be disposed to make use of other actors in the community or
system to further their success?   And when they do, they most likely
engage in politicized forms of behavior akin to that of other special interest
group representatives who try to further their group's winnings by influencing the decision outcomes of issues in which they get involved.

Or take another perspective.   Within any system, decisions are continuously made to allocate or withhold resources with or without the planner's
input, the process having a momentum of its own.   Furthermore, a number
of different interest groups operate on multiple issues to advance their
own policy preferences.   Given this conception of a dynamic, pluralistic,
and complex decision system, planners and planning agencies that are
reluctant to intervene and behave too passively—behavior which the advisory-rational planning model implies—would too often be left at the
starting gate.   So to increase the chances that their "special" interests will
be embodied more in eventual system decisions, many contemporary plan-

ning bodies compensate at times by playing a more active, interventionist role. At the most, they try to manage the outcomes of planning episodes, some being more successful at this than others.

It should not then come as much of a surprise that intervention activity is more commonly engaged in by planners today—at all levels of government and in all types of functional and general purpose agencies—than is generally acknowledged. Since planners spend much of their time in formulating policies, it's understandable that they would develop stakes in seeing these policies put into effect.

Yet, while most planning agencies have numerous opportunities to intervene in policy issues, not all do so. And of those that do, the extent to which they intervene varies considerably. Some agencies rarely act as interventionists for different reasons. Some hew closely to the rational planning model of collecting facts, analyzing them, posing alternative policies, spelling out their consequences and finally stopping at the point of recommending a preferred policy to decisionmakers, because of philosophical convictions. They see this role as the only acceptable one for planners to perform. Others, less philosophically disinclined towards intervention, markedly limit their intervention activities for practical reasons. Either they perceive they lack sufficient staff or sufficient support for the planning function, or they are leery of the possible backlash that a more aggressive intervention role might engender.

But many contemporary planners still have a propensity, however sublimated, to occasionally intervene in policy issues. The characteristics of these issues can vary considerably. At one end are fairly simple issues— where the policy sought is relatively uncontroversial, where few actors are involved, and where opposition is minimal. A single strategy may suffice, with a decision outcome reached in a fairly short period of time. On the other end are exceedingly complex issues—involving many actors, considerable apathy or even formidable opposition, the use of multiple strategies and tactics phased over time, and a time frame of several years to resolve. The point is that planners may choose to intervene in a wide variety of issues having different degrees of complexity.

And when planners do intervene in an issue, they usually play one of three roles—either they try to initiate a policy, modify a policy, or prevent a policy from being enacted. As an *initiator*, the planning body may try to inject certain preferred policies into the community or system decision stream. There may be recently developed policies or ones kept under wraps for awhile. Such policies are often unfamiliar and untested, usually representing something different from the status quo. While latent support for such policies may exist elsewhere, unless nurtured by the planners, it may never materialize in the form of a favorable action decision. By the same token, opposition may arise to the particular policy the planning body tries to initiate. As an interventionist, some of its energies may therefore have to be directed toward either winning the opposition over to its side or neutralizing it.

As mentioned previously, decisions in a community or within a functional system are being made all the time, with or without the planner's involvement. Since the system is dynamic, with many actors and groups trying to get their policy preferences embodied in decisions that are made, a number of ideas, policies, and proposals about things the planning agency is concerned about obviously surface from different quarters—e.g. the mayor's office, legislators, the business community, other governmental agencies, service providers, service beneficiaries, etc. To the extent planners working for government agencies are aware of these proposals in their germinating stages, they tend to assess them according to some planning-derived benchmarks. Is the proposal consistent with planning agency policy? Or, if put into effect, would it undermine planning agency policy? If the answer is the latter, then the planners—if they choose to intervene—can play one of two other roles. More likely, they may try to *modify* the "outside" initiated proposal to make it more consistent with their policy views, but in some instances, they may try to *prevent* the "outside" initiated proposal from being enacted at all.

In my judgment, as the planner's ability to influence the course of public policies and decisions increases, the growing state of unease about the planner's worth as a public sector professional can be reduced. And selectively intervening in policy issues is an important route to pursue in trying to achieve that greater influence. The problem, however, is that many contemporary planners fall considerably short in their policy intervention efforts.

Increasing General Skills and Resources for Intervention

On the whole, they lack sufficient knowledge of what it takes to bring about successful policy interventions. The analyses done to devise intervention strategies are often sparse and spotty. And they are generally unwilling to go as far as they should in their specific interventions. In other words, while many planners know which route to take to increase their policy and decision making influence, they are not particularly adept at traversing the route.

Improvements are needed at two levels. At a more general level, intervention-oriented planning agencies should cultivate on a continuing basis the development of particular skills and resources to increase their chances of success when they engage in specific interventions. And at the specific level, when an agency actually intervenes in an issue to try to affect its decision outcome, the process usually followed to accomplish this has decided shortcomings.

Let me first consider the general level of staff skills and agency resources that are particularly useful for undertaking any kinds of interventions, regardless of the character or complexity of the issues involved. In brief, with respect to staff, skillful strategists and boundary spanners are needed, as well as people with expertise in particular substantive areas. And, as intervention situations unfold, planning agencies should have a pool of general resources to tap into it, if and when needed. Chief among these are support, information, and power resources. Regardless of the quality of staff and agency resources, the intervention planning agency also needs a well-conceived set of policies to serve as normative guideposts toward which its intervention activities are directed, coupled with carefully framed standards of behavior to guide the ethical conduct of its staff members in carrying out intervention activities. When these conditions are substantially met, the chances for planning agency success in particular intervention situations are enhanced. When not met, prospects are diminished for intervention success at the specific issue level.

THE STRATEGIST:

Since intervention planning agencies attempt to affect decision outcomes so that they are more consistent with their policy preferences, they need people who are experts on the workings of the decision process. More specifically, these people should have the ability to accurately analyze decision environments surrounding intervention issues, taking the results of such analyses and translating them into strategies and tactics which can be followed to achieve greater decision impact. Every time a decision is made by an agency to intervene, some strategy course or courses must be plotted to guide its intervention activities. Without people who possess the acumen of the strategist, having the capacity to chart paths of least resistance for the planning agency to follow as it tries to affect decision outcomes, the agency's chances of achieving success in specific intervention situations will be lessened. Strategists should be recognized as key staff members of the intervention planning agency, and be hired for that purpose alone.

One of the deficiencies of current planning education is that it is not generally designed to train planning strategists. Efforts to hone strategic skills among planning students are fairly limited. Since strategists are very much process oriented—their talents useful in any number of different planning settings—coursework in decision theory, organizational behavior, small group dynamics, conflict resolution, coalition management, and communication theory would seem useful. Additionally, more effort should be devoted to developing practicums in which different decision environments are simulated, so that students would have an opportunity to develop their ability to analyze different issues and actors involved in issues as a prelude to devising strategic plans to guide intervention behavior.

THE BOUNDARY SPANNER:

Another kind of process specialist needed by intervention-oriented planning agencies is the boundary spanner. For plans to be accepted and acted upon, planners of all persuasions must become involved in social relations with others. (Bolan, 1971, p. 386). Planners, therefore, should have the capacity to span the boundaries, or reduce the distances, between themselves and other actors in the decision process. They should be adept at building and sustaining social relationships.

The kind of intervention activity that the agency should undertake should flow from the work of the strategist. But many of the tactics to be deployed as the decision process unfolds require people with boundary spanning skills. Ideally, both skills should be possessed by one and the same person. But some who are adept strategists may not be able to translate their theoretical understanding of such fields as small group behavior, organizational behavior, or conflict resolution into the kinds of practical behavior needed to relate satisfactorily to other actors—behavior essential to the proper working of certain strategies designed to influence decision outcomes of specific issues. In such situations, skilled boundary spanners may have to be called upon.

The educational implications of training boundary spanners are several. For one, it may well be that planning schools should pay more careful attention to the social interactional capacities of prospective students at the early admissions stage. Since intervention situations often entail a fair amount of social interacting, it would be helpful if future planners had a modicum of potential in this regard. Moreover, planning schools should seek to sharpen the boundary spanning abilities of their students by teaching persuasion, communication, mediation, bargaining, negotiation, organizing, coalition management, and conflict resolution techniques. In this regard, it would be important to try to simulate different controlled settings where students, themselves, would have the opportunity to practice different kinds of boundary spanning.

THE SUBSTANTIVE AREA SPECIALIST:

Most often, people are hired by planning agencies for their expertise in certain substantive areas, whether that be in transportation, land use, housing, health or some other system. Obviously substantive specialists are important for their knowledge of system structure and functioning and for their ability to analyze system conditions, prepare system plans, and develop formal programs to achieve system plans. But the intervention planning agency needs substantive experts for other reasons. For one, such specialists play the key role in developing the policy base for the normative directions a planning agency seeks to achieve when it acts as

an interventionist.   At the strategy setting stage of any specific intervention episode, the talents of the substantive area expert are also needed.
Consider the following examples. The strategist's analysis reveals that a
key person's support is needed for the agency's intervention to succeed,
yet that person is leery of the agency's policy position on the issue because
it's too dissimilar from what the community has done before. At this
point, the substantive area expert's knowledge of experiences elsewhere
in comparable settings—where the policy in question has been tried and
successfully implemented—can be drawn upon to try to lessen the concern
this key person has about the agency's policy. Or suppose the strategist
needs more fine-grained information about key actors who might become
involved, for example, in a transportation issue the agency wants to influence, as a basis for designing appropriate strategies and tactics. In this
instance, the agency's transportation expert would be a prime source of
information because of that person's knowledge of people who operate in
the community's transportation network.

AGENCY SUPPORT RESOURCES:

   No intervention effort of planners can succeed without support for the
agency's policy position from a core of important groups and actors. Given
the importance of gaining supportive commitments for the agency's position in specific intervention situations, it stands to reason that the base of
general support for the planning agency built up over the years can serve
as an important reservoir to tap at the specific issue level. The larger
that base, the more likely planning interventions will succeed. Conversely,
lacking much of a support base, a planning agency's capacity to affect
specific issue outcomes will be lessened.
   As a general rule, therefore, planning agencies should carefully pursue
institution building efforts on a continuing basis—e.g. providing useful
services to others, seeking the advice and counsel of others, cooperating
with others, showing others it is productive and capable of producing quality technical work, clearly communicating to others, etc.—to increase their
overall potential for achieving success in specific intervention situations.
Since the cast of actors may differ depending on the specific issue, general
institution building efforts should be aimed at many, not just a few groups
and individuals.
   There is, however, a danger to guard against. Achieving success at
general institution building may lead to a greater sense of security. To
sustain its developing support base, the planning agency might avoid the
risks which some intervention situations present. Consequently, it may
fail to capitalize on the general support resources built up over the years,
reducing its capacity to influence decisions because it chooses to stay out
of, rather than inject itself into, specific important issues.

AGENCY INFORMATION RESOURCES:

When planners intervene in an issue, they are obviously handicapped if they lack sufficient knowledge of the issue's technical features and of the groups and actors who may play important roles in determining the issue's outcome. Ideally, planners should muster as full and accurate knowledge as possible about each potential intervention situation beforehand. But some intervention episodes have too short a time span to allow for sufficient information collection. Other times, work pressures may be too heavy to allow enough time to properly research a potential intervention situation. At still other times, avenues for acquiring certain important information might be closed off at the point planners must decide whether or not to intervene in the issue.

For these reasons, planners should build their information base for potential intervention situations on a regular, continuing basis, playing an anticipatory role by identifying potential intervention situations in advance and augmenting their knowledge of the technical aspects of such issues and of likely key actors who may become involved. By acting in advance to stockpile information instead of having to "start from scratch" each time they consider intervening, planners are much further along in the game.

AGENCY POWER RESOURCES:

General support for the planning function is a form of indirect power, convertible into leverage or into a means of exchange to acquire more support. The possession of in-depth information about some issue is also clearly recognized as a form of indirect power. But other forms of power that give planning agencies more direct leverage—ranging from statutory veto power to administratively delegated authority over a particular function—rarely are discussed or publicly sought by planners.

Yet while planners generally avoid openly asking for increases in direct power, many nevertheless quest for such power. In intervention situations, power can obviously be useful at times in trying to influence decision outcomes. Take, for example, the possibility that planners may need to exchange something with another group to obtain that group's support for their position on a particular issue. When they engage in a tradeoff, they obviously have to have something to offer in exchange. Information may be such a resource, but it is often insufficient. Sometimes the tradeoff may be derived from a certain direct power a planning agency possesses. Without that power, the agency may have little to exchange at the crucial point.

Whether planners like it or not, direct powers are resources that can be utilized in intervention situations to affect decision outcomes. So efforts to acquire selective powers and authorities, realistically speaking, become important for planners to pursue to increase their decisionmaking potential. Such efforts should not be casually rejected on principle.

NORMS AND ETHICS:

The preceding discussion has centered on increasing the potential for success in intervention situations by continuing to augment certain staff skills and agency resources over the long haul. But two other concerns should temper the planners' quest for improving their capacity to succeed in intervention situations. These are the norms they choose to achieve and the ethical standards which guide their behavior in intervention situations.

Coming closer to real influence makes it all the more imperative that planners carefully frame their policy preferences so that they meet the general test of social benefit. For if planners achieve greater success in affecting decision outcomes, then the question of what's achieved becomes critical and much less academic. In effect, intervention planners who get things done but achieve non-socially beneficial ends do more harm in the long run than ineffective planners who achieve little or nothing. So it is incumbent upon planning interventionists to scrupulously examine the norms sought to assure that they are socially beneficial and not harmful.[6]

Likewise, intervention activity expands the range of possible tactics that might be used. Consequently, decisions must be made to carefully distinguish ethical from unethical tactics. How far should planners go in the means they employ to try to affect decision outcomes? Persuasive tactics are obviously acceptable. But are tradeoffs? Are efforts to pressure a group by implied threats taboo? Should information ever be withheld? The point is that when planners shed themselves of the protective shrouds of the rational planning approach and increase both the frequency and range of their interactions with other actors in trying to move them closer to their position, the line separating ethical from unethical behavior becomes a real issue to define. The paucity of consensus within the planning profession about ethically acceptable standards of behavior affords little grounds for guidance.[7] Nevertheless, determining what constitutes ethical and unethical behavior becomes a much more important issue for intervention planners to resolve.

While the ability of planners to affect decision outcomes may increase as they become more adept as interventionists, they must guard against achieving socially detrimental ends and using means that are ethically off-limits. Robert Caro's brilliant account of Robert Moses in *The Power Broker: The Decline of New York* (1974) is dramatic evidence that although a planner like Moses achieved tremendous decisionmaking impact, he pursued many socially disruptive ends and deployed numerous clearly unethical tactics in the course of achieving his implementation successes.

Improving the Intervention Process at the Specific Issue Level

Strategists, boundary spanners, and substantive area specialists are the core members of the planning agency's intervention team. Support, information, and power are key resources to draw upon when an agency engages in specific policy issue interventions. Few contemporary planning agencies possess these skills and resources in sufficient supply, although substantive area specialists and support resources are probably relatively the most plentiful. Whatever level of intervention skills and resources a planning agency has, it usually falls short of properly applying and blending them each time it injects itself into an issue as an interventionist, trying to achieve a favorable decision outcome. More often than not, when agencies engage in specific interventions, they devote far too little effort to what needs to be done. In contrast, planners devote considerably more effort and time to formulating planning policies. What's needed at the policy intervention stage is to bring about more parity with the effort usually put in at the policy formulation stage.

Some typical weaknesses in the process followed by contemporary planners when they engage in specific interventions are:

> The analysis done to devise intervention strategies and tactics to influence decision outcomes is often cursory and incomplete, a somewhat haphazard blending of the political intuitions and instincts of the strategy devisers. While strategy sessions on possible intervention issues are usually held, too often, factors and conditions of importance are left out of the analysis, while others of little or no consequence for strategy purposes are included.

> The strategies and tactics that are derived are often insufficiently dimensioned, and at times, inappropriate and misdirected.

> Tactic deployers are sometimes miscast—i.e., the wrong people are used to deploy what might be the right tactics.

> Tactics are sometimes deployed at inappropriate times—i.e., either too soon or too late.

> Little effort goes into monitoring the progress of the implementation plan as phases of it are carried out to determine how things are going, revising strategic and tactical actions of subsequent phases accordingly.

Given these problems with the present state of the art of intervention practice, how can the process be improved to increase the planners' chances of achieving success in specific intervention situations?

In general, each time planners engage in an intervention, they should develop and carry out a coordinated, time-phased strategy plan, consisting of various tactical measures deployed at key participants involved in the issue. Ideally, the choice of strategies and tactics should evolve from a careful analysis of a mix of behavioral, attitudinal and resource characteristics of the key individuals and groups. Exhibit 1 shows the stages in the recommended intervention process.

While each step in the process is important, the key ones—that incidentally are the weakest points in present intervention practice—are the analysis of supporting and opposing target groups and the development of a time-phased strategy/tactics plan. Each step in the process will be briefly discussed.

IDENTIFYING THE WORKING OBJECTIVE(S):

When a planning agency decides to intervene in an issue, it should establish a specific working objective (or objectives). This would represent the outcome or target to be achieved. Each working objective should consist not only of the policy the agency wants to achieve, but also the key decision units—i.e., individual(s) or group(s) who would decide whether or not to accept the policy.

ANALYZING TARGET GROUP CHARACTERISTICS:

Assuming the agency decides to intervene in an issue area and establishes a working objective, the next step is to acquire substantial knowledge about individuals and groups involved, or likely to be involved in the issue who are potential supporters or opponents of the planning agency's position on the issue. By acquiring such understanding, the agency should be better able to devise a strategy/tactics plan that has a better chance of working. Analysis of these target groups [8] is a critical task, one usually given short shrift by planners. Rather than take a quick squint through the curtain folds at a few random features of the most visible target groups—the usual approach—intervention planners should take a good, long, hard look at a number of key attributes of a larger number of target groups.

Certain *general attributes* about each target group should be known because they provide clues on how to gain the support of the target group (or possibly neutralize it), knowledge useful in devising the subsequent strategy/tactics plan. These general attributes are:

self-interest: what self-interests motivate the target group—e.g., power, recognition, status, respect, security, stability, economic gain?

peer group influencers: who are the individuals or groups that the target group has respect for—its peers, in other words?

successful and unsuccessful past tactics: which tactics worked on the target group and which didn't work with respect to other issues in the community previously decided upon or currently being played out?

EXHIBIT 1

STEPS IN THE RECOMMENDED INTERVENTION PLANNING PROCESS

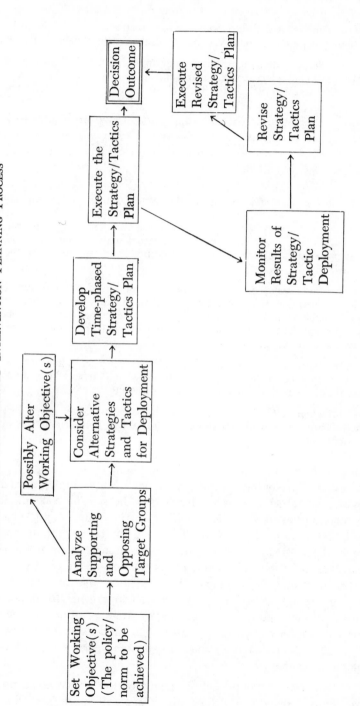

attitude toward the planning agency: what are the target group's feelings about the planning agency—e.g., favorable, neutral, antagonistic?

general resources: what are the target group's performance capacities as a strategist, boundary spanner, or subject area expert? What are its supportive characteristics—the breadth of its sociopolitical contacts?

In addition, other attributes about each target group are useful to know about which relate specifically to *the issue and the planning agency position on the issue.* These also provide important clues for devising appropriate strategies and tactics.

resources in the issue area: what are the target group's control capacities, such as review authority, veto authority, delegated authority? its performance capacities such as how extensive is knowledge of the issue area and specific knowledge of contextual matters like laws and ordinances bearing on the issue? its credibiilty or legitimacy in the issue area?

specific concerns about the planning agency's preferred position: what specific concerns does the target group have about the planning agency's position on the issue—e.g., it's too costly, too uncommon, few of its peers support it, hard to understand, too controversial, consequences too uncertain and risky, etc.

policy preferences in the issue area: does the target group already have a policy preference in the issue area? If so, what is it and how much does it differ from the planning agency's position?

stake/motivation in the issue: how strongly does the target group feel about the issue—e.g., high, medium, low interest in getting involved in the issue?

As a rule, each of these attributes tells the planners something of potential usefulness for developing appropriate tactics. For example, information about a particular target group's self-interest or the specific concerns it has about the planning agency's policy position on the issue provide clues on how that target group might be reached to gain its support or possibly neutralize its opposition. Likewise, the target group's stake in the issue provides a clue about the likelihood of its playing an active role in the intervention situation. A judgment that its stake was low but that it was a peer group influencer of a key decision unit generally opposed to the planning agency's position, might suggest that an effort be made to try to stimulate its interest in the issue—i.e., to raise its stake in the issue so that it might actually exert its influence on the decision unit on behalf of the planning agency.

In the critical target group analysis phase of the intervention process, the key personnel needed to do the analyses are staff strategists. But staff substantive area specialists are also needed. Depending on the nature of the intervention issues—i.e., housing, transportation, health, etc.—the knowledge that substantive area specialists have of selected target group attributes will be invaluable to the strategist. Completely accurate information about attributes of target groups will of course be impossible to obtain. Many judgments will have to be subjective and therefore speculative. But as the agency's planners become more adept at collecting target group attribute information, data reliability should increase. Regardless of the data imperfections, these findings should offer a sounder base for devising more appropriate strategies and tactics than would findings resulting from the more haphazard and hurried investigations usually undertaken.

BRIDGING THE ANALYSIS TO THE STRATEGY/TACTICS PLAN:

In the rational planning process, alternative policies are considered before a preferred policy is selected. Likewise, in the intervention planning process, alternative strategies and tactics should be considered before fixing on a preferred strategy/tactical plan of action. The findings from the target group analysis would provide clues about which alternative strategies and tactics to pursue, with the staff strategists having the best "feel" for interpreting these findings for their strategic and tactical significance. Subtle sifting of the target group analysis findings coupled with reasoned hunches about what might work should guide the strategist at this exploratory stage.

Gaining the support of certain target groups and neutralizing the opposition of others are the two broadest strategy courses to pursue in trying to affect the outcome of a decision in which planners intervene. Support strategies can be further subdivided: building a broad-based coalition among target groups for the planning agency's position on the issue and/or focusing more specifically on trying to gain or solidify the support of one or a few key target groups for the agency's position.

While the more acceptable and less risky strategy course is to build support, reality also dictates the need to be aware that some groups may just not support the agency's position. At times, efforts to neutralize certain target groups may be needed, since some opponents on an issue will stand fast in their opposition to the agency's position, with no amount of reasoned argument effective in changing their minds. If they succeed in their opposition, the planning agency's working objective may be seriously undermined. In such cases a neutralizing strategy may have to be pursued which would take one of two forms: lessening the extent of opposition from certain target groups towards the planning agency's position and/or blocking the efforts of certain target groups to undermine the agency's preferred position.

How to gain support or neutralize opposition is the key question. It is essentially one of tactics. Should exchange tactics, like tradeoffs, be used to gain a key group's support or neutralize its opposition? Should persuasion tactics be chiefly relied upon? If so, what kinds—e.g., attempting to lessen the specific concerns a target group has about the planning agency's policy position on the issue? courting the target group? trying to satisfy the target group's self-interest, perceived specifically as recognition and status? Or should engagement tactics be attempted, for example, trying to get the target group to assist in refining the agency's policy position or in helping to communicate the policy position to others? There are many tactic possibilities to consider that fall under the general headings of persuasion, engagement, exchange, pressure and even deception. While use of pressure or deception tactics might be rejected on ethical grounds, such a decision may be unwise if the ultimate aim is to achieve socially beneficial norms in an often highly competitive decisionmaking environment. Clearly, the intervention planner is faced with an ends-means dilemma. Do the ends, however socially beneficial, justify use of certain tactical means? Turning the question around, is it possible to achieve certain socially beneficial ends in certain situations without at times using certain ethically borderline tactics? The answer is not an easy one. The dilemma, though, highlights the importance of setting ethical parameters to guide the planner's behavior in intervention situations.

DEVELOPING THE STRATEGY/TACTICAL PLAN:

After deriving a first approximation of possible strategies and tactics to deploy on specific target groups, a strategy/tactical plan should be developed. At this point, the focus should shift from target groups to strategies as the central organizing concept, with each strategy phased over time and dimensioned in terms of tactical actions aimed at one or more target groups. In addition, for each tactical action, the party or parties responsible for deploying the tactic and the best forum for deploying the tactic should be identified.

Identifying appropriate tactic deployers is important. Sometimes a tactic may be deployed to affect a target group, but the intended result of either gaining the group's support or neutralizing its opposition does not occur. The fault might not be with the tactic, which might have been entirely appropriate. The problem might be traced to the tactic deployer—e.g., he or she possessed inadequate boundary spanning talents for the job, possibly turning off the target group by exhibiting a blustery or self righteous manner. Likewise, consideration needs to be given to the proper forum for deploying a tactic—i.e., a face-to-face meeting? a memo? a technical report? a committee meeting? more than one of these forums? Knowledge of the target group's prior responsiveness to various forums may aid in selecting the right forum to use.

Deploying tactics at the right time is crucial to the success of any intervention effort. Sometimes a delay in deploying a particular tactic might lead to obtaining the support of a target group or groups, whereas at other times, delaying a tactic too long might negate such an intended effect.

EXECUTING THE STRATEGY/TACTICAL PLAN:

This step is self-explanatory. Once the strategy/tactical plan is prepared and considerations of tactic timing, tactic deployers, and tactic forums built into it, the plan should be carried out. The skills of good boundary spanners are especially important in the execution stage.

MONITORING THE RESULTS OF THE STRATEGY/TACTICS PLAN:

Assessing the results of tactics after they are deployed to see whether they achieve what's intended is a quite important step in the intervention process. As tactics are deployed, either the target group(s) respond as planned or they don't. If they fail to respond as intended, then new efforts may have to be initiated—i.e., subsequent phases of the strategy/tactical plan may have to be altered. This suggests the need for continuous monitoring to gauge the results of tactical actions as they are undertaken.

The importance of monitoring can also be appreciated by recognizing that during the course of any single intervention episode, target group interactions are not just moves in one direction, where the planning agency deploys all the tactics on others. Since the planning agency sometimes encounters opposition, it is well to recognize that some opponents may be actively deploying tactics aimed in effect at counteracting those of the planning agency. Being aware of this possibility should encourage intervention planners to closely monitor the results of their tactics as events transpire.

In any event, the strategy/tactics plan should not be considered immutable or inflexible to change. It would be wise for the intervention planning team to have contingency plans in mind in the event things don't work out as intended. If the strategy/tactics plan has to be revised, a new set of tactics would have to be deployed before reaching the hoped for final decision outcome.

Conclusion

Given the complex and competitive decision environments within which public policies are forged at different governmental levels and within functional systems cutting across governmental levels, public sector planners of all kinds—who generally have little formal authority to begin with—obviously face considerable difficulties in affecting the shape of public policy decisions. Persevering as most planners are, the difficulties, however, haven't stopped them from trying. The question becomes one of making a "choice": how best should they allocate their energies to increase their ability to influence decisions? They might, for example, choose to devote most of their effort to preparing long range comprehensive plans, hoping policy officials and decisionmakers will appreciate the wisdom of their pronouncements and make resource allocation decisions accordingly. Or they might heavily travel the advisory-rational planning route, or some variation of it, in their quest for achieving decision influence.

I have opted in this paper for planners augmenting their intervention efforts as a way of moving up the policy influence ladder. Having said this, I recognize that behaving as interventionists does present certain risks for planners. Such behavior on the part of planners may raise the hackles of some, in the extreme, possibly even resulting in some loss of status or resources. Opposition to planners performing as interventionists may be on philosophical grounds—i.e., "Planners have no right to behave as politicized interventionists. That's the politician's role." Or, some may object on grounds of self-interest, either because of a planning agency's successes in preventing their policy preferences from being incorporated into decisions or because the planning agency successfully initiated policy decisions that they oppose. While the risk factor should be taken into account, it should not intimidate planners from intervening. For, given the nature of the decision environments in which planners operate, they run the higher risk of failing to achieve much decision making impact by avoiding intervening, thus failing to achieve much effectiveness.

But if planners choose to follow the intervention path—which many now are doing—they must improve the present state of the art for their intervention efforts to have much effect. In particular, they must cultivate those skills central to performing intervention activities. They must also augment certain resources of their agencies to strengthen their hand in intervention situations. And they must markedly improve the process they follow when they engage in specific interventions in policy issues aimed at achieving favorable decision outcomes.

Even done well, however, intervention offers no panacea for planners. For, even if the art of intervention practice is elevated to a higher level, the planner's ability to influence public policies and decisions will still be limited overall. The decision process is a tough nut to crack. What can result, however, is a relative gain with planners moving up the influence ladder to a higher notch.

Because it better accommodates to the reality of the difficult, complex and competitive decision environments in which planners operate, the intervention route is an important one for planners to follow. It should lead to increasing the effectiveness of American planning. And if more effective planning occurs, planners can better meet their professional responsibilities in serving to advance social benefit in their respective communities.

NOTES

1. HUD's 1975 policy change, establishing stricter criteria for judging the performance of 701 planning agencies, is a reflection of this type of criticism. Several of these criteria relate to the agency's implementation capabilities. One, quite specifically, applies to the agency's "progress in implementing policies, plans and programs." (AIP Newsletter, November-December 1975, p. 16.)

2. Much of my contact with practicing planners occurred during the 1960's and early '70s when I was employed by the American Society of Planning Officials. While working at ASPO, I served in a consulting capacity to a number of planning agencies at all levels of government, gaining a first hand understanding of how planning really operated in different institutional settings. Since becoming a full time planning educator at the University of Wisconsin-Madison, I have continued my direct contacts with a variety of practicing planners through my research and teaching.

3. This does not mean that the planners' policy preferences are exclusively derived by them—these may be the outcome of a widespread participatory process or more commonly the outcome of numerous informal interactions between planners, their clients and others.

4. In one sense, intervention planners operate like political campaign strategists. The latter are also interventionists who devise certain strategy courses and deploy certain tactical means to achieve certain ends—albeit different ends than planners seek.

5. Exceptions to the latter point would be found in Rabinowitz, *City Politics and Planning* (1969), Catanese, *Planners and Local Politics: Impossible Dreams* (1974), Bolan and Nuttall, *Urban Planning and Politics* (1975), and Needleman and Needleman *Guerillas in the Bureaucracy*, (1974).

6. As a starting point, and only that, planners might examine the policies adopted over the last 10 years by the AIP Board of Governors for normative guidance. These policies, which in large part reflect broader societal concerns that the AIP Board has merely articulated for its membership, represent what some might say are socially beneficial normative directions that planners should work towards achieving.

7. Peter Marcuse's thoughtful article, "Professional Ethics and Beyond: Values in Planning" (*AIP Journal*, July 1976), is an exception. It does provide some helpful guidance for taking planners through the confusing maze of professional planning ethics.

8. These groups and individuals are labeled target groups because they are potential targets for some kind of tactical action to be taken later on in the intervention process.

REFERENCES

Advisory Commission on Intergovernmental Relations, *Regional Decision Making: New Strategies for Substate Districts* (Washington, D.C.: Government Printing Office, 1973).

Edward Banfield, *Political Influence* (New York: The Free Press, 1961).

Edward Bergman and Emil Malizia, "A Case for Practice Research in Planning," U. of North Carolina Deparmtent of City and Regional Planning (May 1975).

Richard Bolan, "The Social Relations of the Planner," *Journal of the American Institute of Planners* (November 1971).

Richard Bolan and Ronald Nuttall, *Urban Planning and Politics* (Lexington: Lexington Books, 1975).

Robert Caro, *The Power Broker: Robert Moses and the Decline of New York* (New York: Alfred A. Knopf 1974).

Anthony Catanese, *Planners and Local Politics: Impossible Dreams* (Beverly Hills: Sage Publications, 1974).

International City Management Association, "Administration of Local Planning: Analysis of Structures and Functions," *Urban Data Service Report* (December 1971).

Norton Long, "The Local Community as an Ecology of Games," *American Journal of Sociology* (November 1958).

Peter Marcuse, "Professional Ethics and Beyond: Values in Planning," *Journal of the American Institute of Planners* (July 1976).

Martin Needleman and Carolyn Needleman, *Guerillas in the Bureaucracy: The Community Planning Experiment in the United States* (New York: John Wiley and Sons, 1974).

Notes on an Expedition to Planland

Brian J. L. Berry

George Sternlieb set me an impossible task when he asked me to contribute to this conference, if, that is, one contemplates a fully responsive answer. "How can the planner be a change agent in an only moderately reactive economic system?" he asked. "Is a planning task to sort out what is and what is not achievable in both the short and the long run?" "Are there within-system, activities that may be undertaken to maximize the quality of life?" "Who are the planners of such activities, and what skills should they have?" Like a naive and foolish social scientist, I agreed to prepare a paper full of answers—which explains in part why I vacillated so long about the task of writing. The other reason is that, in moving from Geography at Chicago to the School of Design at Harvard, I have switched from the world of the social scientist to that of planning, falling now I suppose more clearly than before within the rubric of Marcuse's social scientist turned practitioner in the arena of public policy—one of the characters dissected so ably in the paper by Irving Louis Horowitz.

Yet as I have switched, I have felt much like one of the geographer-explorers of yesteryear, journeying into what, for them, was poorly explored territory and trying to make sense of a jumbled kaleidoscope of new impressions. In the past, the results of such an expedition would have been shared with a scholarly geographical society and duly recorded in its archives. But I only have available the Acton Geographical Society, the most recent and deservedly the least known of such groups, so this conference will have to do instead as a means of communicating my observations. Let me share with you what the archives of the Society now contain about this journey to Planland, for the contents of the notebooks cast light on why it is so difficult to respond to George Sternlieb's questions.

Planland, I should explain, is an island in the Sea of Storms, and the early notebooks describe an almost classical social structure. There are three classes, the chiefs, the priests of Planland's chief god, Plan, and the people. The chiefs engage in endless debate about the collection and redistribution of tribute, being careful that their actions preserve their own position and keep the people happy. The people, preoccupied with self-gratification, seem happiest when left alone. It is the priests of Plan (called colloquially, planners) whom the explorer found most interesting, for they are the philosophers, scientists and magicians. They serve as advisors to the chiefs, called on for solutions most frequently when unexpected storms disturb the normal island tranquility.

The notebooks record that the priests share a common belief that although the people of Planland are not inherently malicious or ill-intentioned, their individual searches for self-gratification create conflict and danger, haphazardness and disorder. The priests also believe that they have been endowed with a unique ability to divine Plan's will. Whenever possible, they advise the chiefs on how to recapture the state of grace from which they believe the people have fallen, and they describe that state by using such words as "balanced," "optimal," "harmonious," "equitable," and "just."

Yet there the agreement ends. The notebooks record how frustrated the priests become when a storm passes and the chiefs assign to them the task of cleaning up (a more frequent event than most will admit), how frustrated the chiefs are that the priests seem unable to predict when storms will occur and what appropriate protective measures might be taken (and with some wonderment that there are as many clans of priests as there are sects in Christendom, and that they disagree as much). The most numerous in all of the temples of Plan are mystics and artists, members of the prismacolor pencil clan. They apparently were more fecund in the past, because they tend to be older on the average than members of other clans (although they still alledgedly breed like rabbits in the boondocks). They can be spotted easily because they build distinctive long houses, called studios. It is in these studios that they have their mystical encounters with Plan, and it is there that—hence their name— they convey his will to the chiefs and the people by drawing sketches of his commandments in bright colors on large sheets of paper. To the people they say "Here is Plan's will, his masterful design. Conform and be happy." And to the chiefs they say "Regulate the people to conform, and Plan's will will be done."

The notebooks also record a peculiar belief of the prismacolor pencil clan, that they receive the most masterful of Plan's edicts directly from his right hand. The notebooks' authors speculate that perhaps this is why among the shrillest of the other clans, and the group not frequently found in opposition, are the lefties. They, apparently, are easily picked out in any crowd because they wear long hair, go beaded and unwashed, and rally around their banner, the bar sinister, as they shout a leftist antithesis to every rightist thesis, find a contradiction in every contribution, and relish in their favorite blood sport, character assassination. Despite their banner, there is a widespread belief among the prismacolor pencil planners that lefties are not conceived normally, albeit on the wrong side of the sheets, but crawl out from beneath rocks.

There are other clans, too, which is why meetings between the chiefs and the priests are generally cacophonous, with much noise but little mutual understanding. There are the model builders, scientists with their super erector sets, full of levers and wheels, trying to engineer better ways for the chiefs to produce greater symmetry and balance by maximizing, minimizing, and optimizing. When their modelling becomes difficult, they frequently can be found going hill climbing. And then there are those who walk ámong the people and, with a little help from Delphi, advocate that Plan's will may best be served by changing the formulas by which tribute is collected, redistributed, and spent . . . and the consultants, for whom Plan's will is the wish of the chiefs . . . and there the notebooks end, except for some cryptic concluding remarks that on any developmental scale, Planland is a pre-paradigm society where many competing schools of thought flourish. Each has its own values and internal logic, its own body of facts that it considers relevant, its own world view. There is the suggestion that the savages will only become civilized, and the priests of Planland become effective change agents in their moderately reactive system, when a single belief system replaces the multitude of viewpoints.

But what shape should this single system take? Should one of the existing clans achieve superiority as advisors to the chiefs, or should a new religion replace the old? In a sense, that is the question David Harvey asks in his conference paper, but he does not develop the implication of his final sentence that "we might even begin to plan the reconstruction of society, instead of merely planning the ideology of planning" —for to rephrase George Sternlieb's questions, who are the "we's"? How do they become effective change agents? And if "we" plan, does it also mean that "we" are in control?

As a much younger geographer, taking my first halting steps into planning in Chicago, I once thought the answer was obvious. What, I asked, might any reasonable and rational man agree is needed to ensure that changing societies make wise decisions? There seemed to be several key ingredients:

Information. Information is needed to tell us what our society is like now, how rapidly and in what ways it is changing, and what scientific and technological alternatives to present practices exist or can be found.

Social analysis. Analysis is needed to determine what relations exist between current actions and future effects, to weigh the merits of alternative priority systems, to derive practical, achievable goals for society, and to determine how best to allocate our finite resources to attain those goals.

Well-informed decisionmakers. Society requires mechanisms to ensure that decisionmakers, including the public, have access to the information they need, have available the results of the analyses carried out, and have alternative courses of action formulated for their consideration.

Appropriate institutions. Institutions are needed to ensure that decisions can be put into practice. They take many forms—political institutions, financial institutions, legal institutions, and educational institutions.

These ingredients led naturally to the idea that key roles for the planner involve:

Forecasting future developments and assessing longer-range consequences of present social trends.

Measuring the probable future impact of alternative courses of action.

Estimating the actual range of social choice indicating what alternative sets of goals might be attainable in terms of available resources and possible rates of progress.

Thence, it was but a short passage to the idea that the key role of social accounts is a reformed system of planning—measurement devices that enable us to assess where we stand and are going with respect to our values and goals, and to evaluate specific programs and determine their impact—with their strong implied cybernetic ingredient, for an active information system demands sensors to determine the consequences of actions, provision for feeding this information back to decision centers, and readiness to change behavior in response to signals that unwanted consequences are occurring or likely to occur.

The need seemed evident. Every day public officials and elected representatives make major decisions in the attempt to change the future states of our social environment. What variables are taken into account? No behavioral scientist will disagree with the basic role that is played by cognition. We have all been trained to believe that the structure of any system operates on behavior through the mediation of cognition and that structure in its turn is composed of aggregations of behavior called "processes." In other words, *decisions rest on beliefs about facts*, and *facts are produced by decisions.* To the extent that beliefs are erroneous or distorted, errors are made in social strategies that waste resources and create future problems by the change processes they set in motion.

Surely, then, better statistics of direct normative interest should help us make balanced, comprehensive and concise judgments about the condition of society. Surely we can benefit if, as many have said, we "apply real science to social affairs," thus eliminating the corruptions of the principle of rationality that arise when decisions about social affairs are made on the basis of beliefs about facts, rather than "true knowledge."

Even in the absence of a trip to Planland, anyone pursuing this line of reasoning confronts his first stumbling block at the most basic level, that of data. In the United States, data have only been gathered when there is reasonable consensus on three issues: that the problem is important; that there is some information which, if available, would be useful; and that the relevant phenomena can be measured. Thus, the probability of any statistical series being developed is directly related to the articulateness and power of the groups whose interests are involved, the perceived susceptibility of the phenomenon to measurement, the extent to which the phenomenon is socially visible, and the preferences and skills of the agency personnel who gather the statistics. Social scientists and planners have contributed little to this determination of the data that are now collected, acting as consumers rather than producers, followers rather than lobbyists.

The interest group issue is the profound one, for it is a product of a society that jealously protects its pluralistic mainstream. Pluralism appears and reappears in many ways. As one turns from questions of data to questions of planning research, it surfaces in the contrasts between disciplinary research and policy research. The object of the former is to advance knowledge in the particular scholarly concerns of a discipline by arriving at empirically valid and theoretically significant conclusions about the phenomena deemed to be relevant by the discipline in question. Such research begins with an intellectual problem posed by previous research or theory, and proceeds at a pace dictated only by the demands of scholarship. The intended audience is the discipline's teachers and researchers; and the self-corrective method employed is the adversary proceeding of replicative studies and scholarly reviews.

Policy research is significantly different from disciplinary research in several respects. Its object is to provide information immediately useful to policy makers in grappling with the problems they believe that they face. Thus, it begins, outside a discipline, with a social problem defined by a decisionmaker. The pace of the research is forced by the policymaker's need to make a decision dictated by non-disciplinary imperatives. The intended audience is the decisionmaker, to whom it must be made intelligible and convincing if it is to be useful. There are no counterparts of disciplinary research's self-corrective methods. Seldom is there time to collect new data or to engage in prolonged analysis. And, most profoundly, the policymaker must contend every day with the differing and changing goals of competing interest groups in a society that values democratic pluralism as an end in itself.

This has been clear and unambiguous implications for the naively assumed priority of the rational planning paradigm. As one commentator remarked to me in those wide-eyed days in Chicago:

"no computer-based simulation model jazzed-up analysis scheme is really going to get very far in terms of adoption if the policymaker has the feeling that he can't control it."

The modus operandi of our government is that elected officials should have the decisive role in determining what programs are developed and how money is spent, and they are the officials who must respond to interest-group and political pressures. Indeed, applied rationality presents fundamental challenges to the traditional American decisionmaking style. For example, the machine-boss politician whose control is based on a hierarchic structure of authority and communication and who remains in power by manipulating interest-group politics and dispersing patronage feels threatened by any attempt to take the ability to bargain and negotiate out of his hands and substitute the results of rational analysis of alternatives. For him, deliberate fuzziness and clouding of the issue is an alternative technique for survival under conditions of increasing complexity. There seems little question that more and better information and analysis intensifies rather than reduces the individual's feelings of anxiety and uncertainty, even though they might help him cope more easily with complexity and change. Thus, the vast majority are not receptive to rational planning techniques, actively opposing them or having a fixed and limited "Bunkeresque" view of exactly what planning activities are legitimate and useful. Yet at the same time there are deep personal frustrations resulting from the conflict between the policymaker's sense of potential power to generate and implement better policies based on more information, and his sense of vulnerability to exposure of personal and organizational insufficiencies. As one of my ex-colleagues commented, "I often feel that politicians don't want issues crystallized. There's a certain kind of defense mechanism that operates in avoiding the crystallization of issues that would conflict and sharpen when they get crystallized." In other words, more rational planning can only result in more groups challenging the policymaker's policies and programs.

Where, then, beyond idealism? First is to admit to the extraordinary strength and resiliency of the mainstream values of democratic pluralism and interest-group politics, reflective of unspoken but overwhelming shared values. Mainstream preservation is reflected in the expression of every planning problem as a threat, and every major program as a war. Indeed, as Harvey notes in his paper, it is this resiliency that has been responsible for the failures of most of the aims of the radical groups of the 1960's. Even the limited successes of the radicals are themselves reflective of the system: another interest group organizing and asserting its right to be heard, and negotiated with.

What, then, is the role of the planner? Can he be a change agent within this only moderately reactive system? One answer emerges from a functional analysis of planners' roles. Consider the mainstream a system responding to exogenous and endogenous inputs and at any point placing values upon its outputs, i.e., upon each element of its present and likely future states. A cluster of negatively valued states is, in common parlance, a problem, and a cluster of problems is a mess. The most common task set for planners is to solve problems and clean up messes; it is reactive, curative. Like the general practitioner, the planner is called upon to restore the health of the sick patient. He must diagnose what is wrong and prescribe a cure. He cannot influence the cause, because it has done its work. Diagnosis has to be based upon symptoms, and while the short-range result of his actions may be to alleviate the condition, the long-range consequences are largely unanticipated and haphazard, because he is intervening in a situation that is subject to continuous change. And because of this continuous change, I see little likelihood that planning will be other than dominantly reactive, past- rather than future-oriented, for many years to come. Most planning will remain the art of the possible, seeking the safety of the broadly acceptable which, freely translated in any situation of complex competing interest groups, means cultivating an unerring aim for the lowest common denominator and the art of the pretty picture.

One step better is, of course, to be able to predict future problems, to understand their causes, and to devise such means of regulation of system behavior that the problems are avoided. This perhaps explains why some of our planning schools are, today, dominated by Keynesian economists and by lawyers, by prediction and prevention rather than cure.

To the systems theorist concerned with growth and change of complex systems, both of the preceding roles are of the most basic and conservative kind. They are system-maintaining behaviors, keeping the mainstream on track and error-free. Only coincidentally, as a result of imperfect understanding, would they result in change. Yet George Sternlieb asked me to consider the likely future role of the planner as *a change agent*, and I am sure he was not thinking of the unintended consequences of less-than-perfect knowledge on the part of the reactive problem solvers or the regulatory manipulators.

Change in complex systems can be incremental and evolutionary, or discontinuous and revolutionary. In the first, sequences of actions result in growth or decline, and in consequential shifts in system form. In the second, one system is replaced by another, which is what Harvey means when he talks about "planning the reconstruction of society, instead of merely planning the ideology of planning." Both types of change are goal-oriented: incrementally one attempts to work *forward* within the system, towards positively-valued future states; but to make a revolution one must work *backwards* from idealized end states to that reconstruction of the system essential if the ends are to be realized.

Yet we have already said that the mainstream is extraordinarily resilient, and indeed, as Boorstin has so ably pointed out, all revolutionary change behaviors throughout American history have quickly been dissolved into special interest-group pleadings.

So this leaves the planner-change agent as incrementalist in a pluralistic mainstream dominated by interest-group politics. But this is probably as it should be, for as Irving Louis Horowitz has already pointed out, "The greater the degree of (system) planning, the lower the degree of innovative capacity; the higher the degree of efficiency, the less the degree of total planning." Effective change agent planning involves interest-group advocacy. Whether in the public agency, the public interest group, or the private corporation, it involves the pursuit of limited rather than systemic goals in an entrepreneurial sense, and it involves access to and acquisition of influence and power. To be sure, the same battery of analytic skills is required, but they are put to another use, the identification, creation and realization of opportunities. Some of the efforts will succeed, others will fail, and the best, in hindsight, will be seen as those foresighted innovations that are the essence of well-planned change.

Planning—An Historical and Intellectual Perspective

Amitai Etzioni

There are two things I will try to contribute to the discussion, one concerns where I believe we are at historically and the other intellectually.

We are on the third leg of a dialectic dealing with the capacity and willingness of a society to engage in deliberate social change. The origin of this attitude which I like to refer to as the active orientation (the desire to change things in line with a deliberate purpose) must find itself in the beginnings of secularization. This is a breaking with the idea that things are given by a superior force, i.e., magical, religious or of some other nature, and the adoption of a notion that at the center of the universe is a person who can crack its coat, understand its forces and make them work to the needs of society. The orientation, as I see it, encompasses nature. The beginning of the industrial revolution and its intellectual and scientific origins lies in the concept that the laws of nature can be opened to both understanding and control.

We then extend this attitude to the body of society and start to use society not as a given, not as a found instrument but rather as an alternative design. In terms of our society, probably the high point of the activist orientation came as a part of the "Great Society," with its almost unbounded appetite to change everything in sight. I don't think I need to ask this group to recall the era in which we were to develop and democratize seventy other nations and eliminate poverty, racial problems, schizophrenia, mental illness, obesity, social abuses and the like.

I'm reminded of David Riesman's paper. He made two suggestions in an attempt to aid the United States in its quest to find roles for its unbounded resources. The first was to bombard Communist China with nylon stockings, washing machines, etc., in order to make that nation a good, God-fearing society like ours. The second was to turn New Orleans into a zoo in which people would live like they did in 1955 so that future Americans could come to New Orleans to see what 1955 Americans lived like.

As another example, the social program of the Eisenhower Administration called for a goal of one and a half times the existing growth of the G.N.P. From this point on we devised mechanisms—social programs abounded. There was a reaction to these programs. This reaction did not challenge specific thrusts, i.e. food stamps, Medicare or welfare, but rather it challenged the very assumption of the capacity to effectuate change. Indeed the central theme of the *Public Interest* volume to which Daniel Bell and others contributed was not to question our capacity to deal with specific items—with criminals or housing or with the problems of the elderly—but with the basic question of our capacity to plan, to engineer, to change, to make things function in line with our design.

I'd like to suggest to you we are entering a third era, which will be the last leg, in which reaction will have corrected the over optimism of the "Great Society" and be ready to engage in a more cautiously optimistic or moderately pessimistic, yet carefully controlled, social activism. Instead of trying to cover everything under the kitchen sink there will be a much shorter list of potential social achievements. Research and development is a key to understanding and meaningful advance. It allows us to correct as we progress. It provides partial insight to areas of admitted ignorance. At the same time it's more commanding, more compelling and more activist than the notion that we can increase and expand already existing commitments or programs.

In the era we are entering now, there will be a need for public policy planners and social scientists. This is because we have learned that we can accomplish a limited number of things if they are approached methodically and carefully. This is where I believe we are historically and, therefore—at the depths of pessimism—I detect, between the lines, an emerging optimism.

As to where we are headed intellectually—several significant concepts will impact on planning of the future. The first is *power*. I believe those engaged in planning will have to deal with the dynamics of power as well as with its component constructs.

To briefly explain: At issue is not the absolute size of a group but rather the political energy it exhibits. The bottom line is how many troops come out, not the size of the troops *if* they came out. Most of our energy is dissipated in fighting each other. In social action, the future belongs to those who can build coalitions and minimize internal strife. Sectarian groups will have their noisy day and go away. The real power base belongs to those who can assemble the larger groups into workable coalitions.

Further, there must be an agreement on goals and directions—*concensus*. It is a bargained sharing in normative principles and bases. The most appropriate power— (control) concensus mix has the best chance of accomplishment.

This blending of control and concensus leads us to another point of necessary compromise—the controversy between Lindblom and the rest of us. I believe it's high time to throw out the extremes: (1) the idea that the only thing you can do is to stumble through history by putting one cautious foot in front of the other, i.e., to "muddle through", as well as (2) the idea that there is such a thing as a grand plan, wih full details for everything that is to occur or be accomplished. Hopefully goals can be arrived at through positive inducement—tax reliefs, payoffs or whatever. These must be flexible, showing direction rather than detail—constantly subject to feedback and editing. If one proceeds via this compromise position, whatever it is to be labeled, we may neither be as hopeless as the muddlers nor as foolish as the grand planners.

Economic Planning in Change—

National Planning, Demand Versus Supply Emphases

On Planning the Ideology of Planning

David Harvey

It is a truism to say that we all plan. But planning as a profession has a much more restricted domain. Fight as they might for some other rationale for their existence, professional planners find themselves confined, for the most part, to the task of defining and attempting to achieve a "successful" ordering of the built environment. In the ultimate instance the planner is concerned with the "proper" location, the appropriate mix of activities in space of all the diverse elements which make up the totality of physical structures—the houses, roads, factories, offices, water and sewage disposal facilities, hospitals, schools, and the like—which comprise the built environment. From time to time the spatial ordering of the built environment is treated as an end sufficient unto itself and some form of environmental determinism takes hold. At other times this ordering is seen as a reflection rather than a determinant of social relations and planning is seen as a process rather than as a plan—and so the planner heaves himself away from the drawing board to attend meetings with bankers, community groups, land developers, and the like, in the hope that a timely intervention here or a preventive measure there may achieve a "better" overall result. But "better" assumes some purpose which is easy enough to specify in general but more difficult to particularize about. As a physical resource complex created out of human labor and ingenuity, the built environment must primarily function to be useful for production, circulation, exchange and consumption. It is the job of the planner to intervene in the production of this complex composite commodity and to ensure its proper management and maintenance. But this poses immediately the question, useful or better for what and to whom?

Planning and the Reproduction of the Social Order

It would be easy to jump from these initial questions straight away into some pluralistic model of society in which the planner acts either as an arbitrator or as a corrective weight in the conflicts amongst a diversity of interest groups, each of which strives to get a piece of the pie. Such a jump leaves out a crucial step. Society works, after all, on the basic principle that the most important activity is that which contributes to its own reproduction. We do not have to enquire far to find out what this activity entails. Consider, for example, the various conceptions of the city as "workshops of industrial civilization," as "nerve centers for the economic, social, cultural and political life" of society, as centers for innovation, exchange and communication and as living environments for people.[1] All of these—and more—are common enough conceptions. And if we accept one or all of them, then the role of the planner can simply be defined as ensuring that the built environment comprises those necessary physical infrastructures which serve the processes we have in mind. If the "workshop" dissolves into a chaos of disorganization, if the "nerve center" loses its coherence, if innovation is stymied, if communication and exchange processes become garbled, if the living conditions become intolerable, then the reproduction of the social order is in doubt.

We can push this argument further. We live, after all, in a society which, for want of a better phrase, is founded on capitalist principles of private property and market exchange, a society which presupposes certain basic social relationships with respect to production, distribution and consumption which themselves must be reproduced if the social order is to survive. And so we arrive at what may appear a rather cosmic question: what is the role of the urban-regional planner in the context of these overall processes of social reproduction? Critical analysis should reveal the answers. Yet it is a measure of the failings of contemporary social science (from which the planning literature draws much of its inspiration) that we have to approach answers with circumspection as well as tact should we dare to depart from the traditional canons as to what may or may not be said. For this reason I shall begin with a brief digression in order to open up new vistas for discussion.

When we consider the economic system, most of us feel at home with analyses based on the categories of land, labor and capital as "factors" of production. We recognize that social reproduction depends upon the perpetual combination of these elements and that growth requires the recombination of these factors into new configurations which are in some sense more productive. These categories, we often admit, are rather too abstract and from time to time we break them down to take account of the fact that neither land nor labor are homogeneous and that capital can take productive (physical) or liquid (money) form. Nevertheless, we seem prepared to accept a high level of abstraction, without too much questioning as to the validity or efficacy of the concepts employed. Yet most of us blanch when faced with a sociological description of society which appeals to the concept of class relations between landlords, laborers and capitalists. If we write in such terms we will likely be dismissed as too simplistic or as engaging in levels of abstraction which make no sense. At worst, such concepts will be regarded as offensive and ideological compared to the supposedly non-ideological concepts of land, labor and capital. Why and on what grounds, philosophical, practical or otherwise, was it decided that one form of abstraction made sense and was appropriate while the other was out of order? Does it not make reasonable sense to connect our sociological thinking with our economics, albeit in a rather simplistic and primitive way? Does it make sense, even, to tell the inner city tenant that the rent paid to the landlord is not really a payment to that man who drives a big car and lives in the suburbs, but a payment to a scarce factor of production? The "scientization" of social science seems to have been accomplished by masking real social relationships—by representing the social relations between people and groups of people as relations between things. The reification implied by this tactic is plain enough to see and the dangers of reification are well-known. Yet we seem to be at ease with the reifications and to accept them uncritically even though the possibility exists that in so doing we destroy our capacity to understand, manage, control and alter the social order in ways favorable to our individual or collective purposes. In this paper, therefore, I will seek to place the planner in the context of a sociological description of society which sees class relations as fundamental.

Class Relations and the Built Environment

In any society the actual class relations which exist are bound to be complex and fluid. This is particularly true in a society such as ours. The class categories which we use are not regarded as immutable. And in the same way that we can disaggregate land, labor and capital as factors of production so we can produce a finer mesh of categories to describe the class structure. We know that land and property ownership comprises residual feudal institutions (the church, for example), large property companies, part-time landlords, homeowners, and so on. We know also that the interests of rentier "money capitalists" may diverge substantially from the interests of producers in industry and agriculture and that the laboring class is not homogeneous because of the stratifications and differentials generated according to the hierarchical division of labor and various wage rates. But in a short paper of this sort I must perforce stick to the simplest categories which help us to understand the planner's role within the social structure. So let us proceed with the simplest conception we can devise and consider, in turn, how each class or fraction of a class relates to the built environment which is the primary concern of the planner.

1. The class of laborers is made up of all of those individuals who sell a commodity—labor power—on the market in return for a wage or salary. The consumption requirements of labor—which are in practice highly differentiated—will in part be met by work within the household and in part be procured by exchanges of wages earned against commodities produced. The commodity requirements of labor depend upon the balance between domestic economy products and market purchases as well as upon

the environmental, historical and cultural considerations which fix the standard of living of labor. Labor looks to the built environment as a means of consumption and as a means for its own reproduction and, perhaps, expansion. Labor is sensitive to both the cost and the spatial disposition (access) of the various items in the built environment—housing, educational and recreational facilities, services of all kinds, etc.—which facilitate survival and reproduction at a given standard of living.

2. We can define capitalists as all those who engage in entrepreneurial functions of any kind with the intent of obtaining a profit. As a class, capitalists are primarily concerned with accumulation and their activities form, in our kind of society, the primary engine for economic development and growth. Capital "in general"—which we will use as a handy term for the capitalist class as a whole—looks to the built environment for two reasons. Firstly, the built environment functions as a set of use values for enhancing the production and accumulation of capital. The physical infrastructures form a kind of fixed capital—much of which is collectively provided and used—which can be used as a means of production, of exchange or of circulation. Secondly, the production of the built environment forms a substantial market for commodities (such as structural steel) and services (such as legal and administrative services) and therefore contributes to the total effective demand for the products which capitalists themselves produce. On occasion, the built environment can become a kind of "dumping ground" for surplus money capital or idle productive capacity (sometimes by design as in the public works programs of the 1930's) with the result that there are periodic bouts of overproduction and subsequent devaluation of the assets embedded in the built environment itself. The "wave-like" pattern of investment in the built environment is a very noticeable feature in the economic history of capitalist societies.[2]

3. A particular faction of capital seeks a rate of return on its capital by building new elements in the built environment. This faction—the construction interest—engages in a particular kind of commodity production under rather peculiar conditions. Much of what happens in the way of construction activity has to be understood in terms of the technical, economic and political organization of the construction interest.

4. We can define landlords as those who, by virtue of their ownership of land and property, can extract a rent (actual or imputed) for the use of the resources they control. In societies dominated by feudal residuals, the landlord interest may be quite distinct from that of capital, but in the United States ownership in land and property became a very important form of investment from the eighteenth century onwards. Under these conditions the "land and property interest" is simply reduced to a faction of capital (usually the money capitalists and the rentiers) investing in the appropriation of rent. This brings us to consider the important role

of property companies, developers, banks and other financial intermediaries (insurance companies, pension funds, savings and loan associations, etc.) in the land and property market. And we should also add that "home-ownership" does not quite mean what it says because most homeowners actually share equity with a financial institution and do not possess title to the property. In the United States, therefore, we have to think of the land and property interest primarily as a faction of capital investing in rental appropriation.

I shall assume for purposes of analytic convenience that a clear distinction exists between these classes and factions and that each pursues its own interests single-mindedly. In a capitalist society, of course, the whole structure of social relations is founded on the domination of capitalists over laborers. To put it this way is simply to acknowledge that the capitalists make the investment decisions, create the jobs and the commodities, and function as the catalytic agents in capitalist growth. We cannot hold, on the one hand, that America was created by the efforts of private entrepreneurs and deny on the other that capital dominates labor. Labor is not passive, of course, but its actions are defensive and at best confined to gaining a reasonable share of the national product. But if labor controlled the investment decisions then we would not be justified any longer in describing our society as capitalist. Our interest here is not so much to focus on this primary antagonism but to examine the myriad secondary forms of conflict which can spin off from it to weave a complex web of arguments over the production and use of the built environment. Appropriators (landlords and property owners) may be in conflict with construction interests, capitalists may be dissatisfied with the activities of both factions, while labor may be at odds with all of the others. And if the transport system or the sewage system does not work then both labor and capital will be equally put out. Let us consider two examples which, in spite of their hypothetical nature, illustrate the complex alliances which can form and shed some light on the kinds of problems which urban planners typically face.

We will start with the proposition that the price of existing resources in the built environment—and, hence, the rate of rental appropriation—is highly sensitive to the costs and rate of new construction. Suppose the construction interests are badly organized, in a slump or unable to gain easy access to cheap land and that the rate of new construction is low and the costs high. Under these conditions those seeking the appropriation of rent possess the power to increase their rate of return by raising rental on, say, housing. Labor may resist, tenant organizations may spring up and seek to control the rate of rental appropriation and to keep the cost of living down. If they succeed, tenant organizations may even drive the rate of return on existing resources downwards to the point where investment with-

draws entirely (perhaps producing abandonment). If labor lacks organization and power in the community but is well-organized and powerful in
the work place, a rising rate of appropriation may result in the pursuit of
higher wages which, if granted, may lower the rate of profit and accumulation. A rational response of the capitalist class under these conditions is
to seek an alliance with labor to curb excessive rental appropriations, to
free land for new construction and to see to it that cheap (perhaps even
subsidized) housing is built for the laboring class. We can see this sort of
coalition in action when large corporate interests in suburban locations join
with civil rights groups in trying to break suburban zoning restrictions
which exclude low-wage populations from the suburbs. An exploration of
this dimension to conflict can tell us much about the structure of contemporary urban problems.

The second case we will consider arises out of the general dynamic of
capitalist accumulation which, from time to time, produces chronic overproduction, surplus real productive capacity and idle money capital desperately in need of productive outlets. In such a situation, money is
easily come by to produce long-term investments in the built environment
and a vast investment wave flows into the production of the built environment which serves as a vent for surplus capital—such was the boom experienced from 1970 to 1973. But at some point the existence of overproduction becomes plain to see—be it office space in Manhattan or of housing
in Detroit—and the property boom collapses in a wave of bankruptcies and
"refinancings" (consider, for example, the fall of the secondary banks associated with the London property market in 1973 and the dismal performance of the Real Estate Investment Trusts in the United States with some
$11 billion in assets, half of which are currently earning no rate of return
at all). What becomes evident in this case is that excessive investment
brings in its wake disinvestment and devaluation of capital for at least some
segment of "the landed interest." The construction interest is also faced
with an extremely difficult pattern of booms and slumps which militates
against the creation of a viable long-term organization for the coherent
production of the built environment. If labor sinks part of its equity into
the property market then it, too, may find its savings devalued by such
processes and, through community organization and political action, it may
seek to protect itself as well as it can. In this case also, we can discern
a structure to our urban problems which is explicable in terms of the conflicting requirements of the various classes and factions as they face up to
the problems created by the use of built environment as a vent for surplus
capital in a period of overaccumulation.

These dimensions of conflict are cut across, however, by a completely
different set of considerations which arise out of the fact that the built
environment is comprised of assets which are typically both long-lived and

fixed and immobile in space. This means that we are dealing with commodities which must be produced and used under conditions of "natural monopoly" in space. It also happens that since the built environment is to be conceived of as a complex composite commodity, the individual elements have strong "externality" effects on other elements. We thus find that competition for use of resources is monopolistic competition in space, that capitalists can compete with capitalists for advantageously positioned resources, that laborers can compete with laborers for survival chances, access, and the like, while land and property owners seek to influence the positioning of new elements in the built environment (particularly transport facilities) so as to gain indirect benefits. The basic structure of class and factional conflicts is therefore modified and in some instances totally transformed into a structure of geographical conflict which pits laborers in the suburbs against laborers in the city, capitalists in the industrial northeast against capitalists in the sunbelt, and so on.

The distinctive role and task of the planner has to be understood against the background of the strong currents of both interclass and factional conflict, on the one hand, and the geographical competition which natural monopolies in space inevitably generate, on the other.

The Production, Maintenance and Management of the Built Environment

The built environment must incorporate the necessary use values to facilitate social reproduction and growth. Its overall efficiency and rationality can be tested and measured in terms of how well it functions in relationship to these tasks. The sophisticated model builders within the planning fraternity have long sought to translate this conception into a search for some idealized *optimum optimorum* for the city or for regional structure. Such a search can be entertaining and it can generate insights into certain typical characteristics of urban structure, but as an enterprise it is utopian, idealized and fruitless. A more down-to-earth analysis suggests that the indications of failure of the built environment to provide the necessary use values are not too hard to spot. The evidence of *crisis* and of failure to reproduce effectively or to grow at a steady rate of accumulation, is a clear indicator of a lack of balance which requires some kind of corrective action.

Unfortunately, "crisis" is a much overused word. Anybody who wants anything in this society is forced to shout "crisis" as loudly as possible in order to get anything done. For the underprivileged and the poor, the "crisis" is permanent and endemic. We will take a narrower view and define a crisis as a particular conjuncture in which the reproduction of capitalist society is in jeopardy. The main signals are falling rates of profit, soaring unemployment and inflation, idle productive capacity and idle money capital lacking profitable employment, financial, institutional and political chaos and civil strife. And we can identify three wellsprings out of which crises in capitalist society typically flow. First, an imbalanced outcome of the struggle between the classes or factions of classes acquires so much power that it can force the wage rate up and the accumulation rate down; finance capital dominates and engages in speculative binges which de-stabilize the system, etc.). Second, accumulation pushes growth beyond the capacity of the sustaining natural resource base at the same time as technological innovation slackens. Third, a tendency towards overaccumulation and overproduction is omnipresent in capitalist societies because individual entrepreneurs, pursuing their own individual self-interest, collectively push the dynamic of aggregative accumulation away from a balanced growth path.

The particular role of the built environment in all of this is complex in its details but simple in principle. Failure to invest in those elements in the built environment which contribute to accumulation is no different in principle than the failure of entrepreneurs to invest and reinvest in fixed capital equipment. The problem with the built environment is that much of it functions as *collective* fixed capital (transport, sewage and disposal systems, etc.). Some way has to be found, therefore, to ensure a flow of investment into the built environment and to ensure that individual investment decisions are coordinated in both time and space so that the aggregative needs of capitalist producers are met. By the same token, failure to invest in the means of consumption for labor may raise the wage rate, generate civil strife or (in the worst kind of eventuality) physically diminish the supply of labor. In both cases failure to invest in the right quantities, at the right times and in the right places can be a progenitor of a crisis of accumulation and growth. Overinvestment in the built environment is, on the other hand, simply a devaluation of capital which nobody, surely, welcomes. And so we arrive at the general conception of the *potential* for a harmonious, balanced investment process in the built environment. Any departure from this path will entail either underinvestment (and a constraint upon accumulation) or overinvestment (and the devaluation of capital). The problem is to find some way to ensure that such a potentiality for balanced growth is realized under the conditions of a capitalist investment process.

The built environment is long-lived, fixed and immobile in space and a complex composite commodity the individual elements of which may be produced, maintained, managed and owned by quite diverse interests. Plainly, there is a problem of coordination because mistakes are very difficult to recoup and individual producers may not always act to produce the proper mix of elements in space. The time stream of benefits to be derived also poses some peculiar problems. The physical landscape created at one point in time may be suited to the needs of society at that point but become antagonistic later as the dynamics of accumulation and societal growth alter the use value requirements of both capital and labor. Tensions may then arise because the long-lived use values embedded in the built environment cannot easily be altered on a grand scale—witness the problems endemic to many of the older industrial and commercial cities in the industrial northeast of the United States at the present time.

Investment in the built environment can be coordinated with general social requirements in one, or a mix of three ways:

1. Allocations can be arrived at through market mechanisms. Elements which can be privately appropriated under the legal relations of private property—houses, factories, offices, stores, warehouses, etc.—can be rented and traded. This sets up the price signals which, under pure competitive bidding, will allocate land and plant to the best-paying uses. The price signals also make it possible to calculate a rate of return on new investments which usually generates a flow of new investment to wherever the rate of return is above that to be had given similar risks in other sectors of the capital market. But the innumerable externality effects and the importance of "public good" items which cannot be privately appropriated —streets, sidewalks, etc.—generate frequent market failures and imperfections so that in no country is investment in the built environment left entirely to competitive market mechanisms.

2. Allocations may be arrived at under the auspices of some hegemonic controlling interest—a land or developer monopoly, controlling financial interests, and the like.[3] This is not an irrational move because a large scale enterprise coordinating investments of many different types can "internalize the externalities" and thereby make more rational decisions from the investor standpoint—the land grant railroads provide an excellent historical example of such monopolistic control, while Rouse's Columbia provides a contemporary example. The trouble with monopolization and hegemonic control is that the pricing system becomes artificial (and this can lead to misallocations) while there is nothing to ensure that monopoly power is not abused.

3. State intervention is an omnipresent feature in the production, maintenance and management of the built environment.[4] The transport system —prime example of a "natural monopoly" in space—has always posed the problem of private gain versus public social benefit, private property rights versus aggregative social needs. The abuse of monopoly power (which it is all too easy to accumulate in spatial terms) has ever brought forth state regulation as a response. The pervasive externality effects have in all countries led to state regulation of the spatial order to reduce the risks which attach to long-term investment decisions. And the "public goods"

elements in the built environment—the streets, sidewalks, sewers and drainage systems, etc.—which cannot feasibly be privately appropriated have always been created by direct investment on the part of the agencies of the state. The theme of "public improvement" has been writ large in the history of all American cities.

The exact mix of private market, monopolistic control and state intervention and provision has varied with time as well as from place to place. Which mix is chosen or, more likely, arrived at by a complex historical process, is not that important. What is important, is that it should ensure the creation of a built environment which serves the purpose of social reproduction and that it should do so in such a manner that crises are avoided as far as is possible.

Urban Planning as Part of the Instrumentalities of State

The proper conception of the role of the state in capitalist society is controversial.[5] I shall simply take the view that the institutions of state and the processes whereby state powers are exercised must be so fashioned that they, too, contribute, insofar as they can, to the reproduction and growth of the social system. Under this conception we can derive certain basic functions of the capitalist state. It should:

1. help to stabilize an otherwise rather erratic economic and social system by acting as a "crisis-manager,"

2. strive to create the conditions for "balanced growth" and a smooth process of accumulation,

3. contain civil strife and factional struggles by repression (police power), cooptation (buying off politically or economically) or integration (trying to harmonize the demands of warring classes or factions).

The State can effectively perform all of these functions only if it succeeds in internalizing within its processes the conflicting interests of classes, factions, diverse geographical groupings, etc. A state which is entirely controlled by one and only one faction, which can operate only repressively and never through integration or cooptation, will likely be unstable and will likely survive only under conditions which are, in any case, chronically unstable. The social democratic State is one which can internalize diverse conflicting interests and which, by means of the checks and balances it contains, can prevent any one faction or class from seizing direct control of all of the instrumentalities of government and putting them to its own direct use. Yet the social democratic State is still a capitalist state in the sense that it is a capitalist social order which it is helping to reproduce. If the instrumentalities of state power are turned against the existing social order, then we see a crisis of the State, the outcome of which will determine whether the social order changes or whether the organization of the State reverts to its basic role of serving societal reproduction.

The urban planner occupies just one niche within the total complex of of the instrumentalities of state power. The internalization of conflicting interests and needs within the State typically puts one branch of the bureaucracy at loggerheads with another, one level or branch of government against another, and even different departments at odds with each other within the same bureaucracy. In what follows, however, we will lay aside these diverse crosscurrents of conflict and seek to abstract some sense of the real limitations placed upon the urban planner by virtue of his or her role and thereby come to identify more clearly the nature of the role itself. To hasten the argument along, I shall simply suggest that the planner's task is to contribute to the processes of social reproduction and that in so doing the planner is equipped with powers vis-à-vis the production, maintenance and management of the built environment which permit him or her to intervene in order to stabilize, to create the conditions for "balanced growth," to contain civil strife and factional struggles by repression, cooptation or integration. And to fulfill these goals successfully, the planning process as a whole (in which the planner fulfills only one set of tasks) must be relatively open. This conception may appear unduly simplistic but a down-to-earth analysis of what planners actually do as opposed to what they or the mandarins of the planning fraternity think they do, suggests that the conception is not far from the mark. And the history of those who seek to depart radically from this fairly circumscribed path suggests that they either encounter frustration or else give up the role of planner entirely.[6]

The Knowledge of the Planner and Its Implied "World View"

In order to perform the necessary tasks effectively, the planner needs to acquire an understanding of how the built environment works in relationship to social reproduction and how the various facets of competitive, monopolistic and state production of the built environment relate to each other in the context of often conflicting class and factional requirements. Planners are therefore taught to appreciate how everything relates to everything else in an urban system, to think in terms of costs and benefits (although they may not necessarily resort to techniques of cost-benefit analysis) and to have some sympathetic understanding of the problems which face the private producers of the built environment, the landlord interest, the urban poor, the managers of financial institutions, the downtown business interests, and so on. The accumulation of planning knowledge arises through incremental understandings of what would be the "best" configuration of investment (both spatial and in terms of quantitative balance) to facilitate social reproduction. But the most important shifts in understanding come in the course of those crises in which something obviously must be done because social reproduction is in jeopardy.

The planner requires something else as well as a basic understanding of how the system works from a purely technical standpoint. In resorting to tools of repression, cooptation and integration, the planner requires justification and legitimation, a set of powerful arguments with which to confront warring factional interests and class antagonisms. In striving to affect reconciliation, the planner must perforce resort to the idea of the potentiality for harmonious balance in society. And it is on this funda-mental notion of social harmony that the ideology of planning is built. The planner seeks to intervene to restore "balance" but the "balance" implied is that which is necessary to reduce civil strife and to maintain the requisite conditions for the steady accumulation of capital. From time to time, of course, planners may be "captured" (by corruption, political patronage or even by "radical" arguments) by one class/faction or another and thereby lose the capacity to act as stabilizers and harmonizers—but such a condition, though endemic, is inherently unstable and the inevitable reform movement will most probably sweep it away when it is no longer consistent with the requirements of the social order as a whole. The role of the planner, then, ultimately derives its justification and legitimacy from intervening to restore that balance which perpetuates the existing social order. And the planner fashions an ideology appropriate to the role.

This does not necessarily mean that the planner is a mere defender of the status quo. The dynamics of accumulation and of societal growth are such as to create endemic tensions between the built environment as is and as it should be, while the evils which stem from the abuse of spatial monopoly can quickly become widespread and dangerous for social re-production. Part of the planner's task is to spot both present and future dangers and to head off, if possible, an incipient "crisis of the built en-vironment". In fact the whole tradition of planning is progressive in the sense that the planner's commitment to the ideology of social harmony—unless it is perverted or corrupted in some way—always puts the planner in the role of "righter of wrongs", "corrector of imbalances" and "defender of the public interest". The limits to this progressive stance are clearly set, however, by the fact that the definitions of the public interest, of imbalance and of inequity are set according to the requirements for the reproduction of the social order which is, whether we like the term or not, a distinctively capitalistic social order.

The planner's knowledge of the world cannot be separated from this necessary ideological commitment. Existing and planned orderings to the built environment are evaluated against some notion of a "rational" sociospatial ordering. But it is the capitalistic definition of rationality to which we appeal.[7] The principle of "rationality" is an ideal—the central core to a pervasive ideology—which itself depends upon the notion of harmonious processes of social reproduction under capitalism. The limits to the planner's understanding of the world are set by this underlying ideological commitment. In the reverse direction, the planner's knowledge is used ideologically, as both legitimation and justification for certain forms of action. Political struggles and arguments may, under the planner's influence, be reduced to technical arguments for which a "rational" solution can easily be found. Those who do not accept such a solution are then open to attack as "unreasonable" and "irrational". In this manner both the real understanding of the world and the prevailing ideology fuse into a world view. I do not mean to imply that all planners subscribe to the same world view—they manifestly do not and it would be disfunctional were they to do so. Some planners are very technocratic and seek to translate all political issues into technical problems while other planners take a much more political stance. But whatever their position, the fusion of technical understandings with a necessary ideology produces a complex mix within the planning fraternity of capacity to understand and to intervene in a realistic and advantageous way and capacity to repress, coopt and integrate in a way that appears justifiable and legitimate.

Civil Strife, Crises of Accumulation and Shifts in the Planner's World View

The planner's world view, defined as the necessary knowledge for appropriate intervention and the necessary ideology to justify and legitimate action, has altered with changing circumstances. But knowledge and ideology do not change overnight. The concepts, categories, relationships and images through which we interpret the world are, so to speak, the fixed capital of our intellectual world and are no more easily transformed than the physical infrastructures of the city itself. It usually takes a crisis, a rush of ideas pouring forth under the pressure of events, radically to change the planner's world view and even then radical change comes but slowly. And while the fundamentals of ideology—the notion of social harmony—may stay intact, the meanings attached must change according to whatever it is that is out of balance. The history of capitalist societies these last two hundred years suggests, however, that certain problems are endemic, problems that simply will not go away no matter how hard we try. Consequently we find that the shifting world view of the planner exhibits an accumulation of technical understandings combined with a mere swaying from side to side in ideological stance from which the planner appears to learn little or nothing, let us illustrate.

The capitalist growth process has been punctuated, at quite regular intervals, by phases of acute social tension and civil strife. These phases are not historical accidents but can be traced back to the fundamental characteristics of capitalist societies and the growth processes entailed. We have not space to elaborate on this theme here, but it is important to note that the organization of work under capitalism is predicated on a separation between "working" and "living," on control of work by the capitalist and alienated labor for the employee, and on a dynamic relation between the wage rate and the rate of profit which is founded on the social necessity for a surplus of labor which may vary quantitatively according to time and place. Generally speaking it is the concentration of low-wage populations and unemployment in either time or space which sets the stage for civil strife.

The response is some mixture of repression, cooptation and integration. The urban planner's role in all of this is to define policies which facilitate social control and which serve to reestablish social harmony through cooptation and integration. Consider, for example, the spatial distribution of the population, particularly of the unemployed and low-wage earners. The revolutions of 1848, the Paris Commune of 1871, the urban violence which accompanied the great railroad strikes of 1877 in the United States and Chicago's celebrated "Haymarket affair" of 1886 demonstrated the revolutionary dangers associated with high concentrations of what Charles Loring Brace called, in the 1870's, "the dangerous classes" of society.[8] The problem could be dealt with by a policy of dispersal which meant that ways had to be found to permit the poor and the unemployed to escape their chronic entrapment in space. The urban working class had to be dispersed and subjected to what reformers on both sides of the the Atlantic called "the moral influence" of the suburbs.[9] Suburbanization facilitated by cheap communication was seen as part of the solution. The urban planners and reformers of the time pressed hard for policies of dispersal via mass transit facilities such as those provided under the Cheap Trains Act of 1882 in Britain and the streetcars in the United States, while the search for cheap housing and means to promote social stability through working class home-ownership began in earnest. In much the same way, planners in the 1960's responded to the urban riots by seeking ways to disperse the ghetto by improved transport relations, promoting homeownership, opening up housing opportunities in the suburbs (although this time round the Victorian rhetoric of "moral influence" was replaced by the more "rational" appeal of "social stability"). In the process, the laboring classes undoubtedly gain in real living standards while the planner acts as advocate for the poor and the underprivileged, raises the cry of social justice and equity, expresses moral outrage at the conditions of life of the urban poor and reaches for ways to restore social harmony.

The alternative to dispersal is what we now call "gilding the ghetto" and this, too, is a well-tried tactic in the struggle to control civil strife in urban areas. As early as 1812, the Reverend Thomas Chalmers raised the specter of a tide of revolutionary violence sweeping Britain as working class populations steadily concentrated in large urban areas. Chalmers saw "the principle of community" as the main bulwark of defense against this revolutionary tide—a principle which sought to establish harmony between the classes around the basic institutions of community.[10]   The principle entailed also a commitment to community improvement, the attempt to instill some sense of civic or community pride capable of transgressing class boundaries. The church was then the most important institution, but we now think of other instrumentalities also—political inclusion, citizen participation, community commitment to educational, recreational and other services as well as the sense of pride in neighborhood which inevitably means a "better" quality to the built environment.   From Chalmers through Octavia Hill and Jane Addams, to Model Cities and citizen participation, we have a continuous thread of an argument which suggests that social stability can be restored in periods of social unrest by an active pursuit of "the principle of community" and all that this means in the way of community betterment and social improvement—and again, the planner typically acts as advocate, as catalyst in promoting the spirit of community improvement.

One dimension to this idea of "improvement" is that of environmental quality.   Olmstead was perhaps the first fully to recognize that the efficiency of labor might be enhanced by providing a compensatory sense of harmony with nature in the living place, although it is important to recognize that Olmstead was building on a rather older tradition.[11]   At issue here is the relation to nature in a most fundamental sense.   Industrial capitalism, armed with the factory system, organized a work process which transformed the relation between the worker and nature into a travesty of its older artisan self.   Reduced to a thing, a commodity, a mere "factor" of production, the worker became alienated from the product of work, the process of production and ultimately from nature itself, particularly in the industrial city where, as Dickens puts it, "Nature was as strongly bricked out as killing airs and gases were bricked in." [12]   The romantic reaction against the new industrial order ultimately led in the practice of urban design and planning to the attempt to counter in the sphere of consumption for what had been lost in the sphere of production.[13]   The attempt to "bring nature back into the living environments" within the city has been a consistent theme in planning since Olmstead's time onwards.   Yet it is, in the final analysis, an attempt based in what Raymond Williams calls "an effective and imposing mystification" for there is something in the relation to nature in the work process which can never be compensated for in the consumption sphere.[14] The planner, armed with concepts of ecological balance and the notion of harmony with nature, acts once more as advocate and brings real gains. But the real solutions to these problems lie elsewhere, in the work process itself.

Civil strife and social discontent provide only one set of problems which the planner must address. The dynamic of accumulation with its periodic crises of overaccumulation pose an entirely different set. The crises are not accidental. They are to be viewed, rather, as major periods of "rationalization," of "shake-outs and shake-downs" which restore balance to an economic system temporarily gone mad. The fact that crises perform this rationalizing function is no comfort to those caught in their midst. And at such conjunctures planners must either simply administer the budget cuts and plan the shrinkage according to the strict requirements of an externally imposed fiscal logic of the sort now being applied to New York, or seek to head up a movement for a forced rationalization of the urban system. The pursuit of the city beautiful is replaced by the search for the city efficient, the cry of social justice is replaced by the slogan "efficiency in government" and those planners armed with a ruthless cost-benefit calculus, a rational and technocratic commitment to efficiency for efficiency's sake, come into their own.

"Rationalization" means, of course, doing whatever must be done to reestablish the conditions for a positive rate of accumulation. When economic growth goes negative—as it did, for example, in 1893, the early 1930's or in 1970 and 1974, then the reproduction of the social order is plainly in doubt. The task at such conjunctures is to find out what is wrong and right it. The physical infrastructure of the city may be congested, inefficient and too costly to use for purposes of production and exchange. Such barriers (which were obvious to all in the progressive era, for example) must be removed and if the planner does not willingly help to do so, then the escalating competition between jurisdictions for "development" at times of general decline will force the planner into action if he or she values the tax base (this kind of competitive pressure often leads communities to subsidize profits). If the problem lies in the consumption sphere—underconsumption or erratic movements in aggregate personal behaviors—then the state may seek to manage consumption either by fiscal devices or through collectivization. The management of collective consumption by means of the built environment at such points becomes a crucial part of the planner's task.[15] If the problem lies in lack or excess of investment in the built environment then the planner must perforce set to work to stimulate investment or to manage and "rationalize" devaluation with techniques of "planned shrinkage," urban renewal and even the production of "planning blight" (which amounts to nothing more than earmarking certain areas for devaluation).

I list these various possibilities because it is not always self-evident as to what must be done in the heat of a crisis of accumulation. At such conjunctures our knowledge of the system and how it works is crucial for action, unless we are to be led dangerously near the precipice of quite cataclysmic depression. And it is exactly at such points that the world view of the planner, restricted as it is by an ideological commitment, appears most defective, while the ideological stance of the planner may have to shift under the pressure of events from advocacy for the urban poor to one dedicated to business rationality and efficiency in government.

But ideologies, we have argued, do not change that easily, nor does our knowledge of the world. And so we find at each of the major turning points in our history, a *crisis of ideology*.[16] Past commitments must obviously be abandoned because they hinder our power to understand and most certainly lose their power to legitimate and justify (imagine trying to justify what is happening currently in New York by appealing to concepts of social justice). And as the pillars to the planner's world view slowly crumble, so the search begins for a new scaffolding for the future. At such a juncture, it becomes necessary to plan the ideology of planning.

Planning the Ideology of Planning—1978 Style

The organizers of this conference suggested in their invitation that the planning inspirations of the 1960's had faded and that our main task here was to define new horizons for planning the 1970's—new technologies, new instrumentalities, new goals . . . new everything in fact *except* a new ideology. Yet if my analysis is correct the real task here is to plan the ideology of planning to fit the economic realities of the 1970's rather than to meet the social unrest and civil strife of the 1960's.

Since many of those who inspired us in the 1960's are still with us and even participating in this conference, it is useful to ask what, if anything, went wrong? The crucial problem of the 1960's was civil strife and in particular the concentrated form of it associated with the urban riots in central city areas. That strife had to be contained by repression, cooptation and integration. In this the planner, armed with diverse ideologies and a variety of world views, played a crucial role. The dissidents were encouraged to go through "channels," to adhere to "procedures laid down" and somewhere down that path the planner laid in wait with a seemingly sophisticated technology, an intricate understanding of the world, through which political questions could be translated into technical questions which the mass of the population found hard to understand. But discontent cannot so easily be controlled and so the other string to the planner's bow was to find ways to disperse the urban poor, to divide and control them and to ameliorate their conditions of life.[17] The management of this process fell very much within the domain of urban planning and it generated conflicting ideological stances and world views within the planning profession itself. At first sight (and indeed at the time) it seemed as if planning theory was fragmented in the 1960's as different segments of the planning fraternity moved according to their position or inclination to one or other pole of the ideological spectrum. With the benefit of hindsight we can see that this process was nothing more than the internalization within the planning apparatus of conflicting social pressures and positions. And this internalization and the oppositions which it provoked proved functional, no matter what individuals thought or did. The technocrats helped to define the outer bounds of what could be done at the same time as they sought for new instrumentalities to accomplish dispersal and to establish social control. The advocates for the urban poor and the instrumentalities which they devised, provided the channels for cooptation and integration at the same time as they pushed the system to provide whatever could be provided, being careful to stop short at the boundaries which the technocrats and "fiscal conservatives" helped to define. Those who pushed advocacy too far were either forced out or deserted planning altogether and became activists and political organizers.

Judged in terms of their own ideological rhetoric, the pursuers of social justice failed, much as they did in the Progressive era, to accomplish what they set out to do, although the position of the "dangerous classes" in society undoubtedly improved somewhat in the late 1960's. But judged in relation to the reduction of civil strife, the reestablishment of social control and the "saving" of the capitalist social order, the planning techniques and ideologies of the 1960's were highly successful. Those who inspired us in the 1960's can congratulate themselves on a job well done.

But conditions changed quite radically in 1969-70. Stagflation emerged as the most serious problem and the negative growth rate of 1970 indicated that the fundamental processes of accumulation were in deep trouble. A loose monetary policy—the most potent tool in the management of the "political business cycle"—saw us through the election of 1972. But the boom was speculative and heavily dependent upon a massive overinvestment in the land, property and construction sectors which easy money typically encourages. By the end of 1973 it was plain that the built environment could absorb no more in the way of surplus capital and the rapid decline in property and construction, together with financial instability, triggered the subsequent depression. Unemployment doubled, real wages began to move downwards under the impact of severe "labor-disciplining" policies, social programs began to be savagely cut and all of the gains made after a decade of struggle in the 1960's by the poor and underprivileged were rolled back almost within the space of a year. The underlying logic of capitalist accumulation asserts itself in the form of a crisis in which real wages must diminish in order that inflation be stabilized and that accumulation (growth) can resume through reinvestment.

The pressure from this underlying logic is felt in all spheres. Local budgets have to shift towards fiscal conservatism and have to alter priorities from social programs to programs to stimulate and encourage development (often by subsidies and tax benefits). Planners talk grimly of the "hard tough decisions" that lie ahead. Those that sought social justice as an end in itself in the 1960's gradually shift their ground as they begin to argue that social justice can best be achieved by ensuring efficiency in government. Those that sought ecological balance and conservation in its own right in the 1960's begin to appeal to principles of rational and efficient management of our resources. The technocrats begin the search for ways to define more rational patterns of investment in the built environment, calculate costs and benefits more finely than ever. The gospel of efficiency comes to reign supreme.

All or this presupposes the capacity to accomplish a transformation of ideological balance within the planning fraternity—a transformation which turns out to be almost identical to that which was successfully accomplished during the progressive era. It can, of course, be done. But it takes effort and fairly sophisticated argument, of the sort which this conference will undoubtedly produce, to do it. And the transformation is made that much easier because the fundamentals of ideology remain intact. The commitment to the ideology of harmony within the capitalist social order remains the still point upon which the gyrations of planning ideology turn.

But if we step aside and reflect awhile upon the tortuous twists and turns in our history, a shadow of doubt might cross our minds. Perhaps the most imposing and effective mystification of all lies in the presupposition of harmony at the still point of the turning capitalist world. Perhaps there lies at the fulcrum of capitalist history not harmony but a social relation of domination of capital over labor. And if we pursue this possibility, we might come to understand why the planner seems doomed to a life of perpetual frustration, why the high-sounding ideals of planning theory are so frequently translated into grubby practices on the ground, how the shifts in world view and in ideological stance are social products rather than freely chosen. And we might even come to see that it is the commitment to an alien ideology which chains our thought and understanding in order to legitimate a social practice that preserves, in a deep sense, the domination of capital over labor. Should we reach *that* conclusion, then we would surely witness a markedly different reconstruction of the planner's world view than we are currently seeing. We might even begin to plan the reconstruction of society, instead of merely planning the ideology of planning.

NOTES

1. These various conceptions of the city can be found in, for example, L. Mumford, *The City in History* (New York, 1961); J. Jacobs, *The Economy of Cities* (New York, 1969); L. Wirth, *On Cities and Social Life* (edited by A.J. Reiss;

Chicago, 1964 ed.); National Resources Committee (of the United States), *Our Cities: Their Role in the National Economy* (Washington, D.C., 1937); R. Meier, *A Communications Theory of Urban Growth* (Cambridge, Mass., 1962).

2. The "long-waves" in economic development and in particular those associated with investment in the various components of the built environment are discussed in B. Thomas, *Migration and Economic Growth* (London, 1973 ed.); M. Abramovitz, *Evidences of Long Swings in Aggregate Construction Since the Civil War* (NBER, New York, 1964); S. Kuznets, *Capital in the American Economy* (Princeton, N.J., 1961); E. Mandel, *Late Capitalism* (London, 1975).

3. Some idea of the extent of hegemonic control exercised by finance capital over the land and property market can be gained from L. Downie, *Mortgage on America* (New York, 1974); G. Barker, J. Penney, and W. Seccombe, *Highrise and Superprofits* (Kitchener, Ontario, 1973); P. Ambrose, and R. Colenutt, *The Property Machine* (Harmondsworth, Middlesex, 1975); D. Harvey, "Class-Monopoly Rent, Finance Capital and the Urban Revolution," *Regional Studies,* 8 (1974): 239-55.

4. The French urbanists have worked on this aspect most carefully as in M. Castells and F. Godard, *Monopolville—l'Enterprise, l'Etat, l'Urbain* (1973), and C.G. Pickvance, ed., *Urban Sociology; Critical Essays* (London, 1976). See also the various essays in *Antipode*, Vol. 7, No. 4,—a special issue devoted to "The Political Economy of Urbanism" and D. Harvey, "The Political Economy of Urbanization in Advanced Capitalist Societies: the Case of the United States," (1975), in G. Gappert and H. Rose, eds., *The Social Economy of Cities* (Urban Affairs Annual, No. 9, Beverly Hills, California).

5. See, for example, E. Altvater, "Notes on Some Problems of State Interventionism", *Kapitalistate*, 1 (1973): 96-108 and 3, pp. 76-83; R. Miliband, *The State in Capitalist Society* (London, 1968); N. Poulantzas, *Political Power and Social Classes* (London, 1973); J. O'Connor, *The Fiscal Crisis of the State* (New York, 1973).

6. A good example of how planners might move down such a path is written up in R. Goodman, *After the Planners* (New York, 1971).

7. The meaning of the concept of "rationality" has been very thoroughly discussed in M. Godelier, *Rationality and Irrationality in Economics* (London, 1972).

8. C.L. Brace, *The Dangerous Classes of New York* (New York, 1889 ed.).

9. J.A. Tarr, "From City to Suburb: the "moral" influence of transportation technology," in A.B. Callow, ed. *American Urban History* (New York, 1973).

10. Reverend Thomas Chalmers, *The Christian and Civic Economy of Large Towns,* 3 Volumes (Glasgow, 1821-26).

11. See, for example, T. Bender, *Towards an Urban Vision* (Kentucky, 1975) and R.A. Walker, *Urban Reform Movements and the Suburban Solution* (Doctoral Dissertation, Department of Geography and Environmental Engineering, The Johns Hopkins University).

12. The phrase can be found in Charles Dickens, *Hard Times,* chapter 10.

13. I have examined this theme in much greater detail in D. Harvey, (forthcoming), "Class Conflict Under the Capitalist Form of Urbanization: Labour, Capital and Conflict over the Built Environment," *Politics and Society.*

14. R. Williams, *The Country and the City* (London, 1973).

15. Again, the French urbanists have discussed this idea at length in, for example, E. Preteceille, *Equipements Collectifs, Structures Urbaines et Consommation Sociale* (Paris, 1975) and M. Castells, "Collective Consumption and Urban Condtarictions in Advanced Capitalist Societies," in L. Lindberg, ed., *Patterns of Advanced Societies* (New York, 1975).

16. There is an important connection between crises in ideology and legitimation—see, for example, J. Habermas, *Legitimation Crisis* (Boston, 1975); for a history of shifting ideology in urban development see R.A. Walker, *Urban Reform Movements*.

17. See F. Piven, and R. Cloward, *Regulating the Poor* (New York, 1971) and R. Cloward and F. Piven, *The Politics of Turmoil* (New York, 1974).

Planning in an Advanced Capitalist State

Robert A. Beauregard

Introduction

Within the advanced capitalist society of the United States, planning has been searched for in a variety of realms. Some have chosen to look in the corporate sector, others have quested after its rudimentary beginnings in the national economic consequences of governmental actions, and those with an administrative bent have scoured the bureaucracies and the environment of large organizations for signs.[1] Still others have been content to treat planning solely as a local phenomenon of little significance for the larger political economy.[2] Despite the paucity of planners in positions of power [3] and the lack of an institutionalized planning apparatus at the national level,[4] the possibility of planning continues to allure academics, activists and policymakers.[5] But as long as no coherent theory of the function of planning in an advanced capitalist society is developed, this multitude of expeditions will continue to forage independently of each other and to bring back only stories of planning once glimpsed. In order to construct an institutionalized planning to be used for moral ends, such a theory should contain an evaluation of the role of planning within the larger political economy and a critical analysis of the interests planning serves.

The ferreting out of the function of planning in the contemporary United States (and in societies in general) must begin with a definition of this activity and an identification of its institutional locus. Planning is an activity in which humans, individually and through their organizations and institutions, attempt to control the present and stabilize the future. This broad conceptualization encompasses all human behavior directed at structuring the natural, built and human environments; preceded by the positing of goals and the calculation of means; and followed by the evaluation of outcomes and the adjustment of initial hypotheses. Such activities, in their most rudimentary form, are performed by most of us as we go about our daily living. But they have also been specialized and hung with the accouterments of various technical skills. The result has been the emergence of a technical expert called the planner whose work is devoted to planning activities.[6] These experts deal with a variety of substantive issues—cities, education, military expenditures, energy, labor markets, corporate profits and income maintenance to name just a few—and thus emerge from a multitude of intellectual disciplines. *What they hold in common are their beliefs in the importance of technical rationality for public policy, the requirement that complex 'systems' must plan, and the political acceptance of State intervention into societal affairs.*[7]

The locus of these individuals and thus of planning, in both advanced capitalist and socialist societies, can be found within the confines of the State. It is in this institution that the activity of planning is legitimized for public consumption. These various levels of government, administration, judiciary, military and police power form that central institution in society which serves as the focus for private demands.[8] The State responds to these requests by developing policy ranging from the symbolic to the concrete. But in order to propagate the more visible programs which regulate private affairs and distribute and redistribute goods and services, the State must expend the monies it has collected through taxation. *These State monies are the State surplus. Through its utilization the State maintains the effectiveness of the political economy and legitimates itself with the major powers within society.*[9]

The specific issue to be addressed here is why the State in advanced capitalist societies engages in planning, and concomitantly, the function planning serves for that State. It will be argued that *planners facilitate the accumulation and legitimation functions of the State through the application of technical expertise to the manipulation of the State surplus. And they do so with a decided bias for efficiency considerations and thus an implicit orientation towards preserving the status quo of power and privilege. These consequences are unacceptable. The future of planning theory must therefore include a reorientation of the technical base of planning and a restructuring of its relationship with the State.*

In order to introduce the reader to the perspective used herein, a brief analysis of the historical development of the State surplus begins the paper. The basic functions of the State are sketched, and, the relationships among this surplus, the State and its planners are analyzed. This discussion focuses upon the use of efficiency criteria by planners and the implications this has for perpetuating inequality within American society. Thus the function of planning in an advanced capitalist State is both described and critically evaluated.

Historical Development of the State Surplus

In subsistence economies in which everyone produced just enough to satisfy own individual and familial needs, any surplus was, by definition, non-existent.[10] As differences in physical and mental abilities led to innovation or simple entrepreneurial activities and crude differences in coercive power developed, resulting in the oppression of some individuals by others, division of labor was extended outside the family. As a consequence of this rudimentary, occupational specialization, productivity increased and workers were exploited by their employees thus producing goods and services beyond basic human needs. Where there were imbalances in power, certain groups were forced to live below their needs and the differential extracted by their oppressors. Both mechanisms, either separately or jointly, resulted in the generation of a surplus, the difference between the socially produced product and the social need.[11] In general, then, the *surplus is the amount and value of productive resources in society beyond that required to satisfy basic human and social needs.*[12] It is financial capital, labor, natural resources, other factors of production, and individual and organizational abilities in excess of that which fulfills all individual and familial needs for food, clothing, shelter and communal well-being and all collective needs for the production, distribution and administration to meet these needs.

This surplus is not equally distributed among all members of society. Some possess and control more than others. Those initially in control of the surplus have a competitive advantage and with technological and organizational advances are able, through judicious use of the surplus already under their control, to increase their advantage.[13] This internal division of society by function and control over resources gave rise to social differentiation based upon an evaluative ranking of these positions—some positions became accepted as more crucial for and thus more valuable to society than others.[14] It is not just that functional differentiation and power differentials allow for the development of a surplus and its accompanying hierarchy, but additionally that *control over this surplus is used to reinforce and solidify positions.* Those people with surplus use part of it in surplus-extracting investments, part to control labor in order to increase productivity thus creating more surplus value, and part to establish mechanisms geared specifically to protect their privileged positions and interests; e.g., armies, exclusive clubs, prep schools and consumption patterns. Achieved and ascribed social characteristics and normative evaluations are utilized to create a more complex and thus less accessible class structure.

As new surplus is generated, it becomes distributed in accordance with the existing distribution of advantages.[15] Consequently, control over the surplus (that is, privilege) now becomes the major dimension of the class structure. Thus direct links are formed between the surplus and the distribution of power and between this distribution and the various classes. With continued utilization, and except for major political and economic upheavals, control over this surplus becomes more and more impenetrable.[16] Although absolute changes within the class structure may occur, relative positions survive essentially unchanged. Thus the distribution of the surplus and the extent of inequality are highly interdependent, with the mediating factors being the distribution of power and the extant class structure. *It is the existence of a surplus which allows the initial differentiation of society and the control over that surplus which perpetuates and strengthens those differences.*

Those controlling surplus soon find it advisable to establish organizations whose function is to protect the system of surplus-extraction; i.e., the exploitation of the surplus-poor population. But with increasing accumulation of the surplus [17] and thus increasing inequality in society, the potential for unrest intensifies. Even if the absolute benefits are expanding for all, the furtherance and crystallization of relative deprivation has similar consequences for upheaval. Institutions—commonly termed governments—are thus founded by the classes controlling the surplus. Their function is to prevent unrest and, failing that, to resolve conflicts. Moreover, these States are claimed to be the authoritative institutions in society and are draped with legitimacy.[18] This increases the probability that the State's decisions will (at least eventually) be accepted, thus substituting authority for resource-depleting coercion.[19] The State becomes the embodiment of concentrated authority, itself being a derivative of the unequal distribution of the surplus.[20]

In order to maintain and perpetuate itself, the State must serve two functions: accumulation and legitimization.[21] The first involves protecting the private appropriation of surplus i.e., facilitating the workings of the economy. The second involves providing goods and services to all groups whose political support is needed by the State. In both instances, those in authority find it to be in their best interest to be concerned with other centers of power and to be responsive to their needs. In addition, since any major upheaval in society might also destroy the existing form of the State, or at least remove those currently in office, the authorities also benefit from maintaining the status quo. This subsumes vast changes in inequality which would upset the relationships among class groups and eventually disrupt control over surplus-extracting and distributing mechanisms. The function of the State is to protect those mechanisms from such threats and thus serve the upper classes, yet also maintain itself through the provision of goods and services to all those who might offer political support.

For the State to undertake these activities, there must exist a State-controlled surplus that will support the State and its members and maintain the effectiveness of the political economy (i.e., the accumulation function) and the acquiescence or support of various class groups (i.e., the legitimization function). And since the State cannot merely generate wealth by fiat (although States have been known to print money without it having any real or social base),[22] this surplus must be extracted in some fashion from the people. Thus arises the need for different forms of transfer payments from the people and their organizations to the State, usually taking the form of taxation. In this sense, then, *transfer payments to the State are that part of the surplus social product used to maintain existing authoritative institutions (the State) which in turn maintains the existing distribution of power and privilege.*

This State surplus, however, cannot be continuously accumulated: some must go to maintaining the State apparatus, some to respond to demands made by citizens, and some to respond to crises, disasters and external threats and relationships. Nor can the State continue to convert a higher and higher amount of private surplus into State surplus. Taxation of the rich and their organizations hinders the profit maximization which they pursue, of the middle classes, hinders their pursuit of relative affluence and of the underclass, threatens their subsistence. At some level, then, surplus extraction by the State undermines other centers of power and negatively impacts upon its functions of accumulation and legitimization. Thus while the State must enhance accumulation and legitimization with the State surplus, it is limited in its ability to do so by the same concerns. To encroach too far upon certain groups could encourage the formation of coalitions of power sources sufficient to replace the State. Thus State authorities realize that they must utilize the surplus and allocate the burden of taxation in a manner which respects the limits imposed by the upper class' desire for accumulation and the State's desire for political support.

On the other hand, the State needs a surplus in order to function, while the demands on it continue to grow.[23] Thus as the adjustments necessary to achieve this delicate balance between extraction and manipulation of the State surplus become more complex (that is, demand more specific knowledge and expertise), some of the State surplus is allocated for the support of experts, individuals whose task is to plan for the extraction and manipulation of the surplus in line with the contradictory demands being made upon the State.[24] These experts provide the technical understanding needed to deal with complex issues surrounding the State surplus while simultaneously clothing in scientism what are essentially issues of power. The latter activity, moreover, further contributes to the legitimization of the State. Because the State is faced with both contradictory functions and increased demands for accountability, more specifically the need to preserve or enhance existing social conditions through the utilization and manipulation of the State surplus, the need for planning arises.

The Political Economy of Planning

The interrelated functions of legitimization and accumulation dominate the utilization of the State surplus. Since planning as a State activity must serve the ends of the State in order to retain its own legitimization, State planners perform their tasks in relationship to these two functions. Within the legitimization function, planning is involved in (1) the efficient allocation and distribution of the surplus in the form of political outputs (e.g., public goods and State programs) and (2) the redistribution of part of the surplus on the basis of equity considerations. Under the accumulation function, planning is involved in four additional activities: (3) decision-making to directly increase the efficiency of the surplus-extracting system itself by alleviating the impact of market imperfections; (4) the absorption of the costs of economic externalities; (5) the reduction of decision costs of certain groups through regulatory and representative activities; and (6) the control of the uncertain costs of change and the future through research, computer simulation, scanning and forecasting, futures planning and planning for alternative courses of action. The role of planners in these six sub-tasks of the State comprises planning's function in the public realm of advanced capitalism.[25]

LEGITIMIZATION FUNCTION

In order to maintain legitimacy, to insure survival as an organization, and for those in incumbent, authoritative positions to strengthen their political future, it is necessary for the State to provide certain goods and services not furnished by private mechanisms of production and allocation and, additionally, to meet specific political demands for more specialized State outputs. The former involves social or public goods that are highly indivisible and whose benefits are not easily confined to particular consumers.[26] Defense and police protection, weather reporting, public health, national parks and justice are a few examples of public goods. This is a traditional activity of the State, provision of which is necessary for legitimization. The latter, on the other hand, involves distributive and redistributive programs, usually delivered in response to demands by powerful organizations or groups, pressure by groups or events threatening the disruption of existing social relationships, or the need for those in authority to accrue additional political support and maintain present and future political relationships. Distributive programs, ideally, maintain the existing apportionment of the surplus (both private and public), while redistributive programs have as their ostensible intent some relative shifting of that surplus. *Public goods and distributive programs both involve planners in the efficient manipulation of the State surplus; redistributive programs have different implications.*

Public Goods and Distributive Programs.

Public goods and services utilize a large portion of the State surplus; the individual costs and benefits are difficult if not impossible to assign (thus strengthening the rationale of predominately collective benefits and costs);

the optimal quantity of goods and services is difficult to ascertain; and they are highly visible to the populace both as surplus-depleting activities (and thus tax inducing) and as indicators of State responsiveness and responsibility. For these reasons and because the State is faced with numerous demands for the State surplus while being limited in its ability to extract private surplus, the *major criterion for designing, justifying and implementing these programs becomes, in most cases, that of efficiency.* Granted there exist political, administrative and substantive concerns which become decision criteria. These, however, have only peripheral impact upon the State surplus within the sphere of public goods, or, they involve the allocation of more or less State surplus to one or another public good without abandoning the criterion of efficiency. These general concerns apply to all uses of the State surplus.

Distributive State programs differ from public goods and services in that the State has a greater range of choice in their allocation. The distributive, political arena usually involves a large number of small, intensely organized interests that act on the basis of mutual non-interference,[27] the end result being the production of State outputs which have the semblance of collective benefits and costs but whose collective impact is much less than that of a public good. Examples might include such programs as water resource development and mass transit expenditures. These programs can easily be disaggregated and dispensed unit by unit, which is not the case for public goods, and thus such political acts as patronage, pork-barreling and log-rolling are associated with distributive programs. Most important though, the even quality of the political competition enables the State to retain use of the efficiency criterion in manipulating its surplus.

Since these goods, services and programs supposedly have collective costs and benefits which greatly outweigh any inequitable impact they might have, then their provision should either not change the existing distribution of resources[28] or change them in favor of those able to benefit from such distributive programs; e.g., groups in major cities that need mass transit monies. Either way, existing class relationships are reinforced even though they may not be further exacerbated.[29] The superimposition of efficiency criterion upon these State outputs further assures that the surplus will not be unequally allocated across participants and provides the cloth of scientism to cloak the political aspects of these programs. In theory, then, society should remain in 'equilibrium' vis-à-vis the distribution of power and privilege.

The *efficient utilization of the State surplus and the most efficient trade-offs among competing State outputs of this nature form the major charges for planners within this sub-task of the legitimization function.* Before the advent of technical decisionmaking aids, efficiency was applied intuitively by focusing upon minimizing expenditures by program and balancing the budget across programs. With the introduction of the Program-Planning-Budgeting System (PPBS), cost-benefit analysis, linear programming, systems analysis, operations research and computerized data handling, not only has the role of experts expanded within the State but the application of efficiency considerations has increased and become more explicit.[30] All of these analytical methods are primarily concerned with efficiency,[31] although in recent years equity criteria have been developed for inclusion in these techniques. The groups supporting these public goods and distributive programs, however, are politically adverse to the application of such considerations.

Although the role of planers may involve the substantive design of these goods and programs, the development of organizations for their implementation, and the establishment of legal and administrative guidelines, even these contain a concern with efficiently conserving resources whether they be the State surplus or the political support which the State has amassed. The critical factor still remains the amount of surplus which is allocated. Organizational and administrative designs merely manipulate the form of its application with their purpose being to control its ultimate expenditure. This objective requires the expertise of planners and it is here that they play an important role.[32]

Redistributive Programs.

Many demands made upon the State are not for actions which have collective benefits but for State outputs which favor some individuals and groups more than others, resulting either in a relative change in the amount of surplus possessed by various class groups or in differential benefits of surplus expenditure. These responses are termed redistributive programs and involve such State outputs as Medicare, Oil Depletion Allowances, Aid to Families of Dependent Children, Farm Subsidies, Work Relief and Manpower (sic) Training. A response of this nature is usually engendered by some group with either a great deal of political influence, a threat of social disruption, or by the perceived need of those in authority to exchange State surplus for political support. And *when these programs impact directly upon the surplus-producing mechanisms of the economy, both accumulation and legitimization concerns can be found supporting one another and motivating State response.*

Certain of these programs, such as Oil Depletion Allowances and Farm Subsidies, redistribute in favor of the rich, thereby increasing the inequality within the class structure. But on the surface, the reality of programs directed at the lower classes would seem to indicate that equality is being pursued—there is an application of equity considerations and thus an implicit recognition by the State of an unacceptable distribution of the private surplus.[33] Privately generated inequalities are thus to be rectified by an unequal distribution of the State surplus. Three points must be made, however: (1) the amount of State surplus devoted to such programs is small compared to actual need, relative deprivation and other non-redistributive programs; (2) the surplus is usually transferred in such a fashion as to be useless in generating more surplus; that is, the benefits are minimal or in goods and services rather than as a straight monetary transfer; and (3) the individual programs, once the initial equity considerations are exhausted, are still designed and implemented on the basis of efficiency.[34] Although surplus is redistributed, it is done so grudgingly. In addition, many of these programs are politically volatile; susceptible to local, state and federal pressures as well as legislative retaliation, geared politically to maintaining existing power centers, and usually involving little participation, and no decisionmaking, by the beneficiaries.[35] These factors further dampen the effect of equity considerations. Thus the rule of efficiency is doubly applied, once fiscally and again administratively, with planners involved in both decision spheres.

State planners both assure and monitor the efficient use of the State surplus, concerning themselves with the monetary, programmatic and administrative criteria which will achieve these ends.[36] The technical aspects of the redistributive programs with which they are involved are similar to those relating to public goods and distributive programs, only here the initial concern is with an unequal application of the State surplus. But the goal is usually restricted to bringing population groups or depressed areas, for example, above some minimal level of need and not to providing enough surplus which will enable them to alter the present distribution of power and privilege; that is, to possess a surplus of surplus which can be used to develop self-sufficiency and thereby cast off dependency on the State or on affluent centers (as is the case with peripheral regions).[37] *Redistributive programs do not alleviate or eliminate inequalities; they merely dampen the excesses, transfer the issues to technical debates and provide them with political notoriety.*

ACCUMULATION FUNCTION

In newly emerging countries, the growth of certain economic sectors usually dominates State economic decisions.[38] Once a certain level of development is reached, however, growth as a major goal is usually augmented by efficiency; that is, for capitalist countries, once industrial capitalism takes hold then the generation of the surplus is no longer problematical and greater efficiency of surplus extraction can be pursued.[39] In most cases, the State (because it has control over large amounts of capital, can institute laws and has organizational abilities) becomes involved in aiding this economic growth. It does so not only to insure the viability

of the economy but also to demonstrate effectiveness to various groups
within society and to display national competence to other States.[40] (The
first is accumulation, the latter two are the domestic and foreign affairs
aspects of legitimization.) As the transition is made from concerns about
growth to those of efficiency, the State tends to remain involved in the
economy to the extent that industry and business profit from this intervention. Such intervention enhances the efficiency of the private, surplus-
extracting mechanisms of the political economy and thus facilitates the
legitimization of the State.

Market Imperfections.

The free, competitive market with its equilibrium of supply and demand
as regards both commodities and factors of production is generally accepted
as either a myth, a paradigmatic simplification, or the core of an ideological
position. It is, of course, all three. The actual market contains many
imperfections: inadequate or non-existent information, the biasing of preferences through advertising, interdependent preferences, non-responsive
interest rates, wage and price inflexibility, the inability to adjust to technological changes, and immobility of labor and capital.[41] These imperfections, if forced to be absorbed and rectified by producers and entrepreneurs,
would seriously hamper the surplus-extracting capacity of the economy by
siphoning off surplus. Thus the efficiency of capital accumulation would
decrease as some or much of the yield would have to be returned as
ameliorative inputs—inputs with no immediate surplus-extracting component.

No mechanisms internal to the economy exist for making producers and
entrepreneurs accountable for these imperfections. And, as the prevailing
value system labels the State as the institution responsible for the failure
of other institutions (the economy, community, family, Church), it takes
on the burden of rectifying the consequences of market imperfections.[42]
In addition, the State has an inherent commitment to the accumulation
function and to any negative consequences of it which might erode State
legitimacy. State intervention thus occurs, allowing industry and business
to hold (or even enhance) their present level of accumulation while spread-
ing the burden of the solutions more broadly across the population.[43] State
provision of employment information, manipulation of the money supply
in order to facilitate investment, minimum wage legislation, grants for
scientific research, tax deductions for moving expenses and consumer protection bureaus are only a few of the State interventions motivated by
market imperfections.[44] But, the imperfections are never wholly eliminated.
The root conflicts within advanced capitalism remain untouched since only
the surface tensions are resolved.

Responses and solutions to these market imperfections involve being able to define the problem, identify its scope and intensity, determine its direct and indirect causes, identify manipulatable policy variables, design possible responses and allocate the State surplus in the form of an efficient solution. It is these tasks in which planners participate and excel. Their role is to identify, quantify and design appropriate solutions to market imperfections and, since resources are scarce, to do so efficiently. The efficiency of the State's response is not as important in this case, however, as the fact that the State is intervening in the capitalist economy in order to maintain or increase the efficiency and yield of the accumulation process. To some extent the State may trade its efficiency for that of the surplus-extracting organizations. Nonetheless, the ultimate effects are to preserve and strengthen the powerful and privileged, for they control the accumulation process and benefit from its protection. Aided by planners, the State assures that market imperfections will not upset the present distribution of inequalities. For State response here is much like that for redistributive programs; that is, remedial and ameliorative. To do more, to restructure capital accumulation itself, would be institutional suicide for the advanced capitalist State. But, to be too generous to those suffering from these imperfections would seriously strain the State surplus beyond what the political importance of these people would dictate.

Externalities.

A special case of market imperfections is that of externalities, secondary effects of production and consumption which fall outside the boundaries of marketplace accountability.[45] Externalities may have either negative or positive consequences.

An example of a negative externality is air pollution by chemical plants. Costs are imposed upon the inhabitants of the community in the form of dirtier air and threats to health, and there exist no strictly economic mechanisms for making polluters directly accountable and responsible. A positive externality would be an increase in adjacent land values following the construction of a new office building. Just as the producers of pollution can avoid the consequences of their acts, so the producers of these increased land values are also unable to capture this addition to the private surplus. In both cases, economic accountability is problematic. Political pressure then compels the State to intervene with a variety of programs; environmental legislation, zoning, and occupational health and safety regulations constitute major areas of State intervention based upon externalities in the economy. Externalities, both negative and positive, form a concern of the State and thus of planners also.

Neither the responsibility nor the costs of externalities fall upon the producers themselves. Thus response is not forthcoming until economic or political pressure is brought to bear upon the State. But if such intervention hinders the process of capital accumulation (as it does with certain environmental programs) then a counter-response calling for the withdrawal of State involvement is engendered. Responsibility thus becomes uncertain and the implications of intervention unclear. It is easy to see why the State does not actively pursue the discovery and alleviation of externalities. Furthermore, while dealing with market imperfections usually involves some benefits to deprived groups (for example, public employment opportunities to the disadvantaged), dealing with externalities, in theory, has no redistributive overtones since solutions are meant only to reimburse or control the costs to the victims, as in the case of negative externalities, or, to assure that the benefits are not dissipated as in the case of positive externalities. The role of planners, on the one hand, is to identify costs and to insure that they are not exceeded by the reimbursement; i.e., that the State surplus is efficiently utilized. On the other hand, these experts develop techniques (such as zoning) that assure both that positive externalities are captured by property owners and that any negative impacts upon land values are prevented. Planners perform roles similar to those they provide for market imperfections; applying technical expertise to threats to accumulation and legitimization. In addition, they are involved in the development of mechanisms (e.g., effluent charges) which distribute the costs to producers (albeit eventually passed on to consumers) thus extricating the State from such involvement. At the moment, however, these mechanisms are weakly developed and externalities fall on consumers or on the State or are exploited by those holding private surplus.

Regulation and Representation.

Two major goals commonly used to characterize planning are those of reducing uncertainty and providing increased rationality for decision-making.[46] In a highly complex environment, uncertainty and the conveying and interpreting of information impose heavy costs on any decisionmaking system, be it economically or State. Economic and bureaucratic efficiency become more difficult to attain as the complexity, instability and diversity of the environment increases. State identification of needs and its response to political demands also loses efficiency. But mechanisms—regulation and representation—exist to reduce these costs.

Regulatory activity is commonly identified with railroads and airlines, the Federal Communications Commission, the Food and Drug Administration, public health, and so on. Implicitly, this activity is viewed as protecting the public. In fact, State regulation first began as a means to maintain competition and to achieve the implications of laissez faire.[47] Much of regulation involves reducing uncertainty for the producer of a good or the seller of a service. Its actual outcome is to decrease uncertainty in the marketplace by stabilizing demand, by assuring a certain profit level, by protecting industries from competition, and by absorbing information costs. The end result is that these industries are better able to produce a surplus, or, at least, are guaranteed a minimum surplus in exchange for State interference. In addition, secured markets prevent any competition from infringing upon this particular area of surplus-extracting possibilities.[48] Regulation thus stabilizes a set of exchange relationships in favor of those already participating. The State absorbs the information and uncertainty costs (supposedly both consumers and producers) and existing relationships become more permanent.

These types of activities are particularly in need of the techniques and expertise of planners for reducing uncertainty and increasing rationality within the regulatory sphere. The determination of fair market prices, the amount of State subsidy to be dispensed, and the identification of excessive monopolization of markets all require technical expertise even though such analyses may not be the basis upon which final decisions are made. Regulatory activity is clothed in technical analysis. And, while the actual tensions between the State regulatory agencies and private organizations are, at their core, issues of capital accumulation versus State legitimization, this is never allowed to surface.

Planning also reduces uncertainty and information costs to the State by performing a representative function. Between a perfect democracy and a totalitarian society, diverse interests must be identified, aggregated, articulated and satisfied. This involves both the gathering and processing of information and the reduction of the costs of uncertainty which might deplete the State surplus. These vary with the degree of representativeness; that is, the more interests and decisionmaking are aggregated, the lower these costs. One way of decreasing this burden is to have an organization that represents collective interests. This intervening bureaucracy, linking organized and even unorganized citizen groups with elected representatives, would then serve to translate citizen demands into a form capable of being understood by representatives and also shield these representatives from those demands which are excessive and unacceptable.

Planners have and do now conceive of themselves in this role—representing the public interest or the specific interests of an homogenous group (advocacy planning, for example) in a comprehensive manner.[49] Those in authority can use planning as a surrogate for collective interest while controlling the boundaries and content of those interests. That is, public demands are shaped and reinterpreted by planners, purged of their ideological implications through transition into technical form, placed within a public interest framework and passed on to elected officials. Those without the power to bypass this intervening layer of planners have their messages dampened, while those able to speak directly to decisionmakers wield much more influence.

The activity of planning thus gives the impression that interests are being represented when in fact it represents only concerns acceptable to those in power and authority. As a result, information costs are reduced by diminishing the number of individuals confronting the State and participating in its decisionmaking. Uncertainty is also reduced because unexpected demands are first posed through an intervening layer of research and bureaucratic intelligence. *Consequently, the State devotes less of its surplus to information collection, citizen participation and uncertainty reduction than it would if no such intervening bureaucracy existed.* The justification is that only limited resources are available for handling these costs. Planning and other representative mechanisms are thus needed to increase the efficient use of the State surplus. The implications are that the legitimate channels for modifying existing power relationships are further controlled, demands for redistribution are filtered through planning organizations and thus deflected and smothered in the bureaucratic maze and the need for "more research", and inequalities remain unconfronted because overcoming the representative mechanisms requires a private surplus which the deprived do not possess.

Change and the Future.

Certain techniques specifically utilized within planning have great potential for reducing the costs of social change and of future events. And since the State must also face these concerns, it funds many of these activities. They include research, computer simulation, scanning and forecasting, the development of alternative courses of action, and futures planning.[50] Research might focus on identifying social and economic trends and monitoring major social processes, while simulation concerns itself with the mathematical modeling of these societal processes and, through computer techniques, projecting them into the future under various sets of constraints. In scanning, potential problems are systematically searched out so that the time available for the formulation of policy and the establishment of new administrative mechanisms can be identified.[51] Forecasting, on the other hand, involves the development of probability statements concerning the incidence of certain events in the future.[52] Designing alternatives is an inherent element of all these various activities, while futures planning is concerned with determining major social relationships under some wholly different, but possible, form of society. Each of these techniques attempts to eliminate future uncertainty, provide alternative paths of action under varying contigencies, and generally give a glimpse of impending sources and uses of the State surplus as well as identify societal changes which might affect the distribution of power, privilege and authority.

Although these activities might not enhance the efficiency of present surplus utilization, planners involvement in them enables the State to be more efficient in future utilization. First, *those in authority are prepared for future contingencies and thus are able to respond with less surprise, more forethought, and hopefully more certainty*—the State surplus will not be wasted due to lack of prior information. Second, *attempts can be made in the present to prevent detrimental events from occurring in the future;* i.e., classic planning can be undertaken. In addition, these planning activities are also conducive to the continued persistence of the State within a changing environment through the anticipation of disruptive influences. Finally, since planning at this level of sophistication is predominately an activity of the State and large-scale, economic organizations,[53] it is the people in control of these institutions who benefit.

Thus planners are fully implicated, to varying degrees, in the functions of accumulation and legitimization which dominate manipulation of the State surplus. In turn this means that these experts at least maintain the existing distribution of power and the extant class system, if not perpetuate it by protecting and enhancing its surplus-extracting efficiency. Although some attention is given to redistribution of the surplus, the amount involved and the manner in which in which it is handled result in little alteration of the patterns of power and privilege. Inequalities prevail with little change, and planners provide essential, supportive activities.

Conclusions

Merely sketching the involvement of planners in the advanced capitalist State is not enough. For by *perpetuating the existing class structure through the application of their technical expertise,* planners are implicated in the inequalities which pervade American society. This is clearly unacceptable to those concerned with abolishing human misery and questing after a society in which invidious distinctions are eliminated and all individuals are allowed to achieve their potentialities. But both convincing others of this position and developing outlines of a new function for planning in the United States are complex tasks. Still, a general outline of the issues can be drawn.

The criticism presented here is that planners' actions help to maintain the existing pattern of power and privilege, although certain of their activities do have countervailing tendencies. Two major aspects of planning have brought this about: first, the *application of technical expertise and*

its attendent efficiency criterion without proper consideration of its ideo-
logical implications, and, second, the embeddedness of planners in the
advanced capitalist State such that their activities are dictated by its con-
cern for accumulation and legitimization. To *eliminate planners' con-*
tribution to perpetuating the existing class structure and send them in
pursuit of more equality requires a reconstruction of the ideology of
technical expertise and of the relationship between planners and the State.

Modification of planning ideology, however, is more amenable to reform
than planners' relationship to the State. The social turmoil of the Sixties
engendered critical analyses of planning and this concern has, with a
Marxist perspective, been extended into the Seventies.[54] But awareness is
not sufficient even though more analyses focusing upon the moral and
political implications of planning theory and practice are needed. The
criteria by which planning decisions are made and the goals which planners pursue must be changed. *Equity considerations must be substituted*
for those of efficiency and the pursuit of greater distributional justice must
replace the goal of minimizing the expenditure of State surplus. Inherent
in such redirection is an understanding by planners of the role they serve
in the larger political economy and of the tendency for scientific techniques
to serve conservative ends if applied uncritically to issues dictated by the
State. In turn, such analyses and understanding may lead to new techniques of planning and the selection of different problems toward which to
direct planners' energies.

But such changes are insignificant when compared to the control of
planners and planning by the State. *Without legal and financial backing*
by the State, it is difficult to picture planning as we know it taking place.
Our ability to conceptualize planning outside of State prerogatives, with
minor exceptions,[55] is ill-developed. That, however, does not seem to be
the path to take into the future. Trying to work within the interstices
of advanced capitalist institutions will only lead to impotence unless a
simultaneous attempt is made to replace those institutions with their socialist counterparts. *To truly disentangle planning from its conservative*
tendencies, it must exist within a political economy based upon socialist
principles of distributive justice.[56] The problems of restructuring American society along these lines and, if attained, of perpetuating it within a
world economy dominated by advanced capitalism are immense.[57] Yet
to acquiesce poses moral perplexities which cry out for resolution. We
cannot move into the future of planning without a critical understanding
of its present function within the advanced capitalism of the United States.
Planning theorists can contribute to planning practice by unearthing its
implications for inequality and suggesting various paths to radical reform.

NOTES

1. John Kenneth Galbraith develops his view of the corporate technostructure and planning system in *The New Industrial State*, (New York, The New American Library, 1967) and *Economics and Public Purpose*, (Boston, Houghton Mifflin Company, 1973). William K. Tabb discusses national economic planning in the United States in "We Are All Socialists Now: Corporate Planning for America," *Social Policy*, 5, 6 (March/April, 1975), pp. 27-34. And Harold L. Wilensky uses the concept of organizational intelligence to investigate an activity akin to planning in complex organizations. See his *Organizational Intelligence*, (New York, Basic Books, Inc., Publishers, 1967).

2. This is true of much of the literature on urban and regional planning. Perusal of the *Journal of the American Institute of Planners* AND *Planning* will quickly reveal this.

3. Robert Moses, of course, is the one exception of an American 'planner' who had power. See Robert Caro, *The Power Broker*, (New York, Alfred A. Knopf, Inc., 1974).

4. See Otis L. Graham, Jr., *Toward A Planned Society*, (New York, Oxford University Press, 1976).

5. Roland Warren discusses and attempts to explain this phenomenon for the social services. See his "Comprehensive Planning and Coordination: Some Functional Aspects," *Social Problems*, 20, 3 (Winter, 1973), pp. 355-64.

6. Planning as used here is synonymous with the use of exprtise in Guy Benveniste's *The Politics of Expertise*, (Berkeley, The Glendessary Press, 1972).

7. See Alan Altshuler, *The City Planning Process*, (Ithaca, Cornell University Press, 1965); Benveniste, *op. cit.*; Graham, *op. cit.*; and Amitai Etzioni, *The Active Society*, (New York, The Free Press, 1968).

8. Ralph Miliband, *The State in Capitalist Society*, (New York, Basic Books Inc., 1969).

9. See James O'Connor, *The Fiscal Crisis of the State*, (New York, St. Martin's Press, 1973), pp. 1-39.

10. The following description is based, in part, upon Harry K. Girvetz, "The Welfare State," *International Encyclopedia of the Social Sciences*, 16 (New York, The Macmillan Company and the Free Press, 1968), pp. 512-21; Gerhard Lenski, *Power and Privilege*, (New York, McGraw Hill Book Company, 1966) and Kurt B. Mayer and Walter Buckley, *Class and Society*, (New York, Random House, Inc., 1969).

11. See Ernest Mandel, *An Introduction to Marxist Economic Theory*, (New York, Pathfinder Press, Inc., 1970), pp. 7-9. The Marxian notion of surplus originates in the capitalist exploitation of labor. See Karl Marx, *Capital*, I (New York, International Publishers, Inc., 1967), pp. 177-230.

12. Paul A. Baran, "The Concept of the Economic Surplus," *The Political Economy of Growth*, (New York, Modern Reader Paperbacks, 1957), pp. 22-43. It should also be noted that such needs will vary from one society to another and from one historical period to the next since they are socially determined. See Ralf Dahrendorf, "On the Origins of Inequality Among Men," *Essays in the Theory of Society*, (Stanford, Stanford University Press, 19668), pp. 151-78.

13. Harry Braverman in his *Labor and Monopoly Capitalism*, (New York, Monthly Review Press, 1974), explores the history of such exploitation under monopoly capitalism.

14. Dahrendorf, *op. cit.* The functionalist theory of stratification has developed this into an apologia for existing inequalities. See Kingsley Davis and Wilbert E. Moore, "Some Principles of Stratification," *American Sociological Review,* 10, 2 (1945), pp. 242-9 and Melvin M. Tumin, "Some Principles of Stratification: A Critical Analysis," *American Sociological Review,* 18 (August 1953), pp. 387-93.

15. Lenski, *op. cit.*

16. Arthur L. Stinchcombe, *Constructing Social Theories,* (New York, Harcourt, Brace and World, Inc., 1968), pp. 121-3.

17. Marx, *op. cit.,* pp. 612-712.

18. Legitimacy involves ". . . by virtue of the doctrines and norms by which it is justified. . . ." a power being able to call upon sufficient other powers to make its power effective. Stinchcombe, *op. cit.,* p. 162.

19. Robert A. Dahl has written: "It is easy to see why leaders strive for legitimacy. Authority is a highly efficient form of influence. It is not only more reliable and durable than naked coercion but also enables a ruler to govern with a minimum of political resources." See his *Modern Political Analysis,* (Englewood Cliffs, N.J., Prentice-Hall, Inc., 1963), p. 19.

20. V. I. Lenin in *The State,* (Peking, Foreign Languages Press, 1970), writes: ". . . as the social division into classes arose and took firm root, as class society arose, the state also arose and took firm root."

21. O'Connor, *op. cit.,* p. 6.

22. Marx discusses this in an interesting way when he deals with relative value. *Op. cit.,* p. 49-62.

23. Daniel Bell, "The Public Household—On 'Fiscal Sociology' and the Liberal Society," *The Public Interest,* 37 (Fall, 1974), pp. 29-68.

24. Ultimately, of course, this involves planners, albeit indirectly, in determining the differential positions of various social groups.

25. These are not mutually exclusive categories and overlap among them is to be expected.

26. Richard A. Musgrave, "A Multiple Theory of the Public Household," *The Theory of Public Finance,* (New York, McGraw-Hill Book Company, 1959), pp. 3-27; Vincent Ostrum and Elinor Ostrum, "Public Choice: A Different Approach to the Study of Public Administration," *Public Administration Review,* 31, 2 (March/April, 1971), pp. 203-12; and Peter O. Steiner, "The Public Sector and the Public Interest," in Robert H. Haveman and Julius Margolis eds., *Public Expenditures and Policy Analysis,* (Chicago, Markham Publishing Company, 1970), pp. 21-58.

27. Theodore Lowi, "American Business, Public Policy, Case Studies and Political Theory," *World Politics,* 16 (July, 1964), pp. 677-715.

28. For an attempt to assess the distributive impact of higher education see W. Lee Hansen and Burton A. Weisbrod, "The Distribution of Costs and Direct Benefits of Public Higher Education: The Case of California," *The Journal of Human Resources,* 4, 2 (Spring, 1969), pp. 176-91.

29. See Stinchcombe, *op. cit.,* pp. 120-5 for an analysis of how institutions are perpetuated by resource utilization. Note also that even though the technical efficiency of individual programs may be deficient and political gains themselves may not be efficiently maximized, one must realize that deviations from 'perfect' efficiency are not a valid criticism of this general argument but only the manifestations of 'imperfect' elites (not to mention the defects of their experts).

30. For a discussion of this within the advanced capitalist State of France see Stephen S. Cohen, *Modern Capitalist Planning*, (Berkeley, University of California Press, 1977).

31. Aaron Wildavsky, "The Political Economy of Efficiency: Cost-Benefit Analysis, Systems Analysis and Program Budgeting," *Public Administration Review*, 26, 4 (December, 1966), pp. 292-310.

32. There is another interpretation of the use of these techniques in the State; i.e., they are merely devices to legitimate decisions previously made using political criteria. I am not willing to admit that this is *merely* the case, rather, it is *also* the case.

33. For an analysis of pre-transfer and post-transfer poverty in the United States see Robert D. Plotnick and Felicity Skidmore, *Progress Against Poverty*, (New York, Academic Press, 1975).

34. For a critique of the present system of public assistance based upon these points see Theodore R. Marmor and Martin Rein, "Reforming 'The Welfare Mess': The Fate of the Family Assistance Plan, 1969-72," in Allan P. Sindler (ed.), *Policy and Politics in America*, (Boston, Little, Brown and Company, Inc., 1973), pp. 3-28.

35. Richard A. Cloward and Frances Fox Piven, *The Politics of Turmoil*, (New York, Pantheon Books, Random House, 1974), pp. 69-170 and Gilbert Y. Steiner, *The State of Welfare*, (Washington, D.C., The Brookings Institution, 1971), pp. 280-313.

36. Theodore Marmor, "On Comparing Income Maintenance Alternatives," *The American Political Science Review*, 65 (March, 1971), pp. 83-96 and Daniel P. Moynihan, *The Politics of a Guaranteed Income*, (New York, Random House, 1973).

37. For a discussion of this in an international context see Andre Gunder Frank, "The Development of Underdevelopment," *Monthly Review*, 18, 4 (September, 1966), pp. 17-31.

38. For a description of this for the United States see Seymour Martin Lipset, *The First New Nation*, (New York, Basic Books, Inc., 1963), pp. 15-60.

39. Walter Weisskopf discusses the historical determinants of impulse control to deal with scarcity of capital and hedonistic consumption in response to demands for growth in his *Alienation and Economics*, (New York, Dell Publishing Company, Inc., 1971).

40. Lipset, *op. cit.*, p. 46.

41. Lester C. Thurow in *Generating Inequality*, (New York, Basic Books, Inc., 1975), pp. 211-30 looks at some of the problems of neoclassical economic theory.

42. This, of course, is compatible with certain arguments as to the origins of the Welfare State. See Girvetz, *op. cit.* and Dorothy Wedderburn, "Facts and Theories of the Welfare State," in Milton Mankoff, ed., *The Poverty of Progress*, (New York, Holt, Rinehart and Winston, Inc., 1972), pp. 190-206.

43. See Benveniste, *op. cit.*, p. 31 for a brief mention of the political consequences of State intervention into the economy.

44. Daniel Fusfeld, "The Rise of he Corporate State," *Journal of Economic Issues*, 11, 1 (March, 1972), pp. 1-22.

45. K. William Kapp, *The Social Costs of Private Enterprise*, (New York, Shocken Books, 1971).

46. Benveniste, *op. cit.*, pp. 23-38 and Ruth P. Mack, *Planning on Uncertainty*, (New York, John Wiley and Sons, Inc., 1971).

47. James Weinstein, *The Corporate Ideal in the Liberal State, 1900-1918*, (Boston, Beacon Press, 1968).

48. See Galbraith, *Economics and the Public Purpose, op. cit.,* pp. 81-175 on the planning system and O'Connor, *op. cit.,* pp. 15-6 on the monopoly sector.

49. Altshuler, *op. cit.,* pp. 299-353 and Paul Davidoff, "Advocacy and Pluralism in Planning," *Journal of the American Institute of Planners,* 31, 4 (November, 1963), pp. 331-8.

50. For a general overview of planning's concern with the future see Charles W. Williams, Jr., "Inventing a Future Civilization," *The Futurist,* 5, 4 (August, 1972), pp. 137-41 and Jib Fowles, "An Overview of Social Forecasting Procedures," *Journal of the American Institute of Planners,* 42, 3 (July, 1976), pp. 253-63.

51. Benveniste, *op. cit.,* p. 66.

52. Ibid., p. 65.

53. Galbraith, *The New Industrial State, op. cit.,* and Ralph Miliband, "Professor Galbraith and American Capitalism: The Managerial Revolution Revisited" in Mankoff, ed., *op. cit.,* pp. 46-58.

54. For a Sixties critique see Alan S. Kravitz, "Mandarism: Planning as Handmaiden to Conservative Politics" in T. L. Beyle and G. T. Lathrop, eds., *Planning and Politics* (New York, The Odyssey Press, 1970), pp. 240-67 and for a Seventies critique see Harvey Goldstein and Thierry Noyelle, "Planning and Social Practice: A Theory of Capitalist Planning in the U.S." in Thierry Noyelle, ed., *1976 Symposium on Planning Theory,* (Philadelphia, Department of City and Regional Planning, University of Pennsylvania, June, 1977), pp. 59-92. These latter authors discuss two types of planning, one dealing with capitalist crises and the other with program management during periods of social tranquility. This paper, obviously, is concerned solely with the latter type.

55. There is, of course, John Friedmann's attempt in *Retracking America,* (Garden City, New York, Anchor Press, 1973).

56. For a discussion of the application of socialism to the United States see Samuel Bowles and Herbert Gintis, *Schooling in Capitalist America,* (New York, Basic Books, Inc., 1976), pp. 264-88 and Michael Harrington, *Socialism,* (New York, Saturday Review Press, E. P. Dutton and Company, Inc., 1972).

57. Mao Tse Tung was ever aware of the threats to Chinese socialism by the capitalist world economy and, since his death, the new rulers of China have begun to succumb. For a good presentation of Mao's approach see E. L. Wheelwright and Bruce MacFarland, *The Chinese Road to Socialism,* (New York, Monthly Review Press, 1970).

The Comprehensive Planning of Location

Britton Harris

This conference as a whole may turn out to have a somewhat old-fashioned flavor, since it involves many of the Old Guard of planning and planning theory. A central question of the conference will revolve around the issue of whether the younger guard—sometimes our students or our students' students—has generated a set of new ideas or new approaches which are more effective in meeting the needs of society than some of the ideas of twenty years ago. At the same time, some of us will be examining our own consciences and we will address the question of whether the changes which have come about in our thinking and the new ideas which we have adopted have themselves made any substantial difference in the practice of planning.

It will not come as a surprise if I report in advance on those aspects of my own thinking which have changed and those which have not changed. I will show in what follows why I still insist on the importance of comprehensive planning, on the importance of systematic method, and on the importance of research and theory-building. At the same time, I will try to show implicitly how my own sense of priorities in planning has changed substantially with the times. Most particularly, I will show how I no longer believe in any serious way in the automaticity of the search for good plans or in the possibility of fully automating such a search. Finally, I will try to show why I believe that some of my colleagues have over-reacted to the social stimuli which have affected us all, in a way which. may have a tendency hopelessly to fragment the field of planning.

To a considerable extent this paper deals not with planning itself, but with a set of ideas or theories about planning. In one of the discussions of the conference, David Harvey elicited considerable amusement when he said that planners tend to regard their ideas as fixed capital, not subject to rapid replacement. In truth, however, I don't regard this remark as a subject for amusement except insofar as in fact the intellectual capital of Harvey and other Marxists is indeed more fixed than that of almost any other intellectual group. There is really nothing wrong with the idea of fixed intellectual capital. The whole of morality, religion, culture, and science (including the putative science of Marxism) is the most permanent set of human creations and the most important for the survival of the species. It is almost certain that Euclid's work will outlast the Parthenon and Newton's Laws of Motion, the work of Christopher Wren. From one point of view, therefore, the conference to which this paper is contributed may be regarded as an exercise in discovering what durable concepts we have in common or what kind of discourse we need to engage in to find and develop such concepts. This paper is offered in that vein.

I intend to limit my consideration largely to the field of locational planning, since this is the field in which, willy-nilly, most city planners are constrained to work. There are important aspects of social and economic planning at various levels of government which have little locational content—but even such matters as health care, education, and employment opportunity are shot through with locational considerations at the level of day-to-day living. National economic and employment policy, for example, cannot ignore the effects of geographic segregation in large metropolitan areas on employment patterns, although it is clear that there are multiple forces acting on this problem and that such segregation is only one of them. To an extent, however, this distinction is beside the point, as I believe that a strong case can be made for similarity among all kinds of planning, including locational planning. I preserve it because some of the characteristics which will be important in this development are more easily identified in locational situations than in less locationally oriented realms.

Almost all of the objectives of our society and of its component actors are influenced by the patterns of habitation and economic activity which develop nationally, regionally, and locally in either planned or unplanned ways. To a considerable extent, these locational patterns are permeated by interdependence among decisions, by economies of scale, and by the nature of public acts. All of these considerations are related in the ordinary case to some form of market failure and consequently to considerations of planned social action. The fact that developmental outcomes might be different from those which would be desired optimally leads to a putative necessity for planning. The same factors, however, which lead to market failure also lead to difficulties in planning to which I shall return later.

In order to lend further point to this analysis, I will review briefly the objectives, public and private, which are to some extent served by locational decisions.

Efficiency is still a major social goal. Under a narrow definition and without regard to the values which it is supposed to serve, the pursuit of efficiency can be corrosive and counterproductive. Nevertheless, over a quarter of our income is devoted to private housing and the transportation of the population on a daily basis. A five percent reduction in these costs would represent a substantial national saving which could be used to augment income or improve social services.

The individual, household, or family, in making its living and working arrangements in accord with its objectives and under the constraints of the housing and job market, is attempting to pursue a number of benefits and avoid a number of difficulties. It seeks adequate shelter; congenial neighbors; good environmental conditions; safety at home, at work, and in transit; and good access to education, health care, employment, recreation, and cultural activities. The pursuit of these objectives is affected in intricate ways by the decisions of government and other locators as well as by the concerned households themselves.

The preservation of the environment and of natural resources is a broad social concern which extends beyond the locational interests of individuals. In part this social concern stems out of the spillovers from activities antagonistic to a sound social or physical environment from one location to another. At least as seriously, it concerns the preservation of natural and manmade variety (which might otherwise be irretrievably lost) for the benefit of future generations.

It is becoming increasingly clear that some form of equity is or should be a matter of central social concern. We have only begun to address the problems of what equity means in locational terms. To some extent, it seems perverse to talk about complete locational equity when our society has very incomplete economic equity. It is also self-deluding to imagine that correcting locational inequities will lead to major adjustments of economic inequities. For this reason, the questions of appropriate definitions of locational equity and inequity and their application to policy need to be carefully pursued.

There is a special aspect of this problem, revolving around questions of segregation and desegregation, which also deserves careful thought. There appears to be in any society a certain amount of natural self-segregation by various groups on the basis of language, culture, income, and other factors. Insofar as this satisfies an individual desire to be in a congenial and comfortable social environment, it may be equitable to permit such segregation. Insofar as the segregation tends to divide society or to permit the perpetuation of pejorative social attitudes within and between groups, the segregation may be inequitable and socially undesirable.

At particular points in its development, a society also may have goals which fulfill a particular need. These may be given the status of programs of considerable importance or saliency. Such programs have included in the past in the United States the drive for universal free public education, the building of canals, railroads, and roads, and the attempt to put a man on the moon. Ongoing programs of substantial current saliency include biomedical research and energy conservation. Since energy conservation is closely connected with locational problems, it deserves consideration as a major current goal of society in this context.

It goes almost without saying that there are some conflicts between these goals, as inevitably happens when a number of objectives are being pursued with limited resources. But it is also possible that some goals are at least to a certain extent synergistic or mutually reinforcing. The desire to preserve the environment for the future is in many respects compatible with improving living conditions today. The conservation of power may result in improved environmental conditions and in the conservation of resources. Probably, however, environmental protection, conservation, and reduced or redirected uses of energy will prove costly in terms of productivity and will involve some sacrifices in other aspects of the standard of living. It is also widely believed that increased equity through the redistribution of income is harmful to incentives and thus leads to further losses in productivity. Both equity and productivity could be better served by a higher level of total employment and economic activity, but this might again conflict with conservation. Finally, both underprivileged classes and underprivileged nations are beginning to realize that one indirect effect of conservation may be to freeze the existing distribution of amenities and resources and prevent a more equitable distribution of access to them. This is a broader application of the quip that a conservationist is a man who already owns a summer home.

This extended discussion of values implicitly suggests that I place some serious reservations on a comment by Mel Webber in another paper for this conference, that science can say nothing about values. The most truth that I can find in this view is that science cannot determine the choice of values by which an individual or society will conduct itself; beyond this, there are serious qualifications. Science can deal with the logic of values, stating whether a set of values in a given social and technical situation either leads to contradictions or leads to a situation in which certain choices are undecidable. Insofar as values may be expressed in constraints, science can frequently make an evaluation of the costs and other implications which these values impose upon choice. Social research can identify or verify the value systems of individuals and groups and can examine the ways in which changes in values occur or are induced. This sketch is certainly incomplete, but the scope of science in studying values is constantly expanding even though at the end there will be an irreducible core of personal and societal free will.

Since the achievement of a variety of objectives requires a harmonization of policy, we should take a brief look at the policy measures which are available to deal with these issues, especially at the local level, and at the way these policy actions are regarded by the people who advocate and employ them. As the number of problems in these various fields multiplies, the number of available measures increases, seemingly without end. Characteristically, each such measure is addressed to a single problem. Since, as I have sketched, all of the problems are closely interrelated, no single measure will in fact accomplish a single purpose without affecting other goals. Measures directed solely at increasing equity, improving the environment, or conserving energy are bound to have unintended consequences—because each such measure reacts on other objectives and other classes of the population besides those which it was primarily intended to serve. In the polemic of today, we are constantly reminded of the unintended consequences of planning based on elitist concepts or on a drive toward engineering efficiency, and our attention is drawn to the political consequences and social destabilization which resulted from these and other causes. It requires more single-mindedness (chosen from a number of available varieties) than I can muster to believe that current single-purpose panaceas will prove less counterproductive and less politically destabilizing than previous one-sided experiments.

All of the foregoing argue, in ways which are not particularly novel, for the importance of comprehensive planning with respect to almost any constellation of problems and of policy decisions needed to resolve them. This is not to say that from time to time it will not be possible to identify key elements in planning and decisionmaking which take some form of priority over other decisions. Such priority decisions are most apt to be identified in situations of extreme emergency, but I do not believe that we face this class of difficulty at the present time. At the national level, such difficulties have appeared periodically and perhaps with increasing frequency during the current century. Some major innovations in local policy have arisen in part as a response to other issues. It is at least arguable that roadbuilding and mortgage insurance, which contributed heavily to suburbanization, were influenced by national recovery considerations at least as much as by their relation to the living conditions of the population.

The priority of particular decisions is sometimes confused with the fact that there obviously exist various levels of decisionmaking. This is easily established by trying to imagine in the extreme case that all of the policy decisions taken in the United States (or for that matter, in the world) represent a total plan because they are not independent and because they thus interact at various levels. One could try to pretend that all of these decisions can be made by a single agency or by a national or world government. Since this is patently absurd, the problem is therefore typically decomposed by function, by geographic or administrative area, and by level of government. This decomposition is loosely organized and not strictly hierarchical. When viewed in this light, its is clear that the higher-level and more comprehensive decisions are not independent of the lower-level and more particular decisions. It is not possible to develop a national policy for transportation or housing without understanding in detail how the delivery of transportation or housing services operates at the local level, or at intermediate levels if there exist relevant organizational activities. Similarly, the fiscal plan for a city cannot be developed without a consideration of the operation of the functional elements of the city system; and a plan for the environmental quality of a metropolitan region depends on sub-plans and sub-activity systems in various parts of the metropolis.

In brief, the coordination of plans requires coordination between functions, areas and levels. At any particular level there continues to be a comprehensive planning problem. Such problems will be variously formulated depending on the level and function being considered, but they will have, in spite of their apparent variety, a common set of characteristics. These characteristics are well elaborated if we keep in mind the overall approach of mathematical programming. Such an approach is suggested here not as a method, but as a pattern or paradigm which should serve as a guide to our thinking and analysis.

Before articulating the way in which the concept of mathematical programming can serve as a paradigm for planning, I must pay some attention to the fact that many people do not regard planning as an optimum-seeking process and indeed contend that there is no such thing as an optimum plan. This opinion seems to me to arise from a number of alternative sources. First, if the society in which planning is embedded does not have a stable established way of making decisions, then it is impossible to talk about optimality. This situation reflects a severe difficulty in the political process and a lack of stability which cannot be attributed to planning. Second, there may be a large number of alternatives which are relatively close in value or desirability; these may be much better than other possibilities, but it may not be important to discriminate between them. This does not deny the existence of an optimum. Finally, the cost of locating an optimum may be excessive and the planning process will display a form of bounded rationality. This may be regarded as a form of optimizing in which the costs of search are included in the objective function. In brief, therefore, since we constantly attempt to improve plans, we must, despite many difficulties, consider ourselves to be engaged in optimum-seeking.

Any plan is designed to serve a set of objectives among which there are trade-offs and substitutions. These objectives include the welfare of the population as it is perceived by that population and measured through its utility functions and as it may be measured by externally established social criteria. It also includes a wide variety of social objectives whose general character I have discussed above. For limited purposes and function objectives, such an objective function or social welfare function may be translated into a cost-benefit measure. There are obviously many difficulties in explicitly constructing a complete social objective function for any level, area, or function for which planning is being done. Thus in the extreme case, such a welfare function is embodied in the thought process and actions of a planner, an executive, a legislature, or a court.

In a complex and interconnected society, it is by no means immediately apparent what the effects of hypothetical decisions will be. Since the objective function places value not primarily on the planning decisions themselves, but on their effects over time, some predictive mechanism is required. Such a mechanism is the subject matter of social science research and model-building, although the application to large and complex systems is not always either obvious, or intended by the social science researcher. There are many other dimensions on which social science prediction may fall short of the realities and needs of planning. The economic model of individual utility optimization certainly does not contain enough social, psychological, and aesthetic variables. To mention a few topics, we do not have adequate models dealing with power, with diversity and conformity, or with the preservation of the environment. Indeed, some models are counterfactual and antisocial, such as economic resource management on the basis of discounted present value. There is thus room for a much closer concatenation of social science and humanism in the predictive process.

The availability of various modes of planning control and guidance tends to define the decision space within which planners and politicians can operate. Since some of these measures can be valued or devalued because of effects which are socially and politically independent of their primary objectives, the use of various measures may enter directly into the objective function. For the same reason, social convention often rules out certain measures from consideration; this is a form of constraint. The process of investigation of the consequences of plans and the search for effective combinations of policy actions frequently leads to new suggestions for laws, regulations, incentives and the like. Such invention may be regarded as an important part of planning.

Most mathematical programming and a great deal of planning operates under constraints. Some of these constraints are physical in nature and hence absolute. Other constraints, arising out of resources, capital stock, productivity, population, and culture, are relatively fixed in the short to medium run. Many constraints, however, represent a crystallization of social policy which may be entirely temporary. Indeed, in many cases, such apparent constraints are unrealistic, and an overconstrained problem proves incapable of solution.

A final element of ordinary mathematical programming is an optimization procedure. Here there arises a real difficulty and the most substantial difference between most planning and straightforward optimizing processes. Conventional optimizing operates on the "principle of the extreme" and thus implicitly assumes that there is only a single optimum—that is, that the objective function is unimodal in the policy space. This assumption is unrealistic in the case where considerable importance attaches to economies of scale, economies of agglomeration, and externalities. Similar considerations tend to invalidate the reality of a classical economic equilibrium, when we consider the effects of monopolies and decreasing cost industries. In these circumstances, methods for finding the extreme value of a function lead at best to a local optimum, and these local optima may be extremely numerous. Mathematical programming has made very little progress in applying branch and bound and dynamic programming to problems of realistic size with multiple optima. Clearly, this creates a situation in which more artful and approximate methods of planning become necessary and where the risk of personal and institutional failure is greatly increased.

It is perhaps appropriate to emphasize in particular the contradiction which arises between this expanded view of the nature of the search for optimal plans and the classical approaches to economics and public policy. Economics refers to the inapplicability of standard economic analysis as "market failure." This term is offensive in the sense that it implies that markets could ordinarily be expected to deal with most of the important phenomena of decisionmaking and choice. For reasons sketched briefly above, this presumption is *prima facie* incorrect and leads economists into many difficulties. In particular, the presumption that solutions to planning problems, or more briefly, plans, can properly be discovered through analysis is false and misleading. While the search for improved plans may be guided and informed both by analysis and by formal optimizing methods, it is ultimately sufficiently complex to take on the nature of an art rather than a science. Analytical methods should therefore be directed not at planning, but at assistance to planning.

If we consider planning as analogous to but not identical with a formal optimum-seeking procedure, then the elements of optimum-seeking enumerated above provide a method by which a planning procedure can be decomposed into interacting components, each of which may be considered in relative independence. As a simple but non-trivial example of such a decomposition, I should like to examine Mel Webber's statement that planning represents a cognitive style which examines questions of the type "what if." We can expand this concept in at least two different ways. First, the question may be rewritten as "If A, then what?" This really consists of two parts; the specification of A is a design problem since we can indeed examine only a very few of all the possible plan and policy configurations—that is, of all possible A's. In the second place, we are dealing with a predictive question which connects the antecedent with the consequence. We want to know what is "what." There is, however, another step. If "what" turns out to be Y, we ask the question, "If A implies Y, do we choose A?" This question obviously involves evaluation of the consequences of A, and still further, a comparison of A with B, C, D, and other designs or plans. Thus, what Webber defines as a cognitive style is really a compressed statement about a very complex process. I would suggest that the foregoing outline yields one very useful way to decompose and examine that process.

There are elements of the folklore of an anti-theory of planning which might merit brief mention. The idea that optima do not exist has been mentioned above. Another of these is the idea that it is impossible to have a fixed plan, since to paraphrase Democritus, it is not possible to step twice in the same river. There is a paradox here in that if you are going to act, at the moment that you do so, the plan upon which you act becomes fixed. If the plan was only generated at that moment, you are not planning, while if it was generated previously, it was fixed over time. The idea of planning with no fixed plan presents a paradox which I think cannot be sustained. Another useful but somewhat perverse idea is that planning procedures are more important than plans. The perversity lies in the implied denial that procedures and processes can be the objects of planning themselves. I believe that this is contrary to fact and that the paradigmatic approach outlined above can be applied not only to physical plans but also to institutions and societies. There are of course many political reasons why the design of new societies does not get discussed in responsible detail, but I think that planning could be, and indeed is, usefully extended in this direction.

Many of the recently fashionable approaches to the theory of planning take up one or a small subset of these planning activities and give this focus a saliency which may or may not be justified. In most cases, I believe that these tendencies neglect very important aspects of planning and lead to a distortion of the problem which will ultimately prove self-defeating.

Apocalyptic approaches have two different aspects which relate to the foregoing discussion. Many of them present the problem of planning for some particular set of purposes as so highly constrained by social reality and resource availability that problems of harmonizing objectives and achieving a good (or better) solution do not exist. This problem corresponds in mathematical programming with the initial step of finding a feasible basis from which improved solutions may be sought. The second stage of this approach (if the author is not himself in complete despair) is to provide a single salient remedy. This may be any one of a variety of familiar nostrums: zero population growth, social revolution, income redistribution, desegregation, improved mass transit, housing allowances, urban decentralization, new towns, and the like. Once the joint application of a collection of remedies is proposed, all of the problems associated with the optimal combinations of policies once again arise.

A practical planner frequently attempts to put himself in the position of imputing virtues to a single solution by emphasizing the binding nature of constraints. Such an excessively practical approach to planning neglects to give proper attention to the process by which constraints are established and therefore begs the whole question of planning.

An emphasis upon enlarging the solution space by adopting or considering for adoption new policies and new technical solutions is usually coupled with an oversimplified view of the consequences of each action or with an oversimplified view of the value system which is to be satisfied for proper planning. Many of the solutions put forward as ways to avoid catastrophe fall into this category.

There is a major concern with information, with its interpretation, and with modeling and prediction which is not as fashionable a focus for planning as it was as little as ten years ago. Nevertheless, this focus persists in the view that a proper analysis of problems will lead to their solution. Such a view might be supportable if there were unique optimal solutions to problems, but there are not. The approach retains an element of truth in that a better understanding of systems is a prerequisite for sound planning, but this kernel of truth will not sustain complete reliance on data, analysis, and modeling.

By far the greatest emphasis in recent years has been placed upon restructuring the social objective function which is used to evaluate planning. The discovery that questions of equity and justice may have been neglected has shocked many planners and led to an exclusive emphasis upon this and related features having to do with the evaluation of plans. Such an approach completely neglects the necessity for realistic prediction and for balancing together a wide variety of social objectives.

To my mind, a most reasonable view of the overall planning process considers it as a part of a process of social learning. As I will suggest, this view must be taken with some caution, but first I should like to review some of the strengths of the social learning point of view, especially as it relates to more popular participation in the planning process, in the context of the paradigm briefly discussed above.

Popular participation can contribute directly to improved understanding of almost every part of the paradigm. First and most important, popular participation helps to define much more clearly the values of society, including the values of equity and social justice, towards various classes and subgroups of the population. Second, popular participation can lead to more accurate predictions of the ways in which plans will function by bringing to the attention of the social scientists and planner trends and realities which for cultural and other reasons they might otherwise have overlooked. The predictive contribution of popular participation may be particularly important with respect to the political consequences of plans. Third, participants in the planning process on a broad scale can provide suggestions for new planning measures and information regarding the effectiveness of old ones, together with an assessment of constraints which can be applied to or removed from planning. Finally, through counter-planning and advocacy planning, the range of search for solutions to planning problems can be greatly widened.

Granted these very substantial advantages, I would demur at making public participation the sole form of planning and social learning. In any case, it is an exaggeration to imagine that social learning as now advocated is an entirely new discovery; all of the social sciences, together with history and literature, represent a constant effort on the part of man to understand himself and his society. It is of course true that new ways in which this process can be speeded and made more effective are useful and perhaps necessary. Social learning must also be distinguished from incrementalism and short-run adaptive planning. This type of adaptation makes it impossible to change drastically the pattern under which affairs are conducted, and implicitly it denies the possibility of avoiding mistakes by foreseeing them instead of by running into and then going around them. Finally, new direct participation by individuals must be distinguished from participation by groups and the representation of interests which have previously been wholly or partially excluded from the decision process. Above the neighborhood level the numbers of individuals involved in public participation become too large for a high level of direct involvement. Some form of delegation of decisionmaking subject to ultimate popular control is a necessity. For this reason, any description of systematic public participation in large-scale regional and national affairs begins to sound increasingly like a description of representative and democratic government. Thus there are issues of the organization of the whole of society so as to ensure more responsible and active participation and a more clear-cut and effective process of social learning. These however become improvements largely in the political sphere rather than in the planning process as an independent structure.

In my view, the immediately preceding remarks are responsive to Mel Webber's inquiry at the conference as to the appropriateness of reviving a kind of Victorian liberalism in his discussions of diversity, pluralism, and individual freedom. I believe that these concepts can be shown to be useful not entirely as ends in themselves, but as means to the total ends of society. In this event, they must be considered carefully in a structured context. Pluralism applies not only to individuals but to groups, to institutions, and to subsidiary cultures. There should be no incentive to preserve a pluralism which rests on unnecessary or unjust circumstances, such as the extreme differences in wealth and education which can be observed in many societies. Since pluralism does not exist for its own sake, there are instances in which some deviations from emerging social norms (such as the perpetuation of slavery) must be suppressed with a possible sacrifice of liberty. On the other hand, the evolution of society requires means of generating and testing new inventions and new adaptations to changing circumstances. The question of diversity, evolution, and social control is an important and universal issue which must be considered realistically in relation to the total long-term needs of society. Rhetoric in favor of unbridled individualism or unqualified social control will not be useful.

Given all of these conditions and qualifications and given the fact that planning has not been outstandingly successful in avoiding the difficulties inherent in political, social, and urban development, we may address the question of what would be a good scheme for the improvement of planning theory and planning teaching in the period ahead.

At the outset, I think it would be wise to approach this problem with some modesty. Planning is not the whole of society nor the whole of the political and social processes by which society undertakes self-guidance. Indeed, it can be fairly argued that many of the failures in recent decades which are sometimes attributed to planning are in fact the product of political shortfalls and difficulties. To assume responsibility for all of these external difficulties seems masochistic on the part of planners.

In examining what can be done in the realm of true planning responsibility, I will examine briefly three aspects of the paradigm set forth above.

First, we need a better understanding of the way in which society functions and evolves. This is the basis on which we approach the problem of predicting the future impacts of plans as well as the future contexts in which they will operate. There are those who maintain that the turbulence of current technical, economic, and social development on a worldwide basis is such as to defy prediction. Since at the same time we know that the effects of many current decisions will have major long-term impacts, taking this assumption would place us in a very difficult position. We would have no simple way to determine how present developments ought to be controlled or reshaped in order to promote welfare or avoid disaster.

There are essentially two solutions to this problem of turbulence. One is to institute rigid planning controls such as might make predictions come true. This course is conservative and authoritarian and contains dangers and uncertainties of its own. Its objectionable features could be mitigated to a substantial extent if the planning measures undertaken included an appropriate effort to reshape and humanize social value systems, but there remains the question of how such reshaping can be planned and conducted. Alternatively, we may take the general approach that turbulence has been exaggerated and the continuity of social life can be uncovered and systematized. This is certainly true at some small scales, and we may have underestimated the power of social science at larger scales. In any event, assertions about the unpredictability of turbulent development remain hypotheses which can never be proved.

The second area in which planning theory and processes can be substantially improved is in the specification of the value systems which govern the development and choice of plans. Not only must we take into account the values and interests of many different groups within the population, but we must also consider that many of the values which influence political and social behavior are hidden and obscure and reflect preferences for things which are not marketed. The strength of these preferences and the variables on which they depend are most difficult to specify and to measure. An understanding of these issues will simultaneously assist planmaking, decisionmaking, and the understanding of social and economic behaviors.

The third area which deserves our close attention is the process of finding or inventing good plans. This is the process which corresponds with a search for an optimum in mathematical programming. I think that a review of planning curricula will show that we teach our students very little about this process, which is essentially how to make plans. Some attention to the matter survives in some places in the form of planning studios, or is being revived in the form of workshops—but these approaches depend largely upon an intuitive understanding of the problem and upon the example of an effective planner or studio master. I believe that we can effectively do much better than this through a systematic investigation and structuring of this problem, but since there has been so little work in the field, this will be a difficult job. Work along these lines may also illuminate questions of change within society, since there may be strong parallels between the emergence of new technologies, new life styles, and new modes of social organization, and their acceptance, and the emergence of one or more plans or policies out of the problem area and into acceptance by the planning agency or by decisionmakers.

Perhaps I may add a footnote with regard to finding and investing good plans. There is a great deal of work in these areas which forms a contrast with two other activities. One of these is paradigm formation, and in the case of planning, normal plan-making activities play the role of normal science in Kuhn's *Structure of Scientific Revolution*. Most planners are engaged in this type of normal planning, which would cover problems like planning a route system for buses, developing a housing program, or designing a new town or subdivision—in each case attempting to meet a given set of goals and contraints. I believe that these normal activities would utilize similar techniques in New Orleans, Nizhni Novgorod, or

Kunming. Normal planning also stands in contrast to planning at the very large-scale political level with respect to major issues like poverty and health. Unfortunately, I believe that there is a somewhat unfavorable tendency for academics and planning theorists to escape from the pragmatic exigencies of normal planning into more romantic and appealing but less exigent realms—less exigent, that is, because these individuals have less responsibilities in these areas.

If we view these three fields as the most important interrelated aspects of a planning paradigm, we can see that they are in different states of development and require different kinds of inputs. Modeling and prediction perhaps are in the strongest position because of the commitment of social scientists and bureaucrats to continuity and to a certain effort to find regularities in life. This field needs more attention to joining the micro-knowledge sociology and economics to the description of large-scale systems. Working on the problems of adequate value systems represents a growing field of research to which both social scientists and politicians have become more sensitized. The problem of searching for plans currently lacks the moral or scientific appeal of these other two fields, but it is the area in which planning theory is furthest behind. A failure to produce original and effective plans is an obvious weakness of the planning process as a whole, and I believe a major one.

I believe that even if one were to subscribe to principles of social reorganization which would greatly change the context in which planning is conducted, these problems would persist, obviously in a modified form. Even further, I feel that a change in society of any kind could not be sustained, developed, and implemented without a planning effort, and such a planning effort would rest on the foundation which I have reviewed —of values, prediction, and the discovery or invention of plans. I therefore see no contradiction between the paradigm which I have briefly described and more specific recommendations for the improvement of society and planning. I simply believe that very limited proposals are in the final analysis not wholly adequate and that counsels of despair create a barrier to seeking solutions to the problems which we all face.

Economics In Urban Planning:
Use, Skills and Supply

Otto A. Davis and Chang-I Hua

Perhaps it is appropriate to begin this paper by noting that it is the joint product of two authors. One is an economist who has enjoyed an interaction (albeit often interrupted and sporadic) with the planning community as his part-time avocation. The other is a planner whose approach is inclined toward economics. Hence, here at the outset we should state that in a conference devoted to exploring the new challenges which are now confronting the planning profession, as well as the alternative responses to those challenges, we make no pretense of complete neutrality. We have an economic viewpoint.

It also may be appropriate to begin our essay by stating our impression of some of the intellectual trends which have been developing in the planning community, particularly with respect to economic thinking. The history of Utopia (in its positive sense) in the West as Martin Meyerson once noticed (Meyerson, 1961), is dominated by two distinct courses—the physical approach and the social approach. Intellects in the two camps have not really communicated, perhaps because they didn't understand each other. Historically, the social utopians regarded the physical approach as limited and non-fundamental while the physical utopians regarded the social approach both as too abstract and as deficient in providing direction for courses of action for implementation. The neoclassical economist's utopian world, a world of Pareto optimality, was not mentioned in Meyerson's essay—that world would probably be viewed as limited by other social utopians. Yet, we would like to argue that the Pareto world, simple and abstract as it is, is more relevant to our real world through its impact on the current science of policy analysis. In our opinion, the theme of this conference can be interpreted as the response of two types of utopians to the challenge provided by economists with a Pareto-type orientation.

To describe contemporary urban planning as being limited to the physical approach is not at all fair or even accurate. Originally growing out of urban design and land use planning, urban planning in the United States, since the early sixties, has been increasingly absorbing knowledges and methods from other social sciences. At the same time it has been becoming idealogically oriented. Among those new inputs to the professional knowledge of planning, economics has probably been accepted more favorably as compared with other social sciences. But the development as a whole has not been perfectly balanced, in our opinion. While both the strength and limitations of applying economics to planning are well recognized by the sophisticated planning educators, the understanding of the potential contribution of economics to urban planning may be inadequate among less sophisticated educators and practitioners at this stage. The limitation and difficulties of economic analysis in policy studies as discovered by economists themselves have been too readily quoted by planners for justifying a non-economic approach. There seems to be a wide-spread opinion that those advocates of economic efficiency in planning are narrow-minded, outdated persons unconcerned with social justice which planners, being in a profession as a vocation, are called for to correct. One can say that the physical utopians' about-face toward social utopians has been complete in that they now seem to regard the Pareto optimizers as naive, if not reactionary.

This attitude may not benefit the planning profession. The deficiency of a tool does not justify discarding it when no substitute is available, particularly when the useful part of the tool has not been fully understood or utilized and when the deficient part is at least partially remediable. It is with this belief that we are doing the unexciting thing of advocating the emphasis of orthodox economic analysis in the professional training of urban planners. To do this we first briefly take stock of economics as it seems to be applied to the practice of urban planning. Then we discuss certain neglected basic economic ideas that could have made more important contribution to the planning profession. The significant shift toward the demand approach, which seems to be the theme of this conference, is subsequently interpreted. Finally, we briefly examine the supply side, the education of the demand oriented planning/analysts, to conclude our observations.

If we are right, the parts of economics that have become familiar to practicing urban planners are limited to certain areas of the discipline. Naturally, the first is the cost analysis of projects. Any serious planner with a concern for implementation must give some thought to cost. Otherwise, a plan would be utopian in the negative sense of the term. This concern about cost is essentially engineering economics in which the goal is simple efficiency. In other words, the basic idea is to minimize cost given a predetermined objective. This branch of economics later became associated with a second area of interest, urban land economics. Starting from the real estate business, urban land economics developed into a specialized subdiscipline and has become one of the major components of the pure academic field of urban economics. The academic field may be gradually slipping away from the practicing planners' understanding. However, the consideration of both project cost and the effect of a project on future land value, together with its tax implications, have been commonly accepted as important and necessary in planning. Knowledge, if not training, in these aspects of applied economics is professionally indispensable.

The third economic area to which the planner has paid attention is community economic base analysis. To understand the local industrial structure and its dynamics in order to predict future employment as a basis of demographic and other studies, the planners have attempted to acquire certain practical techniques, not economic theories, in this area. In fact, the interest in this area is so intense, and economic theories have so little to contribute, that many techniques such as the employment multiplier, the location quotient, and shift-share analysis have been developed and tried by the planners themselves.

This is a crude summary of the major areas of economics in which planners have a general interest. Certain of the basic ideas in economics have not been well received yet and thus are worth a brief discussion. We particularly want to point out the three interrelated ones that have been most neglected or misunderstood in the planning circle. The first one concerns the efficient allocation of resources in a society through the market mechanism; the second one is that consumers' preferences may still be detected without a market for the sake of efficiently allocating resources; and the third is that in many circumstances efficiency does not have to be traded off with equity—in fact, in most circumstances efficiency can be improved without sacrificing anyone's gain.

In respect to the market, the planning profession seems to have embraced a different idea in past years. The intellectual agenda of the profession appeared to have been characterized by a lack of appreciation, or even a distrust, of the allocative forces of the marketplace. In the fields of housing, physical and regional planning, the dominant theme appears to have been that the planner was at least supposed to know what was right for the population and that the major problem was to determine an agenda and plans which might accomplish the given objectives. In this rather extreme characterization, the planner's disregard of the allocative role of the market appears somewhat similar to that of the central planner in a planned economy. These kinds of influences appear to have been more or less embodied in much of the legislation of that date. Thus, urban renewal was designed to remove blight without serious regard to the forces which might have caused it to appear and to migrate. The planner knew that it was undesirable and his role was to devise a program for its demise. Similarly, urban housing programs were designed because certain portions of our population simply deserved "more adequate" housing than they seemed to have. The problem was conceived as one in which the deserved housing had not been provided by the private sector's marketplace so that the solution was simply to provide it publicly. The subtle allocative mechanism of the market was not thought to be relevant. A similar line of thought applies to the other housing subsidy programs of the day, which were oriented towards bringing new stock into being.

The planners' attitude about the market mechanism may be explained by several factors. One is that they had an intuitive belief that the externality problem was pervasive so that the textbook description of market allocation would not be applicable. The other is that they tended to mix the efficiency problem with the equity problem and thus were inclined to seize any opportunity for public intervention to achieve an effect of income redistribution. Another is simply that the profession grew out of a physical tradition, and the visual culture of that tradition makes it difficult to perceive an invisible hand.

Let us hasten to add that at least part of the planner's suspicion of the market mechanism is justified. Externality is a complicated matter which we now find to be more pervasive than we previously thought. Worst of all, it has no general solution, but needs ad hoc treatment depending on the situation (Davis & Whinston, 1966), (Davis & Kamien, 1969). In fact, it is mainly due to this problem that the national economic scene has been moving towards more and more regulation, a trend opposite to what is happening in the urban scene which motivates this conference. Nevertheless, the existence of externality does not necessarily mean the market should be abandoned. It only suggests that the planner's job is to eliminate the externalities as much as possible in order to facilitate the market mechanism. This sounds trite, but the long historical evolution of federal housing subsidy programs in the United States can basically be regarded as a consequence of our learning about the working of the housing market.

It is certainly true that in many planning cases no market exists at all. (This is perhaps another major reason for planners' lack of interest in taking this economic approach seriously). In such cases, a planner should ask himself whether it is indeed impossible for him to create a situation to allow or force people to reveal their true preferences. Granted, the work may be difficult, but, on the other hand, the opportunities for such a revelation are often present in a surprisingly large percentage of the cases. Search for such opportunities can be regarded almost as an art rather than a science, but that fact should make the planning profession more challenging and interesting. Since this task is almost an art, we feel obligated to illustrate it with two cases.

The value of beauty in terms of cold dollars may be unthinkable and profane to many planners. To an economic oriented highway planner, the question can be conceptually and empirically answered at least with respect to certain patterns of the landscaping. For example, the planner might make efforts to improve two highways between two places in order to achieve identical road characteristics, including distance and driving time, except that one is made more scenic than the other. After the two roads are opened, all the travellers between the two places would drive on the scenic road unless the factor of congestion was involved. Now the planner sets a toll both on the scenic road and experiments on the effect of charging the toll on the traffic on the two roads. From this he can estimate the road users' dollar value of enjoying highway beauty and the information should enable him to invest better in highway landscaping in the future. There are many practical and technical problems in the estimation, but in principle, beauty can be evaluated for certain particular situations. In principle, the same experiment can be extended to evaluating other unmarketable resources such as time, which has indeed become a major research topic in transportation planning.

A more pertinent case concerns the provision of public services and a decision about the capital projects in a community. It has been proposed in the context of the Model Cities programs that a simulated market system can be designed to achieve efficiency under the consumer sovereignty (Weismantel, 1969).

Each household in the Model City is offered a credit card. A certain number of dollars, which is determined by the total budget of the Model City and perhaps the need of the household, is credited to the households' accounts and can only be spent on the provided services on a pay-as-you-go basis. Voting in capital investment is tied into the credit system since for each accepted project the cost would be shared and charged against each household. On the supply side, each public agency and each program staff is responsible for establishing its cost account to be converted to the price of its service. The agencies and program staffs thus operate as firms competing for a given market, and their production efficiency might be assumed. The proposal is indeed interesting enough,[1] and there is no reason for not extending its application beyond the context of Model City. But, so far we have heard little about its implementation at any level of public service system. It is not clear whether the lack of response is mainly due to certain technique problems in such approach or due to the planner's lack of appreciation for the idea of consumer sovereignty itself.

Many planners, partially following the traditional belief that the profession must deal with something fundamental to the society, and partially in a reaction to the discovery in the sixties that land use planning is not that fundamentally relevant to the newly surfaced area of social problems, are more inclined to discuss the equity problem than the efficiency problem which we have addressed here. Certain of the fundamentalist planners seem to implicitly assume that the current social problems are a consequence of our capitalistic society which seeks only efficiency. To those planners efficiency really implies a maintenance of the status quo so that efficiency must be traded off with equity, etc. The truth of these assumptions is partially polemic and partially contingent on the level and situation of the problems in question. A Pareto utopian would believe that equity and efficiency are basically two distinct problems and that in the real suboptimum world there is usually substantial room for increasing efficiency at no ones cost (and this should be politically more feasible). Furthermore, utopians like ourselves probably believe that the efficiency problem is a technical one which forms the basis for our professionalism and the equity problem is political so that no profession is entitled to claim expertise in it (except for politics in its positive sense and if it is regarded as a profession).

The last belief runs counter to the convictions of the ideological planners and the issue is not a new one. Here, however, we can again illustrate the difference between ideological planner's thought and our preferences with the foregoing example. (If we replace the Model City with any geographic unit—a city or a neighborhood or any interest group— the point will become clearer). Ideological planners would argue that the most meaningful professional role is to advocate the interest of the client group, particularly when that group is the underprivileged, by maximizing the resources allocable to the group. Our beliefs are different. First, although a redistribution of resources in the larger context of the nation (and the world) is important, it does not appear to us that there are convincing arguments that the professional role of urban planners is redistribution. Second, although a coalition of interests can sometimes be formed to gain resources for the group, there are seldom homogeneous preferences, even among very poor people. To identify the preference structure within a group or a community and to plan or design accordingly is not only a significant accomplishment, but it is also a very technical and artistic one requiring formal training. And third, since such training is currently not adequate in the planning profession, is seems appropriate to make achieving Pareto optimal allocations in the wider physical world as the first task of the profession at this stage.

Based upon our observations about the past controversies concerning the role of the planner, and especially upon our perception of a lack of appreciation or understanding of the role of efficiency in the allocation of resources, we see the subtheme of this conference, *Demand vs. Supply Emphasis,* as most interesting. To an economist, demand and supply are always equally significant and the phrase "shift of emphasis" may not ring a bell to such a person. To a planner, however, the phrase may characterize a long course of evolution of the U.S. Federal Government's role and strategy in urban development, particularly in housing. But, to an economist interested in planning or an economic oriented planner, the phrase has a more fundamental meaning.

It means that planners no longer, at least at the operational level, feel confident in defining what is good or bad for the public. It indicates a recognition of the idea of consumer's sovereignty. In the context of our view of the intellectual history of planning, this is no small shift and, if the trends continue, will change the basic professional role of the planner. However, the change in the basic professional role will require a change in the basic skills which are required for the profession. Analyzing what is and will be demanded in the market is a very different and more difficult job than pronouncing what should be supplied by the government and the private sector. Any student of housing can easily see the differences between the required skills, time, and information in a housing market demand analysis and a housing needs study.

To illustrate more concretely the different skills that will be required from a demand oriented planner, let us consider two questions concerning the impact of a housing subsidy program. The first question, at the macro-level, is whether a massive subsidy program in the form of a housing voucher scheme will cause an inflationary price increase in the market. The very expensive social experimental program now underway in Green Bay and South Bend is intended to answer this query. Specifically, the question is the extent to which the observed increase in housing expenditures of the subsidized families reflects an increased consumption of housing services and the extent to which that increase merely reflects inflated prices of housing services in the market. Notice that both components (the housing services and the prices) of the housing expenditure are unobservable (Lowry, 1971). First-rate housing analysts are being recruited to design and supervise this experimental project. We have some doubt whether the findings that are to be generated from the two urban areas can be generalized and transferred to other metropolitan areas when we consider that each local housing market has it own peculiar structure and pattern of economic growth. A more appropriate approach might be to consider obtaining the answer from a well-designed econometric model continuously estimated from local data. Such an approach would, however, require a local planner who possesses a knowledge of certain economic theories and statistical techniques just to understand and evaluate the work of an expert who might be hired for the job.

The second question, at a macro-level, concerns the external effect which might be attributed to a new house which initiates a chain of household moves. Some people tend to answer the question by tracing the vacancy chain and interpreting the length of the chain as representing the indirect benefit from the new house (Lansing et al., 1972). This is the result of supply oriented thinking and we argue that it is misleading. The length of the chain may not represent the social benefit at all. It is quite reasonable to believe that a shorter chain length might be associated with a situation where there is a housing shortage. The more severe the housing shortage, the larger might be the benefit which accrues to each household included in the chain of moves. In other words, if one wishes to evaluate the secondary benefit from creating a house, one must weigh the expected vacancy chain length with the expected benefit which accrues to each household included in the chain. But to obtain a figure for the latter, one has to use demand analysis and the underlying concept of consumer's surplus, which is a rather intriguing subject.

Incidentally, tracing individual housing vacancy chains has become a popular research undertaking in recent years. Not only is this research costly, but certain chain behaviors cannot be ascertained by the popular approach. The appropriate way is to apply a Markov Chain Model to aggregate data on household moves. Not only is this latter approach much less expensive, but it also provides more insightful information (Hua, 1972). This latter approach, however, requires that the planner be familiar with theories about stochastic processes which have not been regarded as a standard part of the professional tool kit.

It is now appropriate to summarize the major points we have tried to make. First, the shift from supply oriented to demand oriented planning is more than just a strategic change. It may shake the very roots of the planning profession's ideology and aggravate the identity crisis of the profession. More specifically, the normative role of the planner will shrink. Second, if the shift is to be furthered, planning will be increasingly a job of working with the market mechanism rather than opposing or intervening with the mechanism. To create or to improve competitive market conditions, to eliminate the undesirable externality, to break up the "prisoner's dilemma" and other subtle problems associated with externalities will require more information and knowledge than has been associated with the more traditional role. Third, such means can be acquired only through training which emphasizes analytical methods. Applied economics, qualitative techniques, and modeling skills must be more adequately taught and practiced.

Are planners and planning schools ready for such a shift?

The current training of professional planners occurs mainly through master programs of two years duration. Without the support of an undergraduate program for the profession, like that of engineering, the two years time is barely enough for the acculturation to urban problems and the practices of urban planning. Students come from widely different backgrounds and usually are not required to have basic analytic training as a prerequisite to enter the planning program. Data collection and analysis, elementary statistics, and other urban planning techniques are introduced through three or four courses. The core of the program is usually a studio or project course which is meant to force students to synthesize all knowledge learned within and without school and which usually takes a lion's share of the student's total time in formal training. Besides the projects, one or two courses concerned with planning theories, commonly called the "Planning Process," are required. The rest of time is used in electives. Many shools have urban economics as an elective course, mainly designed for increasing the planner's insight into urban problems rather than being an integral part of professional technical training.

This description appears to us to be an accurate if general picture of the current planning curriculum. It might still be a best design for training planners to do what planners are really doing now. However, it is clear that if demand oriented planning is the wave of the future, the current curriculum has to be drastically changed in order to meet the requirements of that orientation. Let us say two solid courses of basic economics plus an urban economics course are the minimum. One course in cost-benefit analysis, one course of intermediate level statistics and one course in econometrics should also be required. One course in mathematical programming, one course in stochastic modeling and one course in operations research might follow. These courses can be taught only if the students already have a good basis in mathematics and statistics. These analytic courses should be regarded as standard tools only. Other substantive courses in urban studies and planning should not be omitted. All these considerations lead to the conclusion that it may be impossible to turn out a demand oriented analyst-planner from the current two-year planning program.

One can argue that some kind of doctoral degree in planning or policy analysis, with approximately four years normal time, may be needed as a replacement for the current masters degree as the professional degree if we want to preserve "competence" in a professional degree. This idea might take another decade to be accepted. Meanwhile, there are only two alternatives to supply certain minimally equipped analyst-planners. One is to train them in an analytically oriented school within a two-year limit. This can be done if two thirds of the curriculum is devoted to the development of analytical tools. The danger of the approach is an orientation towards the production technocrats who do not have the planner's perspective and spirit. The other alternative is to extend the current two-year program in planning school to three years in order to have students more adequately prepared for their future tasks. The problem of this approach is that the applicants might not perceive that their extended investment in human capital will be intellectually and monetarily rewarded. If this is true, then the new program will not take hold. The shortage of such analyst-planners will bid up the wage and that in turn will eventually bring up the supply, an economist would say. But the consequence of a short-run disequilibrium is costly owing to the strategical role played by the planner in our society. One way to shorten the disequilibrium period is to disseminate the information about the forecasted situation to the public. This idea motivated us to present this essay.

NOTES

1. We would like to suggest that the (Pareto) efficiency will be further increased if households are allowed to sell and buy the use of other households' credit cards. Short of this extremity, one can always set a limit for each type of service the use of which can be transacted.

REFERENCES

Otto A. Davis and A. Whinston, "On Externalities Information and the Government Assisted Invisible Hand," *Economica* 33 (August 1966), 303-18.

Otto A. Davis and Morton I. Kamien, "Externalities, Information and Alternative Collection Action," *The Analysis and Evaluation of Public Expenditures: The PPB System* (A Compendium of Papers Submitted to the Subcommittee on Economy in Government of Joint Economic Committee of the Congress of the United States) (Washington, D.C.: U. S. Government Printing Office, 1969), pp. 67-86.

Otto A. Davis, Charles M. Eastman and Chang-I Hua, "The Shrinkage in the Stock of Low-Quality Housing in the Central City: An Empirical Study of the United States Experience Over the Last Ten Years." *Urban Studies* 71 (February 1974), 13-26.

Chang-I Hua, *Modelling Housing Vacancy Transfer* (Ph.D. Thesis for Harvard University, 1972).

John B. Lansing, Charles Wade Clifton and James N. Morgan, *New Homes and Poor People* (Ann Arbor, Michigan: Institute of Social Research, University of Michigan, 1969).

Ira S. Lowry, C. Peter Rydell and David M. de Ferranti, "Testing the Supply Response to Housing Allowances: An Experimental Design" (The Rand Paper Series, WN-7711-UI). (Santa Monica, California: The Rand Corporation, 1971).

Martin Meyerson, "Utopian Traditions and the Planning of Cities," *Daedalus* 90 (Winter 1961), 180-93.

Richard F. Muth, *Cities and Housing* (Chicago: The University of Chicago Press, 1969), Chapter VI.

William Weismantel, "A Credit Card System for Model Cities," *Journal of American Institute of Planners* 35 (January 1969), 49-51.

Section V

Who Are Planners?
What Do Planners Do?

And How are They Prepared for Their Tasks?

Three Crises of American Planning

John W. Dyckman

Planning, Professionalism and the University

All professions periodically engage in stock-taking, but of the American professions none does so more regularly and searchingly than the planning profession. There are many reasons for this. While all professions tend to be continuously changing as their scientific foundations develop and their technical apparatus is modified, planning changes for even more volatile political and social reasons. Programs change, public demands take new forms, and the place of the profession in the society shifts. Planners caught up in these changes are confused, and call for a review of their situation.

In the American case, moreover, there are certain peculiarities in the status of the activity of planning which impose strains on the persons who call themselves planners, and give rise to self-doubts. Meetings such as this are intended, in part at least, to assuage those doubts. In particular, American planning is beset by paradoxes which torment the practitioners of this art. Many of these will come to mind, of which a few seem to me particularly important.

First and foremost, of course, is American ambivalence about public planning itself. Unlike planners in some countries, where planning is honored ideologically, if not in execution, American planners are unsure of the degree of national commitment to their work. Not only do we lack a public ideology committed to planning, but actual support of planning activity fluctuates from administration to administration, and with national political currents.

Thus the flurry of planning proposals, spurred by the bite of the De-pression, which surfaced in the New Deal in 1933 extended hopes which were to founder, but which left a residue of experience that is cherished by the planning memory. (And which are often idealized, both in respect of their social purpose and in the revision of their stumbling execution. As John Kenneth Galbraith has observed, there has rarely been a period of such fuzzy semanticism, but the very fuzziness has left openings for subsequent historians to glamorize the experience.) The stringencies of war added to the planning impulse, and erased some of the bitterness of New Deal frustration in the forties. This made it possible for an early and insistent advocate of planning, Charles E. Merriam, who had himself been a New Deal planning advocate in the National Resource Planning

Board, to say in 1945: "The fear that planning will interfere with the development of free industrial society is groundless. The very purpose of planning is to release human abilities, to broaden the field of opportunity, and to enlarge human liberty. We plan primarily for freedom; the ways and means and instruments are secondary to the main purpose. The right kind of planning—democratic planning—is a guaranty of liberty and the only real assurance in our times that men can be free and make a wide range of choices." [1]

On the other hand, an equally early proponent of planning, Rexford Tugwell, speaking in the fifties, observed that, "Some twenty or thirty years ago some of us believed that planning as a profession, and particularly as part of government, was at the beginning of an exciting expansion. Our optimism originated in two identifiable sources: the acceptance of flow and progression as a theory of social change; and accelerating demand for directed betterment of the human condition; the other led us to believe that a series of managerial devices would allow us to satisfy this demand . . . We were too optimistic. The unfortunate fact is that we are not much better off today than we were then. It is true that there are many more individuals who are called planners and many more planning agencies or departments in city and state governments. But neither these officials nor political scientists generally seem to understand how far short they are of the usefulness we foresaw for them a generation ago. They are busy; they produce maps, statistics and reports; they draft zoning ordinances; they rather apologetically identify trends; but they are mere adjuncts to the more important government agencies. They are regarded as a convenience, but they are not responsible and independent contributors. In the Federal government they exist only as minors in a Bureau whose business is the making of the annual budget. In other governments they have even lower status." [2]

The story is well-known. The fortunes of planning fluctuate, but the planners are not significant actors in the American scene. They have certain local powers, but no generalized influence. Their advisory role is treated as backroom drudge work. Our electoral system elevates men and women who are not much bothered by the facts or details. The machinery of planning at their disposal is treated as confirmatory and symbolic, not as relevant to the actual decisions made, which depend on political sensitivity.

Tugwell's comments point to one of the more troubling paradoxes of contemporary American planning. As the functions of planning become more institutionalized in the American scene, the powers of planning seem to decline. There are perhaps important structural reasons for this. The institutionalization of planning observed by Tugwell is largely at the state and local level, and at this level in the American Federal system, less and less of importance is decided. Or, because the environment of state and local governments is open to the Federal sphere of action, the environment is turbulent, unpredictable, and dependent, and the "plans" of locals are highly contingent, and vulnerable to national action.[3] At the same time that the planners have highly localized powers, they deal with issues less and less concordant with the ideological "grand design" of planning.

And, as Tugwell notes, in the Federal government the planning, such as it is, is not done by the "planners." Despite the emergence in recent times of the Humphrey-Javits bill for the creation of National Economic Planning, planning advocates are suspicious of the prospects. Two examples illustrate this climate of misgivings. In his closing address to the March, 1976 meeting of the American Institute of Planners and the American Society of Planning Officials, Martin Meyerson found a number of obstacles to national planning: doubts about leaders, inexact forecasting devices, and reluctance to experiment. Meyerson found a weakening of government legitimacy, deficiency of planning tools, and deepening cleavage of values as likely impediments.[4]

Another, more recent, paper has argued that the core of the difficulty of achieving meaningful national planning is to be found in the ignorance of the planners. In this paper, Peter Schuck contends that, "The state of the art of social engineering is, to put the very best face on it, rudimentary and underdeveloped. Reasonable persons may differ as to whether this ignorance about the workings of social process is an inescapable consequence of their inherent complexity, or whether our social scientists and policy analysts simply have not yet had enough practice. My own conviction is that the ignorance can be dispelled only marginally at best, and that the kinds of propositions about social causality explicit or implicit in any national plan worthy of the name will be exceedingly problematical."[5] To emphasize this point Schuck points to the failures of urban renewal, national transportation policy, and welfare programs, judged by their stated objectives. He disputes the claims that these failures are due to inadequate coordination or to underfunding, or to the sabotage of hostile bureaucracies. He concludes that, "It seems far more plausible to conclude, however, that we simply do not know how to build urban communities, fashion a national transportation system, or eliminate social disintegration, much less accomplish all of these objectives simultaneously through an integrated strategy or plan."[6]

Reasonable persons, among them planners, may also conclude that we are not prepared to allow an adequate test of these social experiments. In social planning we have too often broken off the exercise before such a test could be made. We are partly to blame for promising too much too quickly. There is no doubt that programs are oversold and that we leap from program to program promising new panaceas. But the fact remains that knowledge of incentives, motivation, and social mobilization is primitive in our planning. The California Transportation Agency's recent experience with a reserved traffic lane on freeways for multiple occupancy vehicles—a device long recommended by planners— suggests that we know too little about individual driver behavior and about the transaction costs and social planning preparation necessary to effect changes in even this small part of a total urban behavior system.[7] We learn only too slowly that intervention in complex interdependent systems of action cannot be predicated on simple conceptions of "system efficiency" and on a one-sided reading of motivation.

Contemporary planning activity in America, spurred by the discovery of social science by academic planners, has shown a disposition to apply social science. Where in physical sciences one can normally go from insufficiently critical and sensitive in its handling of these generalizations, and has been largely unaware of the dangers of such generalization in social science. Where in physical sciences one can normally go from general theory to less general ones, so that the general supersedes the particular, the same is not true of social sciences. We cannot go from general theories of behavior to specific models that encompass individual cases, the more so when the environment of action, controlled or neutralized in physical science, is both exogenous to the models and decisive in the behavior. If in fact planning is to be rooted in the specific political environment in which it acts, and is to take its meaning from that environment, much of our generalization will be futile unless we can have a general theory of such environments.

Implied in this criticism is the charge that there is imperfect communication between academic planning study and the practice of planning. Further, there is an implication of a symmetry in the flow of information. The flows from the academy to the practice are more abundant than the reverse flows from practice to our learning institutions. In American city planning we are burdened with an unfortunately deep distinction between the ideas of academic students of planning and the actions of the working planners. In particular, we suffer from an unhappy distinction between "professionalism" and "theory." Professionalization has spread rapidly and extensively over city and regional planning activities in America, and at the same time the teaching of city planning has become widely diffused in the academy. But in the course of this expansion, the ties between the two types of activity have become increasingly strained. In my view, this is explicable, but unnecessary.

The gulf between the sets of actors is not hard to explain. To begin with, the reward systems of the different spheres of activity are . very different. Individual members of the university must conserve their positions in the university and try to rise in that system. They cannot do so unless they meet the expectations of the university community for publication, and this means the construction of generalizations and ultimately of theoretical systems of explanation. Every professor of planning appreciates the extent of his disadvantage if he has no "theory" to call his own. This obligation is not wholly relieved by the location of planning education in "professional schools." The canons of academic judgment pursue the individual, and determine his success.

Very different criteria are determining for the working professional. That planner may be judged by his fellow professionals, or by the community which he serves, but the criteria will be very different from those of the academic community. Fellow professionals may judge him for the size of the budget or quality of staff he has been able to wrest from the political system, or for the scale of the undertakings he is able to generate, or the innovative methods of analysis and programming he mounts, or even from the publicity he obtains from the media. The community may judge him for his political skills, for his ability to articulate his programs, for his skill in compromising interests, or for his ability to inspire visions of the future. As a recent study by Donald Schon and associates conducted on M.I.T. planning graduates shows, communication skills are valued very highly by working planners, but in the profession such skills may be employed for the most part in the service of persuasion.

Professionalization, moreover, has grown within a framework of bureaucratization of planning. The establishment of planning offices, the qualification of planners in the context of civil service, the integration of planning into local and state governments, and the growth of legal and administrative requirements for planning approvals have powerful implications for the conduct of planners and their intellectual tasks. As Max Weber long ago established, bureaucracy emphasizes and demands "formal," or procedural rationality. Substantive rationality, or what planning is about, takes second place to procedural efficiency in this environment. Any planner preparing environmental impact studies knows that these will be judged more for how they are done than for what they imply. And while universities may be bureaucratic in their practices, different skills are required for advancement in a government bureaucracy and in a university.

Academic planners would warmly endorse the dictum of Charles De Gaulle, who wrote, "The power of the mind implies a diversity that is not to be found in the exclusive practice of a profession, for the same reason that home life is rarely very entertaining." [8]

So the school explores the powers of the mind to stretch our understandings of planning, and the professional planners tend to its home life. A price that planners pay for the bureaucratization of their profession is

the inevitable tedium of bureaucratic life.   Ensconced in the offices of
the state or local government they take on some of the powers of the
state apparatus, but they are constrained by all the rules and requirements
of the office. To the extent that they have internalized the conception of
planning taught in the schools in which they prepared, they are likely to
fall victim to feelings of malaise, or the "what-is-planning-all-about
blues." The feelings of recent planning graduates on entering the job
market are described by one of them as follows: "If he or she is lucky (?)
enough to find a job as a planner, he will seldom use his knowledge of
economics, sociology, psychology, et al., because he will promptly be put
to work coloring maps, making models, or talking with business representatives about the refusal of their petition for a zoning variance. For,
speculate as we will about the future of planning, its present is largely
made up of mundane tasks for the new professional." [9]

Of course, this is partly the nature of life in organizations. The junior
officer rarely has the opportunity to exercise his training in tactics,
strategy and combat logistics. Much of his time is spent in routines, in
barrack inspection, enforcement of regulations, and parade. The newly
minted graduate planner, stuffed with social science and armed with the
image of planning as "societal guidance," is likely to experience stunning
culture shock in the environment of bureaucratic life. The most perceptive
of the planning students recognize this prospect, and shy away from that
commitment. Many drift into research organizations, consulting firms,
think tanks, or strive to remain in the protective cocoon of the university.
Since they cannot start in the bureaucratic game at the top, they no
longer aspire to enter official planning offices and to directly influence
local environments. The growing incongruity of planning education with
planning practice constitutes the first of our planning "crises."

The Development of Planning Theories and the Crisis of Planning Education

The second "crisis" which I wish to address is to be found in the
teaching of planning in the universities. In the environment of the university, planning curricula grow rapidly and spread in many directions.
Both the American Institute of Planners and the Associated Collegiate
Schools of Planning are presently engaged in strenuous efforts to codify
the course contents and to specify a required educational content. We
may view these actions as responses to perceived, threatening disorder.
In general, these efforts represent the desire to "bound" the field, so that
it is not preempted by other disciplines and so that it is not so diluted
as to lose respectability. A recent summary report of a committee of
the Association of Collegiate Schools of Planning addresses this issue in

the following terms: ". . . if there is a working consensus on an explicit definition of planning we can invite attention to the differences between planning and such related fields as urban studies and operations research at a level that is intellectually defensible. Rather than drawing boundaries around planning education on the basis of "proper" or "conventional" academic labels, credentials and professional socialization, we may distinguish between planning schools and other academic enterprises by the presence or absence of specific curricular objectives." [10]

The need to be "intellectually defensible" is felt keenly throughout the profession, but it is most acute in the universities. Largely for this reason, planning education created a demand for planning theory. In the institutional environment of the university, pressures for generality, explanation, and rigorous argument are paramount. Within the walls of the academy, planning teachers would be second-class citizens without their own theory or theories. At a trivial level, intra-university struggles for status would account for a certain amount of the grasping for theory in planning.

At a more important level, however, ideas of planning need guiding theories for the important *organizing function* which they can provide. Put simply, if we had a theory of planning, it ought to help organize the core knowledge in the field. For a theory is a point of reference and a means of validating knowledge. Economic theory, for example, is rigorously organized so as to say what economics deals with and what it excludes. Theory is always changing so as to include additional elements, but at any moment it is *coherent*. Further, relations that are observed, as in regression analysis, are interpreted and *validated* by reference to the theory. Finally, theory is largely the construct of professional scholars. Writing of economic theory, George Stigler saw this as a temporal process, observing that "a basic distinction must be drawn between the period in which a field of study is dominated by controversies over policy (applications) and the period in which it is a discipline pursued by professional scholars." [11] At the same time that theory is the creature of the scholar, it must have application to the work of men of affairs. This requirement is especially strong in the case of theory designed to affect the conduct of a profession, such as planning.

The problem of planning theory, moreover, is that it tends to be pulled apart by these requirements. In the era when applications were stressed and controversies raged principally over policy, theory could be close to the profession, but the theory was itself embryonic at best. As it began to be developed in the academy, theory encountered increasing demands for explanatory power and for rigor. Efforts to develop these characteristics were achieved, if at all, only at the expense of relevance. As Nicki King notes, "There are built-in tensions which, in providing *rigor,* pull theorists too far into the world of abstraction and unreality. Their theories about guidance are impressive intellectual statements that bear no relation to the operation of social systems in a modern world. By the same token, attempts at providing *relevance* often reduce concepts of societal guidance to the level of the case study, which limits their generalizability and usefulness in providing insights into the true nature of the larger system." [12]

These tensions have been with us since the maturing of planning curricula in our universities. The same tensions echo throughout the introduction that I wrote in 1969 to the special issue of the *Journal of the American Institute of Planners* on planning theory.[13] The purpose of that issue was, the introduction said, "to dissect the uses of planning theory through exploration and demonstration of theories of planning that are especially appropriate to professional planners." [14] In other words, it represented an effort to relate theory to the practice of a well-defined group. It was designed to help bridge a gulf that even then was widening between the academics and the professionals. The difficulties that effort encountered are still with us. Not all these obstacles are the result of difficulties in theorizing about planning. Some result from the difficulty of classifying the professional practice to which the theory is supposed to relate.

For the planning "profession" in America is insecure about its professionalism. If we accept the commonly asserted argument that a profession is characterized, at a minimum, but the "exclusive possession of competence in a specified area" [15] and by the acceptance of a common ethic, we confront the reality that the technical arts of planning are shared with a host of other professions, among them architecture, engineering, and politics, and that the substantive area in which the planners work is not their exclusive domain, but is shared with economists, sociologists, lawyers, journalists and businessmen. What is more distinctive of the profession of planning is a common culture, with a core of shared ideology. That culture, just as the theories of the scholars of planning, is in flux. But it retains a common core. This core persists, and guides the orientations of planners, when professional tasks change, and when the public interpretation of the planning role is modified by events. To quote my 1969 position: "The rules of the game in public planning are a source of much disagreement between planners, politicians and bureaucrats. This is the point at which planners plead for rational procedures, for giving weight to "technical" information inputs, for consistency and avoidance of contradiction, and for conduct of decisionmaking greatly at variance with prevailing practices." [16] In short, the core has a set of procedures, an attitude towards the use of information, and above all for a commitment to rationality. Further, the "ethic," or normative guidance, of planning is the ethic of rational action.

The presence of this professional orientation of planning does not imply, however, that the appropriate theory for planning is that of rational decision. Academic critics, in and out of planning, have pointed to the difficulties, limitations, and lack of relevance of rational planning. The difficulties are well known to theorists in economics, business, and public administration. Rational planning models require the processing of enormous amounts of information, require an arbitrary limitation of the levels of repercussions to be considered, and encounter severe problems in the aggregation of individual values. Critics such as Simon, March, Braybrooke and Lindblom have attempted to devise models of "limited rationality" which would be more practical for administrators and other public actors. These have been highly pragmatic, "incrementalist" models, which emphasize problem decomposition, and a series of small adjustments and pragmatic trials. Incrementalism is a popular idea with planners, which is more and more appealing as planners find themselves working in structured governmental situations, as administrators rather than as social critics or "agents of change." For it is the nature of incrementalism that, while starting out to economize on the high cost of information and to achieve a practical "rule," it ends with a model that is uncritical of existing structures and excludes the important large scale changes that are most interesting to planning.

The institutionalization of planning in America, and its absorption into state and local government practice, coincided with the academic critique of thoroughgoing rationalism (which had been based largely on utilitarian economics and on statistical decision theory). The convergence of practical tasks and academic views sounded a retreat from big systems to little systems. Planning theorists were not far behind the administrative theorists in modifying their perspectives. Melvin Webber, for example, was one of the early proponents of the ideas of planning as a "process" of thought and action, separated from the idea of the "plan." Later he refined his views of this process, and incorporated a learning model into his view of planning.[17] John Friedmann, in a succession of papers, also incorporated elements of the process view and the theory of learning systems, eventually adding the ideas of "societal guidance" drawn from Mannheim and Etzioni.[18] It is not my purpose to review this literature; it is in any event familiar to those who read the journals in which academic planners publish. What is important for this paper is that these views do not so much dispense with rationalism, or at least with reason, as they restrict and modify it.

These modifications of planning theory marked the effort to make planning thought more congruent with observed planning behavior, on the one hand, and with modified normative rules on the other. But they leave many questions unresolved. Webber's view leans heavily on the means of making the procedures of planning more effective within relatively strict limits to action. As a guide to procedures it expands the conception of "adaptive" planning by providing a model of purposive adaptation. It is weaker on the subject of the norms which are the substantive ends of the process, and for which efficiency and effectiveness are servants. The norm of reducing error is a very general one. In an overtly interventionist activity one needs more specific substance for his purpose if he is to defend the action. It is difficult to discern, in Webber's model, who is ultimately guiding the action.

John Friedmann has made the question of leadership central in his theory of *transactive planning*. In his view, the convergence of certain social and historical ideological movements has produced the conditions for a learning exchange between the planner and his client, a dialogue through which a self-activating society can be realized.[19] The model of guidance is close to that advocated by Etzioni. Like Etzioni, Friedmann seems to take the expert class as given; there are planners and there are clients. How each got to his role, or how they might be exchanged, is not clear. As King put it, "The role outlined . . . is shadowy, and the author shies completely away from issues of equity; (one suspects that a true democracy is not being advocated here); trust (how the planner becomes accepted enough that his clients believe he will act in their best interests); and power (which is crucial to implementation)."[20]

While his theory may appear elitist to some, Friedmann has the virtue of rooting it in real society. It is not an argument by analogy with organizational or biological systems. Friedmann's planner is respectful of the "other," and enters openly in dialogue with him. But he doesn't offer to change places with him. There are those who have one kind of knowledge and those who have another. Thus he appears to protect professionalism—if the professional is a wise man. The planner in this formulation does not have to defend his legitimacy—it is somehow conferred upon him. (King calls this "trust.") His power to implement is presumably based on persuasion. The theory rests on a partial and questionable theory of the state (the emergent self-activating society), and on an unsubstantiated legitimation of planning.

The "advocate planners" challenge both of these. In their view, the state is the creature of dominant interests and the planner is the servant of those interests. Therefore, countervailing plans which represent the interests of the underrepresented are needed. These plans become the embodiment of the interests of the voiceless. In is interpretation by practicing planners this position becomes cloudy. Sometimes it resembles the adversary model of truth-seeking espoused by Paul Davidoff.[21] This model rests implicity on analogy with the representation of interests in the Law. At other times it takes on radical overtones of class interests. Still others interpret it as raw activism. The need for counter-planning is an obvious response to the bureaucratization of city and regional planning. But the sources of legitimacy of the advocate planners are uncertain. Lisa Peattie and other critics have demonstrated that the advocate planners, as intellectuals and professionals, may be suspect in communities they seek to represent, whose members are neither of those.[22] Such communities, moreover, may have no more consensus on plans than the society as a whole. Clearly, the great weakness of the advocacy planning movement is that it lacks a view of the whole social system. Without that view, its very rationality comes into question. It is difficult to relate the partial actions of the advocates with broader social objectives, except in the case of those whose view is based on the role of classes in the society. And even there the case is hard to make that communities are equivalent to classes. Davidoff thought that the advocacy model would improve rationality in a pluralistic society by allowing for a fuller representation of interests, but his idea of the pluralist society is not fully fleshed-out.

The culture of planning cannot dispense with the need for rationality. The German social philosopher Jurgen Habermas asserts flatly: "The choice of a concept of rationality is decisive for the structure of a planning theory." [23] Habermas, who seeks to synthesize Max Weber, Marx, the neo-Hegelians and some strands of Existentialism in his works, has the most ambitious classification of the uses of rationality that I have encountered. Habermas has classified three major modes of rationality. I will take up his argument in some detail because it offers one organizational frame for the struggles for a planning theory.

The three modes are *purposive rationality, systems rationality,* and *practical rationality.* In the first, "The model of rational action is suited to theories of rational choice and to planning techniques in areas of strategic action. The limits of the model can be seen, however, in the attempt to develop empirically substantive theories of social systems. The theoretical strategy of choosing the concept of subjective rationality of action means a prior decision for normativistic approaches and for methodological individualism." [24] In this class one would lump both the traditional optimizing models of economics and the modified bureaucratic models of the incrementalists. It would also include much of the public choice theorizing (e.g., in Downs, Buchanan and Tullock, and Mancur Olson) which has emerged since Arrow played Pandora and let the Genie out of the box. For these theories preserve the individual as the point of reference (even when he is the politician) and focus on his strategic actions.

In the second mode, "Planning theories laid out in *systems theoretic*" terms are based on a concept of objective rationality that is taken from the paradigm of self-regulated systems. The pattern of *systems rationality* is suited for empirically substantive theories about object domains in which unities that are clearly demarcated from their environment can be identified. Then (but only then) stability or instability can be determined on the basis of a systems maintenance accessible to experience.[25] In this class belong many of the planning models of the systems era. In this spirit we find the work of Churchman, Emery and Trist, Dror, Etzioni and others. As Churchman has often stressed, an essence of the system is a need to postulate the objective teleology of the system. This is a critical point of difference among the writers, but is recognized by all. Thus, for example, Etzioni, in his work *The Active Society* postulates a set of "fundamental needs" of the social system. Others, following the early work of Merton and Parsons, have a "structural" model of the system in which the "functions" or roles depend upon and reinforce the structure. Emery and Trist describe this view as follows: "They have found their main business to be in the analysis of a specific bureaucracy as a complex social system, concerned less with the individual differences of the actors than with the situationally shaped roles they perform." [26] Some studies of the planning profession have combined this role view with the sociology of profession's tradition of Everet Hughes, notably those of Altshuler and Rabinovitz.[27]

Habermas concludes, in his third mode, "Finally, planning theories laid out in *communications-theoretic* terms are based on a concept of practical rationality that can be gained from the paradigm of will-forming discourse (and which can be developed in the form of a consensus theory of truth) . . . It is suited to the critical investigation of constellations of interest that are at the basis of normative structures. This procedure of normative genesis must, of course, be connected to the systems-theoretic approach if it is to contribute to a suitable theory of social evolution." [28] In this formulation, *purposive rationality* leads to diverse strategic planning techniques; *systems rationality* yields bio- or organizational cybernetics, the theory of planning as a political process, and universal functionalism; and *practical rationality* gives us a critical theory of society.

We should note that the keystone of the Habermas *practical rationality* is a "communicative planning." This issue is most explicitly addressed in the work of John Friedmann on "transactive planning." The difference between the works of Habermas and Friedmann is that the end of the Habermas type of planning is the critical examination of society and its ultimate restructuring on the basis of the critical findings. The bulk of the *Legitimation Crisis* is devoted to a critique of the modern state, which Habermas sees to be in a crisis of legitimacy. This is the most important aspect of that work. And it is this emphasis which I wish to address in the final section of the paper.

Planning and the State

The third major crisis of American planning is that of its relations to the American state. We have seen that the advocate planners have posed critical questions about the present political orientation of planning, but lacked complete view of the socio-political system in which they operated. In short, they suffered from an imprecise view about the kind of state they envisaged. Other theories either had romantic visions of power and implementation, or took the legitimacy and the authority of planners for granted. And many others simply do not know what kind of state they are talking about.

American planning thought has suffered from more or less unconscious elitism. The guidance theory of Etzioni and Friedmann is unconscious of the implications of assignment of leadership to the "guides." Dror (admittedly an Israeli) has stressed the validity of utopian rationality in administrative planning. These intellectuals of planning, along with the practicing bureaucrats of planning, have been the targets of a barrage of criticism emanating from conservative quarters. Irving Kristol and Nathan Glazer have published a stream of articles in the *Public Interest* pointing to the futility or the presumptions of specific planning proposals. Aaron Wildavsky, in a series of papers, has berated planners for their lack of understanding of *realpolitik*. The presumption of power by planners has provoked a counter-elitism of political savants.

Planning is nothing without politics, we are told, and the rationalism of planning avails naught against the realities of politicians. Is it because planning is utopian in its vision of rational or scientific politics, or because planners are so unworldly? Do they not understand the workings of the political system? In particular, do they not understand power?

Certainly American planners, particularly city planners, have contributed little to the study of their own situation or to the ideas about American government. It is no accident that the best studies of American city planning have been done by political scientists such as Altshuler and Rabinovitz. The only important views on the crucial place of the organization of the state for planning have been those—admittedly somewhat utopian and elitist, but creative—of Rexford Tugwell.[29] At times ideas from abroad have entered our planning literature, as in Dror's views of the "metasystem" of planning. Planners have ignored Daniel Bell's emphasis on the theory of the "public household." [30]

The condition of planning *vis-à-vis* the state in which it is to be located is not confused so much as it is insentient. Planning is *in* politics, and cannot escape politics, but it is not politics. If it is to be effective it will be more or less institutionalized—either as government planning or as counter-planning. Once institutionalized it must face a set of problems of the most intractable sort. These include the dynamic conservatism observed in institutions by Donald Schon;[31] the ubiquity of ill-defined and therefore "wicked" problems first described by Churchman [32] and applied to planning by Rittel and Webber;[33] the powerful incentives to politics to be couched in ambiguous statements, demonstrated by Downs;[34] the obduracy of individual interests; the gaps in our sciences of social and individual behavior; and its lack of understanding of the political system in which it is situated.

At best the planner does not retreat to the precision of technical competence at the cost of social relevance. But he faces technical and political problems which require ideological guidance. And he lives in a political world whose characteristics are often at odds with his ideology of reason. This is true whatever his world: in the states of capitalist electoral democracies he faces organized interests, the power of capital, and the deliberate obfuscations of the politicians; in the socialist states he faces the fundamental confusion of socialist ideology about planning, the conservatism of bureaucracies, and uncertainties about his professionalism in the socialist system.

Martin Meyerson, in the speech cited earlier, spoke of the obstacles facing planning in America. He noted: doubts about leaders; inexact forecasting devices; and a reluctance to experiment. We could freely add to this list, but it is worth noting that the first obstacle is a political one, the second is technical, and the third combines the political and the technical. This division can stand as a paradigm for the types of problems encountered by planning in our society. Some difficulties are political, some technical, some both. They pertain to both capitalist and socialist societies. I have not discussed the technical difficulties—they are well known to the planners. The political ones are less well known. Yet they are pressing in any modern state.

For the modes of politics and the ideologies of planning are not the same. Some confusion on this point was contributed by incomplete Marxism. In a relatively undeveloped argument, Marxists argued that they were going to replace an organization of society by market (Marx said "commodity") relations by an organization of society by means of planned relations. That is, many Marxists saw planning as integral to political ideology and a basis for organizing the state. In fact, we have learned, it is no more integral to the idea of realizing the socialist state than the capitalist one, and in any event, it smacks of statism to many younger socialists. At best, it has left many socialists confused. For example, Vladimir Bakarić, in a recent article, complains: "Actually, I was not referring to lectures and the teachings of Marx's works. What I wanted to say was that all of this has not provided the necessary concrete background for the changes which should be carried out in the socio-economic system. In a word, the active element was missing." [35]   At worst, some socialists feel planning will have to disappear before the state itself can disappear; others believe it will be necessary to secure the dissolution of the oppressing state by planning.

In fact, I believe that planning is an instrument of the state, and where the state exists cannot be separated from the environment of that state, but is nonetheless an independent intellectual creation whose ideology has grown up in a variety of states, and whose uses have been turned to the advantage of many, states and non-states. In this light, I view the connection of planning with socialism as unformulated and incomplete. Were I to be a free interpreter of history, I would identify it closely with the desire of Marx for a more humane allocative system, and with the fundamental rationalism to which Marx adhered all his life. Marx and Engels viewed communism as the abolition of the state, which Marx saw as a form of oppression, through an intervening period in which planning would supersede the capitalist relations. But what was to be the role of planning was never precise.

This at least had the virtue of a clear conception of the state. We have learned—sometimes to our regret—that the independent development of planning can be used in the service not only of the state, but for the maintenance of the most oppressive states. Indeed, the strength of planning is sometimes in proportion to the conservatism of the state, as Stephen Cohen has shown in his study of French capitalist planning. In American planning we lack the vision of what kind of state and what kind of politics we want. We indulge this ignorance at our peril, both as planners and as citizens. Certainly this is a most pressing challenge to creative planning thinking.

Planning and politics are not the same, but it is true that what we do as public actors is always political, especially since when planning is effective it makes allocations of property rights, and every allocation is in some sense a political one. Moreover, as Engels made clear, property is at the heart of state organization. Every land use decision, every transportation decision, every economic strategy has a political content in the sense that the distribution of benefits and costs of that action falls unequally on people. We can have no illusions about our work in this regard. In this light it is all the more remarkable that American planning has largely ignored the organization of the state. Planning can make itself useful to the state without regard to the nature of the state. In that direction lies the dangers pointed out by Bertram Gross, Irving Horowitz and others. But it can also draw on the independence of its intellectual resources to mount a major criticism of the modern state. Only by performing this critical function can it achieve ultimate substantive rationality and be true to its intellectual charge.

NOTES

1. Charles E. Merriam, *Systematic Politics* (Chicago: University of Chicago Press, 1945): 336.

2. Salvador Padilla, ed., *Tugwell's Thoughts on Planning* (University of Puerto Rico Press, 1974): 27-28.

3. In a paper published ten years ago I observed that "the social democracy which is a precondition to collective social planning in a political democracy depends on social gains which will be engineered, for the most part, from Washington. The achievement of economic democracy, the securing of equality in civil rights, the abolition of gross regional differences in education, and other major social gains will be forged by federal power, or not at all." (J. W. Dyckman, "Social Planning, Social Planners and Planned Society," *Journal of the American Institute of Planners* 32 (1966): 66-76. This quote is cited in Andreas Faludi, *Planning Theory* (Oxford: Pergamon Press, 1973): 193. Faludi feels that the built-in atomism of American society is responsible for the inclination of American writers to "advocate a certain amount of centralization as a precondition of effective implementation of social policy."

4. Martin Meyerson, "The Next Challenge for the Urban Planner," *Journal of the American Institute of Planners* (Oct. 1976).

5. Peter H. Schuck, "National Economic Planning: A Slogan Without Substance," *The Public Interest* (Fall 1976): 68.

6. Ibid., p. 9.

7. See, for example, Peter Gordon, "A Note on Political Ambiguity," Peter Gordon and James D. Hess, mimeographed paper, Department of Economics, University of Southern California.

8. From *Vers l'armee de metier*, p. 200, quoted in Nathan Leites, *The Rules of the Game in Paris* (University of Chicago Press, 1969): 41.

9. Nicki King, "Planning Theory: An Examination of the Linkages Between Implementation, Knowledge and Action," Rand Corporation Paper P5161 (Jan. 1974): 14.

10. Henry Hightower, "Toward a Definition of Square One: The ASCP School Review Committee and Procedural Planning Theory," paper presented at the western regional meeting of the Association of Collegiate Schools of Planning, Port Ludlow, Washington, October 18, 1976, p. 1 of report.

11. George Stigler, "Economic Theory and Economic Planning," *American Economic Review* 1 (May 1960), reprinted in Stigler, *Essays in the History of Economics* (University of Chcago Press, 1965): 19.

12. King, "Planning Theory" pp. 1-2.

13. John W. Dyckman, "The Practical Uses of Planning Theory," *Journal of the American Institute of Planners* (Sept. 1969).

14. Ibid., p. 298.

15. See, for example, Harold L. Wilensky and Charles N. Lebeaux, *Industrial Society and Social Welfare* (New York: The Free Press, 1965): 284.

16. Dyckman, "The Practical Uses of Planning," p. 299.

17. Melvin Webber, "Planning in an Environment of Change," Parts I & II, *The Town Planning Review* (Oct. 1968 & Jan. 1969).

18. See, for example, John Friedmann, "Note on Societal Guidance," *Journal of American Institute of Planners* (Sept. 1969).

19. See "Transactive Planning," Chapter 6 in *Retracking America* by John Friedmann (Garden City, New York: Anchor Press/Doubleday, 1973).

20. King, "Planning Theory," p. 7.

21. Paul Davidoff, "Advocacy and Pluralism in Planning," *Journal of the American Institute of Planners* (Nov. 1965): 331-38.

22. See, Lisa Peattie, "Reflections on Advocacy Planning," *Journal of the American Institute of Planners* 34, 2 (1968): 80-88.

23. Jurgen Habermas, *Legitimation Crisis* (Boston: Beacon Press, 1973): 139.

24. Ibid.

25. Ibid.

26. The quote is actually from A. W. Gouldner, *Patterns of Industrial Bureaucracy* (London: Routledge, Kegan-Paul, 1955), and appears in F. E. Emery and E. L. Trist, "Socio-technical Systems," in C. W. Churchman and M. Verhulst, eds., *Management Science*, Models and Techniques, vol. 2 (London: Pergamon, 1960): 83-97.

27. Alan Altshuler, *The City Planning Process* (Ithaca: Cornell Univ. Press, 1965), and Francine Rabonovitz, *City Politics and Planning* (Chicago: Aldine, 1970).

28. Ibid., p. 140.

29. See, for example his papers on "The Place of Planning in Society," Puerto Rican Planning Board, San Juan, 1958; "The Fourth Power," in Planning and Civic Comment (Apr.-June 1939), and his important emphases on constitutional revision.

30. Daniel Bell, "The Public Household," *The Public Interest* (Fall 1974) n.37.

31. Donald Schon, *Beyond the Stable State* (New York: W. W. Norton, 1971).

32. C. West Churchman, "Wicked Problems," *Management Science* 14, 4 (Dec. 1967): B141-142.

33. Horst Rittel and Melvin Webber, "Dilemmas in a General Theory of Planning," *Policy Sciences* 4 (1973): 155-169.

34. Anthony Downs, *An Economic Theory of Democracy* (New York: Harper and Row, 1957).

35. Vladimir Bakaric, "Why Have We 'Returned' to Marx," *Socialist Thought and Practice*, A Yugoslav Monthly, Belgrade (July-August 1976): 67.

Seven Hills on the Way to the Mountain: The Role of Planning and Planners*

George Sternlieb

Introduction

One of the unending metaphysical hobbies of our time is attempting to define the respective roles of planning and planners. Its metaphysical nature refers to one of the lesser definitions of the word: "Beyond the physical and material; incorporeal, supernatural, or transcendental." Considering that planning is an exercise which typically is involved in the measurable—whether physical or otherwise—this may be thought of as a somewhat strange characterization. The justification for the description, in part, lies in the conflict and lack of complete overlay between planners and planning. The former have a relatively small role in the practice of the latter, while the activity itself, reflecting a real world whose responses and implementation are beyond the art form, is often quite unsatisfactory even to the players of the game. But people, even the professionals among them, are what they do, the measurement of their effectiveness and their social utility much more a function of the results of their activity than the avowed theory or credentialization which may serve as a veneer.

The paper that follows therefore, leaves aside the rhetoric of who plans as well as what is planning, titles and subjects which have been addressed all too profusely. Instead its function is to examine seven basic dilemmas of the planner in whatever garb he or she may be found. The list is far from a definitive one but rather represents a blending of conscience with the scars of personal experience.

I. Defining Virtue

Sin, while it may vary in the eye of the beholder, is I would assert, sometimes more readily definable than virtue. From the planner's point of view, this is particularly evident when he is in the business of delivering basic commodities. A lack of any form of sewerage, of clean and plentiful water, can with few caveats be seen as sins in the planner's lexicon. As societies become more complex however, the ameliorative measures de-

---

*This paper served as the basis for the Dennis O'Harrow Memorial Lecture presented at the 1978 ASPO National Planning Conference held in Indianapolis, Indiana.

signed to combat these sins of omission may have ramifications and consequences which, to borrow an unhallowed phrase, are "counter-intuitive"
in their impact. The planner within a society as complex as that of the
contemporary United States rarely has the luxury of contemplating simple
conflicts between good and evil in the abstract.

Virtue in a sophisticated world is much more than the complement of its
lack and can only be viewed as monolithic and simple in design and
concept to the true believer, i.e., someone whose goals are very clear, to
whom any deviation from those goals is inappropriate, any step toward
their furtherance, good by definition.

The profusion of property interests in a world whose linkages often defy
prediction, to cite merely one example, make a clearcut scorecard nearly
impossible. The sponsor defines the art form—defines the goal structure,
and thus very frequently the planner's goal structure is simplicity itself—
achieve what your client is paying for. But even here, clients—particularly
governmental and neo-governmental ones are actually unclear on their
goals. The planner is brought into a scene that may be more familiar to
the pediatrician than the logician, i.e., a patient who simply says "I hurt.
Figure out why and do something about it." Whether in the fields of
energy provision, job optimization or regional renewal, we are not faced
with a clash between causes which are properly identified specifically as
the sinners versus the virtue holders, but rather the clash between alternate
virtues or rivals; the furtherance of one may be at some level of cost to
the other.

An anecdote on the question of what is virtue perhaps exemplifies the
problem. The Center for Urban Policy Research was invited by the City
of Washington, D.C. to do a study of the cost-revenue implications of
condominium conversion. The City had recently adopted a rent control
ordinance and, as a consequence, owners of rental buildings were con-
verting them into condominiums. The typical case involved units in an
aging apartment house occupied by pensioners who had retired from the
State Department or other public agency on incomes of ten or twelve
thousand dollars per year. The current rental levies were on the order of
$200 and $225 monthly. The condominium conversion that was taking
place usually involved a fairly substantial amount of cosmetic rehabilitation.
The modular price to future occupants of the converted units was approximately $50,000 per unit, with maintenance cost of $300 to $350 monthly.

From the community's point of view condominium conversion represented a fiscal boom; more than a doubling in the value of existing ratables
per site. Yet political pressure was brought to bear on behalf of current
occupants and the city imposed a moratorium on the procedure.

The rationalization was clear. "Here are these people who have been
faithful to our government. They have performed well in their jobs,

worked forty years and now have retired. Doesn't society owe them a right to live the rest of their lives in an apartment house at $225 a month on Connecticut Avenue?" The answer most probably is: "Yes, these are decent people, in fact some of us may even know or be related to some of them."

Then a critic comes along to point out that the schools in Washington are inadequate and one of the reasons they are wanting is that there is a limited ratable base in the city. The fastest way to escalate the ratable base is to promote conversion.

So the question is "What is virtue?" Is virtue the cause and comfort of the retired individual living in a rent controlled apartment or is virtue the deprived child going to a poor school which, perhaps, could be a little bit less lacking if some money was put into it?

Now, my own definition of the planning role is that planners provide the numbers. It is the politicians who must determine the definition of virtue or blend the various spigots of virtue. One of the problems with providing the numbers as well as indulging oneself as an amateur politician decision-maker or public figure, is that the numbers then are presumed to be biased. If you package your numbers and your decision together, there is a bifurcation of response. Part of the audience says, "I love and agree with the decision that this learned individual has come up with and therefore I don't have to look at the numbers."

The remainder responds: "I disagree with his conclusion and therefore distrust and refuse to read his numbers.

It seems to me that a very modest base goal of our art form—and it still is an art form—is to provide some semblance of neutral ground, some reasonable statement of the costs and benefits of various programs.

Actually making the decision as to the preferred course of action, as well as a choice of the hedonic indices or the specific quantifications that determined the specific decision is not our business. It debilitates what is a very important and unique contribution of the planner—the numbers.

Clearly, the role specified here is one which a great many practitioners of planning would quarrel with, finding it much too narrow or, for that matter, completely unrealistic. In the former category, there are the exemplars of planning as philosophy; here the definition of goal structure is clearly one of the major tasks of the practitioner, the pursuit of its accomplishment essential to the profession. As planning becomes more and more a central complement to an ever deepening governmental role, the Europeanization of the process, i.e., the formalization of our priorities, stances and political affirmations clearly are overtaking the innocence (or perhaps the purity?) of the planner as technician. Whether one leans on Marx, or Rawls, or the neo-conservative movement, there is an amazing degree of confidence—(in my opinion, overconfidence) in the casual surety with which virtue can be identified. While I envy the surety of the millennialists, short of such teleological beliefs, the search is far from simple.

There is a second school of critics which, based upon a composite of Freud and Herbert Marcuse, decries the belief in the existence of neutralism. The planner in this view inevitably reflects either his psyche or the society in which he or she has been raised. Thus there is no technical input which is free from some form of subjectivism. And, certainly, there is much truth in these assertions. The very choice of alternatives which are considered may or may not reveal the limitations and prejudices of the planner—and the world of which he or she is a part. My only response is we must try, and try desperately, to maintain some semblance of neutrality. To do this requires not turning one's back upon the critics—but rather being aware of the strength of their arguments and attempting as much as possible to view alternatives, to self-scrutinize, to discuss and, most of all, to start at least with honest arithmetic, while being aware of its limitations.

II. Numbers Do Not Read Themselves

There is a favorite line somewhere in the Bible which reads approximately as follows: "Seek the truth and the truth shall make you free." Even in that most romantic of books it is a remarkably romantic statement. One may present data only to find that the ultimate decisionmaker rejects it. Similarly, much planning research is merely a form of symbolic gesture, a justification for a priori determined action or inaction. And that too is a fact of life—but it does not excuse imprecision. That is one of the risks of the trade. All too frequently, however, there is an even more important problem—the data itself, the capacity to retrieve it, to analyze and screen it, may fail to provide definitive insight. Numbers are, or should be, the prelude to policy. In a number of areas however, we are flooded with data—and yet, we lack its ultimate distillate-information for action. Several examples come to mind.

The *Annual Housing Survey* is a soup-to-nuts structured probability sampling of about 75,000 households. Within the survey a variety of questions are asked about housing. One of the original priorities was to incorporate a whole series of probes which would give some indication of what consumers feel about their housing. There was also a desire to move away from a simple counting of toilets and hot water availability as an indication of housing quality. So functional queries were developed "Does the toilet work? How frequently do you have hot water, et cetera, et cetera."

The results proved very interesting. There is remarkably little variation in the reported demerits of accommodations, regardless of the rent level or value of the housing concerned. The quality of satisfaction expressed is relatively constant from poor to excellent, in slum residences as well as penthouses. Within the state of the art, the criticisms that we get at a relatively constant level regardless of cost or its reflection, affluence. To initiate a policy of replacing low rent units based on age of structure or income of occupant is to ignore the reality of numbers. Both rich and poor perceive a remarkably similar proportion of their housing as good. And similarly, the complaints both in number and substantive area are close to constant.

Another example: The Center has been involved repeatedly in base-line data development as inputs to fiscal impact analysis— how many school-age children are found in a garden apartment, gross income multipliers and other such profundities. In pursuit of the former, in order to establish demographic profiles of residents of specific housing types, we developed a probability sampling of approximately 4,000 households in approximately thirty different towns. As a byproduct of the study a whole series of probes on the personal evaluation of local municipal services were incorporated. The interviewee was asked "There are many services that communities provide. How would you rate the following service—?" The blank was filled in with police, fire, recreational facilities and the like. At a later stage of the interview, we even tried to include measures of significance as well as evaluative indices.

The results are remarkably consistent across communities, if some of the more notorious urban areas are eliminated. About seventy-five to eighty percent of those sampled at the various sites rate their library highly. Police and fire protection also uniformly receive very high ratings. Sanitation and recreational provisions less so, etc. But these responses are largely indifferent to the realities of facilities or personnel. Even if one looks at the data over time, there appears to be no positive correlation between changes in expenditures and satisfaction. *What you discover is that the planning rationalist is probably wrong and the hypothesis of the shopper-consumer is probably right.* There has been a significant measure of locational pre-sorting, with residents buying the mix of levels of services, cum tax rates and shelter which they prefer. The planner may say (1) the people are too uninformed to know what's good for them; I as a planner must tell them" or, (2) "Underneath these calm exteriors there are all sorts of tensions, stresses, and unvoiced desires. By exposing people to the greater light through planning suddenly these will come to the surface." This is part of the great planning dilemma: control versus consensus. Thus while in many instances data (numbers) provide direction as to the necessary mix of components for successful implementation of policy, this is not always the case. *But the assemblage of numbers is our unique area of responsibility, and the reporting of ambiguity rather than the invention of results where they do not exist, a crucial element of it.*

III. Have Regression Will Travel

The tempation to give our unique possession—numbers—greater authority, greater meaning and greater insight, has been much enhanced by the
magic of the black box—the composite of the computer and the statistical
routines which it makes so deceivingly easy to get numbers. Unfortunately,
like every great technological innovation, the mechanics of the computer
have brought a variety of perversions in their wake. In general, the more
competent the statistician, the more modest he is toward the predictive
capacities and even explanatory powers of his mechanics. The converse
is also true. The size of the pretentions of the art form are inversely pro-
portioned to the true learning of its practitioners.

The use and misuse of data, deified through the printout, generated
without theory, analyzed without concept, massaged to keep the 95 percent
confidence level, are not unique in the planning field. They have been
joined by model builders in a variety of other areas as well. Yet the
process has been as brutalized here as anywhere else. Poor sampling
procedures and badly defined data probes abound as well as a failure to
report null findings. My plea here is not to reject either survey methodology or rigorous analysis, but rather to insist on the latter's use, not
merely as a technical term, but as a qualitative one as well.

In addition, we have seen too many studies which will take relationships
traced by regression analyses and blatantly move from associative correlations to causality. Again, the seductiveness of taking the statistical linkages
which at best are historical and making them projective must be fought
against—unless there is a worthwhile conceptual apparatus to justify the
procedure.

The failure to understand that at most the data and techniques provide
tracing of past relationships, reaches its culmination particularly in the
areas of the social planner. In mathematics there is a general rule of the
commutative nature of relationships, i.e., if A equals B, then B equals A.
In social relationships however, time intrudes as an intervening variable.
A may have led to B, but that was in the past; it does not mean that in the
future B will equal A. Perhaps an example is worthwhile to clarify this
issue. A whole host of studies have found that homeownership tends to
have a high correlation with good housing maintenance and satisfaction in
neighborhood, indeed, even with neighborhood stability as a whole. These
findings have been supported by recent rigorous research.

To go from these correlations however, to a policy which says "Let us
take a neighborhood which has bad characteristics and bad housing and
make it whole by fostering homeownership," is an enormous over-simplification, a gap which can only be justified by a fallacious reading of the significance of A's statistical linkage to B, a failure whose results are all too
evident as we institute B (homeownership) to reverse the neighborhood
tides.

Data analysis provides history, not forecast. It can serve as a base line, as a beginning to achieve the latter, but at most it requires a vast supplementation of ingenuity, of ingenuity, of insight, and perhaps most of all, common sense, to foresee the future.

IV. How High the Silhouette?

Whether the numbers are clear in their skew—and/or obscure in their relevance, the difficulties of merchandising them, of getting the public and its leaders to agree on a path of conduct, can often be a harsh and disillusioning process. A cynical description of liberals is that they are "Fascists out of power." The temptation to join (even for a good cause) those ranks must always be guarded against by the technician. The dividing line between presentation and advocacy is far from wide, from advocacy to preaching relatively narrow, and from the latter to viewing the opposition or even the less than enthusiastic follower as barriers to be overcome by whatever means are at hand—that line is practically invisible. There are all too many examples of this seduction which could be cited here—they serve as very chastening road signs to the practitioner.

Planners typically are recruited from the elite of American society. The schools which they have attended (and for that matter the society as a whole) have greatly enhanced the role of the activists—the leader—the doer. (Perhaps we should add to that list the active, successful anti-doer as well.) The temptation, therefore, of the technician to become the conductor of the orchestra is a constant; "to get out there on the line and slug it out." I'm not necessarily criticizing individuals who adopt the role of principals and of protagonists—but rather suggesting that the requirements thereof, and the life force which is absorbed in the process, tend to be antithetical to the planner's unique competence and to successful planning in the long run. Advocacy is a brutal master.

It must be realized that planners are not a unique subset of humanity. They are impacted—as are others—by the tide of current tastes and prejudices. A not uncommon disease of staff personnel is to try also to be line. This is particularly beguiling, given the power vacuums that open in local government combined with the leverage that access to federal funds may provide.

V. A World I Never Made

Genius requires an audience; planners require clients. The limits of execution may not be specific to the plans that are developed—but rather to the society in which those plans are to be brought to consumation.

Planners must accept the limitations of the time and ambience within which they work. Currently, for example, we must deal with an America grown fearful of its future. One of the few data sets on national optimism levels that we have over time is the Cantril Ladder, designed by Hadley Cantril. It's a very clever device. You show the respondent a ladder with ten rungs; the top rung is wonderful, the bottom rung is terrible. Where are you on the ladder now? Where were you five years ago and where do you expect to be five years into the future? A series of stylized questions is then implemented replicating the same procedure for: Where do you think the country is now? Where do you think it was five years ago and where do you think it's going to be five years in the future?

The Cantril Ladder technique has been employed since the late forties in survey after survey in the United States. It is now being undertaken fairly regularly on an annual base. It seems to be remarkably culture free and has been used in about twenty-odd countries. In general, the historical results have been very consistent. Americans were much more optimistic in terms of their country and its future than was true of any European country. The Germans, for example, were always flat. Their typical response was that things used to be a little better and, with luck, they will stay just about where they are now in their degenerate state.

Americans, on the other hand, used to feel that things were better than they were and are going to get even better.

Two years ago, for the very first time in a sequence which extended back to 1949, the American response in terms of the country as a whole changed to a belief that things were better five years ago and that, at best, they would remain constant five years into the future. There are signs of an even more negative note, "Things used to be better than they are now and they will get worse."

This is one measure of a new phenomenon that has considerable bearing on what planners can and cannot do; the felt limitations of the world within which they must practice. The population that employs them is increasingly more afraid of losing what it has than gaining a new and better life. The new generation of growth controls is even more consequential as a symptom than it is as an entity within itself.

Basic to this change is the decline of real income in the United States. This is particularly evident in housing buying power. It is not a momentary aberrant, but rather a long-term phenomenon. The age of cheap money in this country is over and with it much of what we used to attribute to American expertise—the American ability to get things done. The American capacity to deliver a better standard of living is associated with cheap money. It isn't going to be there and its departure is currently being felt. It is symbolized by the disease of multifamily housing. One out of five of all FHA multifamily mortgages, including those going back to the 608 Program, are now in default. The number is increasing very rapidly.

We are talking about a new reality: *the whole relationship between real income and housing costs has shifted quite abruptly over the last decade.* That shift has been marked in new one-family housing. It has not been as definitively measured, but is lurking on the doorstep, in multifamily housing.

And that is going to have very substantial influence on the capacity of the new Administration to generate new housing programs. Just as we have gotten out from under the disposal of the 235s, we are going to inherit a large share of publicly assisted multifamily housing. There's three and a half billion dollars currently in default; there will probably be another three to four billion in default within a year. The rate of private multifamily mortgages that are in default has doubled in two years.

Within this context, the capacity of nay-say, of stopping initiative, has never been greater and the capacity for throughput never quite so frustrating. It is entirely possible to put together a significant negative constituency for any social program, one sizable enough to halt any action. The complement of this, securing a constituency adequate for new action, is much more difficult. The frustrations of assembling a meaningful energy response are just the epitome of this broad phenomenon.

How does one adjust to the society of limitations after being educated to dream no small dreams? The sorrowful answer to that rhetorical question is that there are a number of people who do not adjust, but rather fall into the fantasy of wishful thinking, of seeking soft answers to very hard reality. This is epitomized in the case of the next topic which touches on the shrinking role of the central city, but this is merely one manifestation. The other is an increasing tendency toward millennialism: since this world simply is inadequate to bear my hopes and dreams, incompetent to deliver virtue, it must be changed. My criticism of both these responses is that they tend to shortchange the here and now, to deceive present-day clients who have present-day aches, and present-day needs, who cannot wait for this new millennium—and who cannot be cured, or at the very least succored, without facing the immediacies of reality.

VI. The Sick Man of the Metropolitan Region

There is always a temptation to soft-peddle reality when its harshness is distasteful, both to the analyst and the possible audience. The fear of the self-fulfilling prophecy, of predictions which become dynamic inputs, in and of themselves, of all the cliches that call on us to calm the patient—and the audience of patrons with planners placebos is very real. This is strikingly the case when one deals with a topic as un-American as decline. While one can sympathize with this avoidance mechanism, the price very frequently of Pollyannaism is failure to provide measures of a scale adequate to meet the realities of the problem area. One cannot cure cancer by calling it a common cold. The wasting disease which has afflicted the central city will not go away if we avoid the realities of racial and buying power shifts, of economic decline and a disappearing job base. The horrid facts of teenage minority unemployment cannot be appeased by turning one's back upon the demographic realities and pointing with pride to a handful of brownstones occupied by adventurous whites.

Planners who have addressed the central city problem have as a group faced the past rather than the future, to attempt a return to a past which was foreclosed by technology. And even this nominal goal of reinventing some "Golden Era" often represented fallacious history. As a consequence, they have encouraged the increase of the human problems that attend the city's increasing failure to serve as a successful transmutation instrument from agricultural employment to the new technological requirements of modern day employment.

We probably have had more than enough examination of the urban trauma, but let me cite a very simple but decisive number. Take all the people from 1970 to 1974 who migrated *out of* the Nation's central cities, multiply them by their income, and then do the same for all the people who migrated *into* the central cities during those same four years. The results show a decline in central city residents' buying power of thirty billion dollars a year and with it much of the capacity for boostrapped revitalization.

A splendid phrase was coined by my colleague Robert Lake when he said, "*The city, essentially spawned and developed by private enterprise, is now a ward of the State.*" I think he's right. A glance at the level of transfer payments, and the increases in those payments makes it obvious that the capacity of central cities to gear up for independent action will decline. Further, these past six years have seen a wipeout of a number of subsets that we used to think of either as planning regions or finite places competent to deliver services and infrastructure that could substantially change the lives of the people within them. An excellent example is the limited capacity of states to pull their major cities out of the hole. The recent near-bankruptcy of Massachusetts, the inability of New York State to cope with New York City, of Pennsylvania to support Philadelphia's fiscal squeeze, indicate the problem. The "fair share" bust and the inability of metropolitan areas to require housing opportunity for all incomes in a variety of subunits of government, indicates that planning at the regional level may be necessary, but is insufficient in the light of today's problems. Current history must be used as an input, if not an inexorable one.

The United States, regardless of the objections of conservatives and the newest of the New Left groups, is becoming a centralized entity. The shades of John C. Calhoun and states rights, or fear of "bigness" are often invoked, but the flow of funding dominance is national, bypassing the conventional channels with equivalent alteration inevitable in the levels of decisionmaking. Instead of acknowledging these changes and *optimizing* their implementation, we have left the development of alternate future urban scenarios in the hands of the science fiction writers, at the same time assuring our clients that Humpty-Dumpty could be put back together again, and that history would be reversed.

Yet, while it is easy from the viewpoint of the academic institution to turn to the leadership within a central city and say you must be prepared for a smaller and very different future, it is much harder to be a practitioner in the field faced with the potential loss of either job and/or consulting client in making the same statement. The temptation then becomes all too clear: to assure officials and community groups that all will be well as long as they keep taking pink pills—and renewing the planning contract. We have run out of time in this particular case. Can we afford to go through the same process in additional areas?

VII. In the Good Old Bye and Bye

One of the more popular approaches to avoiding the crunch of hard realities, of resource limitation, of popular electorates that refuse to acknowledge eternal verity—and the enthusiasts' proposals—is to advocate the world as it should be for the world as it is. The temptation toward millennialism, towards an imagined golden era, not to be achieved by the painful struggle with the here and now, but rather in terms of intervention from above (and we will come to the definition of "above" in a moment) is an enormously seductive one. Its current manifestation is to say that the SYSTEM (typically spelled with capital letters) is such as to be beyond redemption, its capacity for bettering individuals within it hopelessly encumbered by past organizational and property interests. As such it is doomed. Indeed, adherents of some of the extreme manifestations view efforts to intervene, to prolong its existence, to soften its effect upon the less fortunate as flying in the face of natural law, prolonging the agony, inhibiting the ultimate Second Coming.

In this context, reformers, gradualists, those who make efforts to optimize within the limitations, may be viewed as true enemies. Their practices, if successful, are seen as merely lengthening the period of relative discomfort, once again before the sweep-out of the old, the onset of the new optimal condition. To the religious fanatic of old, the motivating force which would create this latter state was the Second Coming. To the radical of the extreme left or right today, it is a more secular process in which present governing groups and institutions are swept away by alternatives which in their very purity guarantee the better life. The nihilism of back-to-the-Earth (an Earth which will soon have six billion people on it) joins with totalitarianism for the "good" cause.

Forever is indeed a very long time, and thus I will not take issue with the concept of the Second Coming. But for the moment, we are in the here and now, our business must be with the aches of here and now. Our responsibility is never more clear than in the case of the planner dealing with a current clientage to provide help without imposing too great a future cost. Our instrumentalities are limited, our vision is blurred, the society both in the great and small sense frequently obtuse. But none of these conditions excuse the failure to exercise our capacities within their limitations and to perform our roles. This does not mean that we deify the status quo, but rather that we cannot afford the luxury of assuming its disappearance. Millennialists have been tredding up the mountain and waiting for the sun *not* to rise throughout the history of man. The fact that their numbers are increasing does not mean necessarily that we should join them.

Practical Demand for Analytic Methods

Donald A. Krueckeberg

Introduction

The purpose of this paper is to examine the changing role of analytic methods as one of the urban planner's skills. We will attempt to examine what kinds of technical methods are used, how they are changing, and the stimulus for these changes. We are interested in the role of methods in two areas—(1) planning practice, and (2) planning education. Are the methods taught in schools of planning appropriate, helpful and adequate, as well as responsive to practical needs? Or not?

We need first to define what is meant by methods. We mean analytic tools and skills, primarily quantitative—or at least analytically rigorous— that are used in the practical work of urban planners at city, regional, and state levels of government. Thus we include techniques of survey research; statistical data analysis; computer usage for analysis; models of the urban pattern used to study and forecast population, employment, income, land use, and transportation systems; as well as economic evaluation techniques for impact and cost-benefit analysis, and for the scheduling of implementation. In addition there are quantitative models and techniques applied to problems of housing, health, environmental quality, social services, and others that come under a variety of rubrics such as operations research, regional economic analysis, regional science, etc. We will use the terms model, technique, and method interchangeably to refer to this array of analytic tools.

The data we will examine in pursuing answers to our questions shall be from a number of surveys that have been conducted in the past several decades among practitioners, planning agencies, governments, and planning schools. These twenty studies are listed in Exhibit 1 by author or analyst's name, year of survey, units studied, sample size, and the general nature of the questions or variables focused on by the study. The data fall into two broad groups for our purposes. One set bears evidence on the relative importance of methods to the field of practice as a whole, and in the planning school's curriculum. We shall examine these first. The other set bears more specifically on the usage of particular methods, their relative importance among one another, future needs as perceived by those who use these methods, and relative emphasis given various methods in planning education.

EXHIBIT 1

SURVEYS TREATING THE ROLE OF METHODS IN PLANNING
PRACTICE AND EDUCATION

Survey/Analyst	Date of Survey	Units Surveyed	Number of Units	Variables Treated
1. Adams	1953	Schools	21	Training offered
2. Adams	1953	Agencies	35	Training needs
3. Krueckeberg	1963	Agencies	109	Planning activities
4. Hemmens	1967	Agencies	26	Model usage
5. Cobb and Sweet	1969	Agencies	91	Model usage
6. ICMA	1970	Cities	844	ADP usage
7. Harman	1971	Agencies	954	Planning activities
8. Schon, et al.	1960-71	Planners	90	Skills used
9. ACIR	1972	Agencies	289	COG activities
10. Gerecke	1972	Agencies	52	Canadian planning
11. Jefferson	1972	Agencies	108	Methods: England and Wales
12. Thorwood	1972	Cities	268	Planning and management
13. Kaufman	1973	Planners	5500	Specializations
14. Pack	1973	Agencies	782	Model usage
15. A.I.P.	1972-74	Planners	476	Specializations
16. Isserman	1973-74	Schools	41	Methods taught
17. Isserman	1974	Planners	84	Methods used
18. Susskind	1974	Schools	63	Graduate programs
19. Pack and Pack	1975	Agencies	30	Model usage
20. Logan	1975	Schools	38	Social planning courses

We will move from a general discussion of the role of methods to a specific discussion of alternative methods. The final section of this paper will offer some interpretations of these findings—a conceptual scheme for visualizing how methods, practice, and education have been systematically changing in the past several decades, and some suggestions of where methods might be headed.

The Relative Importance of Methods in Planning

Let's start with the perceived needs of nearly thirty years ago. On October 12, 1947, the American Institute of Planners adopted a statement in Philadelphia on "The Content of Professional Curriculum in Planning" (AIP 1948). It outlined three levels of desired curriculum content: general basic education, basic tools, and specialized education for planning. The basic tools consisted of (1) analytic techniques, (2) presentation techniques, and (3) design techniques. Competence in the basic principles of the statistical method and "some facility with mathematics" was considered "a must for any qualified planner." Again, under the third level of study, specialized education for planners, the "analysis and planning" of "land use and population distribution" was singled out for prominence. "This field as it relates to cities as a whole is the primary field of the city planner and, if any one factor can be so selected, the most important in city planning." Housing, transportation, utilities and other government services and public works were discussed as secondary.

In 1953, with the help of the Bettman Foundation, Frederick Adams, head of MIT's planning program, undertook to see how planning education was doing in the United States. He did this with a survey of the curricula of the twenty-one professional planning schools in American universities and a survey of employers, asking a number of pointed questions about the adequacy of the training of planners (Adams 1954). Only five of the twenty-one schools explicitly mentioned courses in statistics, mathematics, and analytic research methods in their graduate programs.

He then asked the employers what specific technical skills were given too little emphasis in planning schools. Forty-five percent mentioned design techniques, 26 percent mentioned presentation techniques, and 29 percent mentioned techniques of economic and social analysis (half of those specifying skill in statistics and research techniques, the other half on costs and needs assessment). Harvey Perloff's important study of planning education in 1957 offers no conflicting evidence. But are things different today?

The AIP statement and Adams' surveys form an important base line against which we can gauge how much things have changed. They, as cross-sectional data, along with Perloff's more longitudinal study, form an important assessment of planning before the computer. Since the computer, we have seen the large-scale land-use and transportation modelling efforts of the late 1950's and the 1960's, P.P.B.S. and its analytic attendants, the use of regional science and operations research, econometrics, the era of simulation and social indicators and environmental impact analysis, and fiscal impact studies of the early seventies. All this has had a tremendous impact on the priorities of the field. Or has it? Several assessments, such as *Urban Planning in Transition* (Erber 1970) and most of *Planning in America: Learning from Turbulence* (Godschalk 1974) have tried to convince us it has.

Contemporary Planning Practice

But in 1974 Kaufman dared to suggest things have not changed so much as some of us had been assuming (Kaufman 1974). He pointed out that the leading edge is also a thin edge, and quite distant from the center of planning practice. Exhibit 2 presents data from one of his tables, to which one column has been added. The last two columns of numbers represent responses of 5,500 participants in ASPO's 1973 membership survey, indicating percent of members selecting each interest area of most concern (they were allowed to choose three). This is shown for all respondents and for those under twenty-five years of age. The first column of percentages represents the distribution of areas of concentration selected by 476 examinees who passed AIP's membership examination between 1972 and 1974 (AIP 1975). The AIP data seem to reinforce Kaufman's conclusions that few planners show interest in the "newer areas" of social planning, research methods, and health planning—neither the younger ones at entry level nor those at the level of professional examinations for AIP. Three other studies reinforce this seeming stability in topical interest in planning practice and relative importance of problems.

An extensive survey was conducted of metropolitan planning agencies in 1963 (U.S. Senate 1963). A later analysis of these data (Krueckeberg 1969) looked at the frequency with which various kinds of technical studies were conducted by 109 agencies. These results are shown in Exhibit 3. The group most frequently studied includes traditional basic studies of population, land use, transportation ,economic base, and land use controls. The middle frequency group covers a wide array of public services and works that also have been traditional concerns of capital improvement programs. The low frequency group tends toward newer, short-range implementation and policy problems.

In 1972 the Advisory Commission on Intergovernmental Relations conducted a comprehensive evaluation of metropolitan planning agencies, now called Council of Government or COG's (ACIR 1973). It shows few changes in the planning and policy priorities. Pollution, health, and poverty are the programs of high conflict potential and low rates of plan and policy adoption, staff time, and budgeting. Housing, solid waste, and economic development show significant shifts, from low priority in 1963 to relatively high priority in 1972 in terms of staff time, budgets, and policy adoption (1973, pp. 96-99). The 1971 ICMA study of the activities of 954 planning agencies reinforces this image of priority. City-wide planning

EXHIBIT 2
AREAS OF SPECIALIZATION: AIP AND ASPO PLANNERS

	AIP 1972-74 Membership	ASPO	
Specializations	Examinees	All Members	Under 25
Comprehensive Physical/ Land Use Planning	41.5%	19.8%	16.1%
Administration/Management for Planning and Development	20.7	17.0	9.7
Urban design	10.0	6.7	8.1
Transportation Planning	6.3	4.7	7.1
Housing/Urban Renewal Planning and Management	6.1	6.8	9.0
Research Method and Development	5.0	2.4	3.3
Social Planning	3.3	5.5	7.6
Economic Development Planning	2.7	5.0	5.9
Environmental Planning	1.9	12.2	13.2
Planning Law and Land Use Controls	1.5	13.1	12.4
Programming & Budgeting	1.0	3.1	2.5
Resource Development	—	2.4	3.2
Health Planning	—	1.3	1.9
	100.0%	100.0%	100.0%

SOURCE: The first column of percentages is from American Institute of Planners (1975). The second and third columns are from Kaufman (1974).

EXHIBIT 3
FREQUENCY OF TECHNICAL STUDIES CONDUCTED BY METROPOLITAN PLANNING AGENCIES IN 1963

Fr*	Group 1**
99	General Population Study
91	Residential Land Use
87	Industrial Land Use
85	Commercial Land Use
81	General Economic Study

79   Public and Institutional Land Use
79   Open Space Land Use
79   Highway Planning
76   Subdivision Regulations
75   General Comprehensive Plan
70   Parks and Recreation
68   Agricultural Land Use
68   Zoning Codes

Group 2

59   Schools and Educational Institutions
55   Comprehensive Transportation Plans
54   Sewage Disposal
52   Water Supply and Distribution
42   Policies and Schematic Plan
36   Fire Stations
35   Mass Transit
35   Flood Control Plans
34   Airport Planning
34   Capital Improvements Programs
32   Storm Drainage Plans
32   Civic Center Planning
29   Public Buildings Planning

Group 3

29   Housing Studies
27   Hospital and Health Facilities
24   Urban Renewal Programs
23   Solid Waste Disposal
22   Industrial Development Programs
17   Water Pollution
17   Economic Development Programs
13   Relocation Studies
10   Air Pollution
 8   Port and Harbor Development

* Frequency with a sample size of 109.
** Groups were formed by cluster analysis.

SOURCE: Krueckeberg (1969).

EXHIBIT 4
IMPORTANT PLANNING DECISIONS REACHED BY 52 CANADIAN AGENCIES
OVER A FIVE-YEAR PERIOD

	Frequency of Mention	
New zoning bylaw, revisions and amendments	40	— 40
Preparation, adoption or revisions to comprehensive plan	39	
		— 35
		— 30
Parks and schools	27	
Urban renewal-undertake it, abandon it, implement it	24	— 25
Establish, expand or reorganize planning agency	23	
Special area land use policies including development policies	22	
Involvement in, or affected by, regional or metropolitan planning	21	
		— 20
Freeways, major thoroughfares, bridges	14	— 15
Subdivision control and servicing policies	11	
Civic center plans and development; sewer and water projects and schemes	10	
Development control procedures; residential district plans; special projects; waterfront, beautification, mall EXPO	9	— 10
Capital budgeting; comprehensive transportation plans	8	
Annexation issues; promoting and assisting growth including land acquisition, regional shopping and new town centers	7	
Establishment of planning adjuncts; technical committees, planning commissions; one-way streets, parking, airports; public and senior citizen housing	6	
Industrial parks and programs; regulation of signs and gravel pits, others	5	— 5
Flood and environmental control; land use systems, and goals studies for comprehensive planning; rapid transit	4	
Institute community involvement	2	— 0
	Total of 347	

SOURCE: Data compiled from Table 4, Gerecke, 1973.

and project planning, zoning and subdivision administration lead the list of planning functions and professional time use (Harman 1972, p. 61).

These priorities are repeated again in the results of Gerecke's 1972 study of Canadian planning agencies on all levels of government. Exhibit 4 represents important planning decisions arrived at by fifty-two agencies over a five-year period, by frequency of mention. Comprehensive (land use and transportation, we can presume) planning leads the list. Various land use and transportation issues follow. Citizen participation, goals, and rapid transit bring up the rear.

Gerecke also attempted to gauge the role of research methods in this scheme of planning practice. He divided agency functions into five steps in the planning process: goals formation, research, data collection, plan preparation, and implementation. Fifty-six percent of the agencies said they conduct research only for special studies, 26 percent have a continuous research function, 18 percent have no research function. Gerecke concludes that the movement toward social and economic planning, as suggested by the statement of the AIP in *Urban Planning in Transition* (1970), had not materialized.

How Important Are Methods in the Scheme of Practical Skills?

In studying graduates of the MIT planning program from 1960-71, Schon and others asked respondents to check skills they considered very important. The results are shown in Exhibit 5. Data analysis, surveying, formal management techniques, and economic techniques all lie near the middle of the list of nineteen skills, being selected as very important by between 20 percent and 33 percent of the respondents. More technically demanding skills—computer programming and operations research—are viewed as very important by only 8–12 percent of the respondents. Clearly one must conclude that while less important than certain generic skills, such as writing, consulting, organizing, etc., the methods skills are relatively prominent.[1]

A more representative sample is no doubt depicted in Thorwood's sample, stratified by city size, of local officials, surveying the status of planning and management functions in city government. Officials in 264 cities were asked to indicate the important needs for improving planning and management in their cities. These needs are listed in Exhibit 6, in order of preference. Two analytic methods, information gathering and data processing, head the list. Forecasting was mentioned by 34 percent and "PERT, PPBS, etc." by 25 percent. There is a commonality among the three lowest ranking items: goals, evaluation, baseline data. They are prominent terms and notions in the language of social indicators. But like Franklin's comment about the carving on Washington's chair at the Constitutional Convention, it is difficult to tell if the sun is rising or setting on these concepts.

SKILL RANKING AS VERY IMPORTANT: MIT PLANNING GRADUATES

Skill	Definition	Raw number	% of sample
1. Writing	Ability to produce clear reports, memos, news releases, etc.	70	80.5
2. Synthesis	Ability to become familiar with and synthesize large amounts of material	60	68.9
3. Interaction	Ability to work with politicians, negotiation skills, ability to use and adapt to power relationships.	54	62.0
4. Consulting	Ability to work with client, assessing leverage points in a system.	50	57.0
5. Research design	Ability to formulate a problem and plan how best to answer a series of questions.	47	54.0
6. Community organizing	Ability to establish trust with local groups, skills in public situations.	37	42.5
7. Information retrieval	Knowledge of published sources such as the census.	33	37.9
8. Environmental programming	Discovering client needs and matching designs with those needs.	29	33.3
9. Data analysis	Statistical techniques, ability to use and manipulate figures.	29	33.3
10. Teaching	Command of a field, ability to present material coherently.	27	31.0
11. Original information getting	Conducting surveys, interviewing, etc.	26	29.9
12. Management	Formal techniques such as PERT, logistical skills, budgeting.	22	25.3
13. Economic techniques	E.g., cost-benefit analysis, program budgeting, input-output analysis, economic base studies.	18	20.7
14. Spatial design	E.g., drawing, using maps, aesthetic sense.	18	20.7
15. Evaluation	E.g., designing experiments, matched sampling, other assessment techniques.	16	18.4
16. Site planning	No definition given.	16	18.4
17. Computer skills	Ability to effectively interact with a computer.	10	11.5
18. Operations research	Probabilistic analysis, linear programming, etc.	7	8.1
19. Recording	Photography, film-making, video, etc.	4	4.6

SOURCE: Schon, et. al. (1976).

EXHIBIT 6

CITY OFFICIAL'S IMPORTANT NEEDS FOR IMPROVING
PLANNING AND MANAGEMENT

Need	Frequency of Mention (in percent)
1. Information Gathering	64
2. Data Processing	48
3. Additional Personnel	48
4. Multi-Year Planning	38
5. Land Use Plan	38
6. Training	36
7. Improve Planning/Budgeting	35
8. Forecasting	34
9. More Efficient Utilization	32
10. Government Reorganization	29
11. Introduce PERT, PPBS, etc.	25
12. Goals	19
13. Evaluation	9
14. Baseline Data	6

SOURCE: Compiled from Thorwood (1973).

Computers, Models and Methods: Who Does What?

Clearly if we are going to get some concrete answers to our question of the extent of methods used in practice and taught in planning schools, it would help to have a more specific review. We look then to three kinds of data that follow. With some overlapping of content, these surveys cover the extent of computer usage in planning agencies of various types, the extent of and type of usage of urban development models, and the opinions of practitioners as to specifically what methods should be part of the planning training and the extent to which current planning education is matching those expressed needs.

Hemmens conducted a limited survey of large planning agencies in 1967 to gauge the extent of use of computers for data processing and the usage of urban development models. Of his twenty-six respondents, sixteen were metropolitan agencies, six city, two state, one federal, and one consulting. Twenty of the respondents were using data processing, the other six were all planning to do so. Sixteen were using or developing models, three were planning to use them, seven had no plans to use them. Among those seven were five of the six city agencies surveyed. The major problems that agencies were having were a lack of adequate programming personnel and difficulties of accurate communication among the programmers and the planners. In spite of these difficulties, the extent of technical work appears extensive.

Data gathered by the International City Management Association indicates rapid rates of expansion of computer usage by cities. From 1959 to 1964 they document an average of seventeen new installations per year, and from 1965 to 1969, an average of thirty-one per year. A 1968 survey showed 30 percent of all cities using ADP in some aspect of municipal operations (ICMA 1970). By 1970 it was 47 percent.

Exhibit 7 is compiled from results of the ICMA survey. It indicates that among cities over 100,000 population, over 90 percent lease or own computers. The proportion of planning operations using computers increases with size of city, as does the variety of problems to which they are applied. Given that the proportion of cities having planning operations increases with city size, and of those, the size of their professional staff increases markedly with city size—given these considerations and without having all of the numbers, one can quickly come to this conclusion: a very large proportion of the planners in the country are in agencies that use computers.

This conclusion is reinforced by the finding of a survey from the Battelle Institute in 1969 by Cobb and Sweet (1972). In a structured survey sent to 226 agencies with what the authors feel was a representative sample of 91 returns (40 percent), only 30 percent of the responding agencies indicated no use or plan to use either models or computers. Of the other 64 agencies, 26 were currently using computerized models, 25 may use a computer in the future, and 13 planned no computer usage but may use hand computed models. The types of data collected by the 26 user agencies in the Cobb and Sweet survey are ranked by frequency in Exhibit 8. Note again the priorities—population and land use high, health and welfare low. Exhibit 9 shows ranking of these agencies by urgency of needs related to model development. This is particularly interesting—high priority is put on policy models, information systems, small-area data, and impact analysis. Standardization, sensitivity analysis, and behavioral models—these are not so urgent. This low emphasis on behavioral models is consistent with the data-gathering priorities of Exhibit 8, where typically dependent variables rank high and behavioral types and other independent variables (sales, zoning, income, assessment, etc.) are low. Again, of course, we have the rising or setting sun problems of interpretation. (Or is the imputation of movement a mistake?)

The most extensive survey of model usage to date has been under way for several years at the University of Pennsylvania by Janet Rothenberg Pack. Her analysis of 782 responses to a survey of 1,500 agencies does

EXHIBIT 7

MUNICIPAL AUTOMATIC DATA PROCESSING (ADP) AND PLANNING APPLICATIONS

City Size	% of cities leasing or owning ADP machines	Number of cities asked about ADP in application	% of cities asked, using ADP in planning	Mean number of applications to planning per user city
Over 1,000,000	100%	6	83%	6.6
500,000–1,000,000	100	19	53	3.5
250,000–500,000	100	23	57	3.2
100,000–250,000	91	78	35	2.3
50,000–100,000	59	140	14	1.4
25,000–50,000	39	206	5	1.6
10,000–25,000	21	—	—	—
5,000–10,000	11	—	—	—

SOURCE: Compiled from International City Management Association (1970).

EXHIBIT 8

TYPE OF DATA COLLECTED BY 26 PLANNING AGENCIES

Type data	Frequency of Mention	
Land Use	26	— 25
Population	23	
Employment	20	— 20
Housing	19	
Transportation Network	18	
Traffic Volume	17	
School	16	
Origin-Destination	15	— 15
Land Value	10	
Shopping Trip Behavior	10	— 10
Personal Income	10	
Assessment	9	
Zoning	9	
Retail Sales	7	
Agriculture	6	— 5
Migration	6	
Health	2	
Production and Other Economic Data (Input/Output)	2	
Welfare	1	— 0

SOURCE: Compiled from Table B-2 in Cobb and Sweet (1972, p. 245).

EXHIBIT 9

MOST URGENT AGENCY NEEDS RELATED TO MODEL DEVELOPMENT

Frequency of Mention

50	Planning agencies need better information system.
42	Planners need good, reliable small-area data.
40	More effort toward data updating is required.
39	A model to quantify impacts of proposed land-use changes.
39	Land-use and transportation models need to incorporate, to a greater extent, planning policy.
35	Newly developed census tapes should be utilized as they become available.
31	Simpler models which are cheaper to run and therefore may be updated more frequently.
30	New policy-oriented land-use and transportation models need to be developed.
30	Better forecast and allocation models.
29	More effective use of the relationship between aggregate forecasts and allocation to small areas is needed.
28	Agencies must obtain data at the parcel, block face, or census block level then aggregate to tract, traffic zones, etc.
23	Planners and computer programmers need to work more closely together.
20	A standardized package of land-use models similar to the Bureau of Public Roads transportation package.
20	A coordinated grid system, instead of census tracts, census blocks or traffic zones is needed to identify the specific location of all urban activities.
19	Sensitivity analysis should be included in all model evaluation.
10	Planning agencies need more full-time computer-system men.
10	Behavioral models—micro level.
9	Behavioral models—macro level.
1	No new models need be developed to satisfy the needs of this agency.

SOURCE: Reordered from responses reported by Cobb and Sweet (1972, p. 252).

not cover all methods of interest to us, since it is limited to metropolitan land use, transportation, population, and employment models, including housing models. Special purpose operations research models of basic or public services as well as non-urban development oriented analysis is not included.

Pack found about 25 percent of the agencies either using or developing models. Their principal uses are for projection rather than plan evaluation. The models rated most useful were of population and transportation, more than employment, land use, and housing. Exhibit 10 indicates the frequencies with which the agencies surveyed by Pack are either using or developing models of various types. While transportation and land use dominate both categories, the relative proportion of development efforts given to other applications represents a clear shift for the total distribution, as suggested by the last two columns.

EXHIBIT 10

MODELS IN USE AND DEVELOPMENT BY TYPE, 1973.

Type of Model	In Use		In Development		Total	
	Number	%	Number	%	Number	%
Transportation	126	39.6	14	17.1	140	35.0
Land Use	85	26.7	14	17.1	99	24.8
Population Projection	34	10.7	6	7.3	40	10.0
Pop./Employ. Projection	12	3.8	1	1.2	13	3.3
Employment Projection	9	2.8	0	.0	9	2.3
Housing	9	2.8	9	11.0	18	4.5
Environmental Impact	8	2.5	3	3.7	11	2.8
Fiscal Impact	4	1.3	4	4.9	8	2.0
Input-Output	4	1.3	3	3.7	7	1.8
Public Facility Location	4	1.3	3	3.7	7	1.8
Solid Waste	4	1.3	0	.0	4	1.0
Water and Sewer	3	.9	3	3.7	6	1.5
Economic Growth	22	.6	6	7.3	8	2.0
Income Distribution	2	.6	0	.0	2	.5
Retail Location	1	.3	0	.0	1	.3
Not Stated	11	3.5	16	19.5	27	6.8
Total	318	100.0	82	100.2	400	100.4

SOURCE: Data are from J. R. Pack's 1973 survey. This tabulation sent to author in September, 1976. Percentages do not always sum to 100 due to rounding.

The Pack survey was followed in 1975 by case studies and interviews with fifteen agencies on in-depth visits and fifteen more in shorter interviews (Pack and Pack 1975).   This followup study, however, focused on a narrower set of models than the first, this time limited to land use models that allocate exogenously supplied employment and population totals.   One of the most interesting findings deals with why models are adopted by an agency.

First, their findings clearly suggest, in regard to Douglas Lee's "Requiem for Large Scale Models" in 1973, that while it may have been a nearly accurate diagnosis of the patient's health at the time, the patient survived in spite of the doctor's deadly prognosis.   Thus the Packs found that in 1975 there was a substantial amount of modelling effort.

Second, they hoped to find evidence that adoption of models is a rational choice on economic grounds, or by differentials in growth rates and size of the problem area.   Not so; the single clear determinant of model adoption "appears to be the presence in an agency of staff members with some responsibility for program development who were educated in a technical planning or social science discipline or have been part of technical operations at some point in their job history" (Pack and Pack, 1975 pp. 13-14).

J. R. Pack organized a conference on models in 1975 (Pack 1975b).   Two types of participants appeared.   Practitioners describing their use of second generation land use models (e.g., PLUM and EMPIRIC) and scholars offering their judgment of the future and/or proper role of models in planning.   Pack concluded that while the second group of papers gives one the impression that impact analysis is the proper role for models, the practitioners and users of models are not doing that to any great extent. They are generally being used only for more traditional forecasting tasks. This seems a dramatic contrast between theory and practice.   But it simply indicates that urban development models do just that—forecast urban development.   Impact models are a different variety and, as indicated in Exhibit 10, are in addition to, not in place of, urban development models.

The important conclusion we draw from the work of the Pack project with regard to emerging models and the stimulus and causes of model adoption are augmented by a similar study of the adoption of analytic innovation by planning agencies in England and Wales (Jefferson 1973). Surveying agencies at all levels of government, Jefferson initially specified ten methods, relatively new or current technology.   Exhibit 11 lists those techniques and the percentage of agencies using or experimenting with them.

From a simple correlation matrix that Jefferson presents, showing the intercorrelation of the top seven techniques either in use or experimentally under study, I have performed a simple linkage analysis which is portrayed in Exhibit 12.   Two distinct clusters emerge, one around financial appraisal

EXHIBIT 11

FREQUENCY OF TECHNIQUE USAGE AND EXPERIMENTATION
IN 108 PLANNING AGENCIES IN ENGLAND AND WALES

Technique	Using Full Time, %	Experimenting, %	Neither Using Nor Experimenting, %
Financial appraisal	58.4	12.0	29.6
Gravity modelling	38.0	13.9	48.1
Cost-benefit analysis	35.9	25.0	49.1
Multivariate statistical techniques	25.0	21.3	53.7
Computer data bank	25.0	25.9	49.1
Cost-effectiveness studies	21.3	17.6	61.1
Planning balance sheet	14.8	18.5	66.7
Linear programming	13.0	10.2	76.8
Goals achievement matrix	8.3	14.8	76.9
Input-output analysis	3.7	8.3	88.0

SOURCE: Jefferson (1973).

—a cluster of impact analysis techniques—and one around the gravity model—more descriptive techniques suggestive of the gravity or multiple regression forms associated with urban development modelling. Indeed among recently adopted models, Jefferson's subject of study, impact analysis, seems most prominent; nonetheless, the other group of techniques is strong.

The other interesting aspect of Jefferson's study is his finding as to why these innovations were adopted. He was able to statistically attribute about one-half of the variation in adoption behavior to properties of the agencies (staff size, usage of consultants, etc.) and characteristics of the jurisdiction (crowding, tax rate, etc.). The Packs' inability to attribute significant cause of adoption to these kinds of factors may have been due to their narrower focus on metropolitan agencies. Jefferson attributes the balance of the variation largely to the same factor found important by the Packs, individuals who brought ideas into the agency with them from outside.

Practice and Education in Methods Today

We are now going to turn back to the problem we started with, the question of the match between practical demands and educational offerings posed by Adams in 1953. We turn now to what I believe to be the best set of data available: two surveys conducted by Isserman in 1973-74 parallel those conducted twenty years earlier by Adams.

Isserman's study is specific. He asked planning schools which methods, among a long list, were required and which were offered but not required. (He also asked some other questions we will not be examining.) He then conducted a stratified random sample of practitioners, members of AIP, with the same list of methods, to determine which ones they actually used in practice and in which they felt all planning students should receive training. We will now examine several plots of the data taken from Isserman's tables in order to determine the match between practice and education. We first take Isserman's data on each method reporting the percentage of practitioners who feel that *all* students should have a basic introduction to the particular method. In Exhibit 13 we have plotted that data against the data on each method reporting the percentage of planning schools that *require* a basic introduction to the particular method for all students. On first glance the impression is disastrous in terms of educational programs meeting demands. The 45 degree line represents equal valuing by the practitioners and the schools. Any points above the line would represent a proportion of schools requiring the method higher than the proportion of planners feeling the method should be required. The space is empty, but for the one dot representing 17 percent of the schools that have no methods required. Planners' opinions outrank the schools' requirements in every technique.

On studying this distribution, some patterns emerge. I have drawn my interpretation of the groups in Exhibit 14. The large, long cluster at the top nearly parallels the theoretical line of agreement. If we see the difference between the two as the effect of the 17 percent of schools having no required methods, then this group represents basic agreement between practitioners and schools, a set of priorities ranging from population and economic base studies through descriptive and inferential statistics, gravity and regression models, input-output analysis, packaged computer programs, and linear programming. The vertical cluster to the right represents a region of serious difference between practice and education, the most severe difference being housing need studies, then going up to related techniques of market area analysis, cost-revenue and benefit studies, and to questionnaire surveys.

The vertical cluster on the left side of Exhibit 14 is also a set of techniques that practitioners rate about equally, but which schools seem to give varying priority. These are all lower priority items from either point of view, however, and the priorities set by the schools tend to conform to the gradations in mathematical difficulty among the techniques.

The remaining two groups are more difficult to characterize. One contains two transportation techniques, the other crescent-shaped cluster, a miscellany of techniques, all quite sophisticated mathematically or technically.

EXHIBIT 12

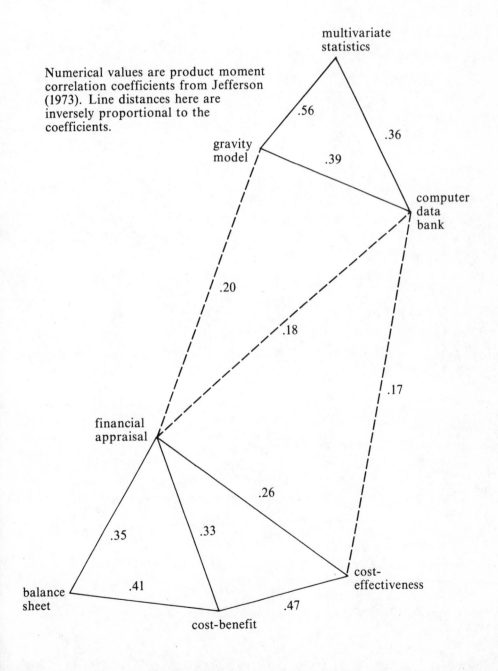

Numerical values are product moment correlation coefficients from Jefferson (1973). Line distances here are inversely proportional to the coefficients.

EXHIBIT 13

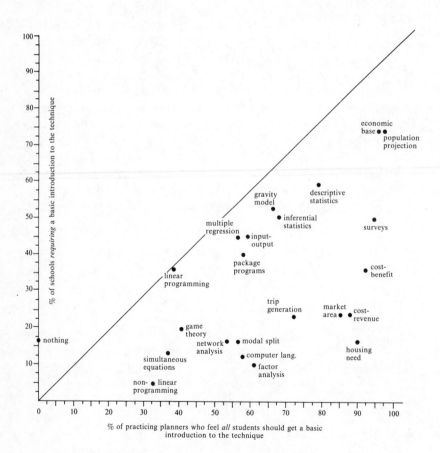

To some, the conclusion is obvious that the schools are not doing an adequate job. But in fairness, perhaps we should look at what the schools offer, rather than what they require. In some smaller schools an offering amounts to a requirement, even though it may not be so, technically speaking. Also we have just passed through a period in which educational fashion has been to reduce or eliminate required courses. Therefore, we have plotted on Exhibit 15 those same preferences by practitioners against the percentage of schools *offering* a basic introduction to the various techniques.

Now the schools look a little better. More than half of the techniques are above the line of agreement. Does this suggest that the schools are now leading the practitioners? Pack and Jefferson, after all, suggested that that might be the case. It is more interesting to look at the particular patterns and configurations. The two major shifts are in the location of housing needs and trip generation, reflecting their frequent study in elective courses in housing and transportation. In order to more clearly generalize the preferences studied in this data, the frequency distribution of each group (schools and planners) was plotted and class intervals selected to designate a high, medium, and low preference for each group. From this classification, the 3 by 3 crosstabulation of Exhibit 16 was constructed. The biggest contrast in preferences now is no longer in housing need studies, which shifted, but in the schools' high frequency of offering linear programming.. The cell of high practitioner preference, low school offering is empty.

Finally, I again offer my own version of a clustering of these methods, by rough subject area, in Exhibit 17. There are two economics clusters, economic base and input-output, more preferred by the schools, and cost-benefit and cost-revenue studies, more preferred by practitioners. The only other group, with the single exception of computer programming, that is entirely on one side of the line of equilibrium is the group of statistical methods more heavily emphasized by the schools. The large sprawling group containing population, gravity models, housing, surveys, housing market studies, and factor analysis form a broadly-defined land use cluster in my mind; a transportation cluster lies in the middle; and to the left are the operations research types of techniques.

Concepts of the Role of Methods in Education and Practice

We have spent a lot of time looking at a lot of data. We now turn to an effort to construct some general concepts that might help tie together those findings and help us perceive some general patterns in it all. We will look at four views of the role: (1) a pure academic view, (2) a pure practice view, (3) a core-periphery view, and (4) a dialectical view of historical thesis, recent antithesis, and emerging synthesis.

EXHIBIT 14

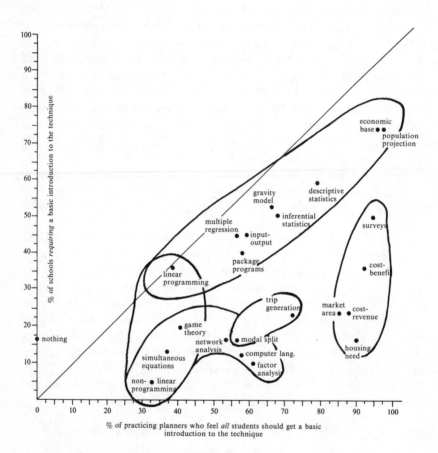

100-
90-
80-
                                                                    economic
                                                                    base ● ●
70-   ● population
                                                                             projection
60-
                                                              descriptive
                                          gravity   statistics
50-   model   ●
                                                          ● inferential
                  multiple   statistics   ● surveys
                  regression   ● input-
40-   output
                                                                                      ● cost-
                           package   benefit
30-   ● linear programs
                    programming
                                        trip
                                       generation   market   ● cost-
20-   ● game   area ●   revenue
                          theory
         ● nothing   network ● ● modal split
                      analysis   ● housing
10- simultaneous   ● computer lang.   need
     equations ●   ● factor
                                analysi
          non- ● linear
            programming

     0   10   20   30   40   50   60   70   80   90   100

% of schools *requiring* a basic introduction to the technique   (vertical axis label)

% of practicing planners who feel *all* students should get a basic
introduction to the technique

EXHIBIT 15

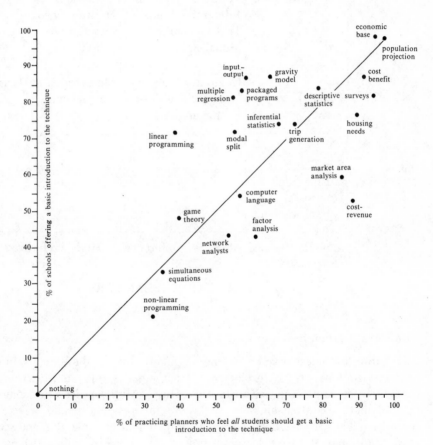

% of schools offering a basic introduction to the technique

% of practicing planners who feel *all* students should get a basic
introduction to the technique

EXHIBIT 16

CROSSTABULATION OF PROPORTION OF SCHOOLS OFFERING METHODS VS.
PROPORTION OF PLANNERS WHO FEEL ALL STUDENTS NEED A BASIC
INTRODUCTION TO THE METHOD

SCHOOLS			
High 70-100%	Linear Programming	Input-output Gravity Model Packaged Computer Programs Multiple Regression Inferential Statistics Trip Generation Modal Split	Population Projection Economic base Cost-benefit Questionnaire Surveys Housing needs Descriptive Statistics
Medium 40-70%	Game Theory	Computer Language Network analysis Factor analysis	Market area analysis Cost-revenue
Low 0-40%	Simultaneous Equations Non-linear Programming		

Low Preference   Medium preference   High Preference
0-50%   50-75%   75-100%

PRACTICING PLANNERS

The Pure Academic View

Probably the oldest way of looking at quantitative methods in planning
has been to look at its development (mathematics and statistics) as a
completely separate and self-sustained entity. Mathematics and compu-
tational methods, after all, do exist quite independently, and have for
centuries. Thus, it has been common for planners to view this endeavor
as a traditional stepwise learning process that begins with arithmetic,
and moves to algebra and geometry, through calculus, to more modern
fields of statistics and mathematical analysis. The way one learns is to
start at one end of this continuum and move as far as one can toward
the other end. One climbs the ladder. This view of quantitative methods
causes problems.

EXHIBIT 17

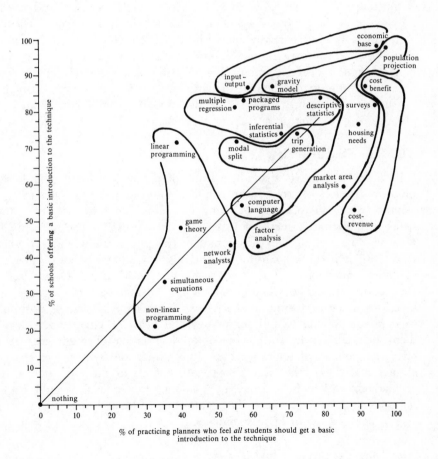

It represents an intellectually conservative view of a world of science and scientific truths and of mathematics as a logical, continuous, and tightly woven fabric of proofs and theorems. This is not a modern, pragmatic view. It is worth noting that the Packs found that planning personnel most resistant to modelling fell into two groups: (1) personnel with planning backgrounds who rejected models because of their mathematical formidability and (2) personnel with backgrounds in the natural sciences and engineering (other than traffic engineering) who dismissed the models because of their mathematical simplicity or from disbelief in the possibility of modelling social processes. One view says the ladder of methods is too tall. The other view says it is not a social science ladder. The problem with the continuous model is that it is only half true. The field of methods is only partially hierarchical. Both views are unfortunately erroneous and were perpetuated through the early development of planning curricula that relied upon course offerings in engineering and statistics entirely outside of the planning departments as the sole source of methods instruction. The pure academic model of the role of methods, in either practice or education, is not a suitable one.

The Pure Practice View

Pure practice asserts that all learning of planning methods should take place on the job. It rejects the notion of professional education in a university. Since there is no planning curriculum in this case, we cannot speak of quantitative methods in it, only outside of it. The pure practice view is a variant of the ladder model, the pure (traditional) academic view. In both cases quantitative methods is a subject wholly outside of planning education. Thus, two seemingly antithetical notions lead to the same result. The schools that require no methods training are open to criticism for perpetuating this view. The effect of such a position is to deprive individuals and, ultimately the field, of competence, leaving them indefensible in the technical-political arena of engineers, economists, environmental scientists, etc. In a profession born out of the conclusion that these other disciplines were not up to the job, such a view of methods widely held today by planning professionals would lead to self-annihilation. Isserman's data indicates, fortunately, that this is not a view held by any of his respondents.

The Core-Periphery View

The core-periphery view holds that there is an inner core of topics to be taught in a planning curriculum which perhaps should be required of all students; that there is a ring around that core of other, more optional substantive and policy courses covering a variety of questions; and that outside of that ring lies the rest of the university and the world. The core often includes planning law, quantitative methods, history and theory of planning, and design and plan preparation.

In the ring around the core, one typically finds an array of substantive courses in housing, transportation, environment, health, and more advanced courses in methods, law, design, etc. In the ring beyond that, lie the other fields allied to planning. It is probably the model most commonly subscribed to by planning schools, and a quick survey of the number of those that have a core of required courses suggests that something over 90 percent of the schools might fit this model (Susskind 1974).

The view has parallels in practice. The planning agency is one of a constellation of public agencies and private interests with varying degrees of interest and authority over certain problems. There are also parallels regarding the organization of methods and models. Pack and Pack refer to the small-area population and land use allocation models as "the bedrock of the planning effort," which are linked with an array of functional models for transportation, air quality, water and sewer, and fiscal impact that take the outputs of the allocation models as their inputs (Pack and Pack, 1974, p. 28). The distribution of priorities found in Isserman's data also suggests that some things are more central than others.

The Dialectical View

This model suggests three stages through which methods in planning are passing. The scheme is displayed in Exhibit 18. The first stage is represented by planning education and practice as they were structured, say before 1950. At that time there were not usually special courses that taught statistics, models of planning, computation, etc., offered by planning faculties. Rather, the models of analysis, as they were applied to various problems of transportation, housing, public utilities, demography, and employment were all imbedded in the substantive courses teaching these subjects. Thus, in a housing course, one learned something about housing market analysis; and in a transportation course, one learned something about transportation analysis. In a course on the comprehensive plan, one learned something about population and employment forecasts as part of land use planning. For more rigorous and thorough training, students were sent to departments of statistics, engineering, and economics. Similarly, in practice, methods were exercised by everyone at about the same level of sophistication. For more sophisticated work, planners looked toward the economists like Haig, Wright, and Hoyt and engineers like Goodrich, Bartholomew, and Lewis. (This was true, of course, regarding architects, landscape architects, and lawyers as well.)

With the growth of methods that occurred in the late 1950's and early 1960's, we saw a transition from this first stage, which we might consider a thesis, to an antithesis. In the second stage of development, which we are now in, the methods of analysis imbedded in each of the substantive areas were pulled out of those courses and centralized in methods courses. The methods and their application had expanded and developed to the point where it no longer made sense to have them dispersed in various courses. At the same time many specialists became available, through the training of Ph.D.'s in planning and cognate programs, to teach these new courses. This second period is the centralization of quantitative functions in specialized courses. There are scale economies that make this an advantageous arrangement. The level of mathematical competence that can be achieved under this arrangement is greatly increased.

What has happened over these fifteen years or so within the field of planning has also happened to the social sciences at large. New disciplines have arisen which have attempted to extract from the whole range of social sciences large packages of quantitative techniques which then become disciplines unto themselves. Witness the rise of regional science, operations research, and some of the policy science programs. The same kind of specialization appears within other established fields, as in the case of psychometrics or econometrics.

And in the area of practice, at least with regard to analysis, there are parallels. Model development, spurred by the advent of the computer and a mushrooming of federal funding, spawned many consulting firms specializing in methods and models. The specialized knowledge (and language) of these techniques and machines required the formation of special branches within planning agencies to deal with the problems and the consultants. Sometimes this required the establishment of special agencies, such as metropolitan transportation study agencies that were often absorbed later into more broadly defined planning agencies. Philadelphia and New York both stand as good examples of this phenomenon.

What the model suggests for the future third stage is interesting. One possible development is that the elevated level of quantitative skills in the field will afford the opportunity to integrate the quantitative methods, or at least many of them, back into the substantive subjects of the planning curriculum. I have seen this happen in some cases. This is especially evident in the area of environmental planning and transportation. I believe it is also on the verge of happening in housing and various social services such as education, health, and criminal justice planning (Logan 1975). The general result will be a more fully integrated curriculum of study with less dependence on service courses from other fields. The common "bedrock" methods, model building, tools of survey and statistics, and computation will remain most efficiently taught in centralized courses which will prepare students for advanced problems in application in substantive policy areas.

EXHIBIT 18

Planning Education
Methods embedded in substantive policy courses (sectors) of housing, land use, transportation, etc. Formal methods training in other disciplines.

Thesis

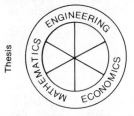

Planning Practice
Methods employed at fairly uniform level of sophistication throughout profession. Technical consultants making major direct innovative applications.

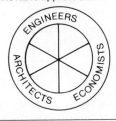

Methods drawn into specialized courses in the core of the curriculum. Heavy reliance on new quantitative outside disciplines for direction and teaching.

Antithesis

Data and modeling functions centralized within agencies and operations. Technical staff developed to work with model consultants (Rand, Consad, A.D. Little, etc.)

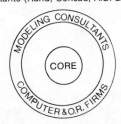

Core retained while methods and models redevelop and diffuse in substantive policy topics such as environment, housing, transportation, social services. Less reliance on outside disciplines for professional levels of instruction.

Synthesis

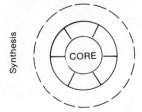

Core data and machine services retained in agencies while methods applications diffuse throughout policy areas.
Less dependence on technical consultants.

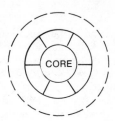

I expect a parallel development in practice. As the entering professional arrives increasingly well prepared in methods, the centralized modelling function will disperse throughout agencies. The development toward impact analysis documented by Pack, Jefferson, Isserman, and even earlier by Cobb and Sweet suggests models more tailored to substantive policy questions well beyond urban development forecasting. This general rise in the level and organization of methods competence in practice may not reduce the level of consultant collaboration, but it should reduce the dependence of many practitioners on consultants. We would still expect some core of data and computation services and in-house consulting to remain in a methods core. Many large agencies already operate under some version of this scheme.[2]

NOTES

1. Unfortunately Schon and his associates distorted these data somewhat in their subsequent formation of skill clusters (Schon 1976, p.198). The nineteen skills were grouped into five clusters using factor analysis. Most groups contained several skills, but "teaching" was a singleton. They then assigned individuals to groups, a form of weighting, using a rule that put a person in the cluster (as one valuing the cluster) if he had rated all but one of the skills in the cluster as "very important." Clearly under this rule, "teaching" got the same 27 persons valuing it as was the case in Table 5 above. The "quantitative skills" cluster contained data analysis, economic techniques, operations research, and computer skills. Since the last two were not often mentioned as "very important," and a person had to rate three of the four items as very important in order to "value" quantitative skills, the cluster ended up with only eight adherents. Most of the Schon group's subsequent analysis was based on this valuing, and consequently quantitative skills look quite unimportant in the balance of its paper.

2. I wish to thank Robert Beauregard and Michael Greenberg for their helpful comments and suggestions on various parts of this paper. I also wish to thank Robert Buck for his skilled editorial contributions and Vera Lee for her valuable assistance in the preparation of the tables and manuscript.

REFERENCES

Frederick J. Adams, *Urban Planning Education in the United States* (Cincinnati: Alfred Bettman Foundation, 1954).

Advisory Commssion on Intergovernmental Relations, *Regional Decision Making: New Strategies for Substate Districts* (Washington: Government Printing Office, 1973).

American Institute of Planners, "The content of professional curricula in planning," *Journal of the American Institute of Planners* 14(1948):4-19.

American Institute of Planners, *National Membership Standards Committee Annual Report 1975* (Washington: American Institute of Planners, 1975).

Robert W. Cobb, and David C. Sweet, "Computer Utilization and Model Development in Urban Planning Programs," in *Models of Urban Structure*, ed. David C. Sweet (Lexington, Mass.: Lexington Books, 1972):243-252.

Ernest Erber, ed., *Urban Planning in Transition* (New York: Grossman, 1970).

Kent Gerecke, "An Evaluation of Canadian Urban Planning." Occasional paper no. 10, Faculty of Environmental Studies, University of Waterloo. *Contact* 5,6 (1973).

David R. Godschalk, ed., *Planning in America: Learning from Turbulence* (Washington: American Institute of Planners, 1974).

B. Douglas Harman, "City planning agencies: organization, staffing and functions," in *The Municipal Year Book 1972* (Washington: International City Management Association, 1972):55-79.

Britton Harris, "New Tools for Research and Analysis in Urban Planning," in *Urban Planning in Transition,* ed. Ernest Erber (New York: Grossman, 1970): 192-202.

Britton Harris, "Planning Method: the State of the Art," in *Planning in America: Learning from Turbulence,* ed. David R. Godschalk (Washington: American Institute of Planners, 1974):62-85.

George C. Hemmens, "Survey of Planning Agency Experience with Urban Development Models, Data Processing, and Computers." *Urban Development Models.* Highway Research Board Special Report 97 (Washington: Highway Research Board, 1968):219-230.

International City Management Association, "Municipal Use of Automated Data Processing," *The Municipal Year Book 1971* (Washington: International City Management Association, 1971):36-50.

Andrew M. Isserman, *Planning Education: Madness in our Methods?* Working Paper 7504, Bureau of Urban and Regional Planning Research, University of Illinois, Urbana, Ill., March, 1975.

Andrew M. Isserman, *Planning Practice and Planning Education: The Case of Quantitative Methods.* Planning Paper 75-10, Bureau of Urban and Regional Planning Research, University of Illinois, Urbana, Ill. Paper read at 57th Annual Conference of the American Institute of Planners, October, 1975, San Antonio, Texas.

Ray Jefferson, *Planning and the Innovation Process* (Oxford: Pergamon Press, 1973).

Jerome L. Kaufman, "Contemporary Planning Practice: State of the Art," *Planning in America: Learning from Turbulence,* ed. David R. Godschalk (Washington American Institute of Planners, 1973):111-137.

Donald A. Krueckeberg, "A Multivariate Analysis of Metropolitan Planning," *Journal of the American Institute of Planners* 35 (1969):319-325.

Douglas B. Lee, Jr., "Requiem for Large-Scale Models," *Journal of the American Institute of Planners* 39 (1973):163-178.

Thomas H. Logan, *The Meaning of "Social" in Planning Curricula: a Review of Courses Offered in Member Schools of the Association of Collegiate Schools of Planning.* Prepared for Task Group on the Social Planning Concentrations of The School of Social Work and the Department of Urban and Regional Planning, University of Wisconsin-Madison, June, 1976.

Howard Pack, and Janet Rothenberg Pack, *The Adoption and Use of Urban Development Models.* Paper read at Conference on the Use of Models by Planning Agencies, 6-7 October 1975, at University of Pennsylvania, Philadelphia, Pa., Sept., 1975.

Janet Rothenberg Pack, "The Use of Urban Models: Report on a Survey of Planning Organizations," *Journal of the American Institute of Planners* 41 (1975): 191-199.

Janet Rothenberg Pack, Introduction. *Proceedings of the Conference on the Use of Models by Planning Agencies,* 6-7 October, 1975, at University of Pennsylvania, Philadelphia, Pa., 1975b.

Harvey S. Perloff, *Education for Planning: City, State and Regional* (Baltimore: The Johns Hopkins Press, 1957).

Donald A. Schon, Nancy Sheldon Cramer, Paul Osterman, and Charles Perry, "Planners in Transition: Report on a Survey of Alumni of M.I.T's Department of Urban Studies, 1960-1971," *Journal of the American Institute of Planners* 42 (1976):193-202.

Lawrence Susskind, *Guide to Graduate Education in Urban and Regional Planning* (East Lansing, Mich.: Association of Collegiate Schools of Planning, 1971).

Michael B. Teitz, "Toward a Responsive Planning Methodology," *Planning in America: Learning from Turbulence,* ed. David R. Godschalk (Washington: American Institute of Planners, 1974):86-110.

Thomas Thorwood, "The Planning and Management Process in City Government." *The Municipal Year Book* 1973 (Washington: International City Management Association, 1973):27-38.

U.S., Congress, Senate, Committee on Government Operations, *National Survey of Metropolitan Planning* (Washington: Government Printing Office, 1963).

Planning Education: The Challenge and the Response

William G. Grigsby

Forty years ago, the Dean of the Law School of the University of California, told entering students that only one out of every six of them could expect to earn a decent living as a lawyer. In the ensuing four decades, the legal profession has made things so complicated that, despite a huge increase in the number of law school graduates, nearly all attorneys can make a decent living at the bar, and a substantial number are thought to make an indecent one.

Judging from the discussion at this conference, the perceived challenge for the planning profession is to do the lawyers one better. And even if this is not the challenge, the response has been clear enough—to talk the subject to death. Both the challenge and the response are in the highest of academic traditions.

Whatever the real challenge—however various persons might describe it—one must worry that city and regional planning programs throughout the country are not fully responding, either in the education they offer or in the research their faculties undertake.

If one looks at planning education in the United States from the end of World War II to the present, I think it could be fairly said that for most of the period, the quality of that education went from bad to worse. In the late 1940's and the 1950's, we lacked the knowledge necessary to provide students with a proper planning education. Some of the needed theory and methods and facts may have been in existence, but they were largely unknown to planning faculties. By the mid 1960's when scholarly rigor, in the traditional sense, had to some extent been achieved, students rejected most of it in favor of things which, though important, planning faculties were not equipped to teach. So many planning students in this era received little education at all. Today the situation seems somewhat better. The content of planning curricula continues to be more and more rigorous, and the broadened vision which was imposed on us by the students of the 1960's has not yet been lost. There remain, however, troublesome old questions about planning education, and new ones as well. Let me mention a few.

The first has to do with the myth of "the planner." In both casual conversation and scholarly journals, it is customary to speak of the moral dilemmas of "the planner," of the best way to train "the planner," etc., in the same way one would refer to "the doctor" or "the lawyer." Yet in other contexts it is argued, and I think persuasively, that planning is a universal activity engaged in by all individuals and organizations. The myth is strengthened in the frequent discussions which contrast "the planner" with "the decisionmaker," ignoring the fact that on any list of outstanding planners appear the names of more than a few persons who not only have made plans but also brought them to fruition. As still another example of the myth, "the planners" are often blamed for the plight of our cities, even though the planners who are discussed in planning journals constitute only a tiny portion of those who determine directions of urban growth and development. If there does exist a group of "the planners"—persons with the power and influence that are often ascribed to "the planners"—99 percent do not come from planning schools, read planning journals, belong to planning associations, come to conferences such as this, or lack decisionmaking responsibilities. Planning schools and the so-called planning profession are very narrowly based. Whether they directly or indirectly influence the other planners in a major way could perhaps be debated. It is likely, however, that development of planning as a discipline will continue to flounder as long as the myth of "the planner" continues to confuse discussions of planning theory, the curricula of planning schools, and direction for the planning profession, if there is one.

The second troubling question is related to the first. Although conceptually there may be no such animal as "the planner," most students who are drawn into urban planning programs and most persons who call themselves planners do have one characteristic which distinguishes them from most doctors, lawyers, teachers, and other professionals. They wish to devote their professional life to improvement and reform. Indeed, when planning is referred to pejoratively, it is frequently by those who recognize and fear the reform instincts of self-identified planners. Persons in other occupations may be no less dedicated to change, but they usually work at it as a collateral activity. It may be wrong to push this idea too far. After a few years in the real world, many starry-eyed graduates of planning schools gradually become comfortable members of conservative bureaucracies. It is also true that planning is not the same as reform. It is, as Jack Dyckman has said, a way of looking at things. Planning theories and methods can be used to achieve a variety of objectives, not simply those which in some fashion enhance fairness and justice. Nevertheless, given the commendable instincts and concerns of planning students, it is worrisome that not a very good job is done in training them for reform roles, however modest. It is not possible to supply them with techniques for determining optimal solutions to complex problems, since by and large such techniques do not exist. And they cannot be taught how to implement optimal solutions in a political setting, since few persons in academia know how to do this themselves. Indeed, it is questionable whether much planning is taught in planning schools. Students learn a bit of quantitative analysis and a good deal about urban systems, but urban analysis and urban planning are, as all would agree, quite different. In any event, most sophisticated public and private planning and most urban reform is not participated in by graduates of planning schools. They do not have the planning tools to do so effectively. The situation could be worse. Melvin Levin has proposed that so-called professional planners take control of planning schools, a suggestion that, if implemented, would move planning backward in time and destroy it as a discipline. But to reject Levin's suggestion is not to ignore his concern. How to move planning education ahead should be a high priority for educators and practitioners alike.

A third disturbing question may not be generally viewed as important by persons outside academia, but it should be. A number of the papers presented here discuss in one way or another the challenge posed to planning by the changing societal environment within which planning takes place. There is also, however, a changing environment within universities, one which has equally important implications for the planning profession. A former colleague of mine recently observed that after 1965 or so, planning schools were no longer exciting places to be. By then, academic interest in urban problems had become so widespread that sociologists, economists and others having a scholarly attraction to such problems no longer had to find refuge in planning programs to pursue these interests. They could be appointed and promoted in departments in their own discipline. As a consequence, planning programs have found it increasingly difficult to recruit persons who are or will become eminent scholars. Unless this problem is solved, planning education will decline in stature, relative to other academic disciplines, and cease to be viewed with respect on university campuses. Such an eventuality could be very unfortunate for cities, for no longer would it be possible to attract and appropriately train the types of individuals needed to fill a number of important urban planning roles.

The problem *is* solvable. Because academic interest in urban planning problems is now so broadly based, and urban related courses so numerous, it is theoretically possible on many campuses for a student to receive a good planning education without being in a planning department at all. At the University of Pennsylvania, for example, planning theory is taught in four departments, urban economics in three departments, urban transportation in three departments, and the list goes on and on, involving fully eighteen different schools and departments within the University. The task is to organize this vast array of resources so as to produce graduates who in ten or twenty years will function effectively in influential positions. Unfortunately, academic inertia prevents this from being accomplished easily. Meantime, a related problem creates immediate difficulties (and opportunities) for planning schools. Again because of the widening scholarly interest in urban planning problems, graduates of planning schools must compete with graduates in a variety of other disciplines—law, business, political science, public administration, economics, and architecture—for planning related jobs in the public and private sector. It is still too early to say whether traditional planning programs will be able to provide these students with the training that will enable them to compete successfully for most of these jobs. It seems likely, however, that complete revamping of planning departments and planning education will be necessary. Whether, despite their presumed orientation to the future, planning faculties are equal to this challenge is a question which will soon be answered.

One final concern. Planning suffers from what might be loosely termed an identity crisis, except that the condition has persisted for so long that "crisis" may not be the correct term. The struggle for identity has been expressed over the years in two ways. The first has been a fear of takeover by alien forces, such as economics, systems analysis, the computer, and aerospace engineers, that have appeared on first glance to have had mythical powers that planning could neither overcome nor acquire. This fear is so well known that elaboration seems unnecessary. The second manifestation of doubt about identity has been the endless heated debates over a number of overlapping planning dimensions:

1. physical versus social or non-physical
2. quantitative versus non-quantitative
3. analytic versus integrative
4. academic versus professional
5. large scale versus urban design scale
6. policy versus design
7. urban and regional versus national
8. planning versus implementation
9. process versus end-state

These debates have typically not been very well constructed, which is perhaps why they continue today long after nothing new is being said. The lack of forward intellectual movement is discouraging.

None of the above remarks tells us very much about where planning education will or should go from here. A few things are apparent, however. In the last twenty-five years, planning has made considerable progress with respect both to its substantive knowledge of cities and the legal tools and financial resources it has helped to mobilize to deal with urban problems. But the ways in which planning of urban areas and regions—not only by so-called professional planners but by all those who determine the future of cities—has actually improved the urban environment rather than make it measurably worse, needs to be specified. Moreover, regardless of whether cities are becoming more or less desirable places in which to live, and regardless of whether there is or is not an urban crisis, metropolitan areas are confronted with three extremely serious and interrelated problems which, despite much public effort, do not appear to be lessening in intensity. These problems may best be expressed as questions:

1. Where within metropolitan areas will social minorities and lower income groups have an opportunity to live? This question relates to school busing, red-lining, unemployment and nearly all other presumably non-housing issues that divide urban society today. It has replaced concern over lack of decent housing as the dominant housing issue today.

2. In growing metropolitan areas, how can the natural and man-made environment be integrated so as to preserve the amenities and functions of nature without sacrificing other important values. Progress on this point is very slow and every delay translates into an unretrievable loss of amenity.

3. How can the decaying central portions of metropolitan areas be recycled and revived in a way that will give support to a vibrant urban society, not just recreate one-class suburbs in an urban setting? Much has been written on both sides of this question. George Sternlieb has described the decline of central areas in a tone that seems to stress the inevitability of the process, while Edmond Bacon and others predict, work for, and document revival.

At the moment, these problems are beyond resolution. New legal institutions are needed, because ultimately questions of turf and conflicting rights of individuals and groups are involved. As I have mentioned in another context, the city is like neither a reservation nor a sandbox. It is like a ship. It would be extremely difficult, perhaps impossible, to plan, build, operate, overhaul, and modernize ships if the rights and responsibilities of owners and crews were distributed as are the rights of citizens in our democracy. But this is precisely what must be done in the case of cities. This is the planning challenge. Recognition of the fact must be central to planning education's response.

A BIBLIOGRAPHY
ON PLANNING THEORY

Carl F. Horowitz

I. PHYSICAL PLANNING IN CHANGE

101. Alonso, William. *Location and Land Use: Towards a General Theory of Land Rent*, Cambridge: Harvard University Press, 1964.

102. Bair, Frederick H. Jr. and Curtis, Virginia, eds. *Planning Cities: Selected Writings on Principles and Practice*, American Society of Planning Officials, 1970.

103. Banz, George. "The Imperial City and its Alternatives," *Habitat*, May 6, 1974, 44-47.

104. Bednar, Michael J., ed. *Barrier Free Environments*, Stroudsburg, Pa.: Dowden, Hutchinson & Ross, 1977.

105. Black, Alan "The Comprehensive Plan" in Goodman, William I. and Freund, Eric C. *Principles and Practices of Urban Planning*, Washington, D.C. International City Managers Association, 1968. pp. 349-378.

106. Branch, Melville C. *City Planning and Aerial Information*, Cambridge, Mass.: Harvard University Press, 1971.

107. ————. *Planning Urban Environment*, Stroudsburg, Pa.: Dowden, Hutchinson, & Ross, 1974.

108. ————. "Continuous City Planning," *ASPO Planning Advisory Service*, April 1973, 1-26.

109. Buder, Stanley. "Ebenezer Howard: The Genesis of a Town Planning Movement," *Journal of the American Institute of Planners* Vol. 35, No. 4, Nov. 1969. pp. 390-398.

110. Chapin, F. Stuart, Jr. *Urban Land Use Planning*, 2nd ed., Urbana, Ill.: University of Illinois Press, 1965.

111. Christakis, Alexander N. "Toward a Symbiotic Appreciation of the Morphology of Human Settlements," *Ekistics* 40 (241), Dec. 1975, 449-63.

112. Christensen, David E. "Geography and Planning: Some Perspectives," *Professional Geographer*, Vol. 29, May 1977, pp. 148-152.

113. Coke, J. G. "Antecedents of Local Planning" in Goodman, William I and Freund, Eric C. *Principles and Practices of Urban Planning*. Washington, D.C. International City Managers Association, 1968, pp. 7-19.

114. Crane, Jacob L. *Urban Planning—Illusion and Reality: A New Philosophy for Planned City Building*, New York: Vantage Press, 1973.

115. Cutler, Lawrence S. and Stephens, Sherrie. *Recycling Cities for People: The Urban Design Process*, Boston: Cahners Books International, 1976.

116. Dantzig, George B. and Saaty, Thomas L. *Compact City: A Plan for a Livable Urban Environment*, San Francisco: W.H. Freeman, 1973.

117. Detwyler, Thomas. *Man's Impact on Environment*, New York: McGraw-Hill, 1971.

118. DeChiara, Joseph and Koppelman, Lee. *Urban Planning and Design Criteria,* 2nd ed., New York: Van Nostrand Reinhold, 1975.

119. Dorney, R.S. & Rich, S.G. "Urban Design in the Context of Achieving Environmental Quality Through Ecosystems Analysis," *Contact* 8, May 1976, 28-48.

120. Downs, R.M. and Stea, David. *Image and Environment: Cognitive Mapping and Spatial Behavior,* Chicago: Aldine, 1973.

121. Doxiadis, Constantinos A. *Building Entopia.* New York, W.W. Norton, 1975.

122. ————. *Ekistics: An Introduction to the Science of Human Settlement.* New York, Oxford University Press, 1968.

123. Dunham, Allison. "Legal Basis for City Planning" in *Columbia Law Review.* Vol. LVIII-5, May 1958, pp. 656, 659.

124. Floyd, Jeff. "Creation of Planning Ideology: Fads and Fashions from High Rise to Local Plans." *Built Environment* 3, 1977, 155-160.

125. Galloway, Thomas D. and Huelster, Ronald J. "Planning Literature and the Environmental Crisis: A Content Analysis," *Journal of the American Institute of Planners,* Vol. 37, No. 4, July 1971, pp. 269-273.

126. Garnham, Harry L. "Maintaining the Spirit of Place: A Guide to Participation in Planning for Small Towns," *Ekistics* 42 (251), 1976, 208-213.

127. Godschalk, David R. "Reforming New Community Planning," *Journal of the American Institute of Planners,* Vol. 39, No. 5, September 1973, pp. 306-315.

128. Goodman, William I., & Freund, Eric C., eds. *Principles and Practice of Urban Planning.* Washington, International City Managers Association, 1968.

129. Greenbie, Barrie. *Design for Diversity-Planning for Natural Man in the Neo-technic Environment: The Ethological Approach,* New York: Elsevier, 1976, 209 pp.

130. Gutman, Robert, ed. *People and Buildings,* New York: Basic Books, 1973.

131. Hall, Peter. *The Theory and Practice of Regional Planning.* London: Pemberton, 1970.

132. Harary, F. & Rockey, J. "A City is Not a Semilattice Either," *Environment and Planning,* 8, 1976, 375-384.

133. Hester, Randolph T. *Neighborhood Space: Use, Needs and Design Responsibility,* Stroudsburg, Pa.: Dowden, Hutchinson, & Ross, 1975.

134. Holling, C.S. and Goldberg, M.A. "Ecology and Planning," *Journal of the American Institute of Planners,* Vol. 37, No. 4, July 1971, pp. 221-230.

135. Houghton-Evans, William. *Planning Cities: Legacy and Portent,* London: Lawrence & Wishart, 1975.

136. Kantarowitch, Ray. "Architectural Utopias: The City Planning Theories of Frank Lloyd Wright and Le Corbusier," *Task* 2, 1941, 30-35.

137. Levin, Melvin R. *Community and Regional Planning*, 2nd ed., New York: Praeger, 1977.

138. Lynch, Kevin. *The Image of the City*, Cambridge, Mass.: MIT Press, 1960.

139. ————. *Site Planning*, Cambridge, Mass.: MIT Press, 1971.

140. Madge, Robert. "Planning by Ideals: The Utopian Trap," *Built Environment* 4, 1975, 66-75.

141. Marsh, William M., ed. *Environmental Analysis for Land Use and Site Planning*, New York: McGraw-Hill, 1978.

142. Mazarec, Robert C. "Let's Put the Plan Back into Planning," *Planning*, May 1977, pp. 12-19.

143. McHarg, Ian. *Design with Nature*, Garden City, N.Y.: Doubleday, 1969.

144. Mocine, Corwin R. "Urban Physical Planning and the New Planning," *Journal of the American Institute of Planners*, Vol. 32 No. 3, July 1966 pp. 26-40.

145. Moseley, M.J. *Growth Centres in Spatial Planning*, New York: Pergamon Press, 1974.

146. Mumford, Lewis. "Arthur Glikson: The Planner as Ecologist," *Journal of the American Institute of Planners*, Vol. 38, No. 1, January 1972, pp. 3-10.

147. Newton, Norman T. *Design on the Land*, Cambridge, Mass.: Harvard University Press, 1973.

148. Papageoriou, Alexander. *Continuity and Change: Preservation City Planning*, New York: Praeger, 1971.

149. Perloff, Harvey S. and Sandberg, Neil C. *New Towns: Why and for Whom?* New York: Praeger, 1973.

150. Peters, Pauhaus, ed. *Design and Planning*, New York: Van Nostrand Reinhold, 1972.

151. Porteous, J. Douglas. *Environment and Behavior: Planning and Everyday Urban Life*, Reading, Mass.: Addison-Wesley, 1977.

152. Row, Arthur. "The Physical Development Plan", *Journal of the American Institute of Planners*, Vol. 26, No. 3, August 1960. pp. 177-185.

153. Saarinen, Eliel. *The City: Its Growth, Its Decay, Its Future*. New York: Reinhold, 1943.

154. Scott, Mel. *American City Planning*. Berkeley Cal.: University of California Press, 1969.

155. Sommer, Robert. *Design Awareness*, San Francisco: Rinehart Press, 1972.

156. Spyer, Geoffrey. *Architecture and Community: Environmental Design in an Urban Society*, New York: Humanities Press, 1971.

157. Stearns, Forrest W. and Montag, Thomas. *The Urban Ecosystem: A Holistic Approach,* New York: Wiley & Sons, 1975.

158. Strong, Ann Louise. *Planned Urban Environments,* Baltimore: Johns Hopkins Press, 1971.

159. Sutcliffe, Anthony. "A Vision of Utopia: Optimistic Foundations of Le Corbusier's Doctrine D'Urbanisme'," in *The Open Hand: Essays on Le Corbusier,* Russell Walden, ed., Cambridge, Mass., MIT Press, 1977, 216-243.

160. Teitz, Michael B. "Technical and Social Bases for Regional Land Use Policy and Planning," *Papers of the Regional Science Association,* Vol. 32, 1974, 203-213.

161. van Dressen, Peter. *Development on a Human Scale,* New York: Praeger, 1973.

162. Wilson, Forrest. *City Planning: The Games of Human Settlement,* Van Nostrand Reinhold, 1975.

163. Wolfe, M.R. and Shinn, R.D. *Urban Design Within the Comprehensive Planning Process,* Washington, D.C.: Department of Housing and Urban Development, 1970.

II. *SOCIAL PLANNING IN CHANGE*

201. Abrahamson, Mark. "The Social Dimensions of Urbanism," *Social Forces,* March 1974, 376-83.

202. Algie, Jimmy. *Social Values, Objectives and Actions,* New York: Wiley & Sons, 1975.

203. Anderson, Stamford, ed. *Planning for Diversity and Choice,* Cambridge, Mass.: MIT Press, 1968.

204. Appleyard, Donald. *Planning a Pluralist City,* Cambridge, Mass.: MIT Press, 1976.

205. Arnstein, Sherry. "But Which Advocate Planner?" *Social Policy,* Vol. 1, No. 2, July/August 1970, pp. 33-34.

206. Bailey, Joseph. *Social Theory for Planning,* Boston: Routledge & Kegan Paul, 1975.

207. Berry, Brian, J.L. *The Human Consequences of Urbanization,* New York: St. Martin's Press, 1973.

208. Berry, David and Steiker, Gene. *The Concept of Justice in Regional Planning: Some Policy Implications,* Philadelphia: Regional Science Research Institute, November 1973.

209. Blackman, Lucy E. *The Social Process in Theory and Practice: Some Effects of Group Structure Upon Participatory Planning and Action Explored in an Open Education Setting,* Los Angeles: School of Architecture and Urban Planning, UCLA, July, 1973.

210. Bolan, Richard S. "The Social Relations of the Planner," *Journal of the American Institute of Planners*, Vol. 37, No. 6, November 1971, pp. 386-396.

211. Brooks, Michael P. *Social Policy in Cities: Toward a Theory of Urban Social Planning*, Ph.D. Dissertation, University of North Carolina at Chapel Hill, Ann Arbor: University Microfilms, 1970.

212. Brown, Lance Jay and Whiteman, Dorothy E. *Planning and Design Workbook for Community Participation: An Evaluation Report*, Princeton, N.J.: Research Center for Urban and Environmental Planning, Princeton University School of Architecture and Urban Planning, 1973.

213. Burke, Edmund M. "Citizen Participation and Strategies," *Journal of the American Institute of Planners*, Vol. 34, No. 5, September 1968, pp. 278-294.

214. Buttimer, Anne. "Sociology and Planning," in *Studies in Social Science and Planning*. Jean Forbes, ed. New York, John Wiley, 1974, 101-128.

215. Cole, Richard L. *Citizen Participation and the Urban Policy Process*, Lexington, Mass.: Lexington Books, 1974.

216. Coroso, Anthony. *The Urban Planner as Inside Advocate*, Monticello, Ill.: Council of Planning Librarians, Exchange Bibliography No. 1218, February 1977.

217. Cullingworth, J.B. *Problems of an Urban Society, Volume I: The Social Framework of Planning*, London: George Allen & Unwin, 1973.

218. ————. *Problems of an Urban Society, Volume III: Planning for Change*, London: George Allen and Unwin, 1973.

219. Davidoff, Paul. "Advocacy and Pluralism in Planning," *Journal of the American Institute of Planners* 31, 1965, 331-338.

220. Davidoff, Paul & Reiner, Thomas A. "A Choice Theory of Planning," *Journal of the American Institute of Planners*, 28, 1962, 103-115.

221. Davidoff, Paul and Linda; Gold, Neil N. "Suburban Action: Advocate Planning for an Open Society," *Journal of the American Institute of Planners*, Vol. 36, No. 1, January 1970, pp. 12-21.

222. de Neufille, Judith Innes. *Social Indicators and Public Policy: Interactive Processes of Design and Application*, New York: Elsevier, 1975.

223. Dyckman, John W. "Social Planning, Social Planners, and Planned Societies," *Journal of the American Institute of Planners*, Vol. 32, No. 2, March 1966, pp. 66-76.

224. Fainstein, Norman I. & Susan S. Fainstein. *Urban Political Movements: The Search for Power by Minority Groups in American Cities*, Englewood Cliffs, N.J.: Prentice-Hall, 1974.

225. Fainstein, Susan S. & Norman I. Fainstein. "Local Control as Social Reform: Planning for Big Cities in the Seventies," *Journal of the American Institute of Planners*, Vol. 42, No. 3, July 1976, pp. 275-285.

226. Finley, Robert K. "The Comprehensive Plan as an Instrument of Social Planning Policy." Washington, D.C.: Center for Metropolitan Studies, 1962 (pamphlet).

227. Frieden, Bernard J. and Kaplan, Marshall. *The Politics of Neglect,* Cambridge, Mass.: MIT Press, 1976.

228. Frieden, Bernard J. and Morris, Robert, eds., *Urban Planning and Social Policy,* New York: Basic Books, 1968.

229. Frieden, Bernard J. "The Changing Prospects for Social Planning," *Journal of the American Institute of Planners,* Vol. 33, No. 5, September 1967, pp. 311-323.

230. Fromm, Erich. "Humanistic Planning." *Journal of the American Institute of Planners,* March 1972, 67-71.

231. Gans, Herbert J. *People and Plans: Essays on Urban Problems and Solutions,* New York Basic Books, 1968.

232. ————. "Social and Physical Planning for the Elimination of Urban Poverty," *Washington University Law Quarterly* 1963 (1), 2-18.

233. Gillingwater, David. *Regional Planning and Social Change,* Lexington, Mass.: Lexington Books, 1975.

234. Godschalk, David R. ed. *Planning in America: Learning from Turbulence,* Washington, D.C.: American Institute of Planners, 1974.

235. Goodman, Percival, and Goodman, Paul. *Communitas: Means of Livelihood and Ways of Life.* Chicago: University of Chicago Press, 1947.

236. Gutenschwager, Gerald. *Planning and Social Theory: A Selected Bibliography,* Exchange Bibliography No. 179. Monticello, Ill., Council of Planning Librarians, 1971.

237. Grabow, Stephen & Heskin, Allan. "Foundations for a Radical Concept of Planning," *Journal of the American Institute of Planners* 39, 1973, 106-113.

238. Gross, Bertram M. "Planning in an Era of Social Revolution," *Public Administration Review,* Vol. 31, 1971, pp. 259-296.

239. Harrison, Bennett. "The Participation of Ghetto Residents in the Models Cities Program," *Journal of the American Institute of Planners,* Vol. 39, No. 1, January 1973.

240. Harrison, M.L. "British Town Planning Ideology and the Welfare State," *Journal of Social Policy,* 4, July 1975, 259-74.

241. Hendon, William S. *Economics of Urban Social Planning,* University of Utah Press, 1975.

242. Honikman, B. *Responding to Social Change,* Stroudsburg, Pa.: Dowden, Hutchinson, & Ross, 1975.

243. Horowitz, Irving L. "Social Science Mandarins: Policy-making as Political Formula," *Policy Sciences,* Vol. 1, 1970, pp. 339-360.

244. Jacobs, Jane. *The Death and Life of Great American Cities*, New York: Alfred A. Knopf, 1961.

245. Kaitz, E.M. and Hyman, H.H. *Urban Planning for Social Welfare: A Model Cities Approach*, New York: Praeger, 1970.

246. Kaplan, Samuel. *The Dream Deferred: People, Politics and Planning in Suburbia*, New York: Seabury Press, 1976.

247. Krumholz, Norman and Bonner, Ernest. "Toward a Workable Program for an Advocate Planning Agency." Paper presented to the annual convention of the American Institute of Planners, San Francisco, Cal., October 24-28, 1971.

248. Liebman, Lance. "Social Intervention in a Democracy," *The Public Interest*, March 1974.

249. Lomas, G.M. *Social Planning at a Metropolitan Scale*, Philadelphia: Regional Studies Association, 1971.

250. Lamb, Curt. *Political Power in Poor Neighborhoods*, New York: Wiley & Sons, 1975.

251. Mann, Lawrence D. "Social Science Advances and Planning Applications: 1900-1965," *Journal of the American Institute of Planners*, Vol. 28, No. 6, November 1972.

252. Marris, Peter and Rein, Martin. *Dilemmas of Social Reform*, New York: Atherton Press, 1969.

253. Marshall, Chris E. and Carter, Keith A. *Needs Assessment for Social Planning: Ideas and Approaches*, Monticello, Ill.: Council of Planning Librarians, Exchange Bibliography No. 1442, January 1978.

254. Maruyama, Magaroh. "Human Futuristics and Urban Planning," *Journal of the American Institute of Planners*, Vol. 39, No. 5, September 1973, pp. 346-357.

255. Mayer, Robert R. *Social Planning and Social Change*, Englewood Cliffs, N.J.: Prentice-Hall, 1971.

256. Mazziotti, Donald F. *Advocacy Planning*, Monticello, Ill.: Council of Planning Librarians, Exchange Bibliography No. 323, September 1972.

257. ————. "The Underlying Assumptions of Advocacy Planning: Pluralism and Reform," *Journal of the American Institute of Planners*, Vol. 40, No. 1, January 1974, pp. 38-47.

258. Miller, S.M. and Rein, Martin. "Participation, Poverty, and Administration," *Public Administration Review*, Vol. 29, No. 1, January/February 1969, pp. 15-21.

259. Moore, Vincent, Jr. "Politics, Planning, and Power in New York State: The Path from Theory to Reality," *Journal of the American Institute of Planners*, Vol. 37, No. 2, March 1971, pp. 66-77.

260. Morris, Robert and Birstock, Robert H. *Feasible Planning for Social Change*, New York: Columbia University Press, 1966.

261. Mudd, John. "Beyond Community Control: A Neighborhood Strategy for City Government," *Publius*, Fall 1976, pp. 113-136.

262. Parsons, Talcott. *The Structure of Social Action* (Vol. I), New York: The Free Press, 1937.

263. Peattie, Lisa R. "Reflections on Advocacy Planning," *Journal of the American Institute of Planners*, Vol. 34, No. 2, March 1968, pp. 80-88.

264. Perloff, Harvey S. "New Directions in Social Planning," *Journal of the American Institute of Planners* 31, 1965, 297-304.

265. Piven, Frances F. "Whom Does the Advocate Planner Serve?" *Social Policy*, May-June 1970, pp. 32-37.

266. Rein, Martin. "Social Planning: The Search for Legitimacy," *Journal of the American Institute of Planners*, Vol. 35, No. 3, May 1969, pp. 233-244.

267. Reiner, Thomas A. *The Place of the Ideal Community in Urban Planning*, Philadelphia: University of Pennsylvania Press, 1963.

268. Ross, Robert J.S. "The Impact of Social Movements on a Profession in Process: Advocacy in Urban Planning," *Sociology of Work & Occupations* 3, 1976, 429-454.

269. Rothman, Jack. *Planning and Organizing for Social Change*, New York: Columbia University Press, 1974.

270. Smith, Richard Warren. "A Theoretical Basis for Participatory Planning," *Policy Sciences* 4, 1973, 275-295.

271. Steggert, Frank X. *Community Action Groups and City Governments*, Cambridge, Mass.: Ballinger 1975.

272. Warren, Donald J. *Black Neighborhood: An Assessment of Community Power*, Ann Arbor, Mich.: University of Michigan Press, 1975.

273. Webber, Melvin C. "Comprehensive Planning and Social Responsibility," in Frieden, Bernard J. and Morris, Robert eds., *Urban Planning and Social Policy*, New York: Basic Books, 1968.

273. Weicher, John C. "A Test of Jane Jacobs' Theory of Successful Neighborhoods," *Journal of Regional Science*, April 1973, 29-40.

III. *POLICY PLANNING IN CHANGE*

301. Aberback, Joel D. and Walker, Jack L. "Citizen Desires, Policy Outcomes, and Community Control," *Urban Affairs Quarterly*, Vol. 7, No. 3, September 1972.

302. Alexander, Ernest R. and Beckley, Robert M., *Going It Alone? A Case Study of Planning and Implementation at the Local Level*, Washington, D.C.: U.S. Department of Housing and Urban Development, Office of Policy Development and Research, 1974.

303. Allenworth, Don T. *The Political Realities of Urban Planning*, New York: Praeger, 1974.

304. Altshuler, Alan A. *The City Planning Process*, Ithaca, N.Y., Cornell University Press, 1964.

305. ————. *Community Control*, New York: Pegasus, 1970.

306. Apgar, Mahlon IV. "Planning for Uncertainty: An Approach for Decision Makers," *Habitat*, Vol. 1, Nos. 3/4, 1976, pp. 231-240.

307. Banfield, Edward C. *The Unheavenly City: The Nature and Future of Our Urban Crisis*, Boston, Little, Brown, & Co., 1970.

308. Beckman, Norman. "The Planner as Bureaucrat," *Journal of the American Institute of Planners*, Vol. 30, No. 5, November 1964.

309. Beyle, Thad L. and Lathrop, George T. *Planning and Politics: The Uneasy Partnership*, New York: Odyssey Press, 1970.

310. Bird, Tony. "The Boundaries of Planning Rationality," *Planner* 61, 1975, 106-108.

311. Bolan, Richard S. "Community Decision Behavior: The Culture of Planning," *Journal of the American Institute of Planners*, Vol. 35, No. 5, September 1969, pp. 301-310.

312. Braybrooke, David and Lindblom, Charles. *A Strategy of Decision*, New York: Free Press, 1963.

313. Buck, Roy C. and Roth, Robert A. "Planning as Institutional Innovation in the Smaller City," *Journal of the American Institute of Planners*, Vol. 36, No. 1, January 1970, pp. 54-64.

314. Caro, Robert A. *The Power Broker: Robert Moses and the Fall of New York*, New York: Alfred A. Knopf, 1974.

315. Cartwright, T. J. "Problems, Solutions and Strategies: A Contribution to the Theory and Practice of Planning," *Journal of the American Institute of Planners* 1973, 179-187.

316. Catanese, Anthony J. *Planners and Local Politics: Impossible Dreams*, Beverly Hills, Cal. Sage Publications, 1975.

317. Catanese, Anthony J. & Steiss, Alan W. *Systematic Planning: Theory and Application*. Lexington, Mass., Heath, 1970.

318. Chadwick, George F. *A Systems View of Planning: Towards a Theory of the Urban and Regional Planning Process*, New York, Pergamon, 1971.

319. Dahl, Robert A. and Lindblom, Charles E. *Politics, Economics and Welfare*, New York: Harper Torchbooks, 1953.

320. Davidoff, Paul and Reiner, Thomas. "A Choice Theory of Planning," *Journal of the American Institute of Planners*, Vol. 28, No. 3, May 1962, pp. 103-115.

321. Davidoff, Paul. "Advocacy and Pluralism in Planning" *Journal of the American Institute of Planners*, Vol. 31, No. 4, Nov. 1965, pp. 331-338.

322. Dickerson, Steven L. and Robertshaw, Joseph E. *Planning and Design: The Systems Approach*, Lexington, Mass.: Lexington Books, 1975.

323. Dror, Yehezekel. *Design for Policy Sciences*, New York: Elsevier, 1971.

324. ————. *Public Policymaking Reexamined*, San Francisco, Cal.: Chandler Publishing Co., 1968.

325. Dyckman, John W. "Planning and Decision Theory" *Journal of the American Institute of Planners*, Vol. 27, No. 4, Nov. 1961, pp. 335-345.

326. Etzioni, Amitai. *The Active Society*, New York: The Free Press, 1968.

327. ————. "Mixed Scanning: A Third Approach to Decisionmaking," *Public Administration Review*, December 1967, pp. 385-392.

328. Fainstein, Susan S. and Norman I. "City Planning and Political Values," *Urban Affairs Quarterly*, Vol. 6, No. 3, September 1971.

329. Friedmann, John. *Retracking America: A Theory of Transactive Planning*, New York, Doubleday, 1973.

330. ————. *An Approach to Policies Planning for Spatial Development*, University of California, Los Angeles, Comparative Urbanization Studies, Occasional Paper No. 7, July 1974.

331. ————. Notes on Societal Action," *Journal of The American Institute of Planners*, Vol. 25, No. 5.

332. ————. "The Public Interest and Community Participation: Toward a Reconstruction of Public Philosophy," *Journal of the American Institute of Planners*, Vol. 39, No. 1, January 1973, pp. 2-12.

333. ————. *Urbanization, Planning, and National Development*, Beverly Hills: Sage Publications, 1973.

334. Friedmann, John and Hudson, Barclay. "Knowledge and Action: A Guide to Planning Theory." *Journal of the American Institute of Planners* 40, 1974, 2-16.

335. Fudge, Colin. "Local Plans, Structure Plans and Policy Planning, *The Planner*, 62, 1976, 174-176.

336. Galloway, Thomas D. *The Role of Urban Planning in Public Policymaking: A Synthesis and Critique of Contemporary Procedural Planning Thought*, Ph.D. Dissertation, University of Washington, Ann Arbor: University Microfilms, 1971.

337. Getter, Russell W. and Elliott, Nick. "Receptivity of Local Elites Toward Planning," *Journal of the American Institute of Planners*, Vol. 42, No. 1, January 1976, pp. 87-95.

338. Getzels, Judith, et al., *Private Planning for the Public Interest*, Chicago: American Society of Planning Officials, 1975.

339. Godschalk, David R. *Participation, Planning, and Exchange in Old and New Communities: A Collaborative Paradigm*, Chapel Hill: Center for Urban and Regional Studies, University of North Carolina, 1971.

340. Gottschalk, Shimon S. *Communities and Alternatives: An Exploration of the Limits of Planning*, New York: Wiley & Sons, 1975.

341. Haar, Charles, "The Master Plan: An Inquiry in Dialogue Form," *Journal of the American Institute of Planners*, Vol. 25, No. 3, August 1959.

342. Hasbrouck, Sherman. *Pragmatic Planning: An Alternative to Comprehensive Planning*, Orono, Maine: University of Maine Press, 1973.

343. Hoos, Ida R. "Information Systems and Public Planning," *Management Science*, Vol. 17, 1971, pp. 658-671.

344. Hughes, James and Mann, Lawrence. "Systems and Planning Theory," *Journal of the American Institute of Planners*, Vol. 35, No. 4, September 1969, pp. 330-333.

345. Jacob, Charles E. *Policy and Bureaucracy*, New York, D. Van Nostrand Company, 1966.

346. King, Nicki. *Planning Theory: An Examination of the Linkages Between Implementation, Knowledge and Action*, Santa Monica: RAND, 1974.

347. Krumholz, Norman; Cogger, Janice M.; and Linner, John H. "The Cleveland Policy Planning Report," *Journal of the American Institute of Planners*, Vol. 41, No. 5, pp. 298-304. (Several responses to this article appear in this issue.)

348. Levine, Robert A. *Public Planning: Failure and Redirection*, New York: Basic Books, 1973.

349. Lichfield, Nathaniel; Kettle, Peter; and Whitehead, Michael. *Evaluation in the Planning Process*, New York: Pergamon Press, 1975.

350. Linowes, R. Robert and Allensworth, Don T. *The Politics of Land Use: Planning, Zoning, and the Private Developer*, New York: Praeger, 1973.

351. Mack, Ruth P. *Planning and Uncertainty: Decision-Making in Business and Government Administration*, New York: Wiley & Sons, 1971.

352. Meyerson, Martin and Banfield, Edward. *Politics and the Public Interest*, New York: The Free Press, 1955.

353. Moffitt, Leonard C. "Value Implicity for Public Planning: Some Thought and Questions," *Journal of the American Institute of Planners*, Vol. 41, No. 6, November 1975, pp. 397-405.

354. Moore, Gary T., ed. *Emerging Methods in Environmental Design and Planning*, Cambridge, Mass.: MIT Press 1970.

355. Nuttall, Ronald L. and Bolan Richard S. *Urban Planning and Politics*, Lexington, Mass.: Lexington Books, 1975.

356. Oberman, Joseph *Planning and Managing the Economy of the City*, New York: Praeger, 1972.

357. Pressman, Jeffrey and Wildavsky, Aaron. *Implementation*, Berkeley: University of California Press, 1973.

358. Pollack, Patricia Baron. "The Planning Pretense," *Maxwell Review*, 8, 1972, pp. 65-71.

359. Public Administration Review. "Special Issue: Essays on Citizens, Politics, and Administration in Urban Neighborhoods," *Public Administration Review*, Vol. 32, No. 5, September/October 1972.

360. Public Administration Review. "Symposium on Policy Analysis in Government: Alternatives to 'Mudding Through,'" *Public Administration Review*, Vol. 37, No. 3, May/June 1977, pp. 221-263.

361. Rabinovitz, Francine. *City Politics and Planning*, New York: Atherton Press, 1969.

362. Ranney, David. *Planning and Politics in the Metropolis*, Columbus, Ohio; Charles Merrill Publishing Co., 1969.

363. Reiner, Thomas A. "The Planner as Value Technician; Two Classes of Utopian Constructs and Their Impacts on Planning," in H. Wentworth Eldridge, ed., *Taming Megalopolis, Vol. I.* New York: Anchor Books, 1967, pp. 232-248.

364. Robinson, Ira M. *Decision-Making in Urban Planning*, Beverly Hills, Cal.: Sage Publications, 1972.

365. Rondinelli, Dennis A. "Politics, Policy Analysis, and Development: The Future of Urban and Regional Planning," in *Urban and Regional Development Planning: Policy and Administration*, Ithaca, N.Y., Cornell University Press, 1975, 237-266.

366. ————. *Urban and Regional Development Planning: Politics and Administration*, Ithaca, N.Y.: Cornell University Press, 1975.

367. ————. "Urban Planning as Policy Analysis: Management of Urban Change," *Journal of the American Institute of Planners*, Vol. 39, No. 1, January 1973, pp. 13-22.

368. Roos, J. P. "Theories of Planning and Democratic Planning Theory," *Government and Opposition* 9, 1974, 331-344.

369. Rothblatt, Donald N. "Rational Planning Reexamined," *Journal of the American Institute of Planners*, Vol. 37, No. 1, January 1971, pp. 26-37.

370. Schnore, Leo F. and Fagin, Henry. *Urban Research and Policy Planning*, Beverly Hills: Sage Publications, 1967.

371. Simon, Herbert. *Administrative Behavior*, New York: The Free Press, 1957.

372. Simon, Herbert A. and March, James G. *Organizations*, New York: John Wiley and Sons, Inc. 1958.

373. Sloan, Allan K. *Citizen Participation in Transportation Planning: The Boston Experience*, Cambridge, Mass.: Ballinger, 1974.

374. Smith, Richard A. "Community Power and Decision-Making: A Replication and Extension of Hawley," *American Sociological Review*, Vol. 41, August 1976, pp. 691-705.

375. Stewart, Thomas R. and Gelberd, Linda. "Analysis of Judgment Policy: A New Approach for Citizen Participation in Planning," *Journal of the American Institute of Planners*, Vol. 42, No. 1, January 1976.

376. Stuart, Darwin G. "Rational Urban Planning," *Urban Affairs Quarterly*, Vol. 4, No. 4, December 1969.

377. Tunnard, Christopher. "The Planning Syndrome in Western Culture," *Annals of the American Academy of Political and Social Science* 405, 1973, 95-103.

378. Walton, John. "Community Power and the Retreat from Politics: Full Circle After 20 Years?" *Social Problems*, Vol. 23, No. 1, February 1976, pp. 292-303.

379. Warfield, John N. *Societal Systems: Planning, Policy, and Complexity*, New York: Wiley & Sons, 1976.

380. Weidenbaum, Murray and Rockwood, Linda. "Corporate Planning versus Government Planning," *The Public Interest*, Winter 1977, pp. 59-72.

381. Webber, Melvin M. *Alternative Styles for Citizen Participation in Transport Planning*, Berkeley, Cal.: Institute of Urban and Regional Development, University of California, 1973.

382. Wildavsky, Aaron. "The Self-Evaluating Organization," *Public Administration Review*, Vol. 32, No. 5, September/October 1972, pp. 509-520.

383. Wilson, James Q. and Banfield, Edward C. *City Politics*, New York: Random House, 1963.

384. Wood, Elizabeth. *Social Planning*, New York: Community Education Program, Pratt University, 1965.

IV. *ECONOMIC PLANNING IN CHANGE*

401. Amson, J.C. "Equilibrium models of Cities: 1. An Axiomatic Theory," *Environment & Planning* 4, 1972, 429-44.

402. Forrester, Jay W. "Urban Goals and National Objectives," *Studies in Comparative Local Government*, Summer 1972, 18-26.

403. Grabow, Stephen and Heskin, Allan. "Foundations for A Radical Concept of Planning," *Journal of the American Institute of Planners,* Vol. 39, No. 2, March 1973, pp. 106-114.

404. Halm, George N. *Economic Systems,* New York: Holt, Rinehart and Winston, Inc., 1958.

405. Hayek, Fred. *The Road to Serfdom,* Chicago: University of Chicago Press, 1944.

406. Lepawski, Albert. "The Planning Apparatus: A Vignette of the New Deal," *Journal of the American Institute of Planners,* Vol. 42, No. 1, January 1976, pp. 16-32.

407. Lindblom, Charles E. "Economics and The Administration of National Planning," in Altshuler, Alan A. *The Politics of The Federal Bureaucracy,* New York: Dodd, Mead and Co. 1968.

408. Long, Norton E. "The City as Political Economy." *National Civic Review,* April 1974, 189-91.

409. Mannheim, Karl. "Planning for Freedom," in Amitai and Eva Etzioni, eds., *Social Change,* New York: Basic Books, 1964.

410. Mayer, Robert R.; Moroney, Robert; and Morris, Robert. *Centrally Planned Change: A Reexamination of Theory and Experience,* Urbana, Ill.: University of Illinois Press, 1975.

411. Meier, Richard L. *Planning for an Urban World: The Design of Resource Conserving Cities,* Cambridge, Mass.: MIT Press, 1975.

412. Meyerson, Martin. "The Next Challenge for the Urban Planner: Linking Local and National Economic Planning," *Journal of the American Institute of Planners,* Oct. 1976, 371-376.

413. Miller, S.M. "Planning: Can It Make a Difference in Capitalist America?" *Social Policy,* Vol. 6, No. 2, Sept.-Oct. 1975, pp. 12-22.

414. Oxley, M.J. "Economic Theory and Urban Planning," *Environment and Planning* 7, 1975, 497-508.

415. Peterson, Wallace. "Planning and the Market Economy," *Journal of Economic Issues,* Vol. 3, No. 1, March 1969, pp. 126-143.

416. Robinson, Joan. *Introduction to the Theory of Employment,* New York: St. Martin's Press, 1960.

417. Rosenberg, G. "The Theory of Socialist Territoried Planning in the German Democratic Republic," *Town Planning Quarterly* 41, December 1975, 22-26.

418. Schuck, Peter H. "National Economic Planning: A Slogan Without Substance," *Public Interest,* Fall 1976, 63-78.

419. Tabb, William K. and Sawyer, Lang. *Marxism and the Metropolis,* New York: Oxford University Press, 1978.

V. GENERAL READINGS IN PLANNING THEORY

501. Ackoff, Russell L. *A Concept of Corporate Planning*, New York: Wiley & Sons, 1970.

502. Alden, Jeremy and Morgan, Robert. *Regional Planning: A Comprehensive View*, New York: Wiley & Sons, 1974.

503. Annals of the American Association of Political and Social Science, Special Issue: *Urban Change and the Planning Syndrome*, January 1973.

504. Bolan, Richard S. "Emerging Views of Planning," *Journal of the American Institute of Planners*, Vol. 33, No. 4, July 1967, pp. 233-246.

505. ————. "Mapping the Planning Theory Terrain," *Urban and Social Change Review* 8, Summer 1975.

506. Branch, Melville C., ed., *Urban Planning Theory*, Stroudsburg, Pa.: Dowden, Hutchinson & Ross, 1975.

507. Cartwright, Timothy J. "Problems, Solutions, and Strategies: A Contribution to the Theory and Practice of Planning," *Journal of the American Institute of Planners*, Vol. 39, No. 3, May 1973, pp. 179-187.

508. Catanese, Anthony J. and Steiss, Alan W. *Systemic Planning Theory and Application*, Lexington, Mass.: Lexington Books, 1970.

509. Coleman, Alice. "Is Planning Really Necessary?" *Geographical Journal*, Vol. 142, November 1976, pp. 411-437.

510. Cowan, Peter, ed. *The Future of Planning*, London, Heinemann. 1973.

511. Dyckman, John. "The Practical Uses of Planning Theory," *Journal of the American Institute of Planners*, Vol. 35, No. 5, September 1969, pp. 298-301.

512. Faludi, Andreas, ed. *A Reader In Planning Theory*, New York: Pergamon Press, 1973.

513. ————. "Towards a Three Dimensional Model of Planning Behavior," *Environment and Planning*, Vol. 3, 1971.

514. Friedmann, John A. "A Conceptual Model for the Analysis of Planning Behavior," *Administrative Science Quarterly*, Vol. 12, 1967, pp. 225-252.

515. Gale, Stephen. "On a Metatheory of Planning Theory," *1975 Symposium of Planning Theory*, Papers in Planning No. 1, University Park, Pa., University of Pennsylvania Department of City and Regional Planning, October 1975, 3-23.

516. Galloway, Thomas D. and Mahayni, Riad G. "Planning Theory in Retrospect: The Process of Paradigm Change," *Journal of the American Institute of Planners*, Vol. 43, No. 1, January 1977, pp. 62-71.

517. Goldstein, Harvey A. "Towards a Critical Theory of Planning," *1975 Symposium of Planning Theory*," Papers in Planning No. 1, University Park, Pa., University of Pennsylvania Department of City and Regional Planning, October 1975, 24-39.

518. Graham, Otis. *Toward a Planned Society—From Roosevelt to Nixon,* New York: Oxford University Press, 1976.

519. Handler, A. Benjamin. "What is Planning Theory?" *Journal of the American Institute of Planners,* Vol. 23, 1957, 144-150.

520. Krieger, Martin H. "Some New Directions for Planning Theories," *Journal of the American Institute of Planners,* Vol. 40, No. 3, May 1974, pp. 156-163.

521. "The Practical Uses of Planning Theory: A Symposium," *Journal of the American Institute of Planners,* 35, September 1969, 298-333.

522. Peterson, William. "On Some Meanings of 'Planning,'" *Journal of the American Institute of Planners,* Vol. 32, No. 3, May 1966, pp. 130-142.

523. Rittel, Horst W. I. & Webber. Melvin M. "Dilemmas in a General Theory of Planning," *DMG-DRS Journal: Design Research & Methods,* Jan-March 1974, 31-39.

524. Skjei, Stephen S. "Urban Problems and the Theoretical Justification of Urban Planning," *Urban Affairs Quarterly,* Vol. 11, No. 1, March 1976, pp. 323-344.

VI. GENERAL READINGS IN PLANNING EDUCATION/PRACTICE

601. AIP Journal, "Reshaping Planning Education," (Special Issue) *Journal of the American Institute of Planners,* Vol. 36, No. 4, July 1970, pp. 229-284.

602. Applebaum, Richard P. "The Future is Made, Not Predicted: Technocratic Planners vs. Public Interest," *Society,* Vol. 14, No. 4, May/June 1977, pp. 49-53.

603. Baer, W.C. "Urban Planners: Doctors or Midwives," *Public Administration Review,* Nov-Dec. 1977, pp. 671-678.

604. Ban, Donald. "The Professional Urban Planner," *Journal of the American Institute of Planners,* Vol. 38, No. 3, May 1972, pp. 155-59.

605. Beauregard, Robert A. "The Occupation of Planning," *Journal of the American Institute of Planners,* Vol. 42, No. 2, April 1976, pp. 187-192.

606. Benveniste, Guy. *The Politics of Expertise.* Berkeley: Glendessary Press, 1972.

607. Branch, Melville C. *Planning: Aspects and Applications,* New York: Wiley, 1966.

608. Buck, James V. *City Planners: The Dilemma of Professionals in a Political Milieu,* Ph.D. Dissertation, Stanford University, Ann Arbor: University Microfilms, 1972.

609. Dyckman, John W. "The Scientific World of City Planners, *American Behavioral Scientist,* Vol. 6, No. 6, February 1963.

610. Dyckman, John W. "What Makes Planners Plan?" *Journal of The American Institute of Planners,* Vol. 27, No. 3, May 1961, pp. 164-167.

611. Erber, Ernest, ed. *Urban Planning In Transition,* New York: Grossman 1970.

612. Friedmann, John. *The Design of Education Systems for Assessing the Quality of the Physical and Social Environment,* Los Angeles: School of Architecture and Urban Planning, UCLA, Discussion Paper No. 26, 1973.

613. —————. "Planning As a Vocation," *Plan Canada,* Vol. 7, July 1966, pp. 1-20.

614. Gillingwater, David and Hart, D. A. *Regional Planners: Problems, Processes, Prescriptions,* Lexington, Mass.: Lexington Books, 1976.

615. Green, Bruce H. *Role Perceptions of City Planners and Their Relevant Others,* Ph.D. Dissertation, Iowa State University, Ann Arbor: University Microfilms, 1970.

616. Hawkins, Brett W. "A Macro Analysis of the Effects of Planning Agency Professionalism on Municipal Planning Outputs," *Journal of the American Institute of Planners,* Vol. 41, No. 6, November 1975, pp. 419-424.

617. Hightower, H. "Planning Theory in Contemporary Education," *Journal of the American Institute of Planners,* Vol. 35, No. 5, September 1969.

618. Howard, John T. "City Planning as a Social Movement, A Governmental Function and a Technical Profession," in Harvey S. Perloff ed., *Planning and the Urban Community,* Pittsburgh: University of Pittsburgh Press, 1961, pp. 150-170.

619. Hudson, Barclay M. "The Crisis in Planning," *Economic Development and Cultural Change,* Vol. 22, No. 3, April 1974, pp. 518-26.

620. Kaplan, Marshall. *Urban Planning in the 1960's: A Design for Irrelevancy,* New York: Praeger, 1973.

621. Krieger, Martin H. "What Do Planners Do?" *Journal of the American Institute of Planners,* Vol. 41, No. 5, September 1975.

622. Lieberman, Susan A. *The Practitioners Viewpoint: An Exploration of Social Policy Planning and Education Part I: The Study,* Chapel Hill: Department of City and Regional Planning, University of North Carolina, 1976.

623. McCallum, J. Douglas "Planning Theory in Planning Education," *Planner* 60, 1974, 738-740.

624. Marcuse, Peter. "Professional Ethics and Beyond: Values in Planning," *Journal of the American Institute of Planners,* Vol. 42, No. 3, July 1976, pp. 264-274.

625. Michael, Donald N. *On Learning to Plan—And Planning to Learn,* San Francisco: Josey-Bass Publishers, 1973.

626. Perloff, Harvey S. *Education for Planning: City, State, and Regional,* Baltimore: The Johns Hopkins Press, 1957.